SUCCESSFUL KNITTING

WH SMITH

EXCLUSIVE
· BOOKS ·

This edition produced 1991 exclusively for W H Smith Ltd by Book Connections Limited, 47 Norfolk Street, Cambridge CB1 2LE.

Based on *Creative Knitting*.
© Eaglemoss Publications Limited 1987.
All rights reserved.

A CIP catalogue record for this book is available from the British Library.

Cover design and production in association with Book Connections Limited, 47 Norfolk Street, Cambridge CB1 2LE.

Printed and bound in Italy.

ISBN 0 906782 52 X

CONTENTS

INTRODUCTION

Here is a book for everyone attracted to the age-old craft of knitting. Whatever level you are at, there is plenty for you. *Successful Knitting* is a detailed reference source for the essential techniques and the wide variety of stitches. It is also a compendium of patterns for all the family.

If you are a beginner you will find fully illustrated step-by-step instructions to take you through the basic techniques you will need to get started. If you have already gained some expertise, there is plenty that will be of value to you, ranging from advice on different methods for particular effects to hints on giving your work the expert finishing touch.

The techniques section at the beginning of the book outlines the methods you will need to follow the patterns that make up the main section. Drawings and photographs make the procedure for everything from casting-on to casting-off easy to follow. Included in this section are instructions for such basic items as gloves and socks – you will find yourself turning to these over and over again.

In the main part of the book is a wide range of patterns coded to show the level of expertise required. There is something here for everyone in the family, and for every level of skill. There are patterns for women, men, children and babies; and there are simple clothes for everyday wear and high-fashion garments for those who want to make an impression.

Knitting is a long-established craft that is gaining in popularity from year to year. It is satisfying, it is practical, it is economical – and it is fun. Become skilled in knitting, and make high-fashion clothes exactly as you want them; make garments for a fraction of the price in the shops; and simply enjoy your expertise in a relaxing and rewarding craft. The range of things you will be able to make is enormous. Yarns are available in a wide range of textures, thicknesses and colours, ranging from chunky ones that can be made into a child's jersey in an evening to fine ones which it will take weeks to turn into a christening robe or a lacy shawl.

Before you start, here is a word of warning. Until you are experienced, do not attempt to adapt patterns or to make them up in any yarn other than the one specified. In particular, do not leave out the basic step of making a tension square, recommended in each pattern. That is the only way to make sure you have enough yarn to finish the garment and that it will be the size intended. Saving a few minutes by skimping on the tension square can mean that you waste hours of time and a considerable amount of yarn. More important, it could mean that you will lose your enthusiasm for a craft that can give you pleasure for a life-time.

There are few crafts that offer so much satisfaction and require so little equipment and expertise. As you grow in skill, the sense of achievement you gain from everything you make will increase.

BEFORE YOU BEGIN

The tools of the trade

Knitting is one of the cheapest crafts to start. There is no expensive equipment to buy – all you need is the yarn and a couple of pairs of needles. Don't start by buying a complete set of needle sizes; simply add to your collection as you need them for a particular pattern.

Knitting needles

Needles come in a range of sizes from 2mm/No14 to 10mm/No000. The smaller sizes are made from plastic-coated metal, while larger needles are made from lightweight rigid plastic. All sizes are also made from bamboo – they cost a little more but do not make the clicking sound of metal or plastic needles which can be irritating for non-knitters.

Pairs of needles come in three standard lengths – 25cm/10in, 30cm/11¾in and 35cm/13¾in – with a knob at one end to stop the stitches falling off. The choice of length is usually one of personal preference but a garment with a large number of stitches will obviously need longer needles.

Sets of needles sold in fours or fives come in the same sizes as pairs and in lengths of 20cm/7¾in and 30cm/11¾in. They have points at both ends and are used for working in rounds to produce narrow tubular items such as socks.

Circular needles are not made in as many sizes as pairs of needles. They consist of two short, pointed needles which are joined together with a length of flexible nylon. The lengths available are 40cm/15¾in, 60cm/ 23½in, 80cm/31½in and 100cm/39½in. They can be used for knitting in rounds or rows but if you are working in rounds it is important to get the right length so that the stitches can reach from needle point to needle point without stretching the knitting.

Cable needles, short needles with a point at each end and sometimes with a V in the middle, are available in two or three sizes.

Additional items

A **needle gauge** is needed to identify unmarked needle sizes.

A **row counter** which fits on to the end of a needle helps to keep track of which row you are on.

Stitch holders hold one set of stitches while you work on another. Several large safety-pins are also useful.

A **tape measure**, made of fibreglass which will not stretch, is essential both for body measurements and measuring the knitting.

Sewing equipment including a pair of sharp scissors, large, glass-headed pins and blunt, large-eyed crewel needles.

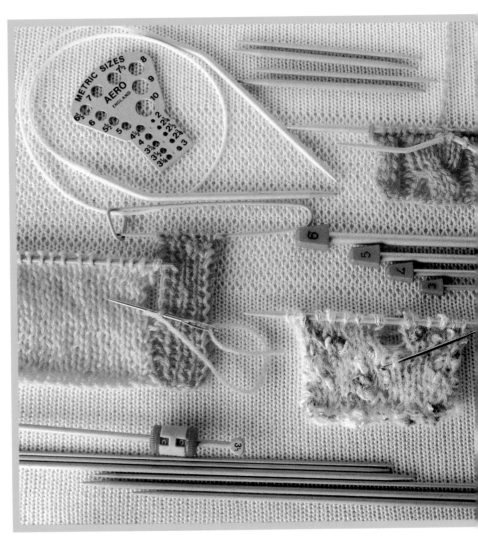

Yarn

There is a huge range of yarns available made from both natural and synthetic fibres, or a combination of the two. The most common natural fibres are wool, angora, alpaca, mohair, silk and cotton. Common synthetic fibres include nylon, acrylic, viscose and polyester. Standard yarns are sold as 2, 3 or 4 ply, double knitting (DK) or chunky. Fancy yarns vary from spinner to spinner and from year to year.

Most yarns are sold by weight. The ball band gives the composition of the yarn, the suggested needle size, instructions for aftercare and the dye lot number. There is often a slight variation in dye lots, so make sure you buy yarn from one lot.

Every pattern in this book has been designed for a specific yarn. If you want to use a different yarn, check with the manufacturer whether it will give a satisfactory result.

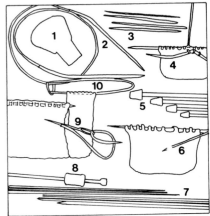

Key

1 Needle gauge. 2 Circular needle. 3 Cable needles. 4 Cable needle. 5 Standard metal knitting needles. 6 Crochet hook. 7 Double-pointed needles. 8 Row counter. 9 Large-eyed blunt needle. 10 Stitch holder.

If the tension of your knitting does not correspond to that of the pattern you are following, you may end up with a garment which is too small or too large or has the wrong sort of texture.

The tension square

The importance of tension in knitting cannot be overstated. Every knitting pattern gives a tension measurement and this refers to the number of stitches and rows which go to make up a square of knitted fabric using the stitch pattern given. The tension is usually given for a 10cm/4in square like this:

21 stitches and 26 rows to 10cm/4in worked in stocking stitch.

This is the tension, shown in the example below, which you must try to achieve.

Different people knit at different tensions – some people naturally knit tightly, others knit loosely and beginners will find their tension alters as they become more proficient.

You should always knit a tension square before starting a pattern. Cast on at least four extra stitches and knit at least four more rows than the given tension so that you can measure it accurately when it is laid on a flat surface.

Adjusting the tension If your sample measures *more* than the given tension you are working too loosely. Change to one size smaller needles and work another tension square.

If your sample measures *less* than the given tension you are working too tightly. Change to a size larger needles and work another tension square.

Yarn used for knitting a tension square is never wasted. A small skein unravelled and stitched into the seam and washed with the garment will be in the same condition and can be used for darning and repairs. Or you can use the yarn to sew up the seams when the garment is completed.

Substituting yarn Some spinners give a recommended tension over stocking stitch on the ball band of the yarn. This is only a guide, but it can also help when you are substituting a different yarn from that recommended by the pattern.

How to hold the yarn and needles

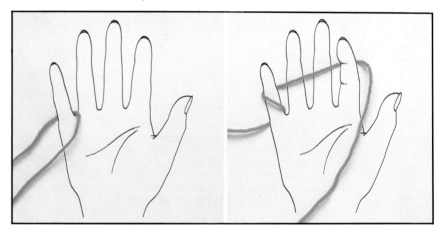

There are several different ways of holding the yarn and needles. The following method is commonly called the English method.

1 Wind the yarn round the little finger of your right hand, behind the middle fingers and over the index finger. This controls the flow of the yarn and helps to maintain the correct tension.

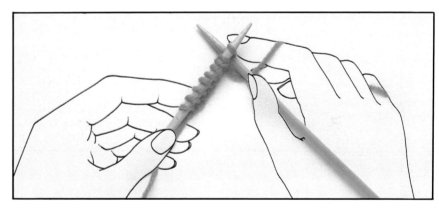

2 Hold the left-hand needle with the stitches with your left hand over the stitches and use the finger and thumb to push the stitches along towards the end of the needle.

3 Hold the right-hand needle like a pencil with the needle resting between the thumb and index finger. Use the index finger to push the yarn round the needle.

The patterns

Both metric and imperial measurements are given for the actual finished size of each garment and both measurements are also used throughout the patterns. The pattern piece diagrams give the measurements in centimetres only.

The standard abbreviations used in the patterns can be found on the next page. Any special abbreviations are given within each pattern.

The yarn quantities quoted are based on average requirements; always buy sufficient yarn to complete the garment and check that it comes from the same dye lot.

Easy or difficult?

To help you choose patterns which suit your ability we have given them the following symbols.

✳	very easy or quick to make
✳✳	easy
✳✳✳	more advanced
✳✳✳✳	advanced, ideal for the more experienced knitter

ABBREVIATIONS

Below are listed the common abbreviations used in all
the patterns. When you are knitting use this page as a handy reference.
Any abbreviations which are specifically used in a
particular pattern will be given at the beginning of that pattern.

alt	alternate(ly)	p2sso	pass 2 slipped stitches over
approx	approximate(ly)	p	purl
beg	begin(ning)	pw	purlwise direction
ch	chain(s)	rem	remain(ing)
cm	centimetre(s)	rep	repeat(ing)
cont	continu(e)(ing)	rev st st	reversed stocking stitch
dc	double crochet	RS	right side of fabric
dec	decreas(e)(ing)	sl	slip
dtr	double treble	sl st	slip stitch(es)
foll	following	skpo	slip 1, knit 1, pass slipped stitch over
g st	garter stitch	sp	space (crochet)
g	gramme(s)	sppo	slip 1, purl 1, pass slipped stitch over
inc	increas(e)(ing) by working twice into a stitch	ss	slip stitch (crochet)
k	knit	st(s)	stitch(es)
kw	knitwise direction	st st	stocking stitch
m	metre(s)	tbl	through back of loop
Mb	make bobble, as specified	tog	together
mm	millimetres	tr	treble
M1	make one by picking up loop lying between needles and knitting through back of loop to increase one	WS	wrong side
		yf	yarn forward
		ytf	yarn to front
		ytb	yarn to back
M1pw	work as for M1, except this time purling through back of loop to increase one	yon	yarn over needle
		yrn	yarn round needle
patt	pattern		
psso	pass slipped stitch over		

USING CHARTS

Some of the most exciting patterns have pictorial or abstract motifs which are worked from charts. If you have never worked from a chart before don't be put off – you will find some handy hints which will make it a lot easier than you expect.

To fit a whole pattern into the space available, some of the charts have to be printed quite small. As long as it is for your own personal use, if you have access to a photocopier which will enlarge, simply enlarge the chart a couple of times, *or* buy some graph paper and copy out the pattern, square by square and line by line.

When working from the chart insert a glass-headed pin at the beginning of each row to keep your place. Move it along as you complete the row.

A line magnifier will enlarge the chart *and* keep track of the line you are working on. Simply slip it over the page and move it up, line by line.

SYMBOLS

* An asterisk in a pattern row means that the stitches after this sign must be repeated.

★ A star at the beginning and end of a patterned section means this section will be repeated later.

[] Instructions in square brackets, mean that this section of the pattern is worked for all sizes.

() Instructions shown in round brackets are for larger sizes.

NEEDLE CONVERSION CHART

Metric	Imperial	Metric	Imperial
2mm	14	5½mm	5
2¼mm	13	6mm	4
2¾mm	12	6½mm	3
3mm	11	7mm	2
3¼mm	10	7½mm	1
3¾mm	9	8mm	0
4mm	8	9mm	00
4½mm	7	10mm	000
5mm	6		

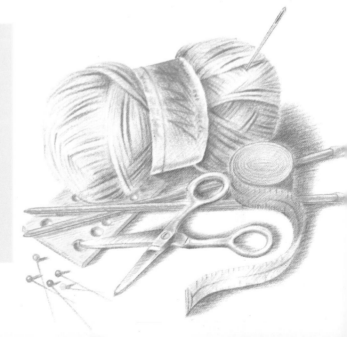

TECHNIQUES
CASTING ON

The one needle method is easy and fast but it does leave a loose edge. Casting on with two needles, known as the cable method, is more commonly used as it gives a neat, firm edge.

Casting on with one needle

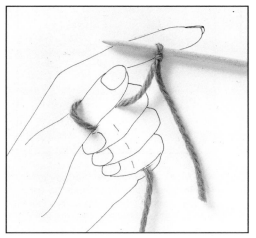

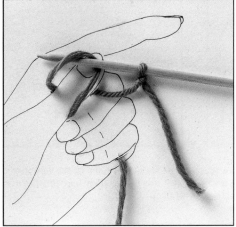

2 Insert the needle through the loop, round the thumb and pull loop off thumb, on to needle.

1 Make a slip loop and place on needle. Hold the needle with the slip loop in the right hand. With thumb and fingers of the left hand, hold yarn as shown.

3 Leave this stitch on the needle and tighten the end of yarn. Wind the end of yarn round the thumb again, ready to make the next stitch. Continue in this way until the required number of stitches are cast on.

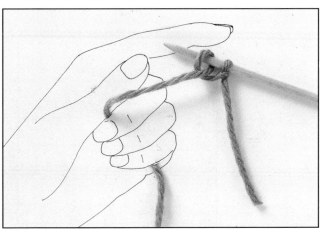

Casting on with two needles

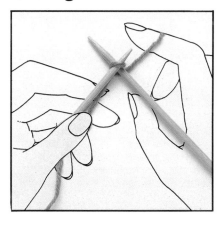

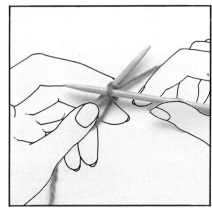

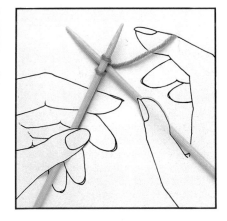

1 Make a slip loop and place on left-hand needle. Tighten loop. Insert the point of right-hand needle into the slip loop from the front to the back, take the yarn under and round the point.

2 Draw the yarn through the slip loop to make a stitch. Place the new stitch on to the left-hand needle.

3 To make next stitch insert needle from front to back *between* the two stitches. Take yarn as before under and round the point of the right-hand needle and draw yarn through. Put new stitch on to left-hand needle. Repeat step 3 until required number of stitches are cast on.

INVISIBLE CASTING ON

This method is used with ribbing and
garter stitch, producing a softer, more elastic edge and a
finish similar to machine-made garments.
It is particularly useful for textured knobbly yarns.

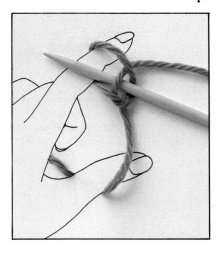

1 Using a length of contrast colour yarn, make a slip loop, place on needle and cast on *half* the number of stitches required, rounding up to the nearest whole stitch.

2 Change to main colour yarn. Knit one stitch, then bring yarn forward to make a stitch.

3 *Knit the next stitch and bring yarn forward again. Repeat from * to last stitch, knit one stitch. (Do not worry if there is one stitch short of the total required at this stage.)

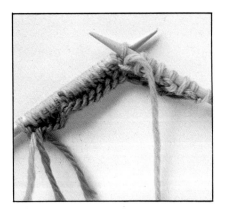

4 On the next row, knit the first stitch, bring the yarn to the front of the work and slip the next stitch purlwise (called sl 1pw).

5 Take the yarn to the back of the work and knit the next stitch. Repeat steps 4 and 5 to the end of the row.

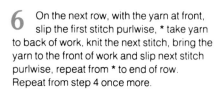

6 On the next row, with the yarn at front, slip the first stitch purlwise, * take yarn to back of work, knit the next stitch, bring the yarn to the front of work and slip next stitch purlwise, repeat from * to end of row. Repeat from step 4 once more.

7 Continue in k1, p1 rib for the required length, increasing one stitch at the end of the first row if needed to give the required number of stitches in pattern. Carefully unpick the contrast yarn (see left), cutting if necessary.

HOW TO KNIT STITCHES

Knitting through front of stitch

1 Hold the needle with stitches in your left hand and the free needle in your right hand. Insert the right-hand needle from the front to the back under the front loop of the first stitch.

2 With the yarn held at the back throughout, take it under and around the point of the needle.

Knitting through back of stitch

1 Hold the needle with stitches in your left hand and the free needle in your right hand. Insert the right-hand needle from the front to the back under the back loop of the first stitch.

2 With the yarn held at the back throughout, take it under and around the point of the needle.

3 Draw the yarn through on to the right-hand needle and allow the first stitch to drop off the left-hand needle. This is called **k1**.
Continue to the end of the row.

3 Draw the yarn through on to the right-hand needle and allow the first stitch to drop off the left-hand needle. This is called **k1 tbl**.
Continue to the end of the row.

 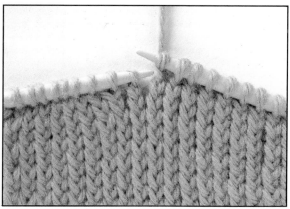

HOW TO PURL STITCHES

Purling through front of stitch

2 With the yarn held at the front throughout, take it over the top and round the point of the needle.

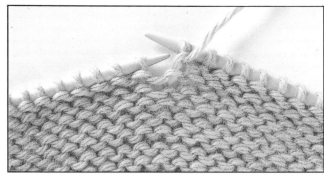

1 Hold the needle with the cast-on stitches in your left hand and the free needle in your right hand. Insert the right-hand needle from right to left into the front loop of the first stitch.

3 Draw the yarn back through the first stitch on to the right-hand needle and allow the first stitch to drop off the left-hand needle. This is called **p1**.
Continue to the end of the row.

Purling through back of stitch

1 Hold the needle with the cast-on stitches in your left hand and the free needle in your right hand. Insert the right-hand needle from right to left into the back of the loop of the first stitch.

2 With the yarn held at the front throughout, take it over the top and round the point of the needle.

3 Draw the yarn back through the first stitch on to the right-hand needle and allow the first stitch to drop off the left-hand needle. This is called **p1 tbl**.
Continue to the end of the row.

LOOSE INVISIBLE CASTING ON

**This method uses the main colour yarn to produce
a neat, loose edge for single rib. Unlike invisible casting on,
this technique cannot be used with knobbly yarns
as the cast on yarn is withdrawn when the rib is complete.**

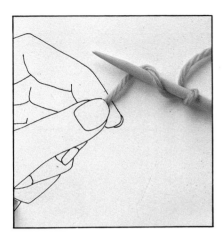

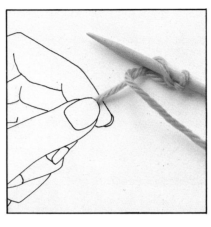

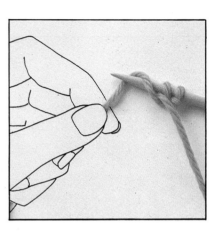

3 Wind the yarn from the ball around the needle once again from front to back.

1 Make a slip loop about 50cm/20in from end of a ball of yarn (this should be enough to make 25 stitches in DK yarn). Place the slip loop on a needle and hold it in your right hand. * With your left hand take the yarn from the ball around the needle once, from front to back.

2 Bring the loose end of yarn from back to front, under the needle and over the main length of yarn, pulling it taut so that the yarn over the needle forms a stitch.

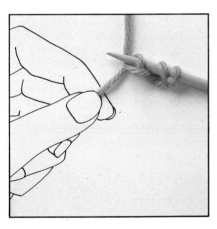

4 Bring loose end of yarn from front to back, under needle and over yarn from the ball, pulling it taut so that the yarn over needle forms a third stitch. It helps to hold the needle with your left hand when bringing the loose end of yarn from back to front and front to back. Rep from * until required number have been cast on.

5 Work the next row with two needles as follows: *k1 tbl, ytf, sl 1 pw, ytb, rep from * to the end of the row, knitting the last stitch if an odd number is required.

6 On the next row knit the slipped stitches and slip the knitted stitches, taking the yarn forward and back between the slipped stitches. If you are using a fine yarn work a third row in this way.
Continue working in k1, p1 rib for the required length. When the rib is complete, pull the loose end of yarn through the first cast-on row to neaten the edge.

INVISIBLE CASTING OFF

These two methods of casting off give a neat
finished edge to a knit one, purl one rib and match the invisible
method of casting on. They are used where the cast-off
edge will show – at neck edges and pocket tops, for example.

Invisible casting off using 2 needles

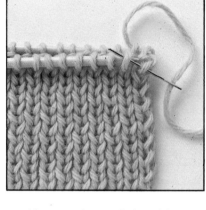

1 Start with an even number of stitches, decreasing 1 stitch if necessary, then two or three rows before casting off, work as follows: * k1, ytf, sl 1, ytb, rep from * to end. Rep this row, slipping the knit stitches and knitting the slipped stitches. Using a pair of double pointed needles, slip alternate stitches on to the needles so that all knit stitches are on one needle and all purl stitches on the other. Break yarn leaving an end 4 times the width of the knitting. Thread a blunt sewing needle with the yarn and, with the knit stitches facing, insert needle from right to left into the first knit stitch on the front needle.

2 Pull yarn through and let the first knit stitch drop off the needle. Insert sewing needle from left to right into the first purl stitch on the back needle and pull yarn through letting stitch drop off needle.

3 * Insert sewing needle from right to left through the previous knit stitch again and then through the next knit stitch on the front needle. Pull yarn through letting stitch drop off needle.

4 Insert sewing needle from left to right through the previous purl stitch again and then, from left to right, through next purl stitch on back needle. Pull yarn through letting stitch drop off needle. Rep from * until all the stitches have been threaded through.
You may find it easier to leave the first threaded knit and purl stitches on the needles until the second stitches have been threaded through.

Invisible casting off using 1 needle

1 Break off yarn leaving an end 4 times the width of the knitting and thread it through a blunt sewing needle. Insert needle through first stitch from right to left and draw through yarn letting stitch drop off needle. Insert sewing needle through next purl stitch from left to right and draw yarn through.

2 * Insert needle from right to left through the previous knit stitch dropped off the knitting needle and then through the next knit stitch on knitting needle. Draw yarn through and slip stitch off needle. Insert sewing needle into the previous purl stitch dropped off knitting needle then, from left to right, through next purl stitch. Draw yarn through and slip stitch off knitting needle. Repeat from * until all the stitches have been threaded through.

CASTING OFF

Casting off is used to finish off a section of
knitting, when making buttonholes or for certain types of
shaping such as armholes and shoulders. Try to
keep the cast off stitches even and darn in the ends neatly.

Casting off with a crochet hook

This method casts off loosely and can
be used for casting off any stitch
pattern.

1 Transfer stitches on to the empty
needle so that the yarn end is at the
opposite end from the point of the
needle. With right side facing, hold the
needle with stitches in your left hand.
Slip the first stitch on to a crochet hook
and insert the hook into next stitch.

2 Draw the second stitch through
the first stitch with the crochet
hook and off the needle. One stitch has
been cast off.

3 Continue to cast off in this way until one stitch
remains. Fasten off yarn end using method
shown overleaf.

Casting off knitwise

1 Knit the first 2 stitches. Insert the point of the left-hand
needle into the first knitted stitch on the right-hand needle.

2 Lift the first knitted stitch over the second and off the
right-hand needle, leaving one stitch on the needle. Knit
another stitch and continue to pass the first stitch over and off
until one stitch remains. This is called **casting off kw**. Fasten
off (see overleaf).

CASTING OFF
AND FASTENING OFF YARN

Casting off purlwise

1 Purl the first 2 stitches. Insert the point of the left-hand needle into the first purled stitch on the right-hand needle.

2 Lift the first purled stitch over the second and off the needle, leaving one stitch on the needle. Purl another stitch and continue to pass the first stitch over and off until one stitch remains. This is called **casting off pw**. Fasten off (see below).

Fastening off

1 Cut yarn leaving about 10cm/4in spare. Thread yarn end through last stitch loop. Pull to tighten.

2 Thread a large-eyed blunt needle with the remaining yarn and thread through **row** ends for 3–4cm/1–1½in. Pull yarn through and trim.

INCREASING STITCHES

To increase means to add a stitch or stitches,
thereby changing the shape of the knitting. Stitches can be
added invisibly or decoratively; slanting to
the left or right; at the edges or in the middle of a row.

Decorative increasing forming eyelet holes

On a knit row, work until position for increase is reached. Bring yarn forward between needles and back over the right-hand needle and knit the next stitch. On the next row, the yarn over needle is worked as a stitch. This is called **yf**.

On a purl row, work until position for increase is reached. Take yarn from front of work over and under right-hand needle and purl the next stitch. On the next row, the yarn round the needle is worked as a stitch. This is called **yrn**.

Increasing invisibly knitwise

1 Pick up yarn lying between the stitch just worked and next stitch on left-hand needle. Place on left-hand needle.

2 Knit into the back of the loop – this twists the stitch and avoids a hole in the fabric. This is called **M1**.

Increasing invisibly purlwise

1 Pick up yarn lying between the stitch just worked and the next stitch on left-hand needle. Place on left-hand needle.

2 Purl into the back of loop by inserting right-hand needle from left to right to twist the stitch – this avoids a hole in the fabric and is called **M1 pw**.

Increasing into a knit stitch

Increasing into a purl stitch

Knit first stitch but do not drop it off the left-hand needle. Insert right-hand needle into back loop of the same stitch and knit again, this time dropping stitch off left-hand needle. This is called **inc kw into next st**.

1 At position of increase, purl next stitch but do not drop it off left-hand needle.

2 Insert right-hand needle into back of loop of same stitch and purl it again, this time dropping stitch off the left-hand needle. This is called **inc pw in next st**.

Increasing to the right on a knit row

Increasing to the left on a purl row

At position of increase, insert right-hand needle into top loop of stitch on row below next stitch on left-hand needle. Knit an extra stitch through this stitch then knit the next stitch on the left-hand needle. The increased stitch slants to the right on the knit side of stocking stitch.

At position of increase, insert right-hand needle from back to front into top loop of stitch on row below next stitch on left-hand needle. Purl an extra stitch through this stitch then purl the next stitch on the left-hand needle. The increased stitch slants to the left on the knit side of stocking stitch.

Increasing several stitches at the beginning of a row

1 It is easier to cast on at the beginning of two consecutive rows than at the beginning and end of the same row. Use the two needle method to cast on the number of stitches required at the beginning of the row. (See page 1.)

2 Work across the cast-on stitches and continue to the end of the row. Cast on the same number of stitches at the beginning of the next row, using the two needle method.

INCREASING SYMMETRICALLY

**The increases can be clearly defined by making
stitches each side of a raised centre stitch or by adding moss or
lacy stitches each side of it. A less obvious
increase is obtained by knitting twice into the centre stitches.**

Picking up stitches

Knit to centre stitch, M1 (make one by picking up loop lying between
needles and knitting through back of loop to increase one), knit
centre stitch, M1, then knit to end.
Next row Purl to end.
Repeat these two rows for the required number of increases.
Note: A second centre stitch can be added for emphasis.

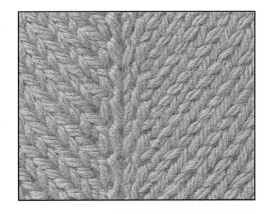

Knitting twice into stitches

Knit to within one stitch of centre stitch. Knit into front and back of
next two stitches, then knit to end.
Next row Purl to end.
Repeat these two rows for the required number of increases.

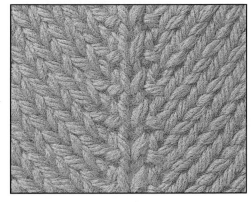

Knitting and purling into stitches

Knit to within one stitch of centre stitch. Knit and purl into next stitch,
knit centre stitch, purl and knit into next stitch, then knit to end.
Next row Purl to end.
Repeat these two rows for the required number of increases.

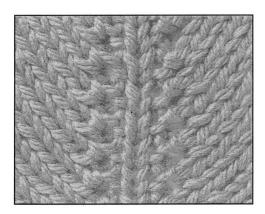

Decorative lacy increases

Knit to centre stitch, bring yarn forward to make a stitch, knit the
centre stitch, bring yarn forward again, then knit to end.
Next row Purl to end.
Repeat these two rows for the required number of increases.

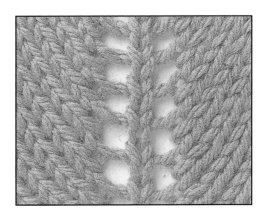

DECREASING SYMMETRICALLY

The decreases are made by knitting stitches together or slipping, knitting together and passing slipped stitches over. The decreased stitch can slant from the left or the right or create a raised centre stitch.

Knitting 3 centre stitches together through back of loops

Knit to within one stitch of centre stitch. Knit the next three stitches together through back of loops, then knit to end.

Next row Purl to end.

Repeat these two rows for required number of decreases.

Knitting and slipping 3 centre stitches

Knit to within one stitch of centre stitch. Knit the next two stitches together through back of loops, slip this stitch back on to left-hand needle purlwise, pass the second stitch on left-hand needle over first stitch and off needle, slip first stitch purlwise back on to right-hand needle, then knit to end.

Next row Purl to end.

Repeat these two rows for required number of decreases.

Slipping and knitting 3 centre stitches

Knit to within one stitch of centre stitch. Slip the next stitch, knit the next two stitches together and pass the slipped stitch over, then knit to end.

Next row Purl to end.

Repeat these two rows for required number of decreases.

Twisting and knitting 3 centre stitches

Work to within one stitch of centre stitch. Insert right-hand needle through next two stitches as if to knit together and slip on to right-hand needle without knitting, knit the next stitch, then pass the slipped stitches over.

Next row Purl to end.

Repeat these two rows for required number of decreases.

Knitting 3 centre stitches together

Knit to within one stitch of centre stitch. Knit the next three stitches together, then knit to end.

Next row Purl to end.

Repeat these two rows for the required number of decreases.

DECREASING STITCHES

To decrease means to take away a stitch or
stitches, thus gradually altering the shape of the knitting.
Stitches can be decreased at the edges or in
the middle of a row, slanting to the right or to the left.

Slip stitch decrease on a knit row

1 Work until decrease position is reached. Slip a stitch on to the right-hand needle, then knit the next stitch.

2 Lift the slipped stitch over the knit stitch and off the needle. The stitch will slant to the left. This is called **skpo**.

Slip stitch decrease on a purl row

1 Work until decrease position is reached. Purl a stitch then slip it back on to the left-hand needle.

2 Pass 2nd stitch on left-hand needle over purled stitch. Return stitch back to right-hand needle by slipping it purlwise. The stitch will slant to the left on the right (knit) side. This is called **sppo**.

Decreasing through back of loops purlwise

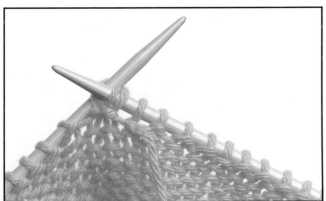 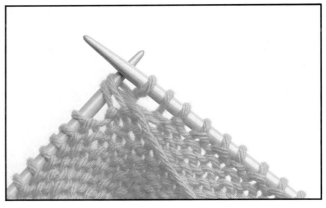

1 Work until decrease position is reached. Insert the right-hand needle through the back loops of the next two stitches.

2 Purl these two stitches together and drop them off the left-hand needle. This stitch will slant to the left on the right (knit) side and is called **p2 tog tbl**.

Decreasing through back of loops knitwise

Work until position for decrease is reached. Insert right-hand needle through back of next two stitches and knit together. This stitch will slant to the left and is called **k2 tog tbl**.

Decreasing through front of loops knitwise

1 Work until position for decrease is reached. Insert right-hand needle knitwise into the next two stitches.

2 Knit these two stitches together. This stitch will slant to the right and is called **k2 tog**.

Decreasing through front of loops purlwise

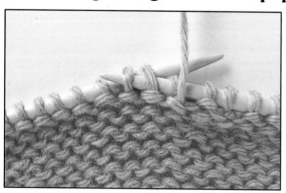

1 Work until decrease position is reached. Insert right-hand needle purlwise into next 2 stitches.

2 Purl these two stitches together. This stitch will slant to the right on the right (knit) side of the fabric and is called **p2 tog**.

WORKING STITCHES TOGETHER

Slipped and passed over stitches are used not only as a method of decreasing but also as part of many lacy stitch patterns. The stitches are replaced by increasing, using yarn forward, yarn over or yarn round needle.

Slip 1, knit 1, pass slipped stitch over

With yarn at back of work, insert right-hand needle into next stitch on left-hand needle and slip it on to right-hand needle without working. Knit next stitch. Insert left-hand needle in the slipped stitch, take it over the knit stitch and off needle. This is called **skpo**

Slip 1, purl 1, pass slipped stitch over

With yarn at front, insert right-hand needle into next stitch on left-hand needle and slip it on to right-hand needle without working. Purl the next stitch. Insert left-hand needle in the slipped stitch, take it over the purl stitch and off needle. This is called **sppo**.

Knit 2 together

Purl 2 together

Insert right-hand needle into next two stitches on left-hand needle and purl in the usual way letting them both drop off needle together. This is called **p2 tog**.

Insert right-hand needle into next two stitches on left-hand needle and knit in the usual way letting them both drop off needle together. This is called **k2 tog**.

Slip 1, knit 2 together, pass slipped stitch over

1 With yarn at back of work slip one stitch on to right-hand needle. Knit the next two stitches together.

2 With right-hand needle, take the slipped stitch over the two stitches worked together and off needle. This is called **sl 1, k2 tog, psso**.

ELONGATED STITCHES

**Elongated stitches are used for lacy and surface
textured patterns and there are several ways of working them.
The most popular method is to wind the yarn
round the needle more than once while knitting the stitch.**

Knit one stitch below

Insert right-hand needle through the centre
of the stitch below the next stitch on left-
hand needle. Wind yarn round point of
needle and draw loop through. Allow stitch
above on left-hand needle to drop off. This
is called **k1B**.

Winding yarn round needle

1 Insert the right-hand needle into the next
stitch on the left-hand needle. Wind yarn
round needle three times and complete knit
stitch in the usual way.

2 On the next row allow the extra loops
made by winding yarn round needle to
drop off the left-hand needle as you work
the elongated stitch. When this method is
used in a row it forms an openwork band.

Elongated stitch

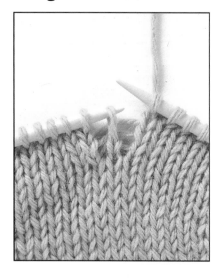

Insert right-hand needle through the centre
of the stitch two rows below the next stitch
on left-hand needle. Allow stitch above on
left-hand needle to drop off and run down to
stitch held on right-hand needle. Place this
stitch back on left-hand needle and knit in
the usual way. This is called **k2B**.

Elongated stitch using crochet hook

1 Knit until position for elongated stitch is
reached..Insert crochet hook into the
centre of the stitch three rows below the
next stitch. Wind yarn round hook and pull
loop through.

2 Place loop on left-hand needle and
knit loop and next stitch on left-hand
needle together through back of loops.

SELVEDGES

**Selvedge stitches are used to neaten the edges of
a piece of knitting when they are left showing and not sewn into
a seam. They are commonly used on the edges of
scarves, collars, and the sides of button and buttonhole bands.**

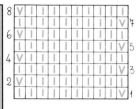

Single chain for garter stitch

At the beginning of every row hold the yarn at the front of the work, slip the first stitch purlwise, then take the yarn to the back of the work and knit to the end of row.

Single chain for stocking stitch

Row 1 Slip the first stitch knitwise, knit to end of row.
Row 2 Slip the first stitch purlwise, purl to end of row.
Repeat these two rows throughout.

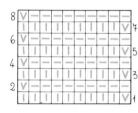

Garter stitch edge

A firm corded edge for stocking stitch.
Row 1 Knit every stitch.
Row 2 Knit the first stitch, purl to last stitch, knit the last stitch.
Repeat these two rows throughout.

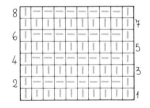

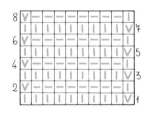

Slip stitch edge

A firm, even border for stocking stitch.
Row 1 Slip the first stitch knitwise, knit to the end of the row.
Row 2 Slip the first stitch knitwise, purl to last stitch, knit this stitch.
Repeat these two rows throughout.

Double garter stitch edge

A very firm border that will not curl.
Row 1 Slip the first stitch knitwise, knit to end of row.
Row 2 Slip the first stitch knitwise, knit one stitch, purl to last two stitches, knit two stitches.
Repeat these two rows throughout.

JOINING IN A NEW BALL OF YARN

A new ball of yarn should, whenever possible, be joined in at the beginning of a row. Sometimes, however, this is not possible or economic, and the join can be made in the middle of a row and the ends darned in for neatness.

At the start of a row

Tie the end of the new ball of yarn to the end of the yarn using a reef knot. Slip the knot up the yarn to the needle and continue to knit using the new yarn. As a rough guide to estimate whether you have enough yarn to knit a complete row, allow about three times the width of the knitting.

With a knot in the middle of a row

As you come to the end of the yarn, use a reef knot to join on the new ball, leaving 6cm/2½in ends. Do not pull the knot too tight. Continue to knit, keeping the yarn ends and knot on the wrong side of the work.
When the piece is finished, and with wrong side facing, untie and retie the reef knot, adjusting the stitches evenly. Use a large-eyed blunt needle to darn in each end separately, vertically down the knitting.

Splicing yarns with a needle

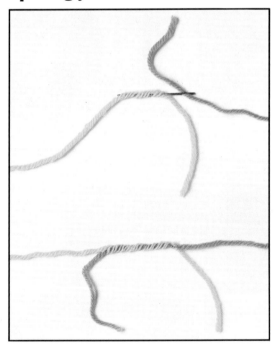

Thread a large-eyed blunt needle with the new yarn, leaving a 10cm/4in end. Starting about 10cm/4in from the end, push the threaded needle through the centre of the old yarn for at least 5cm/2in and pull yarn end through. Unthread needle and knit the next few stitches carefully with the spliced yarn, leaving the loose ends on the wrong side of the work. Darn in the ends as above.
Note Two colours of yarn have been used for clarity.

Using yarn double

1 As you come to the end of the yarn, add in the new ball of yarn and knit a few stitches using the yarns double. Then continue to knit the rest of the row using the new yarn alone leaving both ends hanging down on the wrong side of the work.

2 Trim yarn ends to 10cm/4in and use a large-eyed blunt needle to darn in each end separately, vertically down the knitting.

HORIZONTAL HEMS

Hems can be worked at the beginning or the end of a
piece of work, depending on whether it is knitted upwards or downwards
to create a welt, neckband, waistband or skirt hem.
Contrast coloured yarn has been used here for sewing up for clarity.

Ridge hem at start

Using a size smaller needles and contrast
yarn cast on required number of stitches.
Change to main yarn and work depth of hem
in st st ending with a k row. Knit the next row
thus producing a ridge on RS of work.
Change to correct size needles and
complete garment. Carefully unpick
contrast yarn, slipping stitches on to a needle.

Ridge hem at end

Knit in st st to position of edge to be
turned under ending with a k row. Next
row, knit all the stitches to form a ridge
on RS of work. Change to size smaller
needles and work in st st to required
depth of hem.

Stitching a ridge hem

With WS facing, turn up hem at hemline
ridge. Thread a needle with yarn and
slipstitch each stitch on knitting needle
to corresponding stitch at back of work.

Slip stitch hem at beginning of work

1 Cast on required number of stitches with size smaller needles
than given for main fabric. Work depth of hem ending with WS
row.
Next row * K1, ytf, sl 1 pw, ytb, rep from * to end.

2 Change to correct size needles and complete piece according
to pattern. With WS facing turn up hem at slip stitch line, thread
needle with yarn and slipstitch hem in position.

Knitted in hem

1 Using size smaller needles and contrast yarn, cast on the
required number of stitches. Change to main colour yarn and
work twice the depth of finished hem, ending with a purl row.

2 Carefully unpick contrast yarn, slipping stitches on to a needle
and starting the opposite end from point of needle holding the
stitches. Fold hem in half and, using the correct size needle, knit
together one stitch from each needle to end of row.

Invisible hem at beginning of work

1   Using contrast colour yarn, cast on half required number of stitches, plus one stitch if an uneven number is needed. Change to main colour yarn and knit five rows, ending with a RS row.

2   * Work one stitch then pick up and work a stitch from first row in main colour along line of two colour stitches. Rep from * to end.

3   Complete piece according to rib used in pattern then carefully unpick cast-on row in contrast yarn.

Picot hem at beginning of work

1   Using a contrast colour yarn and one size smaller needles than given for the main fabric, cast on an odd number of stitches (one less than the final total if an even number of sts are given in pattern). Beginning with a knit row, work an even number of rows in stocking stitch to required depth of hem. Change to correct size needles.
Next row * K2 tog, yf, rep from * to last st, k1.
Next row P to end, inc 1 st at beg if an even number of sts is required.

2   When garment is complete and side seams have been joined unpick contrast yarn carefully, slipping stitches on to a circular needle (or set of needles). Thread a large-eyed blunt needle with yarn and slipstitch to wrong side of work.

Grafting a picot hem on right side

1   Work as given above for picot hem but this time using purl side as right side. Thread large-eyed blunt needle with yarn and insert needle through back of loop of first stitch on knitting needle, then purlwise through second stitch on needle dropping both stitches off needle.

2   Insert needle from below through stitch above first stitch dropped off knitting needle and down through stitch above second stitch dropped off needle. Continue in this way until all the stitches have been grafted on to the work.

VERTICAL HEMS AND BORDERS

A turned back border is usually worked on more
tailored garments knitted in stocking stitch to give a neat firm edge
or on a curved edge instead of a ribbed band.
Decorative borders knitted in moss or garter stitch also look neat.

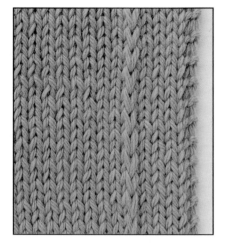

Vertical turned-back border

1 Cast on additional stitches at the edge which is to be turned back to form a hem. Work in stocking stitch, slipping the stitch on the foldline, purlwise, on every knit row.

2 When the garment has been completed, fold the hem to the wrong side along the slip stitch line and sew in place.

Moss stitch border

With the right side facing, pick up and knit required number of stitches along border edge, rounding up or down to an odd number. Work in moss stitch on every row as follows: K1, * p1, k1, rep from * to end. When border is complete, cast off.

Knitted-in border

Using a spare needle and beginning at neck edge, pick up one stitch every two rows along border edge.
Cast on stitches for border.
Row 1 Knit to end, knitting the last stitch together with first stitch from spare needle.
Row 2 Knit to end.
Repeat these two rows until border is complete, then cast off.

Fold-over hem and border

1 Work a ridge hem at start of work, casting on with main colour yarn (see page 19). At the end of the ridge knit row cast on the required number of stitches for turned-back vertical border edge. Continue in stocking stitch, slipping the stitch on the fold-line, purlwise, on every knit row.

2 Fold lower hem along ridge and sew in position. Fold border hem along slip stitch line and over lower hem, then stitch into position.

Mitred fold-over hem and border

A mitred hem reduces the thickness at the corner and is particularly suitable for garments knitted in a thick yarn.

1 Using a size smaller needles cast on required number of stitches for lower edge minus half the number of rows of the completed hem. For example, if the required number of stitches is 50 and the turned back hem is 8 rows deep, cast on 46 stitches, 4 less than the final number.
Beginning with a knit row, work eight rows (or required number for hem) stocking stitch, increasing one stitch at border edge on every purl row.
Knit two rows, increasing one stitch at the end of the second ridge row.
Change to correct size needles and continue in stocking stitch, slipping a stitch purlwise on the foldline and increasing one stitch at border edge on every purl row for eight rows (or until required number of stitches have been increased).
Work straight in stocking stitch, slipping a stitch as before until piece is complete.

2 Fold lower hem and front border to wrong side and oversew mitred edges of corners. Sew lower and border hems in position.

2 Turn hem to wrong side and stitch into place, taking care not to pull the stitching too tight.

Curved fold-over hem

1 With right side facing and using a size smaller needles, pick up required number of stitches round curved edge. Knit one row to form turn ridge. Continue in stocking stitch, increasing evenly along curved parts of edge by knitting into the front and back of a stitch. Cast off loosely.

BUTTONHOLES

Attention to simple details such as buttonholes
gives knitting a professional look. They can be either horizontal
or vertical. Finishing off a buttonhole is
optional. It can be left as it is or hand worked round the edges.

Horizontal buttonhole

1 On the right side knit until position for buttonhole is reached. Cast off 4 stitches (or number given in the pattern). Knit to end of the row.

2 On the wrong side purl to position of buttonhole. Turn work to right side and cast on 4 stitches. Turn work back to purl side again and work to end of the row.

Horizontal buttonhole using crochet hook

1 On right side knit to buttonhole position. Insert crochet hook purlwise into next 2 stitches on left-hand needle and slip both off, drawing second stitch through first to cast it off. Insert hook into next stitch on needle and draw through stitch on hook.

2 Repeat step 1 until the required number of stitches have been cast off. Place last stitch back on to left-hand needle. Turn the work and cast on the number of stitches that have been cast off. Turn work back again and knit to the end of row. This method creates a buttonhole on one row of knitting.

Tailored buttonhole

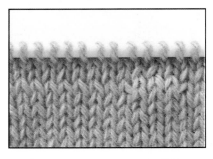

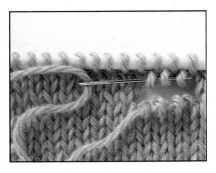

1 Work to position of buttonhole. Using a short length of contrast yarn knit the required number of stitches. Slip these back on left-hand needle and knit them again in main yarn. Knit to end of the row.

2 When garment is complete, remove contrast yarn. Thread a blunt needle with a length of main yarn and run it through all the buttonhole stitches. Finish off with buttonhole stitch (see overleaf).

Vertical buttonhole

1 Work until the position for buttonhole is reached, ending with a right side row. On the next row purl to where buttonhole is required. Turn and leave the last 4 stitches (or number given in pattern) on a stitch holder. Continue across stitches on main part for the number of rows needed to take the size of button, ending with a wrong side row.

2 Return to the stitches on holder. With wrong side facing, join on yarn and purl to end of row. Work the same number of rows as first side of buttonhole, ending with a wrong side row. On the next row knit across all of the stitches to close the buttonhole.

Finishing off with buttonhole stitch

This stitch can be used with horizontal, vertical and loop buttonholes. Thread a blunt needle with yarn and fasten on wrong side. With right side facing bring threaded needle through buttonhole. *Beginning at top left-hand side, insert needle 3mm/⅛in above buttonhole edge and bring it out through buttonhole. Loop yarn from left to right under point of needle and pull needle through to knot thread at buttonhole edge. Repeat from * until buttonhole is covered.

Quick buttonhole

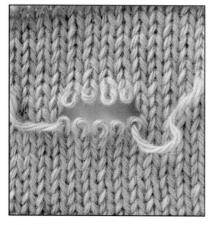

Mark the position for the ends of the horizontal buttonhole with pins. Carefully cut the loop of a central stitch. Unpick the stitches each side to the position of the pins. Finish edges of buttonhole by crotcheting the stitches round the edges (see right) or as for tailored buttonhole on previous page.

Loop buttonhole

A button loop is worked after the garment has been completed. Mark the ends of the button loop with pins. Thread a blunt needle with yarn and use double to make a loop on the edge of the fabric. Using yarn single, cover the loop threads with buttonhole stitch (see top right).

Finishing off with a crochet hook

This stitch is suitable for the tailored buttonhole and the quick buttonhole where the yarn has been cut and stitch loops have been left. Fasten yarn on wrong side and, with right side facing, insert crochet hook into the first stitch. Wind yarn round hook and draw loop through stitch. Insert hook through next stitch, yarn round hook and draw through both stitches on hook. Repeat to end, turning work for second side of buttonhole.

CORRECTING ERRORS

A dropped stitch need not be a disaster. The most
important thing is to stop it running any further down the work.
A wrongly worked stitch, several rows below, can
also be easily corrected using a crochet hook and some patience.

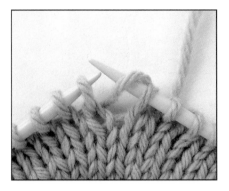

Picking up a dropped knit stitch

1 Stop the stitch from running down any
further by slipping it on to the right-hand
needle. With the point of the right-hand
needle, pick up the loop of yarn between the
second stitch on the right-hand needle and
the first stitch on the left-hand needle.

2 Insert the point of the left-hand needle
through the dropped stitch.

3 Pass the stitch on the right-hand
needle over the loop of yarn and off the
needle, thus 'knitting' it.

4 Pass the stitch back on to the left-hand
needle, taking care not to twist it, ready
to knit in the usual way.

Picking up a dropped purl stitch

1 Stop the stitch from running down any
further by slipping it on to the right-hand
needle. With the point of the right-hand
needle pick up the loop of yarn which runs
between the second stitch on the right-hand
needle and the first stitch on the left-hand
needle.

2 Insert the point of the left-hand needle
through the dropped stitch.

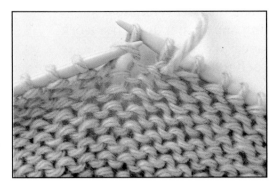

3 Pass the stitch on the right-hand needle over the loop of yarn and off the needle, thus 'purling' it.

4 Pass the stitch back on to the left-hand needle, taking care not to twist it, ready to purl in the usual way.

An error in stocking stitch

1 The stitches are shown on one needle only for clarity. Work to the position directly above the error. Insert a crochet hook into the centre of the stitch below where the mistake is, then drop the stitch directly above this stitch off the needle and let it unravel down to the crochet hook.

2 Use the crochet hook to pick up the bars of yarn in order, making sure you do not split the yarn. Slip the final stitch back on to the left-hand needle and continue working across the row.

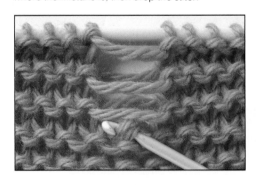

An error in garter stitch

1 The stitches are shown on one needle only for clarity. Work to the position directly above the error. Insert a crochet hook into the centre of the stitch below where the mistake is, then drop the stitch

directly above this stitch off the needle and let it unravel down to the crochet hook. You will see that the bars of yarn run alternately across the back and front of the work. To pick up a bar at the back of the work insert the crochet hook from front to back through the stitch and pick up the bar using the method given above.

2 To pick up the bar at the front of the work insert the crochet hook through from back to front of the stitch and bring it out above the bar. Pull the bar through the stitch. Repeat these two steps until all the bars have been picked up. Slip the stitch back on to the left-hand needle and continue working across the row.

MOVING THE YARN AND STITCHES

There are various ways of moving yarn forwards
and backwards, slipping stitches and twisting stitches. It is
important to use the correct method given in
a particular pattern or the stitch will not knit correctly.

Yarn round needle on a purl row

Take the yarn over the top of the right-hand needle and bring it forward, between the two needles, to the front ready to purl the next stitch. This gives a decorative increase making an eyelet hole and is called **yrn**.

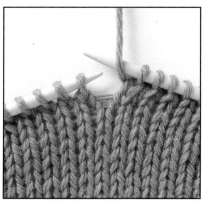

Yarn forward on a knit row

Bring yarn forward between the two needles and over the top of the right-hand needle ready to knit the next stitch. This gives a decorative increase making an eyelet hole and is called **yf**.

Yarn over needle between a purl and knit stitch

Take the yarn from the front of the work, over top of the right-hand needle ready to knit the next stitch. This gives a decorative increase making an eyelet hole and is called **yon**.

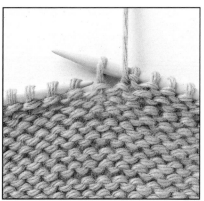

Slip a stitch purlwise

Keeping yarn at front of work, insert the right-hand needle into the next stitch as if to purl it. Slip this stitch on to the right-hand needle without purling it. This is called **sl 1 pw**.

Slip a stitch knitwise

Keeping yarn at back of work, insert the right-hand needle into the next stitch as if to knit it. Slip this stitch on to the right-hand needle without knitting it. This is called **sl 1 kw**.

Yarn over needle between a knit and purl stitch

Bring yarn forward between the two needles, over the top of the right-hand needle and then between the needles to the front again ready to purl the next stitch. This is called **yrn**.

TWISTED STITCHES

Twisting two knit stitches to the right

1 Insert right-hand needle into loop of the second stitch on left-hand needle and knit it *but* do not let stitches fall off left-hand needle.

2 Now knit the first stitch on left-hand needle in the usual way, letting both stitches fall off left-hand needle together. This is called **Tw2R**.

Twisting two knit stitches to the left

1 Insert the right-hand needle through from back of work between the first and second stitches and into the front loop of the second stitch on the left-hand needle and knit it *but* do not let the stitches fall off the left-hand needle.

2 Now knit the first stitch on the left-hand needle in the usual way, letting both stitches fall off the left-hand needle together. This is called **Tw2L**.

Twisting two purl stitches to the right

1 Insert right-hand needle into loop of the second stitch on left-hand needle and purl it *but* do not let stitches fall off left-hand needle.

2 Now purl the first stitch on left-hand needle in the usual way, letting both stitches fall off left-hand needle. This is called **Tw2RP**.

Twisting two purl stitches to the left

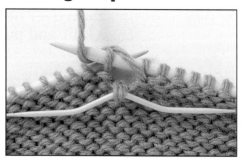

1 Slip the first stitch on the left-hand needle on to a cable needle and hold at front of work. Purl the next stitch but do not let the stitch fall off the left-hand needle.

2 Purl the stitch from the cable needle, letting both of the stitches fall off the needles. This is called **Tw2LP**.

STRANDING AND WEAVING

**Multi-colour knitting will only look professional
if you learn to strand or weave the yarns across the back of the
work correctly. Generally, only two colours are
used in a row although these may change from row to row.**

Weaving yarns in jacquard or Fair Isle

When you are knitting in two colours and there are more than
5 stitches between colour changes, you should weave the yarns in
as you work rather than leave a long loop across the back of the
work. Long loops can be easily caught, on a button for example,
and will pull the knitting out of shape.

Weaving on a knit row

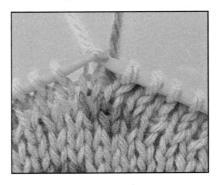

Weaving on a purl row

1 With yarn A, * work to the point where
you need to weave in the second colour
yarn. Insert the right-hand needle into the
next stitch on the left-hand needle as if to
knit it. Take yarn B over yarn A from right to
left and let it drop.

2 Pick up yarn A and knit the stitch.
Repeat from * to the end of the row.

1 With yarn A, * work to the point where
you need to weave in the second colour
yarn. Insert right-hand needle into next
stitch on left-hand needle as if to purl it.
Take yarn B in an anti-clockwise direction
over and round yarn A and let it drop.

2 Pick up yarn A and purl the stitch.
Bring yarn back down over top of
yarn A. Repeat from * to the end of the row.

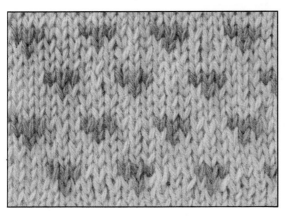

The right side of the knitting.

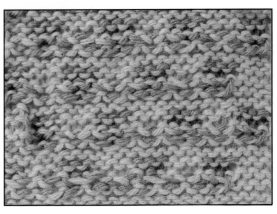

The wrong side of the knitting should look neat
without any loops.

Two colour knitting with yarn in both hands

This technique is used by professional Fair Isle knitters. It may feel awkward at first but as you set up a rhythm you will find it the easiest way of knitting in two colours. Start by learning to knit and purl holding the working yarn in your left hand. When this has been mastered, bring in the second colour in your right hand and continue to knit with a colour in each hand.

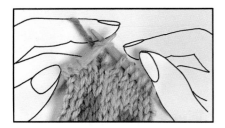

To knit with the left hand

Hold the yarn in the left hand, stranding it across the back of the work from right to left. Insert the right-hand needle into the first stitch on the left-hand needle and pull the yarn through, dropping the stitch off the left-hand needle.

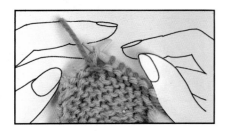

To purl with the left hand

Hold the yarn in the left hand, stranding it across the front of the work from right to left. Insert the right-hand needle purlwise into the first stitch on the left-hand needle and purl the yarn through, dropping the stitch off the left-hand needle.

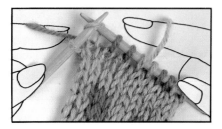

Changing colours on a knit row

Knit the required number of stitches holding yarn A in the right hand, stranding yarn B across the back of the work. Change to yarn B and knit using the method described above, stranding yarn A across the back of the work.

Changing colours on a purl row

Purl the required number of stitches holding yarn A in the right hand, stranding yarn B across the front of the work. Change to yarn B and purl using the method described above, stranding yarn A across the front of the work.

Stranding yarns in jacquard or Fair Isle

When knitting in two colours and changing colours every three or four stitches, you can strand the yarn across the back of the work when not in use. Take care not to pull these loops too tightly or it will affect your tension and distort the knitting. As you practise this technique you will find that you can hold both yarns at the same time, bringing them in one after the other. Some knitters find it helps to use a larger size of knitting needles when working a band of two-colour work on a stocking stitch garment.

Stranding on a knit row

Knit in yarn A to position of colour change. Drop yarn A and bring yarn B over yarn A and continue to knit along the row, making sure the yarn is not pulled too tight.

Stranding on a purl row

Purl in yarn A to position of colour change. Drop yarn A and bring yarn B over yarn A and continue to purl along the row, making sure the yarn is not pulled too tight.

PICKING UP STITCHES

The way you pick up the stitches on a neckband
or border can add the finishing touch to a well-knitted garment.
Here are a few tips to help you pick up stitches
evenly, knitwise or purlwise, and to balance a pattern.

Along row ends or a curve

1 To pick up knitwise, hold the edge in the left hand and the needle and yarn in the right hand. Insert needle through the fabric, from front to back, at least two threads in from the edge. Wind the yarn round the point of the needle and draw the loop through the fabric.

2 Leave this stitch on the needle, then insert needle back through the fabric, a little to the left of the previous stitch, and pick up the next stitch. Continue in this way until the required number of stitches have been picked up.

Along a cast-on or cast-off edge

To pick up knitwise hold the edge in the left hand and the needle and yarn in the right hand. Insert needle, from front to back, under the top two threads of the cast-off or cast-on stitch. Wind the yarn round the point of the needle and draw the loop through the fabric. Leave this stitch on the needle, then insert needle back under the top two threads of the next cast-off or cast-on stitch to the left of the previous stitch, and pick up the next stitch. Continue in this way until the required number of stitches have been picked up.

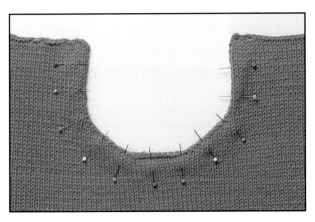

Evenly round a neck

When picking up stitches round a neck, check first with the pattern to see how many stitches need to be picked up. Place pins at 2.5cm/1in intervals along the edge to be picked up. Count how many spaces between the pins there are. Divide the number of stitches to be picked up by the number of spaces; this is then the number of stitches to pick up between each pin.
In the example shown here there are 11 pins giving 12 spaces. The pattern requires you to pick up 48 stitches along the edge. Therefore, divide 48 by 12 to give 4 stitches to be picked up between each pair of pins along the neck edge.

Picking up a stitch purlwise

Usually when you need to pick up stitches, the pattern tells you to pick up and knit the stitch, but ocasionally the pattern will tell you to pick up and purl. This most frequently happens when working an entrelac pattern. To pick up a stitch purlwise work as follows:

1 With the wrong side facing, hold the edge in the left hand and the needle and yarn in the right hand. Insert needle through the fabric, from back to front, at least two threads in from the edge.

2 Wind the yarn round the point of the needle and draw the loop through the fabric. Leave this stitch on the needle, then insert needle back through fabric, a little to the left of the previous stitch, and pick up the next stitch.

Picking up borders on a cardigan

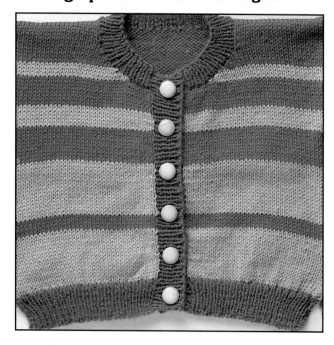

When picking up the button and buttonhole borders of a cardigan with stripes or patterned bands, it is important to make sure that the stripes or bands match up across the front when the cardigan is buttoned up. In order to do this, check first with the pattern to see how many stitches to pick up along each edge, then work as follows.

Even stripes

If the stripes are of an even width, count how many stripes or bands of pattern are in each section, for example from rib to beginning of shaping, from beginning of shaping to shoulder or round the neck. Divide the number of stitches to be picked up in each section by the number of stripes in the section; this is then the number of stitches to pick up along the edge of each stripe.

In the example shown here there are 6 stripes from the rib to neck shaping. The pattern requires you to pick up 30 stitches along this edge. Therefore, divide 30 by 6 to give 5 stitches to be picked up along the edge of each stripe on both the button and buttonhole border.

Uneven stripes

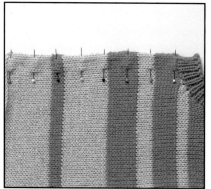

1 If the stripes or patterned bands are uneven, then place pins at 2.5cm/1in intervals along the edge to be picked up. Count how many spaces between the pins there are. Divide the number of stitches to be picked up by the number of spaces; this is then the number of stitches to pick up between each pair of pins.

In the example shown here there are 8 pins. The pattern requires you to pick up 40 stitches along the edge. Therefore, divide 40 by 8 to give 5 stitches to be picked up between each pair of pins along one edge of the cardigan.

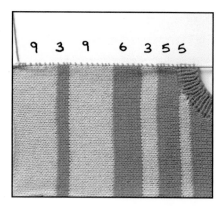

2 Once the stitches have been picked up and the pins removed, make a note of how many stitches have been picked up along the edge of each stripe. When picking up the stitches along the edge of the second front of the cardigan, pick up the same number along the edge of each individual stripe.

ROUND NECKLINES

Before knitting the neckband using any of these methods, join the right shoulder seam. The neckbands are knitted on a pair of needles but several needles were used in the pictures so that the knitting could be laid out flat.

Leaving stitches on needles

Work to position of neck shaping, ending with a WS row. Work across sts for first side of neck as given in patt, turn and leave rem sts, including centre sts on spare needle. Work next row. * On the next row work to last st, turn, leaving st unworked, then work back on rem sts. Rep from * until all neck decreases have been left unworked on needle. Work straight to completion of left front. Leaving sts for centre front neck on a holder, complete right front in the same way. Stitches (shown left) have been left on separate needles for clarity.

   Changing needle size if required, pick up and k sts down straight edge of neck, k across sts held on needle, picking up extra sts in between as necessary to avoid holes, k across sts on centre front neck holder, then complete right side of neck in the same way.

Picking up stitches with crochet hook

With RS facing and beg at shoulder edge of left front neck, insert a crochet hook into the middle of the first st. Wind yarn round hook, pull loop through and place on needle. Rep round neck until required number of sts have been picked up.

Picking up stitches with a needle

With RS facing and beg at shoulder edge of left front neck, insert the point of the needle into the middle of the first st. Wind yarn round needle, pull loop through and leave on needle. Rep round neck until required number of sts have been picked up.

The completed neckband

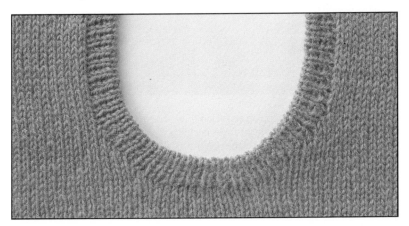

Using any of these methods to pick up stitches round the neck, complete by working in rib for the required measurement. Cast off using the invisible cast off method as shown here (see page 6) or in rib.

SEWN-ON NECKBANDS

Both these neckbands are knitted separately and
then sewn on. Join the right shoulder seam before sewing on the
neckband, then sew the left shoulder and neckband
seam. Contrast colour yarns have been used for clarity.

Ribbed neckband

1 Cast on the required number of sts using
the invisible casting on method (see
page 2). Rib until neckband is correct
length. Join on contrast yarn and work
4 rows st st. Remove sts from needle.

Folded st st neckband

2 With RS of garment facing, pin
neckband in position round neck with
the st st edge overlapping the edge. Thread
a blunt needle with yarn to match garment
and backstitch neckband to neck edge,
inserting needle through the centre of each
rib st.

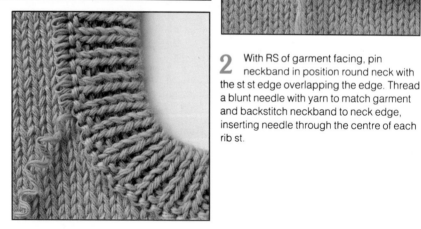

3 Unpick st st worked in contrast yarn,
checking that every rib st has been
stitched to prevent band from unravelling.

1 Cast on the required number of sts to
fit the neck edge. Work twice the
width of the finished neckband, leaving
the sts on the needle.
Thread a blunt needle with matching
yarn and, with RS of neckband facing
WS of garment, oversew band to neck
edge.

2 Fold band to right side and, slipping sts off the
needle, backstitch neckband to neck edge, inserting
sewing needle through centre of every stitch.

V NECKLINES

**The neckband on a V-shaped neckline can be mitred,
with decreases each side of a central stitch, or overlapped at the
centre front. The band is usually knitted in
rib, but garter stitch or stocking stitch can also be used.**

Preparing a V neck

1 A classic V neckline usually starts at the same position as the armhole shaping. With an even number of stitches, divide at the centre and knit each side separately. With an odd number of stitches either decrease the centre stitch before dividing the work or leave it on a safety-pin.

The neck decreases are evenly spaced over the number of rows worked to the shoulder, and are either made at the neck edge or 3 to 4 stitches in from the edge, making a fully fashioned neck.

2 Using needles or a crochet hook, pick up evenly the required number of stitches given in the pattern for the neckband (see page 33).

Garter stitch neckband

Join right shoulder seam and pick up an odd number of stitches round neck. Mark the position of the centre stitch of the V with a loop of contrast yarn. Using a pair of needles work as follows:
Row 1 (WS) K to within 2 sts of centre st, skpo, p centre st, k2tog, k to end of row.
Row 2 K to within 2 sts of centre st, skpo, k centre st, k2tog, k to end.
Repeat these 2 rows until the required depth is reached. Cast off knitwise.

Rib neckband

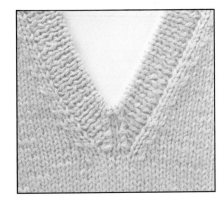

Join right shoulder seam and with RS facing, pick up an even number of stitches round neck plus 1 st from the centre point. Mark the position of the centre stitch with a loop of contrast yarn.
Row 1 (WS) Rib to within 2 sts of centre st, skpo, p centre st, k2tog, rib to end.
Row 2 Rib to within 2 sts of centre st, skpo, k centre st, k2tog, rib to end.
Rep these 2 rows until the required depth is reached. Cast off in rib.

Doubled over rib neckband

Join right shoulder seam and, with RS facing, pick up an even number of stitches round neck, plus 1 st from the centre point.
Row 1 (WS) Rib to within 2 sts of centre st, skpo, p centre st, k2tog, rib to end.
Row 2 Rib to within 2 sts of centre st, skpo, k centre st, k2tog, rib to end.
Rep these 2 rows until required depth is reached, ending with row 1.
Next row Rib to centre st, M1 (pick up loop lying between needles and knit into back of it), k1, M1, rib to end.
Next row Rib to centre st, M1, p1, M1, rib to end.
Rep last two rows for required depth to match first side. Cast off in rib, still increasing each side of centre st. Fold neckband in half to WS and slipstitch in place.

Cross-over neckband

Using a circular needle

Join both shoulder seams. With RS facing and using a circular needle, pick up the required number of stitches round neck, beg and ending at the centre front point. Do not pick up a centre stitch. Work in rib for required depth. Cast off in rib. Overlap edges of neckband and sew down row ends along edge where stitches were picked up.

Using a pair of needles

Join right shoulder seam. With RS facing and beg at left shoulder, pick up the required number of sts down left front neck to centre front point. Work in rib for required depth. Cast off in rib.

With RS facing and beg at centre front point, pick up the required number of sts up right front neck and across back neck. Work in rib for required depth. Cast off in rib.

Join left shoulder and neckband seam, then overlap edges of neckband and sew down row ends as before.

Double rib neckband

Join right shoulder seam. With RS facing pick up an even number of stitches round neck. Mark the 2 centre stitches with loops of contrast yarn. Rib to centre 2 sts, p2, rib to end.

1 Using a pair of needles (four needles have been used here for clarity), rib to within 1 st of 2 centre sts, k2 tog.

2 Slip the second centre stitch on to right-hand needle, knit the next stitch and pass the slipped stitch over the knit stitch. This is called skpo. Rib to end.

3 Repeat these 2 rows until the required depth is reached. Cast off in rib.

COLLAR WITH BUTTON OPENING

**Any pattern with a simple round neck can easily
be adapted to a collar with a placket. At the base of the opening
cast off or leave the centre stitches on a holder,
then complete each side, shaping neck as given in the pattern.**

Picking up stitches each side for placket

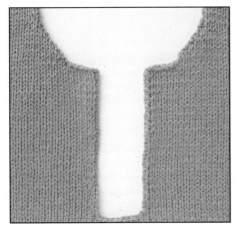

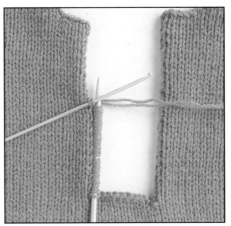

1 * The opening of the placket usually starts at the same position as the armhole. With right side facing, work to within 4 stitches of centre (or required number given in pattern). Turn and slip remaining stitches on to a spare needle. Complete left front neck with shaping, then return to stitches on spare needle *. Join on yarn. Cast off next 8 stitches (or required number), and complete right side of neck to match left side.

2 With right side facing and starting at base of opening, use a crochet hook or needle to pick up and knit stitches up right side of neck.

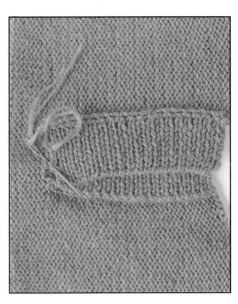

3 Work 16 rows (or required number) in rib, making buttonholes if required. Cast off in rib.
With right side facing and starting at neck edge of opening, pick up and knit the same number of stitches down left side of neck. Cast off in rib.

4 With right side facing, mattress stitch row ends of right neck rib to cast-off edge at base of opening (see page 41).

5 With wrong side facing, place left neck rib over right rib and oversew in position.
Note For a man's jersey add buttonholes on left side of neck.

Picking up stitches from a holder for placket

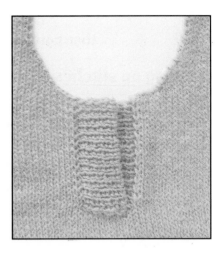

1 Work from * to * as given for step 1 on previous page. Slip next 8 stitches (or required number) on to a holder, join on yarn and complete right side of neck to match left side.

2 With right side facing and starting at base of opening, pick up and knit stitches up right side of neck. Work 16 rows in rib, knitting a stitch from the holder together with the last stitch at the end of each wrong side row and making buttonholes if required. Cast off in rib.

3 With right side facing and starting at neck edge of opening, pick up and knit the same number of stitches up left side of neck. Cast off in rib. Sew row ends on wrong side.
Note For a man's jersey knit stitches from holder and add buttonholes on left side of neck.

Adding a collar

Note The picture shows right side of neck before collar is picked up; left side of neck with stitches being picked up.

1 With right side of work facing and starting at beginning of right neck shaping, pick up and knit the required number of stitches round neckline. Do not pick up the stitches at the top of each placket.

2 Work 12 rows (or required depth) in rib, ending with a wrong side row. Cast off in rib.

BLOCKING AND PRESSING

Care taken in the final stages of finishing the pieces of a garment will help give your knitting a professional look. Careful blocking and pressing is essential, particularly for some modern yarns and textured stitch patterns.

Preparing the pattern pieces

Before you make up a garment you should prepare the pattern pieces carefully.

Darn in the ends

Use a blunt, large eyed needle and carefully darn in all the ends of yarn left at the edges using the method given on page 8.

Block the pattern pieces

This means pinning out each piece on a padded surface such as a table covered with a folded blanket. If you have a piece of evenly-checked gingham use it to cover the blanket. The squares are ideal for making sure the pattern piece is evenly laid out – simply check the number of rows to a square and make sure this is the same all the way up the garment. Use a tape measure to check that the width and length are the same as those given in the pattern and gently pat the piece into shape, particularly where any increasing or decreasing has been done. Some stitch patterns can give the pattern pieces a slight bias and this can be corrected by blocking out the pieces.

If the pieces do not need pressing, simply cover them with a clean wet cloth, well wrung out and leave until completely dry before removing the cloth and unpinning them from the surface.

Pressing

Not all yarns or stitch patterns are suitable for pressing. Consult the ball band of the yarn or check the pressing guide below. Cover

the piece with a clean dry or damp pressing cloth and, with the iron set at the correct temperature, place the iron on the cloth, press and lift it again. Do not move the iron over the surface as you would when ironing normally. Press each area evenly in this way until the whole area has been covered. If you are using a steam iron, allow any steam to evaporate before moving on to the next piece.

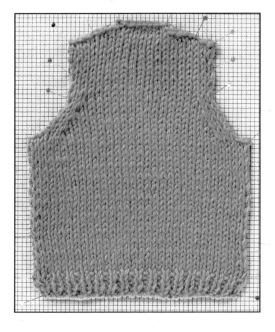

★ **KNIT TIP**

Pressing guide

This is a general guide; always check the ball band first.

Pure wool Press under a damp cloth with a warm iron.

Blends of wool and nylon If the wool content is higher than the nylon, press as for wool.

Blends of wool and acrylic Do not press.

Nylon Press under a dry cloth with a cool iron.

Blends of nylon and acrylic If nylon content is higher than acrylic, press as for nylon.

Acrylic Press under a dry cloth with a cool iron.

Cotton Press under a damp cloth with a warm or hot iron.

Mohair Steam press very lightly.

Angora Steam press very lightly.

Glitter yarn Do not press unless stated on the ball band.

Steam pressing

Place a damp cloth over the piece and set the iron to steam. Begin at the side, holding the cloth just above the surface of the knitting. Allow the iron to come into contact with the cloth but do not press down on to the knitting, so that the steam is forced into the fabric without flattening it.

Press each area in this way and allow the steam to evaporate before moving on to the next pattern piece.

MAKING UP

**After the individual pieces have been blocked
and pressed if necessary, you can start making up the garment.
The method is given in the pattern and can vary
slightly depending on the style, but here is the basic method.**

1 With right sides facing, join the shoulder seams, using one of the methods given on page 41. (In most patterns the neckband is knitted at this stage to avoid the extra weight of the sleeve pulling on the garment and distorting the picked up stitches.)

2 Fold the sleeves in half lengthwise and mark the centre of the sleeve head with a pin.

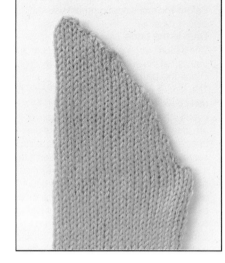

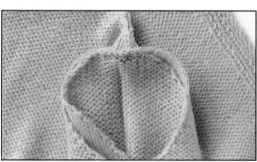

3 With right sides facing, match the centre of the sleeve head with the shoulder seam and pin the sleeve into the garment, slightly stretching the sleeve edge as you go. Sew armhole seams.

4 To finish, pin and sew the side and sleeve seams, working from the armhole to the welt and from the armhole to the cuff.

SEAMS

The making up of a garment needs a lot of care and all the skill which has gone into knitting the stitches is wasted if pieces are badly joined together. A contrast colour yarn is used here to make the stitches clearer.

Swiss darned seams

1 Place the pieces to be joined, edge to edge, right sides facing. Secure yarn with two oversewn stitches on wrong side. Bring the needle up through the right edge stitch. * Insert needle from right to left through the next edge stitch above and the matching left edge stitch.

2 Pull yarn through and insert needle into the base of this stitch and back out under the horizontal thread of the previous stitch. Repeat from * until the seam is complete.

Mattress stitch seams

Place the pieces to be joined, edge to edge, right sides facing. Secure yarn with two oversewn stitches. Pick up the bar between the first and second stitch in from the edge on the right and pull yarn through. Take needle across to the stitch on the same row on the left and pick up bar between first and second stitch. Pass needle back to the next row on the right and pick up bar between stitches. Repeat until seam is complete.

Backstitch seam

Place the right sides of the pieces together. Working from right to left, secure the yarn at the beginning of the seam with two small stitches, one on top of the other. * With the needle at the back of the work insert it one stitch in from the edge and a knitted stitch to the left from the last stitch. Pull yarn through to the front, take needle across the front of the work to the right, re-insert it through to the back where the last stitch was worked. Repeat from * until the seam is completed.

Cross stitch seam

1 Place the pieces to be joined, edge to edge, right sides facing. Secure yarn with two oversewn stitches on the wrong side. * Bring needle out at left side and insert it two stitches above on the right side, bringing it back through horizontally to the left side. Repeat from * to the top of the seam.

2 Beginning at the top of seam, bring needle from last stitch on left and insert it two stitches below from right to left, thus making a cross stitch over previous stitch. Repeat to end of seam. Fasten off yarn securely.

Garter stitch selvedge seam

Place the pieces to be joined, edge to edge, right sides facing. Secure yarn with two oversewn stitches on wrong side. * Insert the needle into the first pip on the right side edge. Pull yarn through. Take needle to left side and insert through pip on matching row. Pull yarn through. Repeat from * picking up stitches alternately until seam is completed.

Invisible flat seam

1 Place the pieces to be joined, edge to edge, right sides facing. Secure yarn with two oversewn stitches on wrong side. Bring needle up through first loop on right side. * Insert needle from right to left through the next edge stitch above, and the matching left edge stitch.

2 Draw yarn through. Insert needle from left to right through next edge stitch above and the matching right edge stitch. Draw yarn through and repeat from * until seam is complete.

Crochet seam

Place right sides together and, working from right to left, insert crochet hook through both pieces, one stitch in from edge. Place yarn round hook and draw through loop leaving a 10cm/4in end. * Insert hook through both pieces, one stitch to the left, yarn round hook and draw loop through. Yarn round hook and draw through both loops on hook. Repeat from * until seam is completed.

Crochet grafting

Note Needles have been removed for clarity; keep stitches on needles until they are worked.
Place the pieces to be joined, edge to edge, right sides facing. Insert crochet hook into first stitch of first piece and draw off needle. Insert hook into first stitch of second piece and draw off needle and through first stitch on hook. Continue to draw stitches alternately off each needle to last stitch. Fasten off.

HOW TO WORK CABLES

Cables are formed by stitches changing places with adjacent stitches. The stitches to be moved are slipped on to a cable needle and held at the back or front of the work while the adjacent stitches are being worked.

Working a cable twist to the left

1 Work until the position for the cable is reached. Slip the next 3 stitches on to a cable needle and leave these at the front of the work. Knit the next 3 stitches on the left-hand needle.

2 Slip the 3 stitches from the cable needle back on to the left-hand needle in readiness to be knitted.
Or bring the cable needle into the position of the left-hand needle in readiness to be knitted.

3 Knit the next 3 stitches from the left-hand needle or the cable needle. Three stitches have been crossed to the left in front of 3 stitches to the right. This 6 stitch cable is called cable 6 front and is abbreviated as **C6F**.

Working a cable twist to the right

1 Work until the position for the cable is reached. Slip the next 3 stitches on to a cable needle and leave these at the back of the work. Knit the next 3 stitches on the left-hand needle.

2 Slip the 3 stitches from the cable needle back on to the left-hand needle in readiness to be knitted.
Or bring the cable needle into the position of the left-hand needle in readiness to be knitted.

3 Knit the next 3 stitches from the left-hand needle or the cable needle. Three stitches have been crossed to the right in front of 3 stitches to the left. This 6 stitch cable is called cable 6 back and is abbreviated as **C6B**.

Cable using two cable needles

1 Work until the position for the cable is reached. Slip the first 3 stitches on to one cable needle and leave at the back of the work, then slip the next 3 stitches on to a second cable needle and leave at the front of the work.

2 Using the right-hand needle knit the next 3 stitches on the left-hand needle.

3 Still using the right-hand needle knit the 3 stitches from the second cable needle.

4 Then knit the 3 stitches from the first cable needle.

5 Three stitches from the left have crossed behind the 3 centre stitches and in front of 3 stitches from the right. Three stitches from the right have crossed to the left at the back. This 9 stitch cable is called cable 9 and is abbreviated as C9.

POMPONS AND FRINGES

Fringes and pompons make bold and striking trimmings to a hat or scarf or even on a garment when the pattern requires them. Make them in matching yarn or add a touch of colour by using up oddments from your workbox.

Pompons

1 Draw two circles the size of the finished pompon on a sheet of thin card, using a pair of compasses or a circular object. Draw a second circle inside the first with a diameter just under a third of the diameter of the first circle. Cut out the circles and their centres carefully.

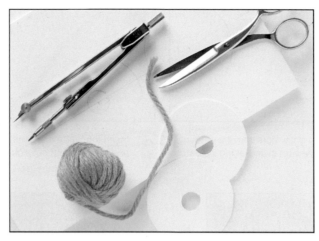

2 Place the two circles together. Thread a blunt needle with a double length of yarn and wind it round the circles as evenly as possible until it is no longer possible to thread any more yarn through the centre hole.

3 Slip one blade of a sharp pair of scissors between the two pieces of card and cut through the yarn all round the outer edges of the circles, taking care not to cut the card.

4 Ease the two pieces of card apart gently and use a length of yarn to tie the centre of the pompon securely. Leave the ends of this yarn to attach the pompon.

5 Continue to ease the circles of card off the pompon carefully – they can be used again to make another pompon.

6 Fluff the pompon into shape, trimming off any uneven lengths of yarn.

FRINGING

1 Cut a strip of firm card to slightly more than the width of the finished fringe. Wind the yarn evenly along the card until it is covered.

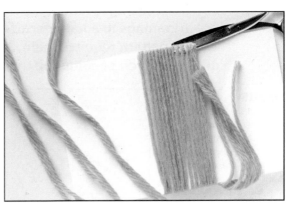

2 Insert the blade of a pair of scissors between the yarn and the card and cut along the edge.

3 Insert a crochet hook at one end of the edge to be fringed and place the centre of two or three strands of yarn (depending on how thick you want each tassel to be) on the hook.

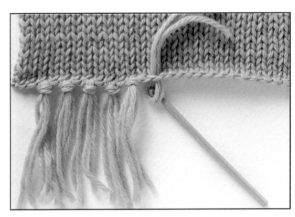

4 Pull the yarn through but do not remove the hook. Wind the ends of the yarn round the hook again and pull them through the loops on the hook.

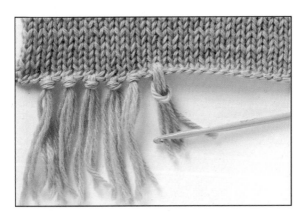

5 Continue making tassels along the edge until it is complete.

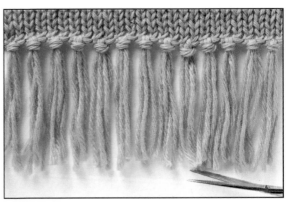

6 Use a pair of sharp scissors to trim any uneven strands in the fringe.

CIRCULAR KNITTING

Knitting on a set of three, four or five double-pointed needles produces a seamless, tubular fabric and is ideal for socks, collars, gloves or hats. When knitting in rounds the right side of the fabric always faces you.

Using double-pointed needles

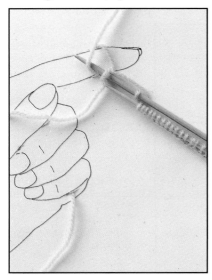

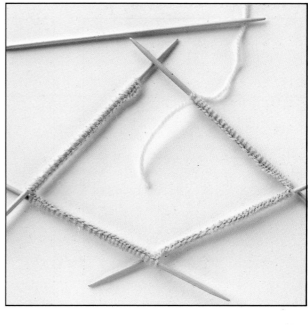

1 Divide the stitches to be cast on equally between four needles (or the number of needles to be used). Cast on the required number of stitches for the first needle. Place the next needle parallel and above the first needle, allowing the point to protrude a little. Cast on the required number of stitches for the second needle.

2 Continue to cast on stitches on the remaining needles. Check that all the stitches face the same way and that none is twisted round the needle. Place a marker – a plastic ring or a loop of different coloured yarn – at the end of the last cast-on stitch. This marks the beginning of every round.

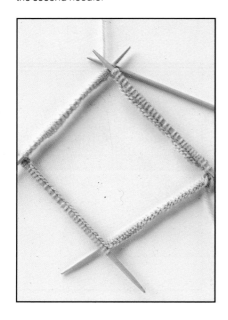

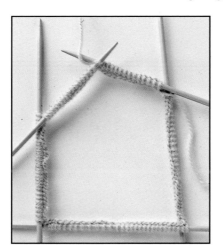

4 Work across the stitches of the first needle, then use this needle to work across the stitches of the second needle, and so on. Always pull the yarn firmly on the first stitch on each needle to avoid a gap.

5 Knit each section of the circle until the coloured marker is reached, then slip the marker without working it and begin the next round.

3 Arrange the four needles in a square (three needles in a triangle) and, using an additional needle, knit into the first cast-on stitch on the first needle, thus closing up the square. Pull the yarn firmly on the first stitch to avoid a gap.

CIRCULAR KNITTING

Circular needles are used to knit in rounds to produce seamless
fabrics of a wider diameter than those produced
by a set of needles. They are also used to knit in rows when
there are a large number of stitches or if the
knitting is particularly heavy, when it can be rested on your lap.

Using a circular needle

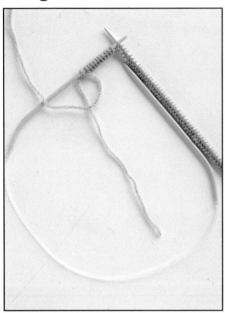

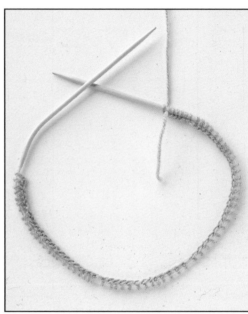

Minimum number of stitches
required for circular needles

TENSION (sts to 10cm/4in)	NEEDLE 40cm 16in	LENGTH 60cm 24in
16	68	93
18	72	105
20	80	117
22	88	129
24	96	141
26	104	153
28	112	164
30	120	176
32	128	188
34	136	200
36	144	212
	80cm 30in	100cm 40in
16	125	156
18	141	176
20	157	196
22	173	216
24	189	236
26	205	255
28	220	275
30	236	294
32	252	314
34	268	334
36	284	353

1 Use a pair of needles to cast on the required number of stitches. Transfer the stitches by slipping them purlwise on to a circular needle.

2 Distribute the stitches evenly around the circular needle, making sure they are not twisted.

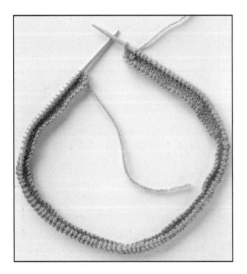

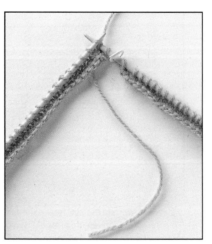

3 Hold the needle with the yarn in your left hand and purl the next row without joining it into a round. Turn and knit the next row without joining the round. Turn and purl the next row without joining it into a round. This prevents the stitches twisting round the nylon strip. The gap in the work can be oversewn with a few stitches when finishing off.

4 Now begin to work in rounds. Place a marker on the right-hand needle to denote the beginning of each round, then knit the next stitch on the left-hand needle, pulling the yarn firmly to close up the circle.

5 Knit around the circle until the marker is reached, slip it and work the next round. Continue working in rounds according to the instructions.

Note When working in rows, work steps 1 to 3 only.
When working in rounds, as you become more experienced you can omit step 3.

BOOTEES

**These bootees are knitted in 4 ply baby yarn,
which is the most suitable for a tiny baby. You will need a
couple of spare needles or large safety-pins
to hold some of the stitches while you are working on the others.**

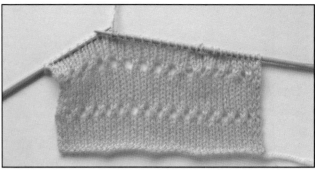

1 Using 3¼mm/No10 knitting needles and 4 ply yarn, cast on 31 sts.

Work 3cm/1¼in st st, ending with a p row.
Picot row 1 K1, * yf, k2 tog, rep from * to end.
Beg with a p row cont in st st until work measures 4cm/1½in from picot row, ending with a p row.
Picot row 2 * K2 tog, yf, rep from * to last st, k1.

2 Beg with a p row cont in st st until work measures 2cm/¾in from the last picot row, ending with a p row.

3 **Next row** K to last 9 sts, turn and leave rem sts on a spare needle or safety-pin.
Next row P13, turn and leave rem sts on a spare needle or safety-pin.
Cont in st st on these 13 central sts until extension measures approx 6cm/2¼in, ending with a p row.
Dec 1 st each end of next and foll 2 alt rows. 7 sts.
P 1 row and k 1 row.

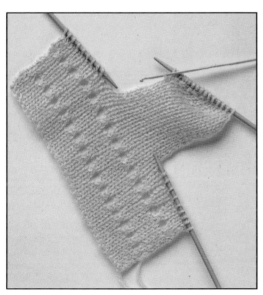

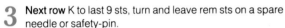

4 With RS facing, pick up and k19 sts along left side of extension.
K9 from left-hand spare needle.
P these 35 sts.

5 With WS facing, pick up and p19 sts along second side of extension.
P9 from rem spare needle. 63 sts.
Work 2cm/¾in st st, ending with a p row.

6 Next row K37, skpo, turn and leave rem 24 sts on needle.
Next row P12, p2 tog, turn and leave rem 24 sts on needle.
Next row K12, skpo, turn and leave rem sts on needle.
Next row P12, p2 tog, turn and leave rem sts on needle.

7 Rep these 2 rows until 6 sts rem on left-hand needle after a p row.

10 Fold top of bootee to WS along first picot row and slipstitch in place.
Thread ribbon or several lengths of yarn through second picot row and tie in a bow.

8 Graft the 6 sts rem on needle to last 6 sts worked (see invisible casting off using 2 needles on page 6).
Slip first 6 sts on needle on to a second needle and graft as before.

9 Mattress stitch the back seam (see page 41).

SOCKS

The traditional way to knit socks is to use a
set of double-pointed needles and work in rounds. This pair is
knitted in reversed stocking stitch and stocking
stitch with a decorative double cable each side of the ankle.

1 These socks are knitted on a set of five double-pointed needles. Start with the ribbed border and work towards the toes, dividing the work into eight parts. This example is worked on 4mm/No8 needles using a DK yarn.

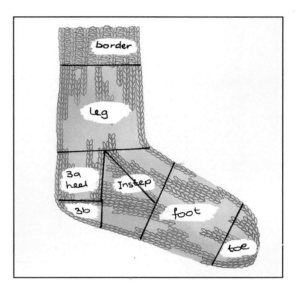

2 Cast on 64 sts, equally divided between the four needles (see Circular knitting, page 47). Work 10 rounds k1, p1 rib.

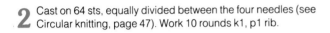

4 **Divide for heel and instep** Using spare needle k across 32 sts from first and 2nd needles for back of heel. Leave rem sts on 3rd and 4th needles for instep. Beg with a p row work 17 rows st st for heel.

5 Turning the heel
Next row K21, K2 tog, turn.
Next row P11, p2 tog, turn.
Next row K11, k2 tog, turn.
Rep the last 2 rows until all side gusset sts have been decreased.

3 Work 29 rounds in reversed stocking stitch (or length required) placing a pair of cables each side as follows:
Round 1 (RS) On to first needle work k4, p12, on to 2nd needle work p11, k4, p1, on to 3rd needle work k4, p11, on to 4th needle work p12, k4, p1.
Round 2 As round 1.
Round 3 C4F, p23, C4B, p1, C4F, p23, C4B, p1.
Round 4 As round 1.
Rep these 4 rounds 6 times more, then round 1 again.

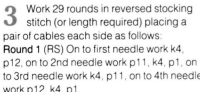
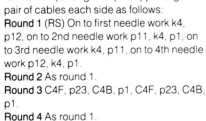

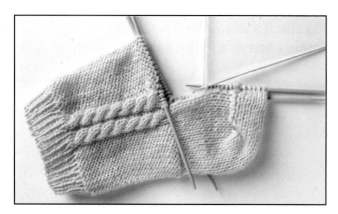

6 **Heel shaping** Leave 6 heel sts on first needle and slip next 6 heel sts on to 2nd needle then, with RS facing, pick up and k18 sts down side of gusset.
Working in rounds, patt across sts on 3rd and 4th needles for instep, then pick up and k18 sts up 2nd side of gusset and k across sts on first needle. 80 sts divided equally between 4 needles.

9 **Decrease for toes** Beg with a k row work in rounds of st st, decreasing by knitting last st on one needle tog with first st on next needle until 16 sts rem.

7 **Decrease for instep** Continuing in rev st st with cables for top of foot and st st for sole of foot, dec as follows:
Next row K20, k2 tog, k2, patt across 3rd and 4th needles for instep, then k2, skpo, k20.
Working 1 st less before and after the decrease, rep this dec row until there are 64 sts.

8 **Work foot** Continue in patt, working in rounds, for 5cm/2in.

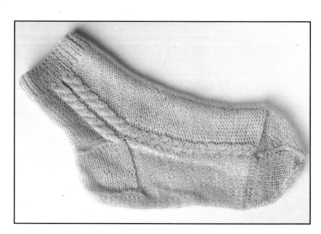

10 Cut off yarn, leaving a length to fasten off with. Thread yarn on to a blunt needle and thread through sts on needles. Pull up yarn and fasten securely on WS of work.

MITTENS

These two methods of making mittens are quite simple. Worked in a DK yarn, they are adult sized; worked in a 4 ply yarn they will fit a child's hand – but check the measurements as you go and alter slightly where necessary.

Mittens – method 1

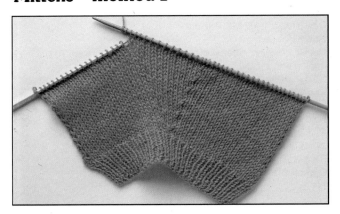

1 Using 3¼mm/No10 needles and a DK yarn, cast on 44 sts. Work 4–5cm/1½–2in k1, p1, rib, ending with a WS row.
Change to 4mm needles and beg with a k row work 2 rows st st.
Next row K21, place slip loop of contrast colour on needle as marker, M1, k2, M1, place slip loop on needle as marker, k21.
* Slipping markers as you reach them, p 1 row.
Next row K21, slip marker, M1, k to next marker, M1, slip marker, k to end.
Rep from * until there are 16 sts between markers.
P 1 row.
Next row K to 2nd marker, remove marker, turn and leave rem sts on holder.
Next row Cast on 2, p to marker, remove marker, turn and leave rem sts on holder.
Next row Cast on 2, k to end. 20 sts.

2 Cont in st st for approx 5cm/2in (length of thumb), ending with a p row.

3 **Next row** * K2 tog, rep from * to end.
P 1 row.
Next row * K1, k2 tog, rep from * to last st, k1.
Cut off yarn, leaving a length long enough to sew up thumb.
Thread yarn through rem sts.
Return to sts on first holder. With RS facing slip sts on to needle, join on yarn and k to end.
Next row P to thumb extension, pick up and p 2 sts from each cast-on edge of thumb then p sts from 2nd holder. 46 sts.
(You may find it easier to pick up the sts if you sew thumb seam before working last row.)

4 Cont in st st until mitten measures approx 10cm/4in from beg of thumb join (length to tip of index finger) ending with a p row.
Next row K1, skpo, k16, k2 tog, k4, skpo, k16, k2 tog, k1.
Next row P to end.
Next row K1, skpo, k14, k2 tog, k4, skpo, k14, k2 tog, k1.
Next row P to end.
Next row K1, skpo, k12, k2 tog, k4, skpo, k12, k2 tog, k1.
Next row P to end.
Cast off, decreasing as before.

5 With right sides together, join thumb seam, then join side and top seams.

Mittens – method 2

1 Using 3¼mm/No10 needles and a DK yarn, cast on 44 sts. Work 4–5cm/1½–2in k1, p1, rib ending with a WS row.
Change to 4mm needles.
Row 1 K1, M1, k1, M1, k to end.
Row 2 P to end.
Row 3 K1, M1, k3, M1, k to end.
Row 4 P to end.
Row 5 K1, M1, k5, M1, k to end.
Row 6 P to end.
Cont in this way, increasing on every k row until there are 70 sts, ending with a k row.
Next row P42, turn and leave rem sts on a holder.
Beg with a k row work 16 rows st st.
Next row K21, turn and leave rem sts on a holder.
Next row * P to end.
Cont in st st, dec 1 st each end of next and every foll 4th row until 11 sts rem.
P 1 row.
Cast off. *

2 Slip sts on 2nd holder on to needle, join on yarn and k to end. Work as given from * to *.

3 Slip sts from first holder on to needle, join on yarn and work 12 rows st st.
Cut off yarn, leaving a length for sewing up seam. Thread yarn on to a large-eyed blunt needle and thread through stitches on needle, pull up yarn and fasten off securely.

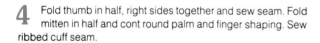

4 Fold thumb in half, right sides together and sew seam. Fold mitten in half and cont round palm and finger shaping. Sew ribbed cuff seam.

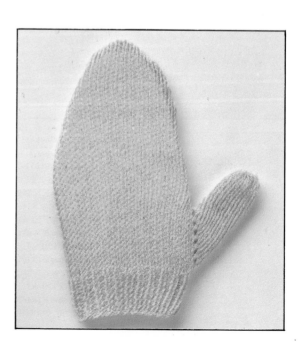

GLOVES

**These gloves are knitted in rounds on a set of
five double-pointed needles and each of the fingers and thumbs
are also worked in rounds. The thumb is placed at
the side of the palm so that each glove will fit either hand.**

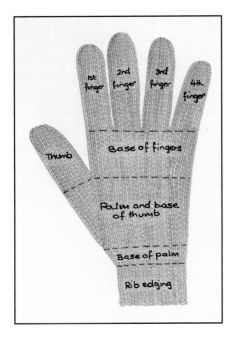

1 Starting at the rib, the palm is divided for the thumb which is worked first, then each of the fingers is knitted separately.

2 Using a set of 2¾mm/No12 needles and a 4 ply yarn, cast on 56 sts, divided equally between 4 needles (see page 47).
Work in rounds of k1, p1 rib for 5cm/2in.

3 Change to a set of 3¼mm/No10 needles, then for the base of the palm work 1.5cm/½in stocking stitch.

4 Increase for right thumb
Next round K28, M1, k28.
Work 1 round.
Next round K28, M1, k1, M1, k28.
Work 1 round.
Next round K28, M1, k3, M1, k28.
Work 1 round.
Cont increasing in this way until there are 75 sts, then work 3 rounds straight.

5 Work thumb
Next round K27 and leave these sts on a length of yarn or large safety-pin, k21 for thumb, then leave rem sts on another thread or safety-pin.
Working on thumb sts only, cast on 3 sts and join into a round.
24 sts. Work in rounds of st st until thumb measures approx 1.5cm/½in less than finished length.
Shape top
Next 2 rounds * K2 tog, k4, rep from * to end. Work 1 round.
Next 2 rounds * K2 tog, k3, rep from * to end. Work 1 round.
Next 2 rounds * K2 tog, k2, rep from * to end. Work 1 round.
Break off yarn, leaving a length to thread through rem sts, draw up and fasten off.

6 Work base of fingers
Return to sts on yarn/safety-pins. Slip first 27 sts back on to a needle, pick up and k3 sts across base of thumb, then k rem 27 sts. 57 sts.
Cont in rounds of st st for approx 2.5cm/1in or for length of palm.

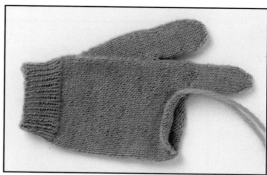

7 First finger
Slip first 20 sts on to a thread, k17 for first finger, then leave rem 20 sts on a thread.
Working on finger sts only, cast on 3 sts and join into a round. 20 sts.
Work in rounds of st st until finger measures approx 6cm/2½in.
Shape top
Next round * K2 tog, k3, rep from * to end.
Work 1 round.
Next round * K2 tog, k2, rep from * to end.
Work 1 round.
Break off yarn, leaving a length to thread through rem sts, draw up and fasten off.

8 Second finger
Slip last 7 sts from front of hand on to a needle, pick up and k3 sts from base of first finger, k7 sts from back of hand then cast on 3 sts and join into a round. 20 sts.
Work in rounds of st st until finger measures approx 6.5cm/2¾in.
Shape top
Next round * K2 tog, k3, rep from * to end.
Work 1 round.
Next round * K2 tog, k2, k2 tog, k1, rep from * to end.
Work 1 round.
Break off yarn, leaving a length to thread through rem sts, draw up and fasten off.

10 Fourth finger
Slip last 6 sts from front of hand on to a needle, pick up and k3 sts from base of third finger, then k6 sts from back of hand and join into a round. 15 sts.
Work in rounds of st st until finger measures approx 5cm/2in.

9 Third finger
Slip last 7 sts from front of hand on to a needle, pick up and k3 sts from base of second finger, k7 sts from back of hand then cast on 3 sts and join into a round. 20 sts.
Work in rounds of st st until finger measures approx 6cm/2½in.
Shape top
Next round * K2 tog, k3, rep from * to end.
Work 1 round.
Next round * K2 tog, k2, rep from * to end.
Work 1 round.
Break off yarn, leaving a length to thread through rem sts, draw up and fasten off.

Shape top
Next round * K2 tog, k3, rep from * to end.
Work 1 round.
Next round * K2 tog, k2, rep from * to end.
Work 1 round.
Break off yarn, leaving a length to thread through rem sts, draw up and fasten off.

GLOVES USING TWO NEEDLES

These gloves are knitted in rows, on only two
needles. Seams are made down each finger and thumb and at the
side of the glove. The thumb is placed at the
side rather than the palm so each glove will fit either hand.

The measurements given here will fit a medium-sized woman's hand. Increase or decrease the stitches slightly to make a larger or smaller glove. Beginning at the cuff, the palm is divided for the thumb which is worked first, then each of the fingers is worked separately. When working on the thumb or a finger, leave remaining stitches on a holder, large safety-pin or a length of yarn. Throughout the pattern this is referred to as a holder.

Using a pair of 3¼mm/No10 needles and a DK yarn, cast on 41 sts.
Rib row 1 K1, * p1, k1, rep from * to end.
Rib row 2 P1, * k1, p1, rep from * to end.
Rep these 2 rows for 5cm/2in.
Change to a pair of 4mm/No8 needles, then for the base of the palm and beginning with a knit row, work 4 rows stocking stitch.

Increase for thumb
Next row K20, M1, k1, M1, k20.
Work 3 rows st st.
Next row K20, M1, k3, M1, k20.
Work 3 rows st st.
Next row K20, M1, k to last 20 sts, M1, k20.
P 1 row.
Rep the last 2 rows until there are 53 sts, ending with a p row.

Work thumb
Next row K20 and leave these sts on a holder, k13 for thumb, then leave rem sts on another holder.
Working on thumb sts only, cast on 2 sts. 15 sts.
Work in st st until thumb measures approx 5cm/2in.
Shape top
Next row * K2 tog, k3, rep from * to end.
P 1 row.
Next row * K2 tog, rep from * to end. 6 sts.
P 1 row.
★ Cut off yarn, leaving an end approx 30cm/12in long. Thread end of yarn through rem sts, draw up and fasten securely, then join side seam of thumb to cast-on sts at base. Turn thumb to right side. ★

Work base of fingers
Return to sts on holders. Slip first 20 sts back on to a needle, join on yarn and pick up and k3 sts across base of thumb, then k rem 20 sts. 43 sts.
Work 11 rows st st on these sts, so ending with a p row.

Increasing for thumb by making a stitch

Cast on 2 stitches at base of thumb

First finger
K15 and leave these sts on a holder, k13 for first finger, then leave rem sts on a holder.
Working on first finger only, cast on 2 sts.
Work in st st until finger measures approx 6cm/2½in, ending with a p row.
Shape top
Next row * K2 tog, k3, rep from * to end.

P 1 row.
Next row * K2 tog, rep from * to end. 6 sts.
P 1 row.
Complete as given for thumb from ★ to ★.

Second finger
Slip last 5 sts from first holder on to a needle, join on yarn at base of first finger, pick up and k3 sts from base of first finger,

Threading yarn through stitches at top of thumb

then k5 from sts at beg of second holder.
Cast on 2 sts, then work in st st until finger
measures approx 6.5cm/2¾in, ending with
a p row.

Shape top

Next row * K2 tog, k3, rep from * to end.
P 1 row.

Next row * K2 tog, rep from * to end. 6 sts.
P 1 row.

Complete as given for thumb from ★ to ★.

Third finger

Slip last 5 sts from first holder on to a
needle, join on yarn at base of second
finger, pick up and k3 sts from base of
second finger, then k5 from sts at beg of
second holder.

Cast on 2 sts, then work in st st until finger
measures approx 6cm/2½in, ending with a
p row.

Shape top

Next row * K2 tog, k3, rep from * to end.
P 1 row.

Next row * K2 tog, rep from * to end. 6 sts.
P 1 row.

Complete as given for thumb from ★ to ★.

Fourth finger

Slip last 5 sts from first holder on to a
needle, join on yarn at base of third finger,
pick up and k3 sts from base of third
finger, then k5 from sts at beg of second
holder.

Work in st st until finger measures approx
5cm/2in, ending with a p row.

Shape top

Next row K1, * k2 tog, k2, rep from * to
end.
P 1 row.

Next row * K2 tog, rep from * to end. 5 sts.
P 1 row.

Cut off yarn, leaving an end approx
50cm/20in long. Thread end of yarn
through rem sts, draw up and fasten
securely, then join side seam of fourth
finger, continuing down side of glove to
cast-on edge.

Picking up stitches
at base of finger

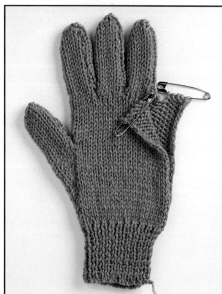

Slip last 5 stitches
from holder on to
needle, then join on
yarn

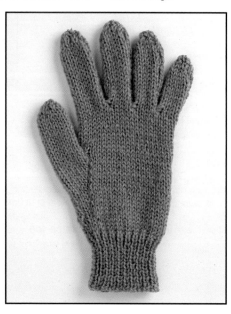

The completed
glove

KNITTED HATS

These two classic hats are simple to make; the pompon hat is just a straight piece of knitting, with a little shaping at the crown and a pompon added. The balaclava is shaped by splitting the crown into three sections.

Pompon hat

Using 3¼mm needles and a DK yarn, cast on 99 sts.

Rib row 1 K1, * p1, k1, rep from * to end.

Rib row 2 P1, * k1, p1, rep from * to end.

Rep these 2 rows for 6cm/2½in, ending with rib row 1.

Change to 4mm needles.

Beg with a k row (so that when ribbed brim is turned back the RS of the cast-on edge will show), work in st st until hat measures 20cm/8in from cast-on edge, ending with a p row.

Shape crown

Dec row 1 * K7, k2 tog, rep from * to end. 88 sts.

Next row P to end.

Dec row 2 * K6, k2 tog, rep from * to end. 77 sts.

Next row P to end.

Dec row 3 * K5, k2 tog, rep from * to end. 66 sts.

Next row P to end.

Dec row 4 * K4, k2 tog, rep from * to end. 55 sts.

Next row P to end.

Dec row 5 * K3, k2 tog, rep from * to end. 44 sts.

Next row P to end.

Dec row 6 * K2, k2 tog, rep from * to end. 33 sts.

Next row P to end.

Dec row 7 * K1, k2 tog, rep from * to end. 22 sts.

Next row P to end.

Cut off yarn, leaving an end approx 40cm/16in long for sewing up.

Thread yarn into a large-eyed, blunt needle, then slip the remaining stitches, one by one, on to the sewing needle. Pull yarn through stitches and draw up tightly, then work a few stitches to secure. Join the seam, reversing the seam at the rib for the folded back brim.

Make a pompon and sew on over gathered up stitches. (See page 45.)

Slipping stitches on to needle

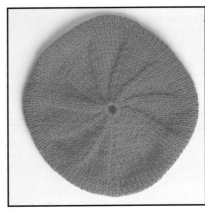

Shaping the crown

The finished pompon hat

Balaclava

Using 3¼mm needles and a DK yarn, cast on 103 sts.
Rib row 1 K1, * p1, k1, rep from * to end.
Rib row 2 P1, * k1, p1, rep from * to end.
Rep these 2 rows for 6cm/2½in, ending with rib row 2.
Cut off yarn.
Change to 4mm needles.
With RS facing, slip the first 11 sts on to a holder, join on yarn and k81, turn and leave rem 11 sts on a holder.
Beg with a p row, work in st st until hat measures 23cm/9in from cast-on edge, ending with a WS row.

Shape crown

Next row K53, skpo, turn.
Next row P26, p2 tog, turn.
Next row K26, skpo, turn.
Rep the last 2 rows until 27 sts rem.
Cut off yarn and leave sts on a holder.

Rib border

With RS facing and using 3¼mm needles, rib across first 11 sts from holder, pick up and k33 sts up side edge to crown, rib across 27 sts from holder, pick up and k33 sts down side edge to rib, then rib across rem 11 sts from holder. 115 sts.
Beg with rib row 2, work 8 rows rib.
Cast off in rib.
Join centre front seam.

Shaping the crown

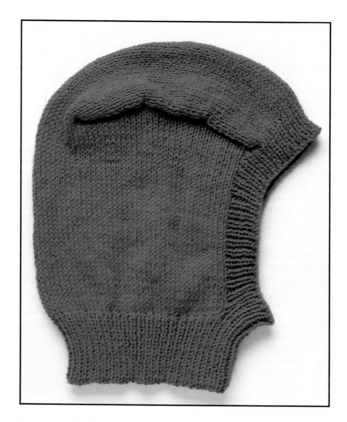

The finished balaclava

WOMEN'S PATTERNS

SLIT NECK JERSEY WITH PATCHWORK STITCH BLOCKS

✳

Moss and Irish moss stitches, various ribs and stocking stitch are all used to effect in this patchwork jersey.

Materials
12×50g balls of Robin New World Chunky
A pair each of 4½mm/No7 and 5mm/No6
  knitting needles

Measurements
To fit bust 97cm/38in
Actual measurements
Bust 116cm/45½in
Length to shoulders 63cm/24¾in
Sleeve seam 44cm/17¼in

Tension
17 sts and 22 rows to 10cm/4in measured
over st st worked on 5mm needles

Back and front (alike)
Using 4½mm needles cast on 98 sts.
Work 5cm/2in k1, p1 rib, ending with a WS
row.
Change to 5mm needles.
Work in patt as follows:
Row 1 K to end.
Row 2 P to end.
Rows 3 to 8 Rep rows 1 and 2 three times.
Rows 9 to 12 P 4 rows.
Row 13 P1, [k1, p1] 31 times, k1, p5, k29.
Row 14 P35, then p1, [k1, p1] 31 times.
Rows 15 to 38 Rep rows 13 and 14 twelve
times.
Row 39 As row 13.
Rows 40 to 44 P 5 rows.
Row 45 K2, * p2, k2, rep from * to end.
Row 46 P2, * k2, p2, rep from * to end.
Rows 47 to 52 Rep rows 45 and 46 three
times.
Rows 53 and 54 P 2 rows.
Row 55 K34, p5, k1, [p1, k1] 29 times.
Row 56 [P1, k1] 29 times, p to end.
Row 57 K34, p5, k1, then [k1, p1] 29 times.
Row 58 [K1, p1] 29 times, p 40.
Rows 59 to 66 Rep rows 55 to 58 twice.
Row 67 As row 55.
Row 68 [P1, k1] 29 times, p1, k to end.
Row 69 P39, k1, then [k1, p1] 29 times.
Row 70 [K1, p1] 29 times, then p1, k to end.
Row 71 P39, k1, [p1, k1] 29 times.
Rows 72 to 75 As rows 68 to 71.
Rows 76 to 78 As rows 68 to 70.
Row 79 P39, k to end.
Row 80 K to end.
Row 81 P to end.
Rows 82 to 85 Rep rows 80 and 81 twice.
Row 86 K to end.
Row 87 * K1, p1, rep from * to end.
Rows 88 to 96 Rep row 87 nine times.
Rows 97 to 100 K 4 rows.
Row 101 * K1, p1, rep from * to end.
Row 102 * P1, k1, rep from * to end.
Rows 103 to 116 Rep rows 101 and 102
seven times.
Rows 117 and 118 K 2 rows.
Rows 119 to 122 Rep rows 80 and 81 twice.
Rows 123 and 124 K 2 rows.
Row 125 * K1, p1, rep from * to end.
Row 126 * P1, k1, rep from * to end.
Row 127 As row 126.
Row 128 As row 125.
Rows 129 and 130 K 2 rows.
Row 131 * K1, p1, rep from * to end.
Rows 132 to 139 Rep row 131 eight times.
Row 140 K to end.
Cast off.

Right sleeve
Using 4½mm needles cast on 36 sts.
Work 5cm/2in k1, p1 rib, ending with a RS
row.
Inc row Rib 4, * M1, rib 3, rep from * to last
2 sts, rib 2. 46 sts.
Change to 5mm needles.
Work in patt as follows.
Row 1 K to end.
Row 2 P to end.
Rows 3 to 8 Rep rows 1 and 2 three times.
Rows 9 to 12 P 4 rows.
Row 13 [P1, k1] 12 times, then k1, p5, k16.
Row 14 P22, [k1, p1] 12 times.
Rows 15 to 39 Keeping the patts correct as
set, rep the last 2 rows increasing and
working into patt 1 st each end of next and
every foll 4th row until there are 60 sts.
Rows 40 to 44 P 5 rows.
Row 45 P1, * k2, p2, rep from * to last 3 sts,
k2, p1.
Row 46 K1, * p2, k2, rep from * to last 3 sts,
p2, k1.
Keeping the rib patt correct, inc and work
into patt 1 st each end of next and foll 4th
row.
Working in rib, patt 3 rows straight. 64 sts.
Rows 55 and 56 K 2 rows.
Row 57 K22, p5, k1, [p1, k1] 18 times.
Row 58 [P1, k1] 18 times, p28.
Row 59 K22, p5, k1, then [k1, p1] 18 times.
Row 60 [K1, p1] 18 times, p28.
Keeping the patt correct, rep the last 4 rows
increasing and working into patt as set 1 st
each end of next and every foll alt row until
there are 74 sts.
Patt 1 row without shaping.
Row 71 P32, [k1, p1] 21 times.
Row 72 [P1, k1] 20 times, p2, k32.
Rows 73 to 82 Rep rows 71 and 72 five
times.
Row 83 P to end.
Row 84 K to end.
Rows 85 to 90 Rep rows 83 and 84 three
times.
Cast off.

Left sleeve
Using 4½mm needles cast on 36 sts.
Work 5cm/2in k1, p1 rib, ending with a RS
row.
Inc row Rib 4, * M1, rib 3, rep from * to last
2 sts, rib 2. 46 sts.
Change to 5mm needles.
Work in patt as follows:
Row 1 K to end.
Row 2 P to end.
Rows 3 to 8 Rep rows 1 and 2 three times.
Rows 9 to 12 P 4 rows.
Row 13 K16, p5, k1, then [k1, p1] 12 times.
Row 14 [P1, k1] 12 times, p22.
Rows 15 to 39 Keeping the patts correct as
set, rep the last 2 rows increasing and
working into patt 1 st each end of next and
every foll 4th row until there are 60 sts.
Rows 40 to 44 P 5 rows.
Row 45 K3, * p2, k2, rep from * to last st, k1.
Row 46 P3, * k2, p2, rep from * to last st, p1.
Keeping the rib patt correct, inc and work
into patt 1 st each end of next and foll 4th
row.
Working in rib, patt 3 rows straight. 64 sts.
Rows 55 and 56 K 2 rows.

Row 57 [K1, p1] 18 times, k1, p5, k22.
Row 58 P28, [k1, p1] 18 times.
Row 59 [P1, k1] 18 times, k1, p5, k22.
Row 60 P28, then [p1, k1] 18 times.
Keeping the patts correct, rep the last 4
rows increasing and working into patt as set
1 st each end of next and every foll alt row
until there are 74 sts.
Patt 1 row without shaping.
Row 71 [P1, k1] 21 times, p32.
Row 72 K32, p2, [k1, p1] 20 times.

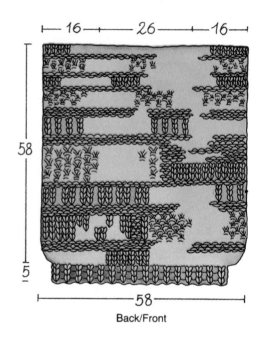

```
  ├─ 16 ─┤├─── 26 ───┤├─ 16 ─┤
```
58
5
```
  ├──────── 58 ────────┤
```
Back/Front

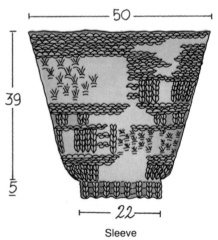

```
  ├──────── 50 ────────┤
```
39
5
```
       ├── 22 ──┤
```
Sleeve

Measurements given in cm

Rows 73 to 82 Rep rows 71 and 72 five
times.
Row 82 P to end.
Row 84 K to end.
Rows 85 to 90 Rep rows 83 and 84 three
times.
Cast off.

To make up
Join shoulder seams for 16cm/6¼in,
leaving the centre open for neck. Fold
sleeves in half lengthwise, then placing
folds to shoulder seams, sew in place.
Join side and sleeve seams.

SIMPLE RIB JERSEY IN SOFT ANGORA

* A loose-fitting jersey with a scoop neck and three-quarter length sleeves.

Materials
10×20g balls of Jaeger Angora Knits As 4 Ply.
A pair each of 3¼mm/No10 and 4mm/No8 knitting needles.

Measurements
To fit bust 86–97cm/34–38in
Actual measurements
Bust 106cm/42in
Length to shoulders 50cm/19½in
Sleeve seam 30cm/12in

Tension
24 sts and 28 rows to 10cm/4in measured over patt worked on 4mm needles

Back
Using 3¼mm needles cast on 129 sts.
Rib row 1 (RS) K1, * p1, k1, rep from * to end.
Rib row 2 P1, * k1, p1, rep from * to end.
Rep these 2 rows once more.
Change to 4mm needles.
Work in patt as follows:
Row 1 K1, * p3, k1, rep from * to end.
Row 2 P1, * k3, p1, rep from * to end.
Rep these 2 rows until back measures 48cm/19in from cast-on edge, ending with a WS row.
Shape neck
Next row Patt 35, turn and leave rem sts on spare needle.
Cast off 2 sts at beg of next and foll alt row. 31 sts.
Patt 2 rows.
Cast off in patt.
Return to sts on spare needle.
With RS facing, slip first 59 sts on to a holder, join on yarn and patt to end.
Work 1 row.
Now complete to match first side of neck.

Front
Work as given for back until front measures 39cm/15½in from cast-on edge, ending with a WS row.
Shape neck
Next row Patt 51, turn and leave rem sts on a spare needle.
Cast off 3 sts at beg of next and foll 2 alt rows, then cast off 2 sts at beg of foll 3 alt rows. 36 sts.
Patt 1 row.
Dec 1 st at neck edge on next and every foll alt row until 31 sts rem.
Work straight until front measures same as back to shoulders, ending with a WS row.
Cast off in patt.
With RS facing, slip first 27 sts on to a holder, join on yarn and patt to end.
Work 1 row.
Now complete to match first side of neck.

Sleeves
Using 3¼mm needles cast on 61 sts.
Work the 2 rib rows as given for back, then work rib row 1 again.
Inc row Rib 5, * M1, k1, M1, rib 5, rep from * to last 2 sts, M1, k1, M1, p1. 81 sts.
Change to 4mm needles.

Working in patt as given for back, inc and work into patt 1 st each end of every 3rd row until there are 137 sts.
Work 1 row.
Cast off in patt.

Neckband
Join right shoulder seam.
With RS facing and using 3¼mm needles, pick up and k35 sts down left side of front neck, k across 27 sts from front neck holder, pick up and k35 sts up right side of front neck and 6 sts down right side of back neck, k across 59 sts from back neck holder, then pick up and k6 sts up left side of back neck. 168 sts.
Work 8 rows k1, p1 rib.
Cast off in rib.

To make up
Join left shoulder and neckband seam. Fold neckband in half to WS and slipstitch into place. Fold sleeves in half lengthwise, then placing folds to shoulder seams, sew into place. Join side and sleeve seams.

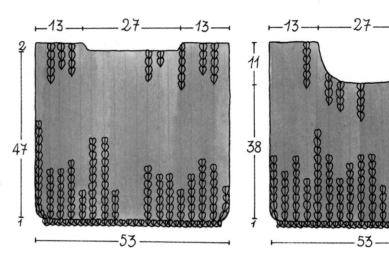

Back   Front

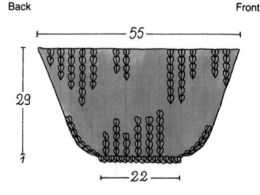

Sleeve

Measurements given in cm

★ **KNIT TIP**

Knitting with fluffy yarns
Keep the fluff at bay when knitting with yarns such as angora and mohair by putting a few balls in a polythene bag in the fridge overnight. A clean tea-towel spread over your knees when knitting will also help to keep your clothes from picking up too many hairs.

IVORY KNIT WITH TEXTURED STITCHES

**

This classic-style jersey is knitted in an Aran yarn which is available in several colours including the traditional one shown here.

Materials

14(14, 15, 16)×50g balls of Emu Superwash Aran

A pair each of 4mm/No8 and 5mm/No6 knitting needles

Cable needle

Measurements

To fit bust 76(81, 86, 91)cm/30(32, 34, 36)in

Actual measurements

Bust 86(90, 98, 106)cm/34(35½, 38½, 41½)in

Length to shoulders 57(60, 62, 64)cm/ 22½(23½, 24½, 25)in

Sleeve seam 44(47, 47, 48)cm/18(18½, 18½, 19)in

Tension

20 sts and 26 rows to 10cm/4in measured over Irish moss stitch worked on 5mm/No6 needles

Special abbreviations

C4B Cable 4 back as follows: slip next 3 sts on to cable needle and leave at back of work, k1, then k3 from cable needle

C4F Cable 4 front as follows: slip next st on to cable needle and leave at front of work, k3, then k1 from cable needle

Notes

The central panel on the front and back of this jersey is knitted in Trinity stitch and the outer panels are Irish moss stitch. The panels are divided by a lobster-claw cable.

Back

Using 4mm needles cast on 80(84, 92, 100) sts.

Work 5cm/2in k1, p1 rib.

Inc row Rib 15(17, 21, 25) sts, [M1, rib 1] 4 times, M1, rib 2, [M1, rib 6] 6 times, M1, rib 5, [M1, rib 1] 5 times, M1, rib 13(15,19,23) 98(102,110,118) sts.

Change to 5mm needles.

Work in patt as follows:

Row 1 [K1, p1] 7(8, 10, 12) times, p2, k9, p48, k9, p2, [k1, p1] 7(8, 10, 12) times.

Row 2 [K1, p1] 7(8, 10, 12) times, k2, p9, k2, [into next st work (k1, p1, k1), p3tog] 11 times, k2, p9, k2, [k1, p1] 7(8, 10, 12) times.

Row 3 [P1, k1] 7(8, 10, 12) times, p2, C4B, k1, C4F, p48, C4B, k1, C4F, p2, [p1, k1] 7(8, 10, 12) times.

Row 4 [P1, k1] 7(8, 10, 12) times, k2, p9, k2, [p3tog, into next st work (k1, p1, k1)] 11 times, k2, p9, k2, [p1, k1] 7(8, 10, 12) times.

These 4 rows form the patt.

Cont in patt until back measures 57(60, 62, 64)cm/22½(23½, 24½, 25)in from cast-on edge, ending with a WS row.

Shape shoulders

Cast off 29(30, 33, 36) sts at beg of next 2 rows.

Cut off yarn and leave rem 40(42, 44, 46) sts on a holder.

Front

Work as given for back until front measures 49(52, 54, 56)cm/19¼(20½, 21¼, 22)in from cast-on edge, ending with a WS row.

Shape neck

Next row Patt 39(40, 43, 46) sts, turn and leave rem sts on spare needle.

Keeping patt correct, cast off 2 sts at beg of

next and every alt row until 29(30, 33, 36) sts rem.

Work straight until front measures same as back to shoulders, ending with a WS row. Cast off.

Return to sts on spare needle.

With RS facing, slip the first 20(22, 24, 26) sts on to a holder, join on yarn and patt to end.

Work 1 row.

Now complete to match first side of neck.

Sleeves

Using 4mm needles cast on 36(36, 40, 40) sts.

Work 6cm/2¼in k1, p1 rib.

Inc row Rib 2(2, 4, 4), * M1, rib 4, rep from * to last 2(2, 4, 4) sts, M1, rib to end, 45(45, 49, 49) sts.

Change to 5mm needles.

Work in patt as follows:

Row 1 [K1, p1] 8(8, 9, 9) times, p2, k9, p2, [k1, p1] 8(8, 9, 9) times.

Row 2 [K1, p1] 8(8, 9, 9) times, k2, p9, k2, [k1, p1] 8(8, 9, 9) times.

Row 3 [P1, k1] 8(8, 9, 9) times, p2, C4B, k1, C4F, p2, [p1, k1] 8(8, 9, 9) times.

Row 4 [P1, k1] 8(8, 9, 9) times, k2, p9, k2, [p1, k1] 8(8, 9, 9) times.

Cont in patt, increasing and working into Irish moss st 1 st each end of next and every foll 4th row until there are 79(87, 93, 97) sts.

Cont in patt until sleeve measures 46(47, 47, 48)cm/18(18½, 18½, 19)in from cast-on edge, ending with a WS row.

Cast off.

Neckband

Join right shoulder seam.

With RS facing and using 4mm needles, pick up and k20(21, 22, 23) sts down left side of front neck, k across 20(22, 24, 26) sts from front neck holder, pick up and k20(21, 22, 23) sts up right side of front neck, then k across 40(42, 44, 46) sts from back neck holder. 100(106, 112, 118) sts.

Work 16 rows k1, p1, rib.

Cast off loosely in rib.

Measurements are given in cm for the smallest size

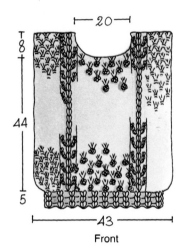

Front

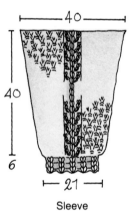

Sleeve

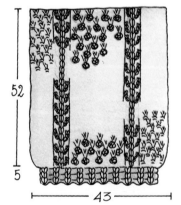

Back

To make up

Join left shoulder and neckband seam.

Fold neckband in half to WS and slipstitch into place.

Fold sleeves in half lengthwise, then placing folds to shoulder seams, sew into place.

Join side and sleeve seams.

KNIT TIP

Substituting patterns

The pattern panels are placed in simple blocks so you can alter the look of this jersey quite easily by substituting a textured stitch pattern which knits to the same tension or a cable which is worked over the same number of stitches.

CANDY-STRIPED SUMMER TOP

✳

The back and front of this cool summer top are knitted exactly the same.

Materials
7×50g balls of Jaeger Monte Cristo in main
    colour A
3 balls same in contrast colour B
A pair each of 3¾mm/No9 and 5mm/No6
    knitting needles

Measurements
To fit bust 81–97cm/32–38in
Actual measurements
Bust 108cm/42½in
Length to shoulders 61cm/24in
Sleeve seam 19cm/7½in

Tension
19 sts and 26 rows to 10cm/4in measured
over patt worked on 5mm needles

Back and front (alike)
Using 3¾mm needles and A, cast on 94 sts.
Work 6cm/2¼in k1, p1, rib.
Inc row Rib 7, * M1, rib 10, rep from * to last
7 sts, M1, rib 7. 103 sts.
Change to 5mm needles.
Joining on and cutting off colours as
required, work in patt as follows:
Row 1 (RS) With A, k1, * p1, k1, rep from * to
end.
Row 2 With A, p1, * k1, p1, rep from * to end.
Row 3 As row 2.
Row 4 As row 1.
Rows 5 and 6 As rows 1 and 2.
Row 7 As row 2.
Row 8 As row 1.
Row 9 As row 1.
Row 10 With A, p to end.
Row 11 With B, k to end.
Row 12 With B, p to end.
Row 13 With A, k to end.
Row 14 With A, p to end.
Rows 15 to 18 As rows 11 to 14.
Rows 19 and 20 As rows 11 and 12.
These 20 rows form the patt.
Cont in patt until work measures approx
37cm/14½in, ending with a 20th patt row.
Shape sleeves and divide for neck
Next row Cast on 36 sts, over these 36 sts
work [k1, p1] 18 times, then [k1, p1] 21
times, turn and leave rem 61 sts on a spare
needle. 78 sts.
Keeping patt correct, work 3 rows straight.
Shape neck
Dec 1 st at neck edge on next and foll 4th
row, then at same edge on foll 3 alt rows. 73
sts.
Work 3 rows straight.
Dec 1 st at neck edge on next and every foll
4th row until 63 sts rem.
Cont without shaping until work measures
61cm/24in, ending with a RS row.
Cast off in patt.
Return to sts on spare needle.
With RS facing, slip first 19 sts on to a
holder, join on A, then [k1, p1] 21 times.
42 sts.
Next row Cast on 36 sts, over these 36 sts
work [k1, p1] 18 times, then [k1, p1] to end.
Keeping patt correct, work 2 rows.
Now complete to match first side of neck.

Neckband (back and front alike)
With RS facing, slip 19 sts from holder on to
a 3¾mm needle, join on A and k3, M1, k4,
M1, k5, M1, k4, M1, k3. 23 sts.

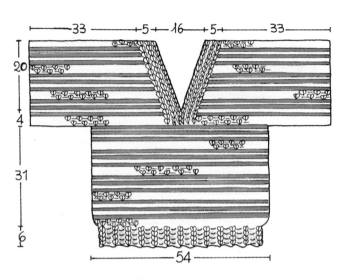

Back/Front

Measurements given in cm for smaller size

Rib row 1 (WS) P1, * k1, p1, rep from * to
end.
Rib row 2 K1, * p1, k1, rep from * to end.
Rep these 2 rows for 4cm/1½in, ending with
rib row 1.
Divide for V neck
Next row Rib 11 and slip these sts on to a
safety-pin, k2 tog, rib to end.
Cont in rib on rem 11 sts until neckband,
when slightly stretched, fits up neck edge to
shoulder.
Cast off in rib.

With WS facing, slip 11 sts from safety-pin
on to a 3¾mm needle and complete to
match first side of neckband.

To make up
Sew neckband into place. Join shoulder
and sleeve seams, reversing seams for
10cm/4in at sleeve edges, then join side
seams. Roll back sleeve edges and catch in
position.

★ KNIT TIP

Joining in colours

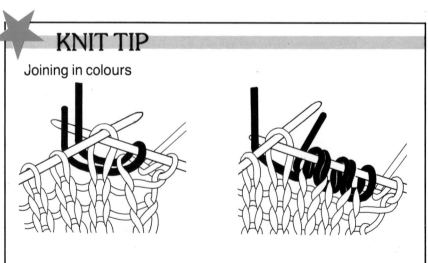

A pattern with a horizontal stripe, such
as this summer top, changes yarn
colours at the beginning of the rows. Use
this method of changing yarn to ensure a
firm start.
Insert the needle into the first stitch and
take both the old and new yarn round the
needle and through the stitch.

Using the new yarn double, knit the next
two stitches. Then continue with the new
yarn singly to the end of the row. On the
return row treat the double yarn as single
stitches and knit the last two stitches
together.

DIAMOND AND BOBBLE PATTERNED JERSEY

** **

Zig-zag lines of bobbles and eyelet holes form an all-over diamond pattern on this summer jersey.

Materials

16×50g balls of Scheepjeswol Mayflower
 Cotton Helarsgarn
A pair each of 4½mm/No7 and 5mm/No6
 knitting needles

Measurements

To fit bust 91–102cm/36–40in

Actual measurements

Bust 110cm/43½in
Length to shoulders 65cm/25½in
Sleeve seam 47cm/18½in

Tension

18 sts and 22 rows to 10cm/4in measured
over pattern worked on 5mm needles

Special abbreviations

Mb Make bobble in next st as follows: all into
next st work [k1, p1, k1, p1 and k1], turn and
k5, turn and p5, then slip 2nd, 3rd, 4th and
5th sts over first and off the needle.

Back

Using 4½mm needles cast on 80 sts.
Work 9cm/3½in k1, p1 rib, ending with a RS
row.
Inc Row Rib 4, * M1, rib 4, rep from * to end.
99 sts.
Change to 5mm needles.
Work in patt as follows:
Row 1 (RS) P5, * yon, skpo, k2, p21, k2,
k2 tog, yon, k1, rep from * to last 4 sts, p4.
Row 2 and every alt row K all the knit sts and
p all the purl, 'yarn over needle' and 'yarn
round needle' sts.
Row 3 P6, * yon, skpo, k2, p19, k2, k2 tog,
yrn, p3, rep from * to last 3 sts, p3.
Row 5 P7, * yon, skpo, k2, p17, k2, k2 tog,
yrn, p5, rep from * to last 2 sts, p2.
Row 7 P8, * yon, skpo, k2, p15, k2, k2 tog,
yrn, p7, rep from * to last st, p1.
Row 9 P9, * yon, skpo, k2, p13, k2, k2 tog,
yrn, p4, Mb, p4, rep from * to end, working
p1 instead of Mb on last rep.
Row 11 P10, * yon, skpo, k2, p11, k2,
k2 tog, yrn, p11, rep from * to end finishing
last rep with p10.
Row 13 P7, * Mb, p3, yon, skpo, k2, p9, k2,
k2 tog, yrn, p3, Mb, p5, rep from * to last
2 sts, p2.
Row 15 P12, * yon, skpo, k2, p7, k2, k2 tog,
yrn, p15, rep from * to end finishing last rep
with p12.
Row 17 P9, * Mb, p3, yon, skpo, k2, p5, k2,
k2 tog, yrn, p3, Mb, p9, rep from * to end.
Row 19 P14, * yon, skpo, k2, p3, k2, k2 tog,
yrn, p19, rep from * to end finishing last rep
with p14.
Row 21 P11, * Mb, p3, yon, skpo, k2, p1, k2,
k2 tog, yrn, p3, Mb, p13, rep from * to end
finishing last rep with p11.
Row 23 P16, * yon, skpo, k3, k2 tog, yrn,
p23, rep from * to end finishing with p16.
Row 25 P13, * Mb, p3, yon, skpo, k1, k2 tog,
yrn, p3, Mb, p17, rep from * to end finishing
last rep with p13.
Row 27 P 18, * yon, sl 1, k2 tog, psso, yrn,

p27, rep from * to end finishing last rep with
p18.
Rows 29, 31 and 33 P.
Row 35 P15, * k2, k2 tog, yon, k1, yon, skpo,
k2, p21, rep from * to end finishing last rep
with p15.
Row 37 P14, * k2, k2 tog, yrn, p3, yon, skpo,
k2, p19, rep from * to end finishing last rep
with p14.
Row 39 P13, * k2, k2 tog, yrn, p5, yon, skpo,
k2, p17, rep from * to end finishing last rep
with p13.
Row 41 P12, * k2, k2 tog, yrn, p7, yon, skpo,
k2, p15, rep from * to end finishing last rep
with p12.
Row 43 P11, * k2, k2 tog, yrn, p4, Mb, p4,
yon, skpo, k2, p13, rep from * to end
finishing with p11.
Row 45 P10, * k2, k2 tog, yrn, p11, yon,
skpo, k2, p11, rep from * to end finishing
last rep with p10.
Row 47 P9, * k2, k2 tog, yrn, p3, Mb, p5,
Mb, p3, yon, skpo, k2, p9, rep from * to end.
Row 49 P8, * k2, k2 tog, yrn, p15, yon, skpo,
k2, p7, rep from * to last st, p1.
Row 51 P7, * k2, k2 tog, yrn, p3, Mb, p9,
Mb, p3, yon, skpo, k2, p5, rep from * to last
2 sts, p2.
Row 53 P6, * k2, k2 tog, yrn, p19, yon, skpo,
k2, p3, rep from * to last 3 sts, p3.
Row 55 P5, * k2, k2 tog, yrn, p3, Mb, p13,
Mb, p3, yon, skpo, k2, p1, rep from * to last
4 sts, p4.
Row 57 P4, k2, * k2 tog, yrn, p23, yon, skpo,
k3, rep from * to end finishing last rep with
k2, p4.

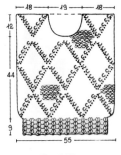

Back/Front

Row 59 P3, k2, * k2 tog, yrn, p3, Mb, p17,
Mb, p3, yon, skpo, k1, rep from * to last
4 sts, k1, p3.
Row 61 P3, k1, k2 tog, * yrn, p27, yon, sl 1,
k2 tog, psso, rep from * to last 33 sts, yrn,
p27, yon, skpo, k1, p3.
Row 62 As row 2.
These 62 rows form the patt.
Cont in patt until back measures 65cm/
25½in from cast-on edge, ending with a WS
row.
Cast off.

Front

Work as given for back until front measures
53cm/21in from cast-on edge, ending with a
WS row.
Divide for neck
Next row Patt 45, turn and leave rem sts on a
spare needle.
Keeping patt correct, cast off 3 sts at beg of
next row.
Dec 1 st at neck edge on every row to
38 sts, then on every foll alt row until 32 sts
rem.
Work straight until front measures same as
back to shoulders, ending with a WS row.
Cast off.
Return to sts on spare needle.
With RS facing, join on yarn and cast off first
9 sts, patt to end. 45 sts.
Work 1 row, then complete to match first
side of neck.

Sleeves

Using 4½mm needles cast on 40 sts.
Work 7cm/2¾in k1, p1 rib, ending with a RS
row.
Inc row Rib 6, * M1, rib 1, rep from * to last
5 sts, rib 5. 69 sts.
Change to 5mm needles.
Work in patt as given for back, inc and
working into patt 1 st each end of 5th and
every foll 6th row until there are 95 sts.
Work straight until sleeve measures 47cm/
18½in from cast-on edge, ending with a WS
row.
Cast off.

Neckband

Join right shoulder seam.
With RS facing and using 4½mm needles,
pick up and k96 sts evenly round neck
edge.
Work 2.5cm/1in k1, p1 rib.
Cast off loosely in rib.

To make up

Join left shoulder and neckband seam.
Place a marker at each side of back and
front 26cm/10¼in below shoulder seam.
Sew in sleeves between markers, then join
side and sleeve seams.

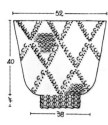

Sleeve

Measurements given in cm

LONG LINE TEXTURED JERSEY

*

Simply by reversing knit and purl stitches in a regular fashion, an attractive textured stitch design can be achieved.

Materials

17×50g balls of Robin New World Chunky
A pair each of 4½mm/No7 and 5½mm/No5
 knitting needles

Measurements

To fit bust 91–97cm/36–38in
Actual measurements
Bust 109cm/43in
Length to shoulders 63cm/24¾in
Sleeve seam 44cm/17½in

Tension

14 sts and 18 rows to 10cm/4in measured
over st st worked on 5½mm needles

Back

Using 4½mm needles cast on 72 sts.
★ Work 8cm/3¼in k2, p2 rib, ending with a
WS row.
Change to 5½mm needles.
Beg with a k row, work in st st until back
measures 25cm/9¾in from cast-on edge,
ending with a p row.
Now work in diagonal st patt as follows:
Row 1 * K6, p2, rep from * to end.
Row 2 P1, * k2, p6, rep from * to last 7 sts,
k2, p5.
Row 3 K4, * p2, k6, rep from * to last 4 sts,
p2, k2.
Row 4 P3, * k2, p6, rep from * to last 5 sts,
k2, p3.
Row 5 K2, * p2, k6, rep from * to last 6 sts,
p2, k4.
Row 6 P to end.
These 6 rows form the patt.
Cont in patt until back measures 41cm/16in

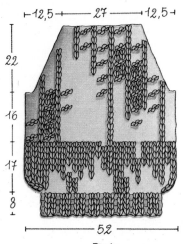

Back

from cast-on edge, ending with a WS row. ★
Shape armholes
Cast off 3 sts at beg of next 2 rows.
Patt 2 rows.
Keeping patt correct, dec 1 st each end of
next and every foll 4th row until 56 sts rem,
then every foll alt row until 38 sts rem,
ending with a WS row.

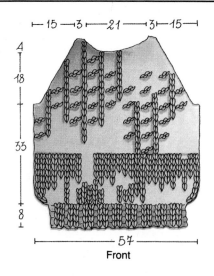

Front

Measurements given in cm

Shape shoulders
Cast off 5 sts at beg of next 2 rows. 28 sts.
Cut off yarn and leave rem sts on a holder.

Front

Using 4½mm needles cast on 80 sts.
Work as given for back from ★ to ★.
Shape armholes
Cast off 3 st at beg of next 2 rows.
Patt 2 rows.
Keeping patt correct, dec 1 st each end of
next and every foll alt row until 48 sts rem,
ending with a WS row.
Shape neck
Next row Work 2 tog, patt 17, turn and leave
rem sts on a spare needle.
Continuing to dec at armhole edge on every
foll alt row as before, dec 1 st at neck edge
on every row until 5 sts rem.
Cast off.
Return to sts on spare needle.
With RS facing, slip first 10 sts on to a
holder, join on yarn and patt to last 2 sts,
work 2 tog. 18 sts.
Now complete to match first side of neck.

Sleeves

Using 4½mm needles cast on 38 sts.
Rib row 1 K2, * p2, k2, rep from * to end.
Rib row 2 P2, * k2, p2, rep from * to end.
Rep these 2 rows for 8cm/3¼in, ending with
rib row 1.
Inc row Rib 4, * M1, rib 1, M1, rib 2, rep from
* to last st, rib 1. 60 sts.
Change to 5½mm needles.
Work in horizontal st patt as follows:
Row 1 * k4, p6, rep from * to end.
Row 2 and every alt row P to end.
Row 3 K to end.
Row 5 P5, * k4, p6, rep from * to last 5 sts,
k4, p1.
Row 7 K to end.

Row 8 P to end.
These 8 rows form the patt.
Continuing in patt, work 2 rows, then inc and
work into patt 1 st each end of next and
every foll 6th row until there are 72 sts.
Work straight until sleeve measures 36cm/
14in from cast-on edge, ending with a WS
row.
Now cont in vertical st patt as follows:
Row 1 P3, * k1, p5, rep from * to last 3 sts,
k1, p2.
Row 2 K2, * p1, k5, rep from * to last 4 sts,
p1, k3.
Rows 3 to 6 Rep rows 1 and 2 twice.
Row 7 * K1, p5, rep from * to end.
Row 8 * K5, p1, rep from * to end.
Rows 9 to 12 Rep rows 7 and 8 twice.
These 12 rows form the patt.
Continuing in patt, work 2 rows.
Shape top
Keeping patt correct, cast off 3 sts at beg of
next 2 rows.
Cast off 2 sts at beg of next 2 rows, then dec
1 st at beg of next 2 rows.
Rep these 4 rows until 18 sts rem.
Cast off 3 sts at beg of next 4 rows, 6 sts.
Cast off.

Neckband

Join right shoulder seam.
With RS facing and using 4½mm needles,
pick up and k20 sts down left side of front
neck, k10 sts from front neck holder, pick up
and k20 sts up right side of front neck, then
k across 28 sts from back neck holder.
78 sts.

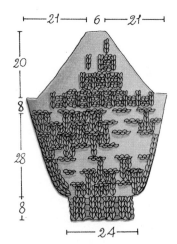

Sleeve

Beg with rib row 2, work 6 rows in rib as
given for sleeves.
Cast off loosely in rib.

To make up

Join left shoulder and neckband seam.
Sew in sleeves, then join side and sleeve
seams.

CABLE AND RIB SUMMER JERSEY

**

This classic summer jersey has an unusual cable twist to add an interesting touch.

Materials

12×50g balls of Emu Cotton DK
A pair each of 4mm/No8 and 4½mm/No7 knitting needles
2 cable needles.

Measurements

To fit bust 86–91cm/34–36in
Actual measurements
Bust 104cm/41in
Length to shoulders 66cm/26in
Sleeve seam 49cm/19¼in

Tension

17 sts and 44 rows to 10cm/4in measured over rib patt worked on 4½mm needles

Special abbreviations

k1B Knit one below as follows: insert right-hand needle into stitch below next stitch on left-hand needle and knit in the usual way, slipping stitch above off needle.
C7B Cable 7 as follows: slip the next 3 sts on to the first cable needle and leave at back of work, slip the next st on to the second cable needle and leave at back of work, over the next 3 sts work k1B, k1, k1B, now knit 1 from second cable needle, then working on sts from first cable needle, k1B, k1, k1B.

Back

Using 4mm needles cast on 80 sts.
Work 8cm/3in k1, p1 rib, ending with a RS row.
Inc row P5, [M1, p9] 8 times, M1, p3. 89 sts.
Change to 4½mm needles.
Work in patt as follows:
Row 1 (RS) K2, * k1B, k1, rep from * to last st, k1.
Row 2 K1, * k1B, k1, rep from * to end.
Rows 3 to 6 Rep rows 1 and 2 twice.
Row 7 K2, [k1B, k1] 6 times, * C7B, k1, [k1B, k1] 5 times, rep from * twice, C7B, k1, [k1B, k1] 6 times, k1.
Row 8 As row 2.
Rows 9 to 12 Rep rows 1 and 2 twice.
These 12 rows form the patt.
Cont in patt until back measures 45cm/17¾in from cast-on edge, ending with a WS row.
Shape armholes
Keeping patt correct, cast off 4 sts at beg of next 2 rows then 2 sts at beg of foll 6 rows. 69 sts.
Cont in patt until back measures 66cm/26in from cast-on edge, ending with a WS row.
Shape shoulders
Cast off 21 sts at beg of next two rows.
Patt 1 row on rem 27 sts.
Cut off yarn and leave rem sts on a holder.

Front

Work as given for back until front measures 56cm/22in from cast-on edge, ending with a WS row.
Shape neck
Next row Patt 29, turn and leave rem sts on a spare needle.
Keeping patt correct, cast off 2 sts at beg of next and every foll alt row until 21 sts rem.
Work straight until front measures the same as back to shoulder, ending with a WS row.
Cast off.
Return to sts on spare needle.
With RS facing, join yarn to next st, patt 11

and slip these sts on to a holder for neckband, patt to end. 29 sts.
Patt 1 row.
Now complete to match first side of neck.

Sleeves

Using 4mm needles cast on 42 sts.
Work 8cm/3in k1, p1 rib, ending with a RS row.
Inc row P3, [M1, p9] 4 times, M1, p3. 47 sts.
Change to 4½mm needles.
Row 1 K2, * k1B, k1, rep from * to last st, k1.
Row 2 K1, * k1B, k1, rep from * to end.
Rows 3 to 6 Rep rows 1 and 2 twice.
Row 7 K2, * C7B [k1, k1B] 5 times, k1, rep from * once more, C7B, k2.
Row 8 As row 2.
Rows 9 to 12 Rep rows 1 and 2 twice.
Cont in patt, inc and work into rib patt 1 st each end of next and every foll 10th row until there are 73 sts.
Work straight until sleeve measures 49cm/19½in from cast-on edge, ending with a WS row.

Shape top

Keeping patt correct, cast off 5 sts at beg of next 2 rows then 2 sts at beg of next 13 rows. 37 sts.
Cast off.

Neckband

Join right shoulder seam.
With RS facing, and using 4mm needles, pick up and k33 sts down left side of neck, k across 11 sts from front neck holder, pick up and k33 sts up right side of neck, then k across 27 sts from back neck holder. 104 sts.
Work 4cm/1½in k1, p1 rib, ending with a WS row.
Cast off loosely in rib.

To make up

Join left shoulder and neckband.
Fold sleeves in half lengthwise, then placing folds to shoulder seams, sew into place.
Join side and sleeve seams.

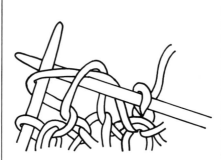

KNIT TIP

Knitting into the stitch below

Insert the right-hand needle through the centre of the stitch below the next stitch on the left-hand needle. Wind yarn under and over the point of the right-hand needle and draw a loop through. Allow the stitch above on the left-hand needle to drop off.

By knitting into the stitch below you are knitting the stitch below and the loop of the stitch above together. This means you have to knit 2 rows to form one 'knit' stitch on the right side of the fabric (you get approximately 2 rows of fisherman's rib to every 1 row of k1, p1 rib). However, as the fabric spreads more than simple rib you need fewer stitches to achieve the same width and every stitch is knitted which speeds up the process. This rib stitch can be worked on every row, as given in this pattern, when it is known as English fisherman's rib or k1B, p1 on every alternate row with the row in between knitted, when it is called fisherman's rib.
The effect of both these stitch patterns is to give a more pronounced ridged rib, making them particularly suitable for all-over ribbed designs.

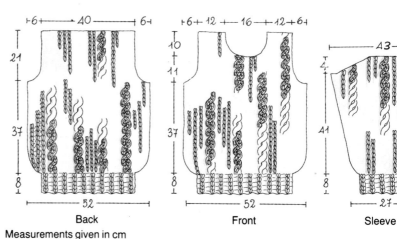

Back

Front

Sleeve

Measurements given in cm

LONG LACY PATTERN CARDIGAN

✳✳✳

Bands of a lacy V stitch pattern separate areas of tucks on this long line cardigan.

Materials

13(14)×50g balls of Patons Beehive Soft Blend DK
A pair each of 3¼mm/No10 and 4mm/No8 knitting needles
6 buttons

Measurements

To fit bust 86(91)cm/34(36)in
Actual measurements
Bust 94(104)cm/37(41)in
Length to shoulders 69cm/27in
Sleeve seam 37cm/14½in

Tension

25 sts and 48 rows to 10cm/4in measured over patt worked on 4mm needles

Special abbreviation

tuck 1 as follows: using right-hand needle pick up the st worked 6 rows below next st on left-hand needle and place it on left-hand needle, p this st tog wiith next st on left-hand needle

Note

Owing to the large stitch pattern repeat, the extra stitches for the second size have all been added to the back: the figures given for the left and right fronts are the same for both sizes.

Back

Using 3¼mm needles cast on 110(134) sts.
Rib row 1 K2, * p2, k2, rep from * to end.
Rib row 2 P2, * k2, p2, rep from * to end.
Rep these 2 rows for 7cm/2¾in ending with rib row 2.
Inc row Rib 8(4), * M1, rib 5(6), rep from * to last 7(4) sts, M1, rib to end. 130(156) sts.
Change to 4mm needles.
P 1 row.
Work in patt as follows:
Row 1 (RS) K to end.
Row 2 P to end.
Rows 3 to 6 Rep rows 1 and 2 twice.
Row 7 As row 1.
Row 8 * P8, tuck 1, [p1, tuck 1] 5 times, p7, rep from * to end.
Rows 9 to 12 Rep rows 1 and 2 twice.
Row 13 As row 1.
Row 14 * P7, [tuck 1, p1] 6 times, tuck 1, p6, rep from * to end.
Rows 15 and 16 As rows 1 and 2.
Row 17 P2, * yon, skpo, k5, k2 tog, yrn, p4, rep from * to last 11 sts, yon, skpo, k5,

k2 tog, yrn, p2.
Row 18 K2, * p9, k4, rep from * to last 11 sts, p9, k2.
Row 19 P2, * k1, yfon, skpo, k3, k2 tog, yf, k1, p4, rep from * to last 11 sts, k1, yfon, skpo, k3, k2 tog, yf, k1, p2.
Row 20 As row 18.
Row 21 P2, * k2, yfon, skpo, k1, k2 tog, yf, k2, p4, rep from * to last 11 sts, k2, yfon, skpo, k1, k2 tog, yf, k2, p2.
Row 22 As row 18.
Row 23 P2, * k3, yfon, sl 1, k2 tog, psso, yf, k3, p4, rep from * to last 11 sts, k3, yfon, sl 1, k2 tog, psso, yf, k3, p2.
Row 24 As row 2.
Rows 25 to 28 Rep rows 1 and 2 twice.
Row 29 As row 1.
Row 30 As row 14.
These 30 rows form the patt.
Cont in patt until back measures approx 69cm/27in from cast-on edge, ending with row 24.
Cast off.

Left front

Using 3¼mm needles cast on 46 sts.
Work 7cm/2¾in rib as given for back, ending with rib row 2.
Inc row Rib 3, * M1, rib 8, rep from * to last 3 sts, M1, rib 3. 52 sts.
Change to 4mm needles.
P 1 row.
Work in patt as given for back until front measures approx 61cm/24in from cast-on edge ending with row 15. (End with row 16 for right front.)
Shape neck
Keeping patt correct, cast off 6 sts at beg of

Measurements given in cm for smaller size

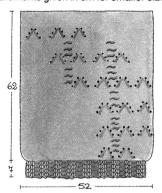

Back

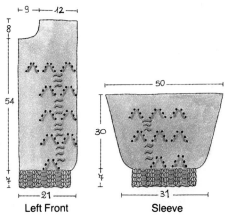

Left Front   Sleeve

next row.
Dec 1 st at neck edge on every row until 30 sts rem.
Work straight until front measures same as back to shoulder, ending at side edge.
Cast off.

Right front

Work as given for left front, noting exception given in brackets

Sleeves

Using 3¼mm needles cast on 42 sts.
Work 7cm/2¾in rib as given for back ending with rib row 2.
Inc row Rib 3, * M1, rib 1, rep from * to last 3 sts, rib 3. 78 sts.
Change to 4mm needles.
P 1 row.
Working in patt as given for back, inc and work into patt 1 st at each end of 3rd and every foll 5th row until there are 126 sts.
Cont in patt until sleeve measures approx 37cm/14½in from cast-on edge, ending with row 24.
Cast off.

Neckband

Join shoulder seams.
With RS facing and using 3¼mm needles, pick up and k24 sts up right front neck, 62(82) sts across back neck and 24 sts down left front neck. 110(130) sts.
Work 12 rows rib as given for back.
Cast off in rib.

Buttonhole border

Using 3¼mm needles pick up and k150 sts evenly up right front edge.
Work 5 rows rib as given for back.
Buttonhole row 1 Rib 4, * cast off 2, rib 26 including st used in casting off, rep from * to last 6 sts, cast off 2, rib to end.
Buttonhole row 2 Rib to end, casting on 2 sts over those cast-off on previous row.
Work a further 5 rows rib.
Cast off in rib.

Button border

Work as given for buttonhole border omitting buttonholes.

To make up

Fold sleeves in half lengthwise, then placing folds to shoulder seams, sew into place.
Join side and sleeve seams. Sew on buttons.

SIMPLE JERSEY WITH TEXTURED STITCHES

✳

Aran yarns are no longer only produced in traditional natural shades but come in a wide range of colours for today's knitters.

Materials
17×50g balls of Water Wheel Pure Wool
 Superwash Aran
A pair each of 5mm/No6 and 6mm/No4
 knitting needles
Shoulder pads (optional)

Measurements
To fit bust 86–91cm/34–36in
Actual measurements
Bust 100cm/39½in
Length to shoulders 60cm/23½in
Sleeve seam 45cm/17½in

Tension
16 sts and 30 rows to 10cm/4in measured
over rice st worked on 6mm needles

Special abbreviation
k1B Knit 1 below as follows: insert right-
hand needle into st below next st on
left-hand needle and knit in the usual way,
allowing stitch above to drop off needle

Back and front (alike)
Using 5mm needles cast on 81 sts.
Rib row 1 (RS) P1, * k1, p1, rep from * to
end.
Rib row 2 K1, * p1, k1, rep from * to end.
Rep these 2 rows for 5cm/2in, ending with
rib row 2.
Change to 6mm needles.
Work in patt as follows:
Row 1 [K1, p1] 15 times for Irish moss st,
k29 for st st, [k1, p1] 11 times for moss st.
Row 2 [P1, k1] 11 times for moss st, p29 for
st st, [k1, p1] 15 times for Irish moss st.
Row 3 [P1, k1] 14 times, p1 for Irish moss st,
k29 for st st, [p1, k1] 11 times, p1 for moss
st.
Row 4 [P1, k1] 11 times, p1 for moss st, p29
for st st, [k1, p1] 14 times, k1 for Irish moss
st.
Row 5 [K1, p1] 14 times for Irish moss st,
k29 for st st, [k1, p1] 12 times for moss st.
Row 6 [P1, k1] 12 times for moss st, p29 for
st st, [k1, p1] 14 times for Irish moss st.
These 6 rows establish the patt.
Cont in patt, working 1 st less in Irish moss
st and 1 st more in moss st so moving the
central st st panel over on every RS row until
a row has been worked thus: [p1, k1] 14
times for moss st, p29 for st st, [k1, p1] 12
times for Irish moss st.
Next row [P1, k1] 11 times, p1 for Irish moss
st, k29 for st st, [p1, k1] 14 times for moss st,
p1 for rev st st.
Next row K1 for rev st st, [k1, p1] 14 times
for moss st, p29 for st st, [k1, p1] 11 times,
k1 for Irish moss st.
Next row [K1, p1] 11 times for Irish moss st,
k29 for st st, [k1, p1] 14 times for moss st, p2
for rev st st.

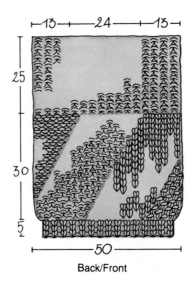

Back/Front

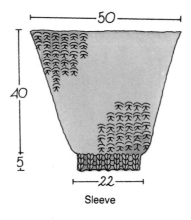

Sleeve

Measurements given in cm

Next row K2 for rev st st, [p1, k1] 14 times
for moss st, p29 for st st, [k1, p1] 11 times
for Irish moss st.
Next row [P1, k1] 10 times, p1 for Irish moss
st, k29 for st st, [p1, k1] 14 times for moss st,
p3 for rev st st.
Next row K3 for rev st st, [k1, p1] 14 times
for moss st, p29 for st st, [k1, p1] 10 times,
k1 for Irish moss st.
Next row [K1, p1] 10 times for Irish moss st,
k29 for st st, [k1, p1] 14 times for moss st, p4
for rev st st.
Next row K4 for rev st st, [p1, k1] 14 times
for moss st, p29 for st st, [k1, p1] 10 times
for Irish moss st.
Cont in patt, working 1 st less in Irish moss
st and 1 st more in rev st st so moving the
central st st and moss st panel over on every
RS row until a row has ben worked thus: k23
for rev st st, [k1, p1] 14 times for moss st,
p29 for st st, k1 for Irish moss st.
Next row K29 for st st, [k1, p1] 14 times for
moss st, p24 for rev st st.
Next row K24 for rev st st, [p1, k1] 14 times
for moss st, p29 for st st. Working st st, moss
st and rev st st, cont to move the panels over
1 st on every RS row as before until a row
has been worked as follows: k28 for rev st st,
[p1, k1] 14 times for moss st, p25 for st st.
Work in rice st as follows:
Row 1 (RS) P to end.
Row 2 K1, * p1, k1B, rep from * to last 2 sts,
p1, k1.
These 2 rows form the patt.
Cont in patt until work measures 60cm/
23½in from cast-on edge, ending with a RS
row.
Cast off in patt for shoulders and neck.

Sleeves
Using 5mm needles cast on 43 sts.
Rep the 2 rib rows for 5cm/2in, ending with a
WS row.
Change to 6mm needles.
Work rice st as given for back and front
increasing and working into patt 1 st each
end of 9th and every foll 6th row until there
are 79 sts.
Cont in patt until sleeve measures 45cm/
17½in from cast-on edge, ending with a RS
row.
Cast off in patt.

To make up
Join shoulder seams leaving approx 24cm/
9½in open at centre for neck. Place
markers 25cm/10in below shoulders on
back and front. Set in sleeves between
markers, then join side and sleeve seams.
Sew in shoulder pads if required.

LARGE JERSEY IN A BROCADE STITCH PATTERN

✳✳

A combination of simple stitches used in a totally random design gives texture to this loose-fitting jersey with deep ribs.

Materials

16×50g balls of Water Wheel Concorde
  Chunky
A pair each of 5½mm/No5 and 6½mm/No3
  knitting needles

Measurements

To fit bust 86–97cm/34–38in
Actual measurements
Bust 114cm/45in
Length to shoulders 75cm/29½in
Sleeve seam 43cm/17in

Tension

13 sts and 22 rows to 10cm/4in measured
over patt using 6½mm needles

Back and front (alike)

Using 5½mm needles cast on 74 sts.
Rib row 1 K2, * p2, k2, rep from * to end.
Rib row 2 P2, * k2, p2, rep from * to end.
Rep these 2 rows for 8cm/3in, ending with
rib row 2.
Change to 6½mm needles.
Work in patt from chart, reading RS rows
from right to left and WS rows from left to
right, noting that areas in white are knitted in
st st, areas in dark pink in rev st st and areas
in pale pink in moss st.

Sleeves

Using 5½mm needles cast on 38 sts.
Work 8cm/3in rib as given for back, ending
with a WS row.
Change to 6½mm needles.
Work in patt from chart as indicated for
sleeves, working increases where shown.

Neckband

Join right shoulder seam.
With RS facing and using 5½mm needles,
pick up and k16 sts down left side of front
neck, 24 sts across front neck, 16 sts up
right side of front neck, 16 sts down left side
of back neck, 24 sts across back neck and
16 sts up right side of back neck. 112 sts.
Work 8cm/3in k2, p2 rib.
Cast off in rib.

To make up

Join left shoulder seam.
Fold sleeves in half lengthwise, then placing
folds to shoulder seams, sew into place.
Join side and sleeve seams.

Back/Front

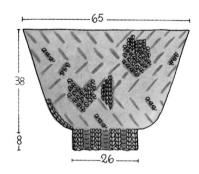

Measurements given in cm

Sleeve

Cast off for neck

knit
purl
k on RS rows and p on WS rows
p on RS rows and k on WS rows

Back/Front   Sleeve

TUCK STITCH JERSEY WITH A ROLLOVER COLLAR

*

The looped slip stitches in a contrast colour yarn make the brick pattern on this jersey.

Materials

9(10,10,11,11,12,12)×50g balls of Jaeger Monte Cristo (DK cotton) in main colour A
2(2,2,2,2,3,3) balls of same in contrast colour B
A pair each of 3¼mm/No10 and 4½mm/No7 knitting needles

Measurements

To fit bust 81(86,91,97,102,107,112)cm/32(34,36,38,40,42,44)in
Actual measurements
Bust 97(103,109,115,119,123,129)cm/38¼(40½,43,45¼,47,48½,50¾)in
Length to shoulders 59cm/23¼in
Sleeve seam 42(42,42,43,43,43,43)cm/16½(16½,16½,17,17,17,17)in

Tension

20 sts and 28 rows to 10cm/4in measured over patt worked on 4½mm needles

Front

★ Using 3¼mm needles and A, cast on 90(98,102,110,114,118,122) sts.
Rib row 1 K2, * p2, k2, rep from * to end.
Rib row 2 P2, * k2, p2, rep from * to end.
Rep these 2 rows for 7cm/2¾in, ending with rib row 1.
Inc row Rib 9(11,9,11,13,13,10), * M1, rib 12(19,14,22,22,23,17), rep from * to last 9(11,9,11,13,13,10) sts, M1, rib to end. 97(103,109,115,119,123,129) sts. ★
Change to 4½mm needles.
Join on and cut off colours as required.
Work in patt as follows:
Row 1 (RS) With B, k6(9,12,3,5,7,10), * winding yarn 3 times round needle k1, k11, rep from * to last 7(10,13,4,6,8,11) sts, winding yarn 3 times round needle k1, k6(9,12,3,5,7,10).
Row 2 With A, p6(9,12,3,5,7,10), * dropping extra loops off needle sl 1 pw, p11, rep from * to last 7(10,13,4,6,8,11) sts, dropping extra loops off needle sl 1 pw, p6(9,12,3,5,7,10).
Row 3 With A, k6(9,12,3,5,7,10), * sl 1 pw, k11, rep from * to last 7(10,13,4,6,8,11) sts, sl 1 pw, k6(9,12,3,5,7,10).
Row 4 With A, p6(9,12,3,5,7,10), * sl 1 pw, p11, rep from * to last 7(10,13,4,6,8,11) sts, sl 1 pw, p6(9,12,3,5,7,10).
Rows 5 to 12 Rep rows 3 and 4 four times.
Row 13 With B, k12(3,6,9,11,13,4), * winding yarn 3 times round needle k1, k11, rep from * to last 13(4,7,10,12,14,5) sts, winding yarn 3 times round needle k1, k12(3,6,9,11,13,4).
Row 14 With A, p12(3,6,9,11,13,4), * dropping extra loops off needle sl 1 pw, p11, rep from * to last 13(4,7,10,12,14,5) sts, dropping extra loops off needles sl 1 pw, p12(3,6,9,11,13,4).
Row 15 With A, k12(3,6,9,11,13,4), * sl 1 pw, k11, rep from * to last 13(4,7,10,12,14,5) sts, sl 1 pw, k12(3,6,9,11,13,4).

Row 16 With A, p12(3,6,9,11,13,4), * sl 1 pw, p11, rep from * to last 13(4,7,10,12,14,5) sts, sl 1 pw, p12(3,6,9,11,13,4).
Rows 17 to 24 Rep rows 15 and 16 four times.
These 24 rows form the patt.
Cont in patt until front measures approx 50cm/19½in from cast-on edge, ending with row 24.
Next row With B, patt 30(33,36,39,41,43,46), k to last 30(33,36,39,41,43,46) sts, patt to end.

Front

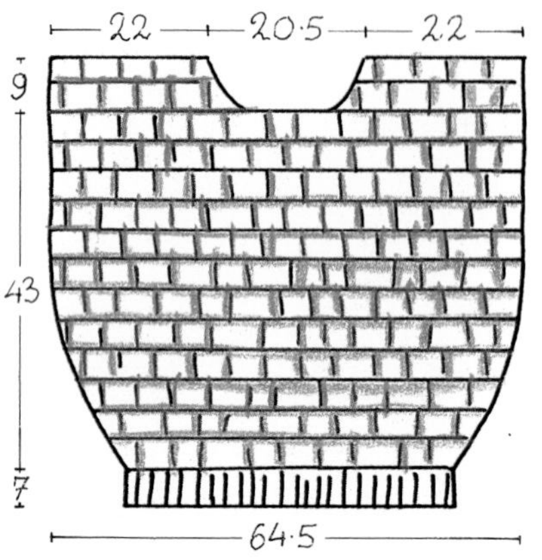

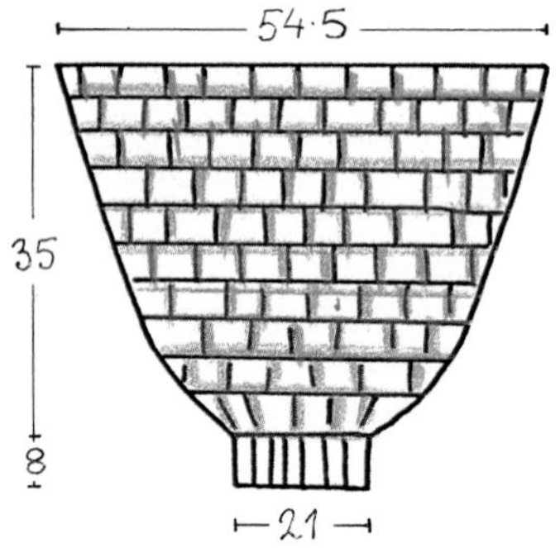

Next row With A, patt 30(33,36,39,41,43,46), p to last 30(33,36,39,41,43,46) sts, patt to end.
Shape neck
Next row Patt 40(43,45,48,50,52,55), turn and leave rem sts on a spare needle.
Keeping patt correct, dec 1 st at neck edge on every row until 29(32,34,37,39,41,44) sts rem.
Work straight until front measures approx 58.5cm/23in from cast-on edge, ending with row 24.
Next row With B, k to end.
Next row With A, p to end.
(For second side of neck, k 1 more row in A.)

Sleeve

Measurements given in cm for largest size

With A, cast off.
Return to sts on spare needle.
With RS facing, join on A and cast off 17(17,19,19,19,19,19) sts, then patt to end. 40(43,45,48,50,52,55) sts.
Now complete to match first side of neck noting the exception in brackets.

Back

Work as given for front from ★ to ★.
Change to 4½mm needles.
Beg with row 13, work in patt as given for front until back measures 2 rows less than front to shoulders, so ending with row 12.
Next row With B, k to end.
Next row With A, p to end.
Shape shoulders
With A, cast off 29(32,34,37,39,41,44) sts at beg of next 2 rows.
Cast off rem 39(39,41,41,41,41,41) sts.

Sleeves

Using 3¼mm needles and A, cast on 38(38,42,42,42,46,46) sts.
Work 7(7,7,8,8,8,8)cm/2¾(2¾,2¾,3,3,3,3)in rib as given for back, ending with rib row 1.
Inc row Rib 3(3,5,5,5,7,7),* M1, rib 2, rep from * to last 3(3,5,5,5,7,7) sts, M1, rib to end. 55(55,59,59,59,63,63) sts.
Change to 4½mm needles.
Working in patt as given for the 4th(4th,5th,5th,5th,6th,6th) size on front, inc and work into patt 1 st each end of 5th(3rd,5th,3rd,3rd,3rd,3rd) and every foll 4th row until there are 97(99,101,103,103,107,107) sts.
Work straight until sleeve measures approx 41(41,41,42,42,42,42)cm/16¼(16¼,16¼,16½,16½,16½,16½)in from cast-on edge, ending with row 24.
Next row With B, k to end.
Next row With A, p to end.
With A, cast off.

Collar

Join right shoulder seam.
With RS facing, using 3¼mm needles and A, pick up and k26 sts down left side of front neck, 20(20,22,22,22,22,22) sts across front neck, 26 sts up right side of front neck and 42(42,44,44,44,44,44) sts across back neck. 114(114,118,118,118,118,118) sts.
Beg with a p row, work 19 rows st st.
Cast off.

To make up

Join left shoulder and collar seam, reversing collar seam for second half and allowing it to roll to right side. Fold sleeves in half lengthwise, then placing folds to shoulder seams, sew into place. Join side and sleeve seams.

SLEEVELESS COTTON TOP WITH FAN STITCH PATTERN

✳✳

The pretty
fan-like
stitch
patterns
are set in
alternating
positions each
side of this
summer top.

Materials

10(12,14)×50g balls of Twilley's Stalite Perlespun
A pair each of 4mm/No8 and 5½mm/No5 knitting needles
Cable needle

Measurements

To fit bust 76-81(86-91,97-102)cm/30-32(34-36,38-40)in

Actual measurements
Bust 94(104,115)cm/37(41,45½)in
Length to shoulders 59(61,63)cm/23(24,25)in

Tension

17 sts and 22 rows to 10cm/4in measured over rev st st worked on 5½mm needles and using yarn double

Special abbreviations

Tw2L Twist 2 left as follows: p into back of 2nd st on left-hand needle, then k first st, slipping both sts off needle together
Tw2R Twist 2 right as follows: k into front of 2nd st on left-hand needle, then p first st, slipping both sts off needle together
C8 Cable 8 as follows: Slip next 4 sts on to cable needle and leave at front of work, k3, p1, then [p1, k3] from cable needle

Note

Yarn is used double throughout.

Back

Using 4mm needles and yarn double, cast on 75(83,93)sts.
Rib row 1 K1, * p1, k1, rep from * to end.
Rib row 2 P1, * k1, p1, rep from * to end.
Rep these 2 rows for 5cm/2in, ending with rib row 1.
Inc row Rib 14, * M1, rib 12(14,16), rep from * to last 13(13,15) sts, M1, rib to end. 80(88,98) sts.
Change to 5½mm needles.
Work in patt as follows:
Row 1 (RS) P54(59,66), k3, p2, k3, p to end.
Row 2 K18(21,24), p3, k2, p3, k to end.
Rows 3 and 4 As rows 1 and 2.
Row 5 P50(55,62), Tw2R, p1, Tw2R, k2, p2, k2, Tw2L, p1, Tw2L, p to end.
Row 6 K14(17,20), p1, k2, p1, k1, p2, k2, p2, k1, p1, k2, p1, k to end.
Row 7 P49(54,61), Tw2R, p1, Tw2R, k3, p2, k3, Tw2L, p1, Tw2L, p to end.
Row 8 K13(16,19), p1, k2, p1, k1, p3, k2, p3, k1, p1, k2, p1, k to end.
Row 9 P51(56,63), Tw2R, k4, p2, k4, Tw2L, p to end.
Row 10 K15(18,21), p1, k1, p4, k2, p4, k1, p1, k to end.
Row 11 P50(55,62), Tw2R, k5, p2, k5, Tw2L, p to end.
Row 12 K14(17,20), p1, k1, p5, k2, p5, k1, p1, k to end.
Row 13 P49(54,61), Tw2R, k6, p2, k6, Tw2L, p to end.

Row 14 K13(16,19), p1, k1, p6, k2, p6, k1, p1,k to end.
Row 15 P48(53,60), Tw2R, k7, p2, k7, Tw2L, p to end.
Row 16 K12(15,18), p1, k1, p7, k2, p7, k1, p1, k to end.
Row 17 P47(52, 59), Tw2R, k8, p2, k8, Tw2L, p to end.
Row 18 K11(14,17), p1, k1, p8, k2, p8, k1, p1, k to end.
Row 19 P46(51,58), Tw2R, p1, k8, p2, k8, p1, Tw2L, p to end.
Row 20 K10(13,16), p1, [k2, p8] twice, k2, p1, k to end.
Row 21 P45(50,57), Tw2R, p1, Tw2R, k7, p2, k7, Tw2L, p1, Tw2L, p to end.
Row 22 K9(12,15), p1, k2, p1, k1, p7, k2, p7, k1, p1, k2, p1, k to end.
Row 23 P44(49,56), [Tw2R, p1] twice, k7, p2, k7, [p1, Tw2L] twice, p to end.
Row 24 K8(11,14), [p1, k2] twice, p7, k2, p7, [k2, p1] twice, k to end.
Row 25 P43(48,55), [Tw2R, p1] twice, Tw2R, k6, p2, k6, Tw2L, [p1, Tw2L] twice, p to end.
Row 26 K7(10,13), [p1, k2] twice, p1, k1, p6, k2, p6, k1, p1, [k2, p1] twice, k to end.
Row 27 P45(50,57), [Tw2R, p1] twice, k6, p2, k6, [p1, Tw2L] twice, p to end.
Row 28 K9(12,15), [p1, k2] twice, p6, k2, p6, [k2, p1] twice, k to end.
Row 29 P47(52,59), Tw2R, p1, Tw2R, k5, p2, k5, Tw2L, p1, Tw2L, p to end.
Row 30 K11(14,17), p1, k2, p1, k1, p5, k2, p5, k1, p1, k2, p1, k to end.
Row 31 P46(51,58), [Tw2R, p1] twice, k5, p2, k5, [p1, Tw2L] twice, p to end.
Row 32 K10(13,16), [p1, k2] twice, p5, k2, p5, [k2, p1] twice, k to end.
Row 33 P48(53,60), Tw2R, p1, Tw2R, k4, p2, k4, Tw2L, p1, Tw2L, p to end.
Row 34 K12(15,18), p1, k2, p1, k1, p4, k2, p4, k1, p1, k2, p1, k to end.
Row 35 P47(52,59), [Tw2R, p1] twice, k4, p2, k4, [p1, Tw2L] twice, p to end.
Row 36 K11(14,17), [p1, k2] twice. p4, k2, p4, [k2, p1] twice, k to end.
Row 37 P49(54,61), Tw2R, p1, Tw2R, C8, Tw2L, p1, Tw2L, p to end.
Row 38 K13(16,19), p1, k2, p1, k1, p3, k2, p3, k1, p1, k2, p1, k to end.
Row 39 P9(12,15), Tw2R, p1, Tw2R, k7, p2, k7, Tw2L, p1, Tw2L, p13(15,19), [Tw2R, p1] twice, k3, p2, k3, [p1, Tw2L] twice, p to end.
Row 40 K12(15,18), [p1, k2] twice, p3, k2, p3, [k2, p1] twice, k13(15,19), p1, k2, p1, k1, p7, k2, p7, k1, p1, k2, p1, k to end.
Row 41 P8(11,14), [Tw2R, p1] twice, k7, p2, k7, [p1, Tw2L] twice, p14(16,20), Tw2R, p1, Tw2R, k2, p2, k2, Tw2L, p1, Tw2L, p to end.
Row 42 K14(17,20), p1, k2, p1, k1, p2, k2, p2, k1, p1, k2, p1, k14(16,20), [p1, k2] twice, p7, k2, p7, [k2, p1] twice, k to end.
Row 43 P7(10,13) [Tw2R, p1] twice, Tw2R,

k6, p2, k6, Tw2L, [p1, Tw2L] twice, p12(14,18), Tw2R, p1, Tw2R, k3, p2, k3, Tw2L, p1, Tw2L, p to end.
Row 44 K13(16,19), p1, k2, p1, k1, p3, k2, p3, k1, p1, k2, p1, k12(14,18), [p1, k2] twice, p1, k1, p6, k2, p6, k1, p1, [k2, p1] twice, k to end.
Row 45 P9(12,15), [Tw2R, p1] twice, k6, p2, k6, [p1, Tw2L] twice, p16(18,22), Tw2R, k4, p2, k4, Tw2L; p to end.
Row 46 K15(18,21), p1, k1, p4, k2, p4, k1, p1, k16(18,22), [p1, k2] twice, p6, k2, p6, [k2, p1] twice, k to end.
Row 47 P11(14,17), Tw2R, p1, Tw2R, k5, p2, k5, Tw2L, p1, Tw2L, p17(19,23), Tw2R, k5, p2, k5, Tw2L, p to end.
Row 48 K14(17,20), p1, k1, p5, k2, p5, k1, p1, k17(19,23), p1, k2, p1, k1, p5, k2, p5, k1, p1, k2, p1, k to end.
Row 49 P10(13,16), [Tw2R, p1] twice, k5, p2, k5, [p1, Tw2L] twice, p15(17,21), Tw2R, k6, p2, k6, Tw2L, p to end.
Row 50 K13(16,19), p1, k1, p6, k2, p6, k1, p1, k15(17,21), [p1, k2] twice, p5, k2, p5, [k2, p1] twice, k to end..
Row 51 P12(15,18), Tw2R, p1, Tw2R, k4, p2, k4, Tw2L, p1, Tw2L, p16(18,22), Tw2R, k7, p2, k7, Tw2L, p to end.
Row 52 K12(15,18), p1, k1, p7, k2, p7, k1, p1, k16(18,22), p1, k2, p1, k1, p4, k2, p4, k1, p1, k2, p1, k to end.
Row 53 P11(14,17), [Tw2R, p1] twice, k4, p2, k4, [p1, Tw2L] twice, p14(16,20), Tw2R, k8, p2, k8, Tw2L, p to end.
Row 54 K11(14,17), p1, k1, p8, k2, p8, k1, p1, k14(16,20), [p1, k2] twice, p4, k2, p4, [k2, p1] twice, k to end.
Row 55 P13(16,19), Tw2R, p1, Tw2R, C8, Tw2L, p1, Tw2L, p15(17,21), Tw2R, p1, k8, p2, k8, p2, Tw2L, p to end.
Row 56 K10(13,16), p1, [k2, p8] twice, k2, p1, k15(17,21), p1, k2, p1, k1, p3, k2, p3, k1, p1, k2, p1, k to end.
Row 57 P12(15,18), [Tw2R, p1] twice, k3, p2, k3, [p1, Tw2L] twice, p13(15,19), Tw2R, p1, Tw2R, k7, p2, k7, Tw2L, p1, Tw2L, p to end.
Row 58 K9(12,15), p1, k2, p1, k1, p7, k2, p7, k1, p1, k2, p1, k13(15,19), [p1, k2] twice, p3, k2, p3, [k2, p1] twice, k to end.
Row 59 P14(17,20), Tw2R, p1, Tw2R, k2, p2, k2, Tw2L, p1, Tw2L, p14(16,20), [Tw2R, p1] twice, k7, p2, k7, [p1, Tw2L] twice, p to end.
Row 60 K8(11,14), [p1, k2] twice, p7, k2, p7, [k2, p1] twice, k14(16,20), p1, k2, p1, k1, p2, k2, p2, k1, p1, k2, p1, k to end.
Row 61 P13(16,19), Tw2R, p1, Tw2R, k3, p2, k3, Tw2L, p1, Tw2L, p12(14,18), [Tw2R, p1] twice, Tw2R, k6, p2, k6, Tw2L, [p1, Tw2L] twice, p to end.
Row 62 K7(10,13), [p1, k2] twice, p1, k1, p6, k2, p6, k1, p1, [k2, p1] twice, k12(14,18), p1, k2, p1, k1, p3, k2, p3, k1, p1, k2, p1, k to end.

Row 63 P15(18,21), Tw2R, k4, p2, k4, Tw2L, p16(18,22), [Tw2R, p1] twice, k6, p2, k6, [p1, Tw2L] twice, p to end.
Row 64 K9(12,15), [p1, k2] twice, p6, k2, p6, [k2, p1] twice, k16(18,22), p1, k1, p4, k2, p4, k1, p1, k to end.
Row 65 P14(17,20), Tw2R, k5, p2, k5, Tw2L, p17(19,23), Tw2R, p1, Tw2R, k5, p2, k5, Tw2L, p1, Tw2L, p to end.
Row 66 K11(14,17), p1, k2, p1, k1, p5, k2, p5, k1, p1, k2, p1, k17(19,23), p1, k1, p5, k2, p5, k1, p1, k to end.
Row 67 P13(16,19), Tw2R, k6, p2, k6, Tw2L, p15(17,21), [Tw2R, p1] twice, k5, p2, k5, [p1, Tw2L] twice, p to end.
Mark each end of last row with a coloured thread to denote beg of armhole.
Row 68 K10(13,16), [p1, k2] twice, p5, k2, p5, [k2, p1] twice, k15(17,21), p1, k1, p6, k2, p6, k1, p1, k to end.
Row 69 P12(15,18), Tw2R, k7, p2, k7, Tw2L, p16(18,22), Tw2R, p1, Tw2R, k4, p2, k4, Tw2L, p1, Tw2L, p to end.
Row 70 K12(15,18), p1, k2, p1, k1, p4, k2, p4, k1, p1, k2, p1, k16(18,22) p1, k1, p7, k2, p7, k1, p1, k to end.
Row 71 P11(14,17), Tw2R, k8, p2, k8, Tw2L, p14(16,20), [Tw2R, p1] twice, k4, p2, k4, [p1, Tw2L] twice, p to end.
Row 72 K11(14,17), [p1, k2] twice, p4, k2, p4, [k2, p1] twice, k14(16,20), p1, k1, p8, k2, p8, k1, p1, k to end.
Row 73 P10(13,16), Tw2R, p1, k8, p2, k8, p1, Tw2L, p15(17,21), Tw2R, p1, Tw2R, C8, Tw2L, p1, Tw2L, p to end.
Row 74 K13(16,19), p1, k2, p1, k1, p3, k2, p3, k1, p1, k2, p1, k15(17,21), p1, [k2, p8] twice, k2, p1, k to end.
Rows 75 to 96 As rows 39 to 60.
Row 97 P13(16,19), Tw2R, p1, Tw2R, k3, p2, k3, Tw2L, p1, Tw2L, p to end.
Row 98 K49(54,61), p1, k2, p1, k1, p3, k2, p3, k1, p1, k2, p1, k to end.
Row 99 P15(18,21), Tw2R, k4, p2, k4, Tw2L, p to end.
Row 100 K51(56,63), p1, k1, p4, k2, p4, k1, p1, k to end.
Row 101 P14(17,20), Tw2R, k5, p2, k5, Tw2L, p to end.
Row 102 K50(55,62), p1, k1, p5, k2, p5, k1, p1, k to end.
Row 103 P13(16,19), Tw2R, k6, p2, k6, Tw2L, p to end.
Row 104 K49(54,61), p1, k1, p6, k2, p6, k1, p1, k to end.
Row 105 P12(15,18), Tw2R, k7, p2, k7, Tw2L, p to end.
Row 106 K48(53,60), p1, k1, p7, k2, p7, k1, p1, k to end.
Row 107 P11(14,17), Tw2R, k8, p2, k8, Tw2L, p to end.
Row 108 K47(52,59), p1, k1, p8, k2, p8, k1, p1, k to end.
Row 109 P10(13,16), Tw2R, p1, k8, p2, k8, p1, Tw2L, p to end.

Row 110 K46(51,58), p1, [k2, p8] twice, k2, p1, k to end.
Row 111 P9(12,15), Tw2R, p1, Tw2R, k7, p2, k7, Tw2L, p1, Tw2L, p to end.
Row 112 K45(50,57), p1, k2, p1, k1, p7, k2, p7, k1, p1, k2, p1, k to end.
Row 113 P8(11,14), [Tw2R, p1] twice, k7, p2, k7, [p1, Tw2L] twice, p to end.
Row 114 K44(49,56), [p1, k2] twice, p7, k2, p7, [k2, p1] twice, k to end.
Row 115 P7(10,13), [Tw2R, p1] twice, Tw2R, k6, p2, k6, Tw2L, [p1, Tw2L] twice, p to end.
Row 116 K43(48,55), [p1, k2] twice, p1, k1, p6, k2, p6, k1, p1, [k2, p1] twice, k to end.
Row 117 P9(12,15), [Tw2R, p1] twice, k6, p2, k6, [p1, Tw2L] twice, p to end.
Row 118 K45(50,57), [p1, k2] twice, p6, k2, p6, [k2, p1] twice, k to end.
Row 119 P11(14,17), Tw2R, p1, Tw2R, k5, p2, k5, Tw2L, p1, Tw2L, p to end.
Row 120 K47(52,59), p1, k2, p1, k1, p5, k2, p5, k1, p1, k2, p1, k to end.

2nd and 3rd sizes only
Row 121 P13(16), [Tw2R, p1] twice, k5, p2, k5, [p1, Tw2L] twice, p to end.
Row 122 K51(58), [p1, k2] twice, p5, k2, p5, [k2, p1] twice, k to end.
Row 123 P15(18), Tw2R, p1, Tw2R, k4, p2, k4, Tw2L, p1, Tw2L, p to end.
Row 124 K53(60), p1, k2, p1, k1, p4, k2, p4, k1, p1, k2, p1, k to end.

3rd size only
Row 125 P17, [Tw2R, p1] twice, k4, p2, k4, [p1, Tw2L] twice, p59.
Row 126 K59, [p1, k2] twice, p4, k2, p4, [k2, p1] twice, k17.
Row 127 P19, Tw2R, p1, Tw2R, C8, Tw2L, p1, Tw2L, p to end.
Row 128 K61, p1, k2, p1, k1, p3, k2, p3, k1, p1, k2, p1, k19.

All sizes
Next row Cast off 22(25,29) sts, patt until there are 36(38,40) sts on right-hand needle, cast off rem 22(25,29) sts. Leave rem sts on a holder.

Front
Work as given for back until row 104(106,110) has been completed.
Shape neck
Next row Patt across 31(34,38) sts, turn and leave rem sts on a spare needle.
★ Keeping patt correct, cast off 3 sts at beg of next row and 2 sts at beg of foll alt row.
Dec 1 st at neck edge on foll 4 alt rows.
Work 5(7,7) rows straight.
Cast off rem 22(25,29) sts. ★
Note Do not work a cable twist on the last rep for the 3rd size, but work [k3, p2, k3] over the 8 cable sts.
Return to sts on spare needle.
With RS facing, slip first 18(20,22) sts on to a holder, join on yarn and patt to end.
Now complete as given from ★ to ★.

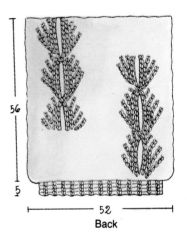

56

5

52

Back

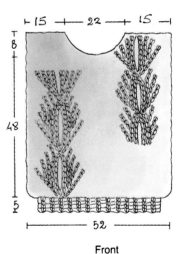

15 — 22 — 15

8

48

5

52

Front

Measurements given in cm for second size

Neckband

Join right shoulder seam.
With RS facing and using 4mm needles, pick up and k18(20,20) sts down left side of front neck, k18(20,22) sts from front neck holder, pick up and k18(20,20) sts up right side of front neck, then increasing 1 st at centre k36(38,40) sts from back neck holder. 91(99,103) sts.
Work 5 rows rib as given for back.
Cast off in rib.

Armhole borders

Join left shoulder and neckband seam.
With RS facing and using 4mm needles, pick up and k97(105,109) sts evenly along armhole edge between markers.
Work 5 rows rib as given for back.
Cast off in rib.

To make up

Join side and armhole border seams.

KNIT TIP

A balanced pattern

The fans each side of the front and back are worked alternately. This means that the cable twist on one side is at the level of the widest part of the fan on the opposite side. If you would prefer a more balanced look or would like to simplify the pattern, you can work both fans at the same time starting at the welt.

Back

Work rib rows and increase row as given in pattern. Change to 5½mm needles and work in patt as follows:
Row 1 (RS) P16(20,25), k3, p2, k3, p31, k3, p2, k3, p16(20,25).
Row 2 K16(20,25), p3, k2, p3, k31, p3, k2, p3, k16(20,25).
Rows 3 and 4 As rows 1 and 2.
Row 5 P12(16,21), * Tw2R, p1, Tw2R, k2, p2, k2, Tw2L, p1, Tw2L *, p24, rep from * to *, p to end.
Row 6 K12(16,21), * p1, k2, p1, k1, p2, k2, p2, k1, p1, k2, p1 *, rep from * to *, k to end.
Row 7 P11(15,20), * Tw2R, p1, Tw2R, k3, p2, k3, Tw2L, p1, Tw2L *, p22, rep from * to *, p to end.
Row 8 K11(15,20), * p1, k2, p1, k1, p3, k2, p3, k1, p1, k2, p1 *, k22, rep from * to *, k to end.
Row 9 P13(17,22), * Tw2R, k4, p2, k4, Tw2L *, p26, rep from * to *, p to end.
Row 10 K13(17,22), * p1, k1, p4, k2, p4, k1, p1 *, k26, rep from * to *, k to end.
Row 11 P12(16,21), * Tw2R, k5, p2, k5, Tw2L *, p24, rep from * to *, p to end.
Row 12 K12(16,21), * p1, k1, p5, k2, p5, k1, p1 *, k24, rep from * to *, k to end.
Row 13 P11(15,20), * Tw2R, k5, p2, k5, Tw2L *, p22, rep from * to *, p to end.
Row 14 K11(15,20), * p1, k1, p6, k2, p6, k1, p1 *, k22, rep from * to *, k to end.
Row 15 P10(14,19), * Tw2R, k7, p2, k7, Tw2L *, p20, rep from * to *, p to end.
Row 16 K10(14,19), * p1, k1, p7, k2, p7, k1, p1 *, k20, rep from * to *, k to end.

Row 17 P9(13,18), * Tw2R, k8, p2, k8, Tw2L *, p18, rep from * to *, p to end.
Row 18 K9(13,18), * p1, k1, p8, k2, p8, k1, p1 *, k18, rep from * to *, k to end.
Row 19 P8(12,17), * Tw2R, p1, k8, p2, k8, p1, Tw2L *, p16, rep from * to *, p to end.
Row 20 K8(12,17), * p1, [k2, p8] twice, k2, p1 *, k16, rep from * to *, k to end.
Row 21 P7(11,16), * Tw2R, p1, Tw2R, k7, p2, k7, Tw2L, p1, Tw2L *, p14, rep from * to *, p to end.
Row 22 K7(11,16), * p1, k2, p1, k1, p7, k2, p7, k1, p1, k2, p1 *, k14, rep from * to *, k to end.
Row 23 P6(10,15), * [Tw2R, p1] twice, k7, p2, k7, [p1, Tw2L] twice *, p12, rep from * to *, p to end.
Row 24 K6(10,15), * [p1, k2] twice, p7, k2, p7, [k2, p1] twice *, k12, rep from * to *, k to end.
Row 25 P5(9,14), * [Tw2R, p1] twice, Tw2R, k6, p2, k6, Tw2L, [p1, Tw2L] twice *, k12, rep from * to *, p to end.
Row 26 K5(9,14), * [p1, k2] twice, k1, p6, k2, p6, k1, p1, [k2, p1] twice *, k12, rep from * to *, k to end.
Row 27 P7(11,16), * [Tw2R, p1] twice, k6, p2, k6, [p1, Tw2L] twice *, p14, rep from * to *, p to end.
Row 28 K7(11,16), * [p1, k2] twice, p6, k2, p6, [k2, p1] twice, k14, rep from * to *, k to end.
Row 29 P9(13,18), * Tw2R, p1, Tw2R, k5, p2, k5, Tw2L, p1, Tw2L *, p18, rep from * to *, p to end.
Row 30 K9(13,18), * p1, k2, p1, k1, p5, k2, p5, k1, p1, k2, p1 *, k18, rep from * to *, k to end.
Row 31 P8(12,17), * [Tw2R, p1] twice, k5, p2, k5, [p1, Tw2L] twice *, p16, rep from * to *, p to end.
Row 32 K8(12,17), * [p1, k2] twice, p5, k2, p5, [k2, p1] twice *, k16, rep from * to *, k to end.
Row 33 P10(14,19), * Tw2R, p1, Tw2R, k4, p2, k4, Tw2L, p1, Tw2L *, p20, rep from * to

*, p to end.
Row 34 K10(14,19), * p1, k2, p1, k1, p4, k2, p4, k1, p1, k2, p1 *, k20, rep from * to *, k to end.
Row 35 P9(13,18), * [Tw2R, p1] twice, k4, p2, k4, [p1, Tw2L] twice *, p18, rep from * to *, p to end.
Row 36 K9(13,18), [p1, k2] twice, p4, k2, p4, [k2, p1] twice *, k18, rep from * to *, k to end.
Row 37 P11(15,20), * Tw2R, p1, Tw2R, C8, Tw2L, p1, Tw2L *, p22, rep from * to *, p to end.
Row 37 P11(15,20), * Tw2R, p1, Tw2R, C8, Tw2L, p1, Tw2L *, p22, rep from * to *, p to end.
Row 38 K11(15,20), * p1, k2, p1, k1, p3, k2, p3, k1, p1, k2, p1 *, k22, rep from * to *, k to end.
Row 39 P10(14,19), * Tw2R, p1, Tw2R, k7, p2, k7, Tw2L, p1, Tw2L *, p20, rep from * to *, p to end.
Row 40 K10(14,19), * [p1, k2] twice, [p3, k2] twice, p1, k2, p1, k20, rep from * to *, k to end.
Rows 5 to 40 form the patt.
Rep rows 5 to 40 twice more then rows 5 to 12(16,20) again.
Cast off 22(25,29) sts, patt until there are 36(38,40) sts on right-hand needle, cast off rem 22(25,29) sts.
Leave rem sts on a holder.

Front

Work rib rows, inc row and 40 patt rows as given for back.
Rep rows 5 to 40 once more then rows 5 to 32(34,38) again.
Shape neck
Work as given in main patt for front from ★ to ★.
Return to sts on spare needle.
With RS facing, slip first 18(20,22) sts on to a holder, join on yarn and patt to end.
Now complete as given for first side of neck from ★ to ★.

LACY PANEL MOHAIR JERSEY

✳✳✳

A single heart-shaped lacy motif from the centre panel is placed on each sleeve, one at the shoulder, the other at the cuff.

Materials

10(11, 12)×50g balls of Phildar Phil'Mohair 50
A pair each of 5mm/No6 and 6mm/No4
knitting needles

Measurements

To fit bust 86(91,97)cm/34(36,38)in
Actual measurements
Bust 104(108,112)cm/41(42½,44)in
Length to shoulders 66cm/26in
Sleeve seam 39(40,41)cm/15½(15¾,16)in

Tension

15 sts and 20 rows to 10cm/4in measured
over st st worked on 6mm needles

Back

Using 5mm needles cast on 66(70,74) sts.
Rib row 1 K2, * p2, k2, rep from * to end.
Rib row 2 P2, * k2, p2, rep from * to end.
Rep these 2 rows for 10cm/4in, ending with
rib row 1.
Inc row Rib 3(5,2), * M1, rib 6(6,7), rep from
* to last 3(5,2) sts, M1, rib to end.
77(81,85) sts.
Change to 6mm needles.
Work in patt as follows:
Row 1 (RS) K27(29,31), * k1, [yf, k2 tog]
twice, k1, yf, k1, [k2 tog, yf] twice, k1,
[yf, skpo] twice, k1, yf, k1, [skpo, yf] twice,
k1 *, k27(29,31).
Row 2 P27(29,31), * p6, all into yf of
previous row work [k1, p1, k1 and p1], p11,
all into yf of previous row work [k1, p1, k1 .
and p1], p6 *, p27(29,31).
Row 3 K27(29,31), * k1, [yf, k2 tog] twice,
k4, k3 tog, yf, k2 tog, yf, k3, yf, skpo, yf, sl 1,
k2 tog, psso, k4, [skpo, yf] twice, k1 *,
k27(29,31).
Row 4 P to end.
Row 5 K27(29,31), * k1, [yf, k2 tog] twice,
k2, k3 tog, yf, k2 tog, yf, k5, yf, skpo, yf, sl 1,
k2 tog, psso, k2, [skpo, yf] twice, k1 *,
k27(29,31).
Row 6 P to end.
Row 7 K27(29,31), * k1, [yf, k2 tog] twice,
k3 tog, yf, k2 tog, yf, k3, yf, skpo, k2, yf,
skpo, yf, sl 1, k2 tog, psso, [skpo, yf] twice,
k1 *, k27(29,31).
Row 8 P to end.
Row 9 K27(29,31), * k1, yf, k2 tog, k3 tog, yf,
k2 tog, yf, k2, k2 tog, yf, k1, yf, skpo, k2, yf,
skpo, yf, sl 1, k2 tog, psso, skpo, yf, k1 *,
k27(29,31).
Row 10 P to end.
Row 11 K27(29,31), * k2, [k2 tog, yf] twice,
k2, k2 tog, yf, k3, yf, skpo, k2, [yf, skpo]
twice, k2 *, k27(29,31).
Row 12 P to end.
Row 13 K27(29,31), * k1, [k2 tog, yf] twice,
k2, k2 tog, yf, k1, yf, sl 1, k2 tog, psso, yf, k1,
yf, skpo, k2, [yf, skpo] twice, k1 *,
k27(29,31).
Row 14 P to end.
Row 15 K27(29,31), * [k2 tog, yf] twice,
k2 tog, k3, yf, skpo, yf, k1, yf, k2 tog, yf, k3,
skpo, [yf, skpo] twice *, k27(29,31).
Row 16 P to end.
These 16 rows form the patt.
Cont in patt until back measures approx
42(41,40)cm/16½(16¼,15¾)in from
cast-on edge, ending with row 16(14,12).
Shape raglans
Cast off 3 sts at beg of next 2 rows.
Next row K2, skpo, patt to last 4 sts, k2 tog,
k2.
Next row Patt to end.
Rep the last 2 rows until 25(27,29) sts rem,
ending with row 16.
Cut off yarn and leave sts on a holder.

Front

Work as given for back until 45(47,49) sts
rem when shaping raglans, ending with
row 12 of patt.
Shape neck
Next row K2, skpo, patt 12, turn and leave
rem sts on a spare needle.
Continuing to dec at raglan edge on every
alt row, dec 1 st at neck edge on next and
foll 4 alt rows. 6 sts.
Keeping neck edge straight, cont to dec at
raglan edge on next and every foll alt row
until 2 sts rem.

Work 1 row. Work 2 tog and fasten off.
Return to sts on spare needle.
With RS facing, slip first 13(15,17) sts on to a
holder, join on yarn and patt to last 4 sts,
k2 tog, k2. 15 sts.
Now complete to match first side of neck.

Left sleeve

★ Using 5mm needles cast on
30(30,34) sts.
Rib row 1 K2, * p2, k2, rep from * to end.
Rib row 2 P2, * k2, p2, rep from * to end.
Rep these 2 rows for 8cm/3in, ending with
rib row 1.
Inc row Rib 1(2,1), * M1, rib 1, M1, rib
3(2,3), rep from * to last st, M1, rib 1.
45(49,51) sts. ★
Change to 6mm needles.
Work in patt as follows:
Row 1 (RS) K11(13,14), rep from * to * on
row 1 of back once, k11(13,14).
Row 2 P11(13,14), rep from * to * on row 2
of back once, p11(13,14).
Row 3 K11(13,14), rep from * to * on row 3
of back once, k11(13,14).
Row 4 P to end.
These 4 rows set position of 16 row patt.
Keeping patt correct, inc and work into st st
1 st each end of next and every foll 4th row
until there are 51(55,57) sts.
Patt 3 rows straight.
Now continuing in st st only, inc 1 st each
end of next and every foll 4th row until there
are 71(75,77) sts.
Work straight until sleeve measures
39(40,41)cm/15½(15¾,16)in from cast-on
edge, ending with a WS row.
Shape raglan
Cast off 3 sts at beg of next 2 rows.
Next row K2, skpo, k to last 4 sts, k2 tog, k2.
Next row P to end.
Rep the last 2 rows until 19(21,21) sts rem,
ending with a WS row. Cast off.

Right sleeve

Work as given for left sleeve from ★ to ★.
Change to 6mm needles.
Beg with a k row, work in st st increasing 1 st
each end of 5th and every foll 4th row until
there are 71(75,77) sts.
Work straight until sleeve measures
39(40,41)cm/15½(15¾,16)in from cast-on
edge, ending with a WS row.
Shape raglan
Cast off 3 sts at beg of next 2 rows.
Next row K2, skpo, k to last 4 sts, k2 tog, k2.
Next row P to end.
Rep the last 2 rows until 57(61,63) sts rem,
ending with a WS row.
Now work in patt as follows:
Row 1 K2, skpo, k13(15,16), rep from * to *
on row 1 of back once, k13(15,16), k2 tog,
k2.
Row 2 P16(18,19), rep from * to * on row 2
of back once, p16(18,19).
Row 3 K2, skpo, k12(14,15), rep from * to *
on row 3 of back once, k12(14,15), k2 tog,
k2.
Row 4 P to end.
These 4 rows set the position of the 16 row
patt.
Keeping patt correct, cont to dec for raglan
shaping on next and every foll alt row as
before until 41(45,47) sts rem.
Patt 1 row.
Working in st st only, cont to dec for raglan
shaping as before until 19(21,21) sts rem,
ending with a WS row. Cast off.

Neckband

Join raglan seams, leaving left back raglan
open. With RS facing and using 5mm
needles, pick up and k12(14,14) sts across
top of left sleeve and 14 sts down left side of
front neck, decreasing 1 st each end
k across 13(15,17) sts from front neck
holder, pick up and k14 sts up right side of
front neck and 12(14,14) sts across top of
right sleeve, then decreasing 1 st each end
k across 25(27,29) sts from back neck
holder. 86(94,98) sts.
Beg with rib row 2, work 7 rows rib as given
for back. Cast off loosely in rib.

To make up

Join left back raglan and neckband seam.
Join side and sleeve seams.

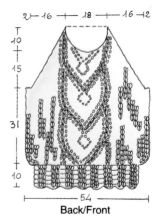

Back/Front

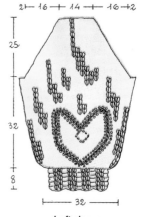

Left sleeve

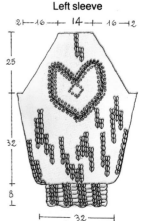

Right sleeve

Measurements given in cm
for second size

JERSEY WITH RELIEF STITCH PATTERNS

✳

Two relief stitch patterns are used on this simple jersey knitted in a soft brushed yarn.

Materials

6(6,7)×100g balls of Patons Diana Brushed Chunky

A pair each of 4½mm/No7 and 5mm/No6 knitting needles

Measurements

To fit bust 81(91,102)cm/32(36,40)in

Actual measurements

Bust 90(106,120)cm/35½(41½,47)in

Length to shoulders 61(62,63)cm/24(24½,25)in

Sleeve seam 43(44,45)cm/17(17½,17¾)in

Tension

16 sts and 27 rows to 10cm/4in measured over brick patt worked on 5mm needles

17 sts and 22 rows to 10cm/4in measured over triangle patt worked on 5mm needles

Special abbreviation

Loop 1 as follows: insert right-hand needle between stitch just worked and next stitch on left-hand needle 6 rows below, wind yarn round needle and pull loop through then place this loop on left-hand needle. Knit loop together with next stitch on left-hand needle

Back

Using 4½mm needles cast on 66(74,82) sts.

Rib row 1 K2, * p2, k2, rep from * to end.

Rib row 2 P2, * k2, p2, rep from * to end.

Rep these 2 rows for 7cm/2¾in, ending with rib row 1.

Inc row Rib 8(6,2), * M1, rib 10(7,6), rep from * to last 8(5,2) sts, M1, rib to end. 72(84,96) sts.

Change to 5mm needles.

Work in brick patt as follows:

Row 1 (RS) P to end.

Row 2 K to end.

Row 3 K to end.

Row 4 P to end.

Rows 5 and 6 As rows 1 and 2.

Row 7 K3, loop 1, * k5, loop 1, rep from * to last 2 sts, k2.

Row 8 P to end.

Rows 9 to 12 Rep rows 3 and 4 twice.

Rows 13 to 16 As rows 1 to 4.

Rows 17 and 18 As rows 1 and 2.

Row 19 K6, loop 1, * k5, loop 1, rep from * to last 5 sts, k5.

Row 20 P to end.

Rows 21 to 24 Rep rows 3 and 4 twice.

These 24 rows form the brick patt.

Rep rows 1 to 24 once more then work rows 1 to 16 again.

Now work in triangle patt as follows:

Row 1 K5, * p1, k11, rep from * to last 7 sts, p1, k6.

Row 2 P5, * k3, p9, rep from * to last 7 sts, k3, p4.

Row 3 K3, * p5, k7, rep from * to last 9 sts, p5, k4.

Row 4 P3, * k7, p5, rep from * to last 9 sts, k7, p2.

Row 5 K1, * p9, k3, rep from * to last 11 sts, p9, k2.

Row 6 P to end.

Row 7 K11, * p1, k11, rep from * to last st, p1.

Row 8 K2, * p9, k3, rep from * to last 10 sts, p9, k1.

Row 9 P2, * k7, p5, rep from * to last 10 sts, k7, p3.

Row 10 K4, * p5, k7, rep from * to last 8 sts, p5, k3.

Row 11 P4, * k3, p9, rep from * to last 8 sts, k3, p5.

Row 12 P to end.

These 12 rows form the triangle patt.

Shape armholes

Cast off in patt 8(10,12) sts at beg of next 2 rows. 56(64,72) sts.

Cont in triangle patt until work measures 24(25,26)cm/9½(9¾,10¼)in from beg of armhole shaping, ending with a WS row.

Cast off for back neck and shoulders.

Front

Work as given for back until armholes measure 17(18,18)cm/6¾(7,7)in from beg of shaping, ending with a WS row.

Shape neck

Next row Patt 21(24,27), turn and leave rem sts on a spare needle.

Keeping patt correct, dec 1 st at neck edge on every row until 17(20,22) sts rem.

Work straight until front measures the same as back to shoulder, ending with a WS row. Cast off.

Return to sts on spare needle.

With RS facing, slip first 14(16,18) sts on to a holder, join on yarn, then patt to end. 21(24,27) sts.

Now complete to match first side of neck.

Sleeves

Using 4½mm needles cast on 38(42,42) sts.

Work 6.5cm/2½in rib as given for back, ending with rib row 1.

Inc row Rib 5(4,4), * M1, rib 3(2,2), rep from * to last 6(4,4) sts, M1, rib to end. 48(60,60) sts.

Change to 5mm needles.

Working in brick patt as given for back inc and work into patt 1 st each end of 7th and every foll 6th row to 68(80,80) sts.

Patt 3 rows.

Now working in triangle patt as given for back, inc and work into patt 1 st each end of 3rd and every foll 4th(6th,6th) row until there are 80(84,86) sts.

Work straight until sleeve measures 43(44,45)cm/17(17¼,17¾)in from cast-on edge, ending with a WS row.

Mark each end of last row with a coloured thread.

Work 10(12,16) rows straight, so ending with a WS row.

Cast off.

Neckband

Join right shoulder seam.

With RS facing and using 4½mm needles, pick up and k14 sts down left side of front neck, k across 14(16,18) sts from front neckholder, pick up and k14 sts up right side of front neck and 22(24,28) sts across back neck. 64(68,74) sts.

Work 4cm/1½in k2, p2 rib.

Cast off in rib.

To make up

Join left shoulder and neckband seam. Sew in sleeves, joining row ends to markers on sleeves to cast-off sts at underarm on back and front. Join side and sleeve seams.

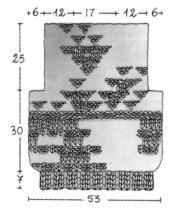

Back

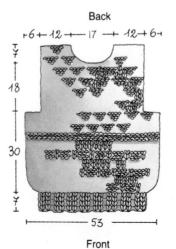

Front

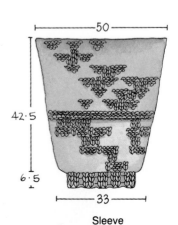

Sleeve

Measurements given in cm for second size

DECORATED MOHAIR CARDIGAN

✳✳✳✳

If you
choose a
dark
background
for this cardigan
make sure the
motifs are knitted
in brightly
coloured yarns.

Materials

8(9)×50g balls of Robin Dynasty in main
  colour A (black)
2 balls of same in contrast colour B (royal)
1 ball of same in each of contrast colours
  C (blue), D (pink) and E (turquoise)
A pair each of 5mm/No6 and 5½mm/No5
  knitting needles
8 buttons

Measurements

To fit bust 86–91(97–102)cm/34–36
(38–40)in
Actual measurements
Bust 107(118)cm/42(46½)in
Length to shoulders 67cm/26¼in
Sleeve seam 42cm/16½in

Tension

18 sts and 20 rows to 10cm/4in measured
over st st worked on 5½mm needles

Left front

★ Using 5mm needles and A, cast on
39(43) sts.
Rib row 1 K1, * p1, k1; rep from * to end.
Rib row 2 P1, * k1, p1, rep from * to end.
Rep these 2 rows for 6cm/2½in, ending with
rib row 1.
Inc row Rib 2, * M1, rib 4, rep from * to last
st, M1, rib 1. 49(54) sts. ★
Change to 5½mm needles.
Use separate balls of yarn for each area of
colour and twist yarns together on WS of
work when changing colour to avoid making
a hole.
Reading odd numbered (k) rows from right
to left and even numbered (p) rows from left
to right, work from chart for left front as
follows:
Row 1 (RS) With A, k to end.
Row 2 With A, p to end.
Rows 3 to 12 Rep rows 1 and 2 five times.
Row 13 *For 2nd size only* k1B, 2A, 2C, *for
both sizes* * k5A, 2C, 2A, 2B, 1A, 2B, 2A,
2C, rep from * once more, k5A, 2C, 2A, 2B,
1A, 1B.
Row 14 P3A, * 2B, 2A, 2C, 3A, 2C, 2A, 2B,
3A, rep from * once more, p2B, 2A, 2C, 3A,
1C, *for 2nd size only* p1C, 2A, 2B.
Cont working from chart for left front,
shaping as indicated for armhole and neck
edges, until row 122 has been completed.
Cast off.

Right front

Work as given for left front from ★ to ★.
Change to 5½mm needles.
Now work from chart for right front as
follows:
Row 1 (RS) With A, k to end.
Row 2 With A, p to end.
Rows 3 to 12 Rep rows 1 and 2 five times.
Row 13 K1B, 1A, 2B, 2A, 2C, * k5A, 2C, 2A,
2B, 1A, 2B, 2A, 2C, rep from * once more,
k5A, *for 2nd size only* k2C, 2A, 1B.
Row 14 *For 2nd size only* p2B, 2A, 1C, then
for both sizes p1C, 3A, 2C, 2A, 2B, 3A
* p2B, 2A, 2C, 3A, 2C, 2A, 2B, 3A, rep from
* once more.
Cont working from chart for right front,
shaping as indicated for armhole and neck
edges, until row 123 has been completed.
Cast off.

Back

Using 5mm needles and A, cast on 75(81)
sts.
Rib row 1 K1, * p1, k1, rep from * to end.
Rib row 2 P1, * k1, p1, rep from * to end.
Rep these 2 rows for 6cm/2½in, ending with
rib row 1.
Inc row Rib 9(6), * M1, rib 3, rep from * to
last 9(6) sts, M1, rib to end. 95(105) sts.
Change to 5½mm needles.

Now work from chart for back as follows:
Row 1 (RS) With A, k to end.
Row 2 With A, p to end.
Rows 3 to 12 Rep rows 1 and 2 five times.
Row 13 *For 2nd size only* k1B, 2A, 2C, *for
both sizes* * k5A, 2C, 2A, 2B, 1A, 2B, 2A,
2C, rep from * to last 5(10) sts, k5A, *for 2nd
size only* k2C, 2A, 1B.
Row 14 *For 2nd size only* p2B, 2A, 1C, *for
both sizes* p1C, 3A, * p2C, 2A, 2B, 3A, 2B,

Left Front

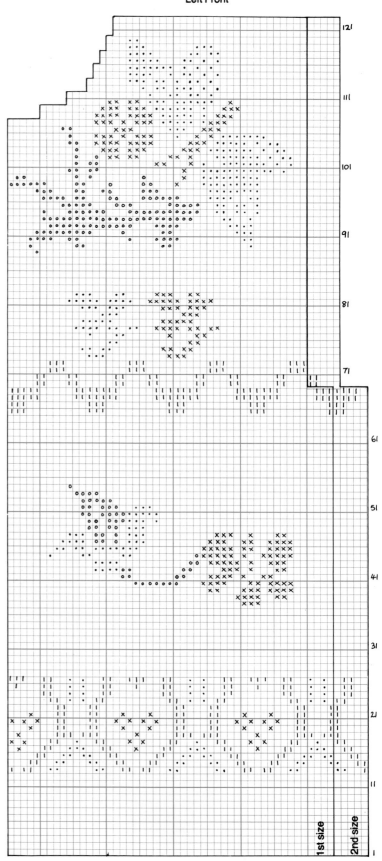

Key
☐ main colour A
▥ contrast colour B
⊡ contrast colour C
☒ contrast colour D
◉ contrast colour E

Back and Right Front

Right Front

Back

2A, 2C, 3A, rep from * to last 1(6) sts, p1C,
for 2nd size only p1C, 2A, 2B.
Cont working from chart for back, shaping
as indicated for armholes and shoulders,
until row 124 has been completed.
Cast off.

Sleeves

Using 5mm needles and A, cast on 45 sts.
Rib row 1 K1, * p1, k1, rep from * to end.
Rib row 2 P1, * k1, p1, rep from * to end.
Rep these 2 rows for 6cm/2½in, ending with
rib row 1.
Inc row Rib 1, * M1, rib 6, rep from * to last
2 sts, M1, rib to end. 53 sts.
Change to 5½mm needles.
K 1 row and p 1 row.
Now work from chart for sleeve as follows:
Row 1 (RS) K2A, 2C, 2A, 2B, * k1A, 2B, 2A,
2C, 5A, 2C, 2A, 2B, rep from * once more,
k1A, 2B, 2A, 2C, 2A.
Row 2 P1A, 2C, 2A, 2B, * p3A, 2B, 2A, 2C,
3A, 2C, 2A, 2B, rep from * once more, p3A,
2B, 2A, 2C, 1A.
Cont working from chart for sleeve,
increasing as indicated at each end of next
and every foll 4th row until there are 83 sts
and row 70 has been completed.
Now with A, k 1 row and p 1 row.
Cast off.

Button border

With RS facing, using 5mm needles and A,
pick up and k115 sts down left front edge.
Rib row 1 (WS) P1, * k1, p1, rep from

* to end.
Rib row 2 K1, * p1, k1, rep from * to end.
Rep these 2 rows twice more, then rib row 1
again.
Cast off in rib.

Buttonhole border

With RS facing, using 5mm needles and A,
pick up and k115 sts up right front edge.
Work 3 rows in rib as given for button
border.
Next row Rib 3, * cast off 2, rib 14 including
st on needle after cast off, rep from * to last
16 sts, cast off 2, rib to end.
Next row Rib to end, casting on 2 sts over
those cast off in previous row.
Rib 2 rows. Cast off.

Neckband

Join shoulder seams.
With RS facing, using 5mm needles and A,
pick up and k33 sts up right side of front
neck, 31 sts across back neck and 33 sts
down left side of front neck. 97 sts.
Work 3 rows rib as given for button border.
Next row Rib 3, cast off 2, rib to end.
Next row Rib to end, casting on 2 sts over
those cast off in previous row.
Rib 2 rows. Cast off.

To make up

Sew in sleeves, joining cast-off sts at
armholes on back and fronts to row ends at
top of sleeves. Join side and sleeve seams.
Sew on the buttons.

Measurements given in cm
for smaller size

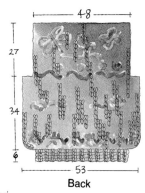

Back

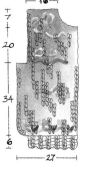

Right Front

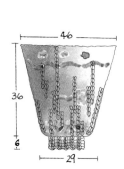

Sleeve

Sleeves

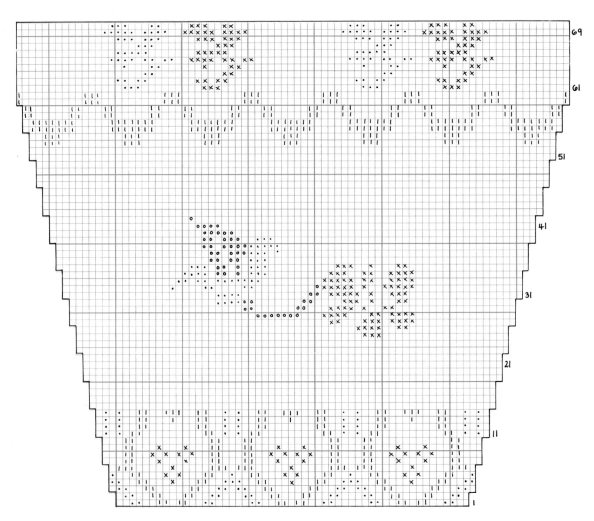

SILKY SLIP STITCH CARDIGAN

*

This elegant
cardigan is
knitted in a
simple
four row
pattern
with the slip
stitch forming an
attractive looped
ridge.

Materials
12(13, 14)×50g balls of Emu Cotton DK
A pair each of 3mm/No11 and 4mm/No8
knitting needles
4 buttons

Measurements
To fit bust 91(97,102)cm/36(38,40)in
Actual measurements
Bust 114(120,126)cm/45(47,49½)in
Length to centre back neck 52(54,56)cm/
20½(21½,22)in
Sleeve seam (with cuff turned back)
39(40,41)cm/15¼(15¾,16)in

Tension
25 sts and 44 rows to 10cm/4in measured
over patt worked on 4mm needles

Left front
★ Using 3mm needles cast on
63(67,71) sts.
Rib row 1 K1, * p1, k1, rep from * to end.
Rib row 2 P1, * k1, p1, rep from * to end.
Rep these 2 rows for 12cm/4¾in, ending
with rib row 1.
Inc row Rib 3(5,4), * M1, rib 8(8,9), rep from
* to last 4(6,4) sts, M1, rib to end.
71(75,79) sts.
Change to 4mm needles.
Work in patt as follows:
Row 1 (RS) K to end.
Row 2 P to end.
Row 3 P1, * sl 1 pw, p1, rep from * to end.
Row 4 P1, * k1, p1, rep from * to end.
These 4 rows form the patt.
Cont in patt until front measures
27(28,28)cm/10¾(11,11)in from cast-on
edge, ending with a WS row. ★
Shape front edge
Dec 1 st at end of next and every foll 4th row
until 68(72,75) sts rem.
Patt 3 rows, so ending at side edge.
Shape raglan
Next row Cast off 5(6,6) sts, patt to last 2 sts,
work 2 tog.
Patt 1 row.
Next row K1, p1, skpo, patt to end.
Next row Patt to last 3 sts, p3.
Next row K1, p1, skpo, patt to last 2 sts,
work 2 tog.
Next row Patt to last 3 sts, p3.
Rep the last 4 rows until 14 sts rem.
Keeping front edge straight, cont to shape
raglan edge as before until 3 sts rem,
ending with a WS row.
Next row K2 tog, k1.
Next row P to end.
K2 tog and fasten off.

Right front
Work as given for left front from ★ to ★
Shape front edge

Dec 1 st at beg of next and every foll 4th row
until 67(71,74) sts rem.
Shape raglan
Next row Cast off 5(6,6) sts, patt to end.
Next row Patt to last 4 sts, k2 tog, p1, k1.
Next row P3, patt to end.
Next row Work 2 tog, patt to last 4 sts,
k2 tog, p1, k1.
Next row P3, patt to end.
Rep the last 4 rows until 14 sts rem.
Keeping front edge straight, cont to shape
raglan edge as before until 3 sts rem,
ending with a WS row.
Next row K1, k2 tog.
Next row P to end.
K2 tog and fasten off.

Back
Using 3mm needles cast on
123(131,137) sts.
Rib row 1 K1, * p1, k1, rep from * to end.
Rib row 2 P1, * k1, p1, rep from * to end.
Rep these 2 rows for 12cm/4¾in, ending
with rib row 1.
Inc row Rib 5(9,11), * M1, rib 6, rep from * to
last 4(8,12) sts, M1, rib to end.
143(151,157) sts.
Change to 4mm needles.
Work in patt as follows:
Row 1 (RS) K to end.
Row 2 P to end.
Row 3 P1, * sl 1 pw, p1, rep from * to end.
Row 4 P1, * k1, p1, rep from * to end.
These 4 rows form the patt.
Cont in patt until back measures same as
fronts to beg of raglan shaping, ending with
a WS row.
Shape raglans
Cast off 5(6,6) sts at beg of next 2 rows.
Next row K1, p1, skpo, patt to last 4 sts,
k2 tog, p1, k1.
Next row P3, patt to last 3 sts, p3.
Rep the last 2 rows until 37(39,41) sts rem,
ending with a WS row.
Cast off.

Left sleeve
★★ Using 3mm needles cast on
47(51,55) sts.
Rib row 1 K1, * p1, k1, rep from * to end.
Rib row 2 P1, * k1, p1, rep from * to end.
Rep these 2 rows for 12cm/4¾in, ending
with rib row 1.
Inc row Rib 4(3,5), M1, rib 8(15,15), rep from
* to last 3(3,5) sts, M1, rib to end.
53(55,59) sts.
Change to 4mm needles.
Work in patt as follows:
Row 1 (RS) K to end.
Row 2 P to end.
Row 3 P1, * sl 1 pw, p1, rep from * to end.
Row 4 P1, * k1, p1, rep from * to end.
These 4 rows form the patt.

Continuing in patt, inc and work into patt 1 st
each end of next and every foll 4th row until
there are 103(107,111) sts.
Work straight until sleeve measures
45(46,47)cm/17¾(18¼,18½)in from
cast-on edge, ending with a WS row.
Mark each end of last row with a coloured
thread to denote beg of raglan shaping.
Shape raglan
Next row K1, p1, skpo, patt to last 4 sts,
k2 tog, p1, k1.
Next row P3, patt to last 3 sts, p3.
Rep the last 2 rows until 11 sts rem, ending
with a WS row. ★★
Next row K1, p1, skpo, patt to end.
Next row Cast off 4 sts, patt to last 3 sts, p3.
Next row K1, p1, skpo, patt to end.
Cast off.

Right sleeve
Work as given for left sleeve from ★★ to
★★.
Next row Cast off 4 sts, patt to last 4 sts,
k2 tog, p1, k1.
Next row P3, patt to end.
Cast off.

Button border
Join raglan seams.
With RS facing and using 3mm needles,
pick up and k21(23,25) sts from centre back
neck to beg of left sleeve, 9 sts across top of
left sleeve, 76(78,82) sts down left front to
beg of front shaping and 43(45,45) sts down
left front to cast-on edge. 149(155,161) sts.
Rib row 1 P1, * k1, p1, rep from * to end.
Rib row 2 K1, * p1, k1, rep from * to end.
Rep these 2 rows twice more, then rib row 1
again.
Cast off in rib.

Buttonhole border
With RS facing and using 3mm needles,
pick up and k43(45,45) sts up right front to
beg of front shaping, 76(78,82) sts up right
front to beg of right sleeve, 9 sts across top
of right sleeve and 21(23,25) sts to centre
back neck. 149(155,161) sts.
Work 3 rows in rib as given for button
border.
Next row Rib 5, * cast off 2 sts, rib next 9 sts,
rep from * twice more, cast off 2, rib to end.
Next row Rib to end, casting on 2 sts over
those cast off.
Rib 2 rows.
Cast off in rib.

To make up
Join side and sleeve seams, reversing cuff
seams for 6cm/2¼in. Join back neck border
seam. Sew on the buttons and turn back the
cuffs.

Measurements given in cm
for second size

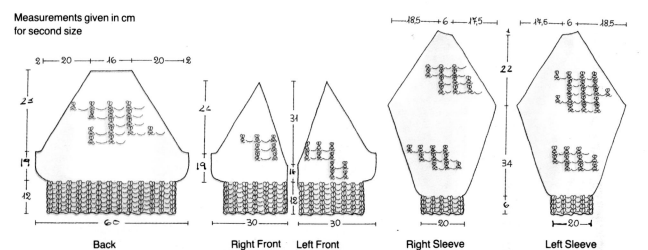

Back   Right Front   Left Front   Right Sleeve   Left Sleeve

FLUFFY JERSEY WITH BOLD MOTIFS

***

These simple geometric motifs are easy to follow from the charts making this an ideal jersey for the beginner to learn motif knitting.

Materials
3(3, 3, 4, 4)×100g balls of Water Wheel
Fluffy DK in main colour A
1 ball of same in contrast colour B
A pair each of 3¼mm/No10 and 4mm/No8
knitting needles

Measurements
To fit bust 81(86,91,97,102)cm/
32(34,36,38,40)in
Actual measurements
Bust 96(102,106,112,117)cm/
38(40¼,42,44¼,46)in
Length to shoulders 64cm/25¼in
Sleeve seam 43(43,44,45,45)cm/
17(17,17¼,17¾,17¾)in

Tension
19 sts and 25 rows to 10cm/4in measured
over st st worked on 4mm needles

Front
★ Using 3¼mm needles and A, cast on
71(73,75,77,79) sts.
Rib row 1 (RS) K1, * p1, k1, rep from * to
end.
Rib row 2 P1, * k1, p1, rep from * to end.
Rep these 2 rows for 9cm/3½in, ending with
rib row 1.
Inc row Rib 7(2,12,9,8), * M1, rib 3(3,2,2,2),
rep from * to last 7(2,13,10,9) sts, M1, rib to
end. 91(97,101,107,111) sts.
Change to 4mm needles.
Beg with a k row and A, work 8 rows st st.
With B, work 6 rows st st.
With A, work 4 rows st st.
Use separate balls of yarn for each area of
colour and twist yarns together on WS of
work when changing colour to avoid making
a hole.
Reading odd numbered (k) rows from right
to left and even numbered (p) rows from left
to right, work from chart 1 until row 76 has

been completed.
Continuing in A only and beg with a k row,
work in st st until front measures 56cm/22in
from cast-on edge, ending with a p row. ★
Shape neck
New row K39(42,43,46,48), turn and leave
rem sts on a spare needle.
Cast off 3(3,3,3,4) sts at beg of next row and
2(2,2,3,3) sts at beg of foll alt row.
Dec 1 st at neck edge on every row until
31(33,34,36,37) sts rem.
Work straight until front measures
64cm/25¼in from cast-on edge, ending
with a p row.
Cast off.
Return to sts on spare needle.
With RS facing, slip first 13(13,15,15,15) sts
on to a holder, join on A and k to end.
39(42,43,46,48) sts.
Work 1 row.
Now complete to match first side of neck.

Back
Work as given for front from ★ to ★.
Cont straight in st st until back measures
same as front to shoulders, ending with a p
row.
Cast off 31(33,34,36,37) sts at beg of next 2
rows.
Cut off yarn and leave rem
29(31,33,35,37) sts on a holder.

Right sleeve
★★ Using 3¼mm needles and A, cast on
37(39,41,43,45) sts.
Work 9cm/3½in rib as given for front,
ending with rib row 1.
Inc row Rib 5(1,2,3,4), * M1, rib 3(4,4,4,4),
rep from * to last 5(2,3,4,5) sts, M1, rib to
end. 47(49,51,53,55) sts. ★★
Change to 4mm needles.
Working in st st and increasing 1 st each
end of 3rd and every foll alt row, work 6 rows

A and 4 rows B.
With A, inc 1 st each end of next and every
foll 4th row until there are
69(71,73,75,77) sts, ending with a p row.
Now place motif from chart 2 as follows;
Next row With A k25(26,27,28,29), following
row 1 of chart 2 k19B, then with A
k25(26,27,28,29) sts.
Next row With A p25(26,27,28,29), following
row 2 of chart 2 p19B, then with A
p25(26,27,28,29) sts.
Continuing in patt from chart 2 as set, inc
and work into st st 1 st each end of next and
every foll 4th row until row 30 has been
completed. 83(85,87,89,91) sts.
Using A only, cont to inc 1 st each end of
next and every foll 4th row until there are
91(93,95,97,99) sts.
Work 5(5,7,9,9) rows straight, so ending
with a p row.
Cast off.

Left sleeve
Work as given for right sleeve from ★★ to
★★.
Change to 4mm needles.
Working in st st, inc 1 st each end of 3rd and
every foll alt row until there are
55(57,59,61,63) sts, then inc 1 st each end
of next and every foll 4th row until there are
61(63,65,67,69) sts, ending with a p row.
Now place motif from chart 3 as follows:
Next row With A k18(19,20,21,22), following
row 1 of chart 3 k1B, 23A, 1B, then with A
k18(19,20,21,22) sts.
Next row With A p18(19,20,21,22), following
row 2 of chart 3 p2B, 21A, 2B, then with A
p18(19,20,21,22) sts.
Continuing in patt from chart 3 as set, inc
and work into st st 1 st each end of next and
every foll 4th row until row 54 has been
completed. 87(89,91,93,95) sts.
Using A only, inc 1 st each end of next and
foll 4th row. 91(93,95,97,99) sts.
Work 5(5,7,9,9) rows straight, so ending
with a p row.
Cast off.

Neckband
Join right shoulder seam.
With RS facing, using 3¼mm needles and
A, pick up and k28 sts down left side of front
neck, k across 13(13,15,15,15) sts from
front neck holder, pick up and k28 sts up
right side of front neck, then decreasing 1 st
at centre k across back neck sts from
holder. 97(99,103,105,107) sts.
Beg with rib row 2, work 5cm/2in rib as
given for front.
Cast off loosely in rib.

To make up
Join left shoulder and neckband seam. Fold
sleeves in half lengthwise, then placing
folds to shoulder seams, sew into place.
Join side and sleeve seams. Fold neckband
in half to WS and slipstitch into position.

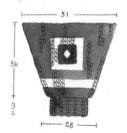

Measurements given in cm for fourth size

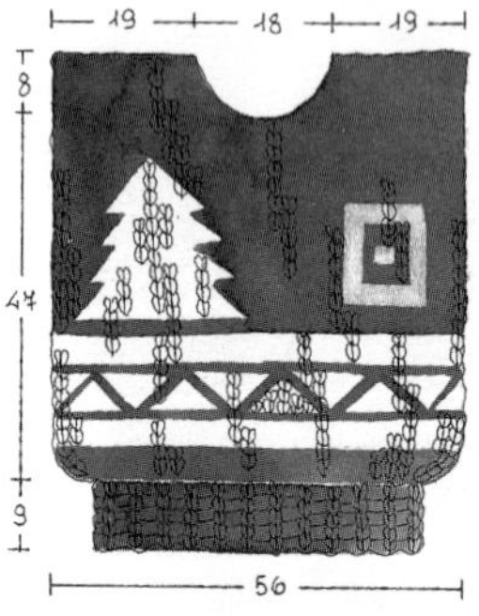

Back/Front   Right Sleeve   Left Sleeve

Chart 1

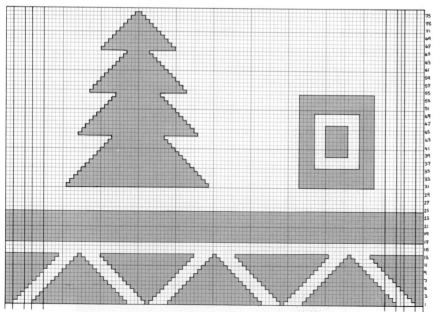

Chart 2

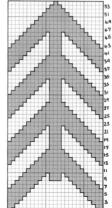

Chart 3

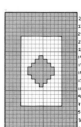

OPENWORK SLEEVELESS TOP

*

This simple
cotton top with
an alternating
stitch pattern
is quick to knit.

Materials

4(5,5)×50g balls of Twilleys Stalite Perlespun No 3 (4 ply cotton)
A pair each of 3¾mm/No9 and 4½mm/No7 knitting needles

Measurements

To fit bust 81–86(91–97,102–107)cm/ 32–34(36–38,40–42)in
Actual measurements
Bust 92(103,114)cm/36¼(40½,45)in
Length to shoulders 56(57,57)cm/ 22(22½,22½)in

Tension

18 sts and 22 rows to 10cm/4in measured over patt worked on 4½mm needles

Special abbreviation

Tw1 Twist 1 st as follows: dropping extra loop off needle sl 1 pw, insert point of left-hand needle from right to left into the st just slipped, taking it back on to left-hand needle, so twisting the st, then p1 tbl to twist the st once again

Back and front (alike)

Using 3¾mm needles cast on 75(87,93) sts.
Rib row 1 K3, * p3, k3, rep from * to end.
Rib row 2 P3, * k3, p3, rep from * to end.
Rep these 2 rows for 5cm/2in, ending with rib row 1.
Inc row Rib 3(3,2), * M1, rib 10(16,10), rep from * to last 2(4,1) sts, M1, rib to end. 83(93,103) sts.
Change to 4½mm needles.
Work in patt as follows:
Row 1 (RS) P4, * [winding yarn twice round needle k1] 5 times, p5, rep from * to last 9 sts, [winding yarn twice round needle k1] 5 times, p4.
Row 2 P4, * [Tw1] 5 times, p5, rep from * to last 9 sts, [Tw1] 5 times, p4.
Row 3 K1, [winding yarn twice round needle k1] 3 times, * p5, [winding yarn twice round needle k1] 5 times, rep from * to last 9 sts, p5, [winding yarn twice round needle k1] 3 times, k1.
Row 4 P1, [Tw1] 3 times, * p5, [Tw1] 5 times, rep from * to last 9 sts, p5, [Tw1] 3 times, p1.
These 4 rows form the patt.

Cont in patt until work measures 36cm/ 14¼in from cast-on edge, ending with a WS row.
Shape armholes
Cast off 3(4,4) sts at beg of next 2 rows.
Dec 1 st each end of next and every foll alt row until 65(75,83) sts rem.
Cont straight until work measures 46cm/18¼in from cast-on edge, ending with a WS row.
Shape neck
Next row Patt 21(25,29), turn and leave rem sts on a spare needle.
Dec 1 st at neck edge on every row until 10(12,12) sts rem.
Cont straight until work measures 56(57,57)cm/22(22½,22½)in from cast-on edge, ending with a WS row.
Cast off.
Return to sts on spare needle.
With RS facing, slip first 23(25,25) sts on to a holder, join on yarn and patt to end. 21(25,29) sts.
Now complete to match first side of neck.

Neckband

Join right shoulder seam.
With RS facing and using 3¾mm needles, pick up and k24(25,25) sts down left side of front neck, decreasing 1 st at centre k across front neck sts from holder, pick up and k24(25,25) sts up right side of front neck and 24 sts down right side of back neck, k across back neck sts from holder, then pick up and k24 sts up left side of back neck. 141(147,147) sts.
Rib row 1 P3, * k3, p3, rep from * to end.
Rib row 2 K3, * p3, k3, rep from * to end.
Rep these 2 rows 3 times more, then work rib row 1 again.
Cast off in rib.

Armhole borders

Join left shoulder and neckband seam.
With RS facing and using 3¾mm needles, pick up and k105(111,111) sts evenly round armhole edge.
Beg with rib row 1 work 9 rows rib as given for neckband.
Cast off in rib.

To make up

Join side and armhole border seams.

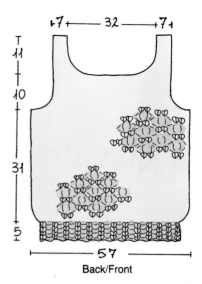

Back/Front

Measurements given in cm for largest size

CHUNKY RIB JACKET

*

This simple ribbed
jacket, with a
turned back front
border and collar,
is quick to knit.

Materials

18(20,22,24)×50g balls of Neveda Donegal Tweed (Aran weight)

A pair each of 5½mm/No5 and 7mm/No2 knitting needles

Measurements

To fit bust 81–86(91–97,102–107,112–117)cm/32–34(36–38,40–42,44–46)in

Actual measurements

Bust 97(108,120,132)cm/38(42½,47½,52)in

Length to shoulders 66cm/26in

Sleeve seam 38cm/15in (with cuff turned back)

Tension

12 sts and 15 rows to 10cm/4in measured over st st worked on 7mm needles using yarn double

16 sts and 15 rows to 10cm/4in measured over rib worked on 7mm needles using yarn double

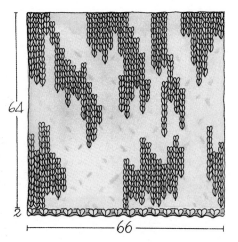

Back

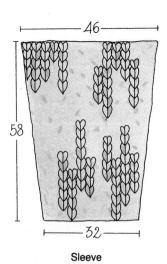

Sleeve

Measurements given in cm for third size

Note

Yarn is used double throughout.

Back

Using 5½mm needles and yarn double, cast on 58(64,72,80) sts.

Work 4 rows k1, p1 rib.

Change to 7mm needles.

Beg with a k row, work in st st until back measures 66cm/26in from cast-on edge, ending with a p row.

Shape shoulders

Cast off 17(20,24,28) sts at beg of next 2 rows.

Cut off yarn and leave rem 24 sts on a holder.

Right front

★ Using 5½mm needles and yarn double, cast on 43(47,51,55) sts.

Rib row 1 K1, * p1, k1, rep from * to end.

Rib row 2 P1, * k1, p1, rep from * to end.

Rep these 2 rows once more. ★

Next row [K1, p1] 7 times, change to 7mm needles and k to end.

Next row P29(33,37,41), turn and leave rem 14 sts on a holder.

Beg with a k row, work in st st until front measures 44cm/17¼in from cast-on edge, ending with a p row.

Shape front edge

Dec 1 st at beg of next and every foll alt row until 17(20,24,28) sts rem.

Work straight until front measures same as back to shoulder, ending with a p row.

Cast off.

Left front

Work as given for right front from ★ to ★.

Change to 7mm needles.

Right Front

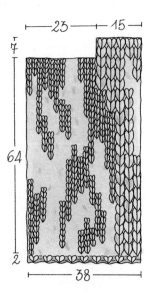

Right Front

Next row K29(33,37,41), turn and leave rem sts on a holder.

Beg with a p row, work in st st until front measures 44cm/17¼in from cast-on edge, ending with a k row.

Shape front edge

Dec 1 st at beg of next and every foll alt row until 17(20,24,28) sts rem.

Work straight until front measures same as back to shoulder, ending with a p row.

Cast off.

Sleeves

Using 5½mm needles and yarn double, cast on 51(53,55,57) sts.

Rib row 1 K1, * p1, k1, rep from * to end.

Rib row 2 P1, * k1, p1, rep from * to end.

These 2 rows form the rib patt.

Rep rib rows 1 and 2 twice more.

Change to 7mm needles.

Cont in patt, inc and work into patt 1 st each end of 5th and every foll 6th row until there are 73(75,77,79) sts.

Work straight until sleeve measures 48cm/19in from cast-on edge, ending with rib row 2.

Cast off in rib.

Right border and collar

Join shoulder seams.

With WS facing, using 5½mm needles and yarn double, rib across 14 sts from right front holder.

Keeping rib patt correct, work straight until border, slightly stretched, fits up right front to beg of front shaping, ending with a RS row.

Shape for collar

Inc 1 st at beg of next and at this same edge on every foll 3rd row until there are 25 sts.

Work straight until collar, slightly stretched, fits up right front and round to centre back neck.

Cast off in rib.

Left front border and collar

With RS facing, using 5½mm needles and yarn double, rib across 14 sts from left front holder.

Keeping rib patt correct, work straight until border, slightly stretched, fits up left front to beg of front shaping, ending with a WS row.

Now complete to match right front collar.

To make up

Join centre back collar seam. Sew collar and border into place up right front edge, across back neck and down left front edge.

Fold collar and rib border back to RS and stitch into place at lower edge of borders.

Fold sleeves in half lengthwise, then placing folds to shoulder seams, sew into place.

Join side and sleeve seams, reversing seams for 10cm/4in at cuff edge.

Turn back cuffs.

TEXTURED STITCH JERSEY

* * *

Three stitch
patterns, moss,
stocking stitch
and reversed
stocking
stitch
are used to create
a well-known three
dimensional cube
effect on this
attractive jersey.

Materials

10(11,12) × 50g balls of Wendy Miami (DK cotton)
A pair each of 3¼mm/No10 and 4mm/No8 knitting needles
2 buttons (optional)

Measurements

To fit bust 81–86(91–97,102–107)cm/32–34(36–38,40–42)in

Actual measurements

Bust 90(100,110)cm/35½(39½,43¼)in
Length to shoulders 65cm/25½in
Sleeve seam 48cm/19in

Tension

24 sts and 31 rows to 10cm/4in measured over patt worked on 4mm needles

Back

Using 3¼mm needles cast on 91(99,107) sts.
Rib row 1 K1, * p1, k1, rep from * to end.
Rib row 2 P1, * k1, p1, rep from * to end.
Rep these 2 rows for 9cm/3½in, ending with rib row 1.
Inc row Rib 5(9,5), * M1, rib 5(4,4), rep from * to last 6(10,6) sts, M1, rib to end. 108(120,132) sts.
Change to 4mm needles.
Work in patt as follows:
Rows 1 and 2 * P5, k1, p1, k5, rep from * to end.
Rows 3 and 4 * P4, [k1, p1] twice, k4, rep from * to end.
Rows 5 and 6 * P3, [k1, p1] 3 times, k3, rep from * to end.
Rows 7 and 8 * P2, [k1, p1] 4 times, k2, rep from * to end.
Rows 9 and 10 * P1, k1, rep from * to end.
Rows 11 and 12 * K1, p1, rep from * to end.
Rows 13 and 14 * K2, [p1, k1] 4 times, p2, rep from * to end.
Rows 15 and 16 * K3, [p1, k1] 3 times, p3, rep from * to end.
Rows 17 and 18 * K4, [p1, k1] twice, p4, rep from * to end.
Rows 19 and 20 * K5, p1, k1, p5, rep from * to end.
Rows 21 and 22 * K6, p6, rep from * to end.
Rows 23 and 24 * P1, k5, p5, k1, rep from * to end.
Rows 25 and 26 * K1, p1, k4, p4, k1, p1, rep from * to end.
Rows 27 and 28 * P1, k1, p1, k3, p3, k1, p1, k1, rep from * to end.
Rows 29 and 30 * [K1, p1] twice, k2, p2, [k1, p1] twice, rep from * to end.
Rows 31 and 32 * P1, k1, rep from * to end.
Rows 33 and 34 * K1, p1, rep from * to end.
Rows 35 and 36 * [P1, k1] twice, p2, k2, [p1, k1] twice, rep from * to end.

Rows 37 and 38 * K1, p1, k1, p3, k3, p1, k1, p1, rep from * to end.
Rows 39 and 40 * P1, k1, p4, k4, p1, k1, rep from * to end.
Rows 41 and 42 * K1, p5, k5, p1, rep from * to end.
Rows 43 and 44 * P6, k6, rep from * to end.
These 44 rows form the patt.
Cont in patt until back measures approx 65cm/25½in from cast-on edge, ending with row 42.

Shape shoulders

Cast off 30(36,42) sts at beg of next 2 rows.
Cut off yarn and leave rem 48 sts on a holder.

Front

Work as given for back until front measures approx 57cm/22½in from cast-on edge, ending with row 18.

Shape neck

Next row Patt 42(48,54), turn and leave rem sts on a spare needle.
Dec 1 st at neck edge on next 12 rows. 30(36,42) sts.
Work straight until front measures same as back to shoulder, so ending with row 42.
Cast off.
Return to sts on spare needle.
With RS facing, slip first 24 sts on to a holder, join on yarn and patt to end.
Now complete to match first side of neck.

Sleeves

Using 3¼mm needles cast on 49 sts.
Work 8cm/3in rib as given for back, ending with rib row 1.
Inc row Rib 3, * M1, rib 2, rep from * to last 2 sts, M1, rib to end. 72 sts.
Change to 4mm needles.
Working in patt as given for back, inc and work into patt 1 st each end of 5th and every foll 6th row until there are 110 sts.
Work straight until sleeve measures 48cm/19in from cast-on edge, ending with a WS row. Cast off.

Neckband

Join right shoulder seam.
With RS facing and using 3¼mm needles, pick up and k30 sts down left side of front neck, decreasing 1 st at centre k the front neck sts from holder, pick up and k30 sts up right side of front neck, then decreasing 1 st each end k the back neck sts from holder. 129 sts.
Beg with rib row 2, work 16 rows rib as given for back. Cast off in rib.

To make up

Join left shoulder and neckband seam.
Fold sleeves in half lengthwise, then placing folds to shoulder seams, sew into place. Join side and sleeve seams. Sew buttons securely to left shoulder seam if required, as shown in photograph.

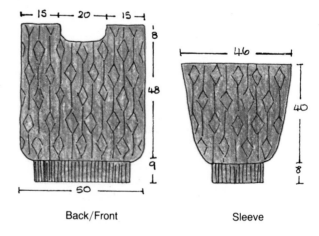

Back/Front   Sleeve

Measurements given in cm for second size

LONG LINE CARDIGAN IN BROKEN RIB

✳

The broken rib stitch makes a dense warm fabric for this cardigan with saddle shoulders.

Materials

20(22,24)×50g balls of Water Wheel Pure Wool Superwash Aran
A pair each of 4mm/No8 and 5mm/No6 knitting needles
A 4mm/No8 circular needle 60cm/24in long
7 buttons

Measurements

To fit bust 86–91(97–102,107–112)cm/ 34–36(38–40,42–44)in
Actual measurements
Bust 107(115,124)cm/42(45¼,49)in
Length to centre back neck 61(62,64)cm/ 24(24½,25)in
Sleeve seam 39(41,42)cm/15½(16,16½)in

Tension

23 sts and 26 rows to 10cm/4in measured over patt worked on 5mm needles

Left front

★ Using 4mm needles cast on 61(67,71) sts.
Rib row 1 P1, * k1, p1, rep from * to end.
Rib row 2 K1, * p1, k1, rep from * to end.
Rep these 2 rows for 7cm/2¾in, ending with rib row 2 and increasing 1 st at centre of last row on first and third sizes only. 62(67,72) sts.
Change to 5mm needles.
Work in patt as follows:
Row 1 (RS) P2, * k3, p2, rep from * to end.
Row 2 K2, * p3, k2, rep from * to end.
Row 3 As row 1.
Row 4 K to end.
These 4 rows form the patt.
Cont in patt until work measures 37cm/ 14½in from cast-on edge, ending with a RS row. ★
Next row Work 2 tog, patt to end. 61(66,71) sts.
Mark beg of last row with a coloured thread.
Shape neck
Row 1 Patt to last 3 sts, k2 tog, p1.
Row 2 K1, p1, patt to end.
Rep these 2 rows 3 times more.
Shape armhole
Next row Cast off 2 sts, patt to last 3 sts, k2 tog, p1.
Next row K1, p1, patt to end.

Next row Work 2 tog, patt to last 3 sts, k2 tog, p1.
Next row K1, p1, patt to end.
Rep these 2 rows 3 times more.
★★ Keeping armhole edge straight, cont to dec at neck edge on next and every foll alt row until 33(40,47) sts rem, then on every foll 4th row until 30(35,40) sts rem, ending at armhole edge.
Shape shoulder
Cast off 10(12,14) sts at beg of next and foll alt row.
Patt 1 row.
Cast off the rem 10(11,12) sts. ★★

Right front

Work as given for left front from ★ to ★.
Next row Patt to last 2 sts, work 2 tog. 61(66,71) sts.
Mark end of last row with a coloured thread.
Shape neck
Row 1 P1, skpo, patt to end.
Row 2 Patt to last 2 sts, p1, k1.
Rep these 2 rows 3 times more, then row 1 again.
Next row Cast off 2 sts, patt to last 2 sts, p1, k1.
Next row P1, skpo, patt to end.
Next row Work 2 tog, patt to last 2 sts, p1, k1.
Next row P1, skpo, patt to end.
Rep last 2 rows twice more, then the first row again.
Now complete as given for left front from ★★ to ★★.

Back

Using 4mm needles cast on 121(131,141) sts.
Work 7cm/2¾in rib as given for left front, ending with a WS row and increasing 1 st at centre of last row. 122(132,142) sts.
Change to 5mm needles.
Work in patt as given for left front until back measures same as fronts to armholes, ending with a WS row.
Shape armholes
Cast off 2 sts at beg of next 2 rows, then dec 1 st each end of next and every foll alt row until 110(120,130) sts rem.
Work straight until back measures same as fronts to shoulders, ending with a WS row.

Shape shoulders
Cast off 10(12,14) sts at beg of next 4 rows, then 10(11,12) sts at beg of foll 2 rows.
Cast off.

Sleeves

Using 4mm needles cast on 47(51,57) sts.
Work 7cm/2¾in rib as given for left front, ending with a WS row and increasing 1 st at centre of last row on 2nd size only. 47(52,57) sts.
Change to 5mm needles.
Working in patt as given for left front, inc and work into patt 1 st each end of 3rd and every foll 4th row until there are 87(92,97) sts.
Work straight until sleeve measures 39(41,42)cm/15½(16,16½)in from cast-on edge, ending with a WS row.
Shape top
Cast off 2 sts at beg of next 2 rows.
Next row K2, skpo, patt to last 4 sts, k2 tog, k2.
Next row P3, patt to last 3 sts, p3.
Rep these 2 rows until 17(18,19) sts rem, ending with a WS row.
Cast off.

Button and buttonhole borders

With RS facing and using the 4mm circular needle, pick up and k95 sts up right front to marker, 58(62,66) sts up right front neck, 11(13,14) sts across first sleeve, 45 sts across back neck, 11(13,14) sts across 2nd sleeve, 58(62,66) sts down left front neck to marker and 95 sts down left front to cast-on edge. 373(385,395) sts.
Beg with rib row 1, work 3 rows rib.
Buttonhole row 1 Rib 3, * cast off 2 sts, rib 13 (including st used in casting off), rep from * 5 times more, cast off 2 sts, rib to end.
Buttonhole row 2 Rib to end, casting on 2 sts over the cast-off sts in previous row.
Rib 2 more rows.
Cast off in rib.

To make up

Join row ends of shaped sleeve top to cast off sts on shoulders of back and front, then sew in remainder of sleeves. Join side and sleeve seams. Sew on buttons.

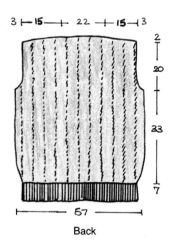

Back

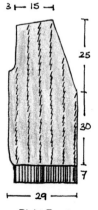

Right Front

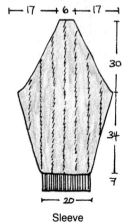

Sleeve

Measurements given in cm for second size

V NECK TOP
IN LACE SQUARES

**

The only
shaping
given
in this
pattern is for
the V neck, and
the pattern is a
reasonably easy
one to keep going.

Materials

7(8)×50g balls of Pingouin Corrida 4 (DK cotton)

A pair each of 3¾mm/No9 and 5½mm/No5 knitting needles

Measurements

To fit bust 81–86(91–97)cm/32–34(36–38)in

Actual measurements

Bust 94(109)cm/37(43)in

Length to shoulders 54cm/21¼in

Tension

18 sts and 22 rows to 10cm/4in measured over patt worked on 5½mm needles

Special abbreviations

Tw2L Twist 2 left as follows: k into back of 2nd st on left-hand needle, then k first st, dropping both sts off needle tog

Tw2R Twist 2 right as follows: k into front of 2nd st on left-hand needle, then k first st, dropping both sts off needle tog

Back

★ Using 3¾mm needles cast on 75(85) sts.

Rib row 1 K1, * p1, k1, rep from * to end.

Rib row 2 P1, * k1, p1, rep from * to end.

Rep these 2 rows for 6cm/2½in, ending with rib row 1.

Inc row Rib 6, * M1, rib 7(6), rep from * to last 6(7) sts, M1, rib to end. 85(98) sts.

Change to 5½mm needles.

Work in patt as follows:

Row 1 (RS) K1, k2 tog, yf, k1, yf, skpo, * Tw2L, k4, Tw2R, k2 tog, yf, k1, yf, skpo, rep from * to last st, k1.

Row 2 and every foll alt row K1, p to last st, k1.

Row 3 K1, k2 tog, yf, k1, yf, skpo, * k1, Tw2L, k2, Tw2R, k1, k2 tog, yf, k1, yf, skpo, rep from * to last st, k1.

Row 5 K1, k2 tog, yf, k1, yf, skpo, * k2, Tw2L, Tw2R, k2, k2 tog, yf, k1, yf, skpo, rep from * to last st, k1.

Row 7 As row 1.

Row 9 As row 3.

Row 11 As row 5.

Row 13 K1, * k2 tog, yf, rep from * to last 2(1) sts, k2(1).

Row 14 K1, p to last st, k1.

These 14 rows form the patt.

Cont in patt until work measures approx 29cm/11½in from cast-on edge, ending with row 8.

Shape sleeves

Keeping patt correct, inc and work into patt 1 st each end of next and foll 3 alt rows. 93(106) sts.

Patt 1 row.

Cast on 12 sts at beg of next 2 rows. 117(130) sts. ★

Work straight in patt until back measures approx 54cm/21¼in from cast-on edge, ending with row 18.

Shape shoulders

Cast off 46(52) sts at beg of next 2 rows.

Cast off rem 25(26) sts.

Front

Work as given for back from ★ to ★.

Work straight in patt until front measures approx 34cm/13½in from cast-on edge, ending with row 6.

Divide for neck

Next row Patt 56(63), k2 tog, turn and leave rem sts on a spare needle.

Patt 1 row.

Dec 1 st at neck edge on next and every foll alt row until 52(59) sts rem, then every foll 4th row until 46(52) sts rem.

Work straight in patt until front measures approx 54cm/21¼in from cast-on edge, ending with row 8.

Cast off.

Return to sts on spare needle.

First size only

With RS facing, slip first st on to a safety-pin, join on yarn, skpo, patt to end. 57 sts.

2nd size only

With RS facing, join on yarn, skpo, patt to end. 64 sts.

Both sizes

Patt 1 row.

Dec 1 st at neck edge on next and every foll alt row until 52(59) sts rem, then every foll 4th row until 46(52) sts rem.

Work straight in patt until front measures approx 51cm/21¼in from cast-on edge, ending with row 9.

Cast off.

Neckband

Join right shoulder seam.

With RS facing and using 3¾mm needles, pick up and k43 sts down left side of front neck, *for 1st size only* k st from safety-pin, and *for 2nd size only* pick up loop between sts at centre front and k into back of it, *for both sizes* mark this st with a coloured thread, then pick up and k49 sts up right side of front neck and 28 sts across back neck. 121 sts.

Rib row 1 [P1, k1] to within 2 sts of marked st, skpo, p centre st, k2 tog, [p1, k1] to end.

Rib row 2 Rib to within 2 sts of marked st, skpo, k centre st, k2 tog, rib to end.

Rep these 2 rows once more, then work rib row 1 again.

Cast off in rib, decreasing each side of centre st as before.

Sleeve borders

Join left shoulder and neckband seam.

With RS facing and using 3¾mm needles, pick up and k106 sts evenly round lower edge of sleeve.

Next row K2 tog, * p2 tog, k2 tog, rep from * to end. 53 sts.

Beg with rib row 1, work 6 rows rib as given for back.

Cast off in rib.

To make up

Join side, sleeve and border seams.

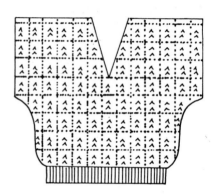

Measurements given in cm for larger size

JERSEY WITH A WIDE PATTERNED BAND

**

The coloured
triangles are
worked on the
front and the back
of this jersey.

Materials

8(9, 10)×50g balls of Robin New World DK in main colour A
1×50g ball of same in each of contrast colours B, C, D, and E
A pair each of 3¼mm/No10 and 4½mm/No7 knitting needles

Measurements

To fit bust 86(97,107)cm/34(38,42)in
Actual measurements
Bust 97(109,121)cm/38(43,47¾)in
Length to shoulders 57.5(61,64)cm/22½(24,25)in
Sleeve seam 42.5cm/16¾in

Tension

20 sts and 24 rows to 10cm/4in measured over st st worked on 4½mm needles

Back

Using 3¼mm needles and A, cast on 86(98,110) sts.
Work 8cm/3in in k1, p1 rib, ending with a RS row.
Inc row Rib 3(4,5), * M1, rib 8(9,10) rep from * to last 3(4,5) sts, M1, rib to end.
97(109,121) sts.
Change to 4½mm needles.
Beg with a k row, work in st st until back measures 32.5(36,39)cm/13(14,15¼)in from cast-on edge, ending with a WS row.
Using separate small balls of yarn for each area of colour and twisting yarns together on WS of work when changing colour to avoid making a hole, work in patt as follows:
Rows 1 and 2 With B, k to end.
Row 3 With A, k to end.
Row 4 P18A, [1B, 11A] 5(6,7) times, 1B, 18A.
Shape armholes
Row 5 Cast off 5 sts, then k12A, [1B, 11A] 5(6,7) times, 1B, 18A. 92(104,116) sts.
Row 6 Cast off 5 sts, then p12A, [1B, 11A] 5(6,7) times, 1B, 13A. 87(99,111) sts.
Row 7 K2 tog, k10A, [3B, 9A] 5(6,7) times, 3B, 10A, k2 tog. 85(97,109) sts.
Row 8 P2 tog, p9A, [3B, 9A] 5(6,7) times, 3B, 9A, p2 tog. 83(95,107) sts.
Row 9 K2 tog, k8A, [3B, 9A] 5(6,7) times, 3B, 8A, k2 tog. 81(93,105) sts.
Row 10 P2 tog, p6A, [5B, 7A] 5(6,7) times, 5B, 6A, p2 tog. 79(91,103) sts.
Row 11 K2 tog, k5A, [5B, 7A] 5(6,7) times, 5B, 5A, k2 tog. 77(89,101) sts.
Row 12 P6A, [5B, 7A] 5(6,7) times, 5B, 6A.
Row 13 K5A, [7B, 5A] 5(6,7) times, 7B, 5A.
Row 14 P5A, [7B, 5A] 5(6,7) times, 7B, 5A.
Row 15 As row 13.
Row 16 With A, p to end.
Rows 17 and 18 With C, k to end.
Row 19 With A, k to end.
Row 20 P8A, [1C, 11A] 5(6,7) times 1C, 8A.
Row 21 K8A, [1C, 11A] 5(6,7) times, 1C, 8A.
Row 22 As row 20.
Row 23 K7A, [3C, 9A] 5(6,7) times, 3C, 7A.
Row 24 P7A, [3C, 9A] 5(6,7) times, 3C, 7A.
Row 25 As row 23.
Row 26 P6A, [5C, 7A] 5(6,7) times, 5C, 6A.
Row 27 K6A, [5C, 7A] 5(6,7) times, 5C, 6A.
Row 28 As row 26.
Row 29 K5A, [7C, 5A] 6(7,8) times.
Row 30 P5A, [7C, 5A] 6(7,8) times.
Row 31 As row 29.
Row 32 As row 16.

Rows 33 and 34 With D, k to end.
Row 35 As row 19.
Row 36 P8A, [1D, 11A] 5(6,7) times, 1D, 8A.
Row 37 K8A, [1D, 11A] 5(6,7) times, 1D, 8A.
Row 38 As row 36.
Row 39 K7A, [3D, 9A] 5(6,7) times, 3D, 7A.
Row 40 P7A, [3D, 9A] 5(6,7) times, 3D, 7A.
Row 41 As row 39.
Row 42 P6A, [5D, 7A] 5(6,7) times, 5D, 6A.
Row 43 K6A, [5D, 7A] 5(6,7) times, 5D, 6A.
Row 44 As row 42.
Row 45 K5A, [7D, 5A] 6(7,8) times.
Row 46 P5A, [7D, 5A] 6(7,8) times.
Row 47 As row 45.
Row 48 As row 16.
Rows 49 and 50 With E, k to end.
Row 51 As row 19.
Row 52 P8A, [1E, 11A] 5(6,7) times, 1E, 8A.
Row 53 K8A, [1E, 11A] 5(6,7) times, 1E, 8A.
Row 54 As row 52.
Row 55 K7A, [3E, 9A] 5(6,7) times, 3E, 7A.
Row 56 P7A, [3E, 9A] 5(6,7) times, 3E, 7A.
Row 57 As row 55.
Row 58 P6A, [5E, 7A] 5(6,7) times, 5E, 6A.
Row 59 K6A, [5E, 7A] 5(6,7) times, 5E, 6A.
Row 60 As row 58.
Shape neck
Row 61 Patt 30(34,38), turn and leave rem sts on a spare needle.
Row 62 Cast off 15(17,19) sts, patt to end.
Using A only work 2 rows st st.
Cast off.
Return to sts on spare needle.
With RS facing, slip first 17(21,25) sts on to a holder, join on yarn, then patt to end.
30(34,38) sts.
Patt 1 row, then complete to match first side of neck.

Front

Work as given for back until row 50 has been completed.
Shape neck
Next row K30(34,38)A, turn and leave rem sts on a spare needle.
★ Keeping patt correct, cast off 5(7,9) sts at beg of next row and 3 sts at beg of foll alt row.
Dec 1 st at neck edge on every row until 15(17,19) sts rem.
Patt 3 rows.
Cast off. ★
Return to sts on spare needle.
With RS facing, slip first 17(21,25) sts on to a holder, join on yarn, then k to end.
30(34,38) sts.
Patt 1 row, then complete as given for first side of neck from ★ to ★.

Sleeves

Using 3¼mm needles and A, cast on 42 sts.
Work 5.5cm/2in k1, p1 rib, ending with a RS row.
Inc row Rib 1 * M1, rib 1, M1, rib 2, rep from * to last 2 sts, [M1, rib 1] twice. 70 sts.
Change to 4½mm needles.
Beginning with a k row and working in st st, inc 1 st each end of 5th and every foll 6th row until there are 98 sts.
Work straight until sleeve measures 42.5cm/16¾in from cast-on edge, ending with a p row.
Cast off 5 sts at beg of next 2 rows, then dec 1 st each end of next 5 rows. 78 sts.
P 1 row.
Cast off.

Neckband

Join right shoulder seam.
With RS facing, using 3¼mm needles and A, pick up and k18(20,22) sts down left side of front neck, k17(21,25) sts from front neck holder, pick up and k18(20,22) sts up right side of front neck and 16(17,19) sts down right side of back neck, k17(21,25) sts from back neck holder, then pick up and k16(17,19) sts up left side of back neck. 102(116,132) sts.
Work 9 rows k1, p1 rib. Cast off in rib.

To make up

Join left shoulder and neckband seam. Fold sleeves in half lengthwise, then placing folds to shoulder seams, sew into place. Join side and sleeve seams.

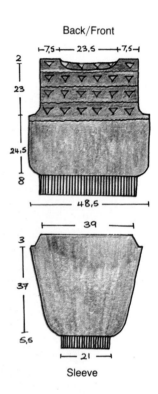

Back/Front

Sleeve

Measurements given in cm for smallest size

ARAN JACKET WITH A BOLD DIAMOND PANEL

✳✳✳

The pocket has been fitted into the diamond panel of this cardigan knitted in traditional Aran stitch patterns.

Materials
11(12)×100g skeins of Rowan Magpie (Aran)
A pair each of 4mm/No8 and 5mm/No6 knitting needles
Cable needle   4 buttons

Measurements
To fit bust 86–91(97–102)cm/ 34–36(38–40)in
Actual measurements
Bust 98.5(106.5)cm/38¾(42)in
Length to shoulders 60cm/23¾in
Sleeve seam 41.5cm/16¼in

Tension
Diamond panel (26 sts) measures 11cm/ 4½in worked on 5mm needles
26 rows to 10cm/4in measured over patt worked on 5mm needles

Special abbreviations
Cr3R Cross 3 right as follows: slip next st on to cable needle and leave at back of work, k2, then p1 from cable needle
Cr3L Cross 3 left as follows: slip next 2 sts on to cable needle and leave at front of work, p1, then k2 from cable needle
C4F Cable 4 front as follows: slip next 2 sts on to cable needle and leave at front of work, k2, then k2 from cable needle
Mb Make bobble as follows: all into next st work [k1, k1 tbl, k1 and k1 tbl], turn and [p2 tog] twice, turn and k2 tog

Pocket linings (make 2)
Using 5mm needles cast on 26 sts.
Work 11cm/4½in rev st st, ending with a k row. Cut off yarn and leave these sts on a holder.

Left front
★ Using 4mm needles cast on 51(57) sts.
Rib row 1 K1, * p1, k1, rep from * to end.
Rib row 2 P1, * k1, p1, rep from * to end.
Rep these 2 rows for 6cm/2½in, ending with rib row 1. ★
Inc row Rib 1, M1, rib 2, [M1, rib 4] twice, [M1, rib 2] 8 times, M1, rib 5, [M1, rib 3] twice, [M1, rib 6] 2(3) times, M1, rib 1. 68(75) sts.   Change to 5mm needles.
Work in patt as follows:
Row 1 (RS) P3, [k3, p4] 2(3) times, k4, p4, k3, p10, Cr3R, Cr3L, p10, k3, p4, k4, p3.
Row 2 and every foll alt row K all the knit sts and p all the purl sts.
Row 3 P3, [k1, Mb, k1, p4] 2(3) times, C4F, p4, k1, Mb, k1, p9, Cr3R, p2, Cr3L, p9, k1, Mb, k1, p4, C4F, p3.
Row 5 P3, [k3, p4] 2(3) times, k4, p4, k3, p8, Cr3R, p4, Cr3L, p8, k3, p4, k4, p3.
Row 7 P3, [k1, Mb, k1, p4] 2(3) times, C4F, p4, k1, Mb, k1, p7, Cr3R, p6, Cr3L, p7, k1, Mb, k1, p4, C4F, p3.
Row 9 P3, [k3, p4] 2(3) times, k4, p4, k3, p6, Cr3R, p8, Cr3L, p6, k3, p4, k4, p3.
Row 11 P3, [k1, Mb, k1, p4] 2(3) times, C4F, p4, k1, Mb, k1, p5, Cr3R, p10, Cr3L, p5, k1, Mb, k1, p4, C4F, p3.
Row 13 P3, [k3, p4] 2(3) times, k4, p4, k3, p4, Cr3R, p5, [Mb] twice, p5, Cr3L, p4, k3, p4, k4, p3.
Row 15 P3, [k1, Mb, k1, p4] 2(3) times, C4F, p4, k1, Mb, k1, p4, Cr3L, p12, Cr3R, p4, k1, Mb, k1, p4, C4F, p3.
Row 17 P3, [k3, p4] 2(3) times, k4, p4, k3, p5, Cr3L, p10, Cr3R, p5, k3, p4, k4, p3.
Row 19 P3, [k1, Mb, k1, p4] 2(3) times, C4F, p4, k1, Mb, k1, p6, Cr3L, p8, Cr3R, p6, k1, Mb, k1, p4, C4F, p3.
Row 21 P3, [k3, p4] 2(3) times, k4, p4, k3, p7, Cr3L, p6, Cr3R, p7, k3, p4, k4, p3.
Row 23 P3, [k1, Mb, k1, p4] 2(3) times, C4F, p4, k1, Mb, k1, p8, Cr3L, p4, Cr3R, p8, k1, Mb, k1, p4, C4F, p3.
Row 25 P3, [k3, p4] 2(3) times, k4, p4, k3, p9, Cr3L, p2, Cr3R, p9, k3, p4, k4, p3.
Row 27 P3, [k1, Mb, k1, p4] 2(3) times, C4F, p4, k1, Mb, k1, p10, Cr3L, Cr3R, p10, k1, Mb, k1, p4, C4F, p3.
These 28 rows form the diamond panel and bobble and cable panel.
Place pocket
Next row Patt 28(35), slip next 26 sts on to a holder, then in their place work across sts from one pocket lining as follows: p10,

Cr3R, Cr3L, p10, then patt to end. 68(75) sts.
Beg with row 2, patt 15 rows.

Shape front edge
Keeping patt correct, dec 1 st at end of next and every foll alt row until 56(64) sts rem, ending with a WS row.
Shape armhole
Next row Cast off 7 sts, then patt to last 2 sts, work 2 tog. 48(56) sts.
Cont to dec at front edge on every foll alt row until 46(53) sts rem.
Dec 1 st at front edge on every foll 4th row until 44(51) sts rem.
Work straight until left front measures approx 60cm/23¾in from cast-on edge, ending with row 28. Cast off in patt.

Right front
Work as given for left front from ★ to ★.
Inc row Rib 1, [M1, rib 6] 2(3) times, [M1, rib 3] twice, M1, rib 5, [M1, rib 2] 8 times, [M1, rib 4] twice, M1, rib 2, M1, rib 1. 68(75) sts.
Change to 5mm needles.
Work in patt as follows:
Row 1 (RS) P3, k4, p4, k3, p10, Cr3R, Cr3L, p10, k3, p4, k4, [p4, k3] 2(3) times, p3.
Row 2 and every foll alt row K all the knit sts and p all the purl sts.
Row 3 P3, C4F, p4, k1, Mb, k1, p9, Cr3R, p2, Cr3L, p9, k1, Mb, k1, p4, C4F, [p4, k1, Mb, k1] 2(3) times, p3.
Row 5 P3, k4, p4, k3, p8, Cr3R, p4, Cr3L, p8, k3, p4, k4, [p4, k3] 2(3) times, p3.
Row 7 P3, C4F, p4, k1, Mb, k1, p7, Cr3R, p6, Cr3L, p7, k1, Mb, k1, p4, C4F, [p4, k1, Mb, k1] 2(3) times, p3.
These 7 rows set position of the diamond panel and bobble and cable panel.
Keeping patt panels correct patt 21 rows, so ending with row 28 of diamond panel.
Place pocket
Next row Patt 14, slip next 26 sts on to a holder, then in their place work across sts from second pocket lining as follows: p10, Cr3R, Cr3L, p10, then patt to end. 68(75) sts.
Beg with row 2, patt 15 rows.
Shape front edge
Keeping patt correct, dec 1 st at beg of next and every foll row until 55(63) sts rem, ending with a RS row.
Shape armhole
Next row Cast off 7 sts, then patt to end. 48(56) sts.
Dec 1 st at front edge on next and foll alt row 1(2) times. 46(53) sts.
Decreasing 1 st at front edge on every foll 4th row, complete to match left front.

Back
Using 4mm needles cast on 101(113) sts.
Work 6cm/2½in rib as given for left front, ending with rib row 1.
Inc row Rib 2, M1, rib 5(6), [M1, rib 5] 1(2) times, [M1, rib 3] twice, * M1, rib 5, [M1, rib 2] 8 times, M1, rib 5 * , [M1, rib 3] 4 times, rep from * to * once, [M1, rib 3] twice, [M1, rib 6] 2(3) times, M1, rib 1. 134(148) sts.
Change to 5mm needles.
Work in patt as follows:
Row 1 (RS) P3, [k3, p4] 2(3) times, k4, p4, * k3, p10, Cr3R, Cr3L, p10, k3 * , [p4, k4] twice, rep from * to * once, p4, k4, [p4, k3] 2(3) times, p3.
Row 2 and every foll alt row K all the knit sts and p all the purl sts.
Row 3 P3, [k1, Mb, k1, p4] 2(3) times, C4F, p4, * k1, Mb, k1, p9, Cr3R, p2, Cr3L, p9, k1, Mb, k1* , [p4, C4F] twice, p4, rep from * to * once, p4, C4F, [p4, k1, Mb, k1] 2(3) times, p3.
Row 5 P3, [k3, p4] 2(3) times, k4, p4, * k3, p8, Cr3R, p4, Cr3L, p8, k3 * , [p4, k4] twice, rep from * to * once, p4, k4, [p4, k3] 2(3) times, p3.
These 5 rows set position of the diamond panels and bobble and cable panels.
Keeping patt panels correct, cont in patt until back measures same as front to beg of armholes, ending with a WS row.

Shape armholes
Cast off in patt 7 sts at beg of next 2 rows. 120(134) sts.
Work straight until back measures same as fronts to shoulders, ending with row 28.
Cast off in patt.

Sleeves
Using 4mm needles cast on 47 sts.
Work 6cm/2½in rib as given for left front, ending with rib row 1.
Inc row Rib 5, * [M1, inc in next st, M1, rib 1, M1, rib 2] twice, M1, inc in next st, M1 * , rib 3, [M1, rib 1] 6 times, M1, rib 2, [M1, rib 1] 5 times, M1, rib 3, rep from * to * once, rib 5. 82 sts.
Change to 5mm needles.
Row 1 (RS) P2, k3, [p4, k4] twice, p4, k3, p10, Cr3R, Cr3L, p10, k3, [p4, k4] twice, p4, k3, p2.
Row 2 K all the knit sts and p all the purl sts.
Row 3 Inc in first st, p1, k1, Mb, k1, [p4, C4F] twice, p4, k1, Mb, k1, p9, Cr3R, p2, Cr3L, p9, k1, Mb, k1, [p4, C4F] twice, p4, k1, Mb, k1, p1, inc in last st. 84 sts.
These 3 rows set position of the diamond panel and bobble and cable panels.
Keeping patt correct, inc and work into bobble patt 1 st each end of every foll 3rd row until there are 140(142) sts.
Work straight until sleeve measures approx 43.5cm/17¼in from cast-on edge, ending with row 14 of diamond panel.
Cast off in patt.

Buttonhole border
Join shoulder seams.
With RS facing and using 4mm needles, pick up and k49 sts up right front to beg of front edge shaping, 77 sts to shoulder and 15 sts to centre back neck. 141 sts.
K 1 row.
Work 4 rows rib as given for left front.
Buttonhole row 1 (RS) Rib 4, [cast off 2 sts, rib 13 including st left on needle after cast off] 3 times, cast off 2 sts, rib to end.
Buttonhole row 2 Rib to end, casting on 2 sts over those cast off in previous row.
Rib 4 rows. Cast off in rib.

Button border
Work to match buttonhole border, omitting buttonholes.

Pocket tops
With RS facing and using 4mm needles, k the sts from holder decreasing 1 st at centre. 25 sts.
K 1 row.
Work 9 rows rib as given for left front.
Cast off.

To make up
Joining row ends at tops of sleeves to cast-off edges for armholes, sew in the sleeves.
Join side and sleeve seams. Join borders seam. Sew pocket linings and row ends of pocket tops into position. Sew on buttons.

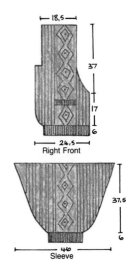

Right Front

Sleeve

Measurements given in cm for first size

SLEEVELESS LUREX TOP

*

An elegant
evening top with
taway armholes
nd a high neck.

Materials
9(10,11,12)×25g balls of Twilleys
 Goldfingering (4 ply lurex)
A pair each of 2¼mm/No13 and 3mm/No11
 knitting needles

Measurements
To fit bust 81(86,91,97)cm/32(34,36,38)in
Actual measurements
Bust 86(91,96,102)cm/34(36,37¾,40¼)in
Length to shoulders 56(57,58,59)cm/
22(22½,22¾,23¼)in

Tension
33 sts and 42 rows to l0cm/4in measured
over st st worked on 3mm needles

Back
Using 2¼mm needles cast on
126(134,142,152) sts.
Work 8cm/3in k1, p1 rib.
Inc row Rib 10(7,11,8), * M1, rib 7(8,8,9),
rep from * to last 11(7,11,9) sts, M1, rib to
end. 142(150,158,168) sts.
Change to 3mm needles.
Work in st st until back measures
36.5(37,37.5,38)cm/14¼(14½,14¾,15)in
from cast-on edge, ending with a p row.
Shape armholes
Cast off 6(6,7,8) sts at beg of next 2 rows
and 3 sts at beg of next 4 rows.
Dec 1 st each end of next and every foll alt
row until 72(76,80,86) sts rem.
Dec 1 st each end of every foll 4th row until
66(70,72,76) sts rem.
Work straight until armholes measure
19.5(20,20.5,21)cm/7¾(8,8¼,8½)in from
beg of shaping, ending with a p row.
Shape shoulders
Cast off 6(8,8,10) sts at beg of next 2 rows.
Cut off yarn and leave rem 54(54,56,56) sts
on a holder.

Front
Work as given for back until
72(76,80,84) sts rem.
P 1 row.

Shape neck
Next row K27(29,30,32), turn and leave
rem sts on a spare needle.
Decreasing 1 st at armhole edge on 2nd
and every foll 4th row as before, dec 1 st at
neck edge on every row until
14(16,12,14) sts rem.
Keeping armhole edge straight, cont to dec
at neck edge on every row until
6(8,8,10) sts rem.
Work straight until front measures same as
back to beg of shoulder shaping, ending at
armhole edge.
Cast off.
Return to sts on spare needle.
With RS facing, slip first 18(18,20,20) sts on
to a holder, join on yarn and k to end.
27(29,30,32) sts.
Now complete to match first side of neck.

Neckband
Join right shoulder seam.
With RS facing and using 2¼mm needles,
pick up and k24 sts down left side of front
neck, k the front neck sts from holder, pick
up and k24 sts up right side of front neck,
then k the back neck sts from holder.
120(120,124,124) sts.
Work 4.5cm/1¾in k1, p1 rib.
Cast off in rib.

Armhole borders
Join left shoulder and neckband seam.
With RS facing and using 2¼mm needles,
pick up and k140(144,148,152) sts round
armhole edge.
Work 2.5cm/1in k1, p1 rib.
Cast off in rib.

To make up
Join side and armhole border seams.

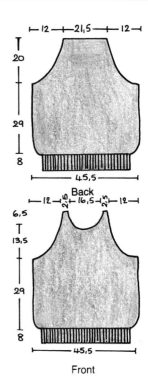

Back

Front

Measurements given in cm for second size

SIMPLE BASKETWEAVE JERSEY

*

Knitted
in a soft
brushed yarn using
a simple stitch
pattern, this is
an ideal jersey
for a beginner.

Materials
6(7,8,8)×50g balls of Scheepjeswol
 Voluma (brushed DK)
A pair each of 3¾mm/No9 and 4½mm/No7
 knitting needles

Measurements
To fit bust 86(91,97,102)cm/34(36,38,40)in
Actual measurements
Bust 96(104,112,120)cm/38(41,44,47)in
Length to shoulders 53(55,57,59)cm/
20¾(21¾,22½,23¼)in
Sleeve seam 46cm/18in

Tension
20 sts and 26 rows to 10cm/4in measured
over patt worked on 4½mm needles

Back and front (alike)
Using 3¾mm needles cast on
90(94,98,102) sts.
Work 4cm/1½in k1, p1 rib, ending with a
RS row.
Inc row Rib 3(2,3,8), * M1, rib 17(10,7,5),
rep from * to last 2(4,9) sts, M1, rib to
end. 96(104,112,120) sts.
Change to 4½mm needles.
Work in patt as follows:
Row 1 (RS) K2, * p4, k4, rep from * to last
6 sts, p4, k2.
Row 2 P2, * k4, p4, rep from * to last 6 sts,
k4, p2.

Rows 3 and 4 As rows 1 and 2.
Row 5 P2, * k4, p4, rep from * to last 6 sts,
k4, p2.
Row 6 K2, * p4, k4, rep from * to last 6 sts,
p4, k2.
Rows 7 and 8 As rows 5 and 6.
These 8 rows form the patt.
Cont in patt until work measures
49(51,53,55)cm/19¼(20,20¾,21½)in from
cast-on edge, ending with a WS row and
increasing 1 st at centre of last row.
Rib row I K1, * p1, k1, rep from * to end.
Rib row 2 P1, * k1, p1, rep from * to end.
Rep these 2 rows for 4cm/1½in, ending
with rib row 2.
Cast off in rib.

Sleeves
Using 3¾mm needles cast on
42(44,46,48) sts.
Work 7cm/2¾in k1, p1 rib, ending with a
RS row.
Inc row Rib 1(1,5,2), * M1, rib 8(6,4,4) rep
from * to last 1(1,5,2) sts, M1, rib to end.
48(52,56,60) sts.
Change to 4½mm needles.
Work in patt as follows:
Row 1 (RS) K2(4,2,4), * p4, k4, rep from
* to last 6(8,6,8) sts, p4, k2(4,2,4).
Row 2 P2(4,2,4), * k4, p4, rep from * to last
6(8,6,8) sts, k4, p2(4,2,4).

Rows 3 and 4 As rows 1 and 2.
Row 5 Inc in first st, p1(3,1,3), * k4, p4, rep
from * to last 6(8,6,8) sts, k4, p1(3,1,3), inc
in last st. 50(54,58,62) sts.
Row 6 *For 2nd and 4th sizes only* p1, *for all
sizes* k3(4,3,4), * p4, k4, rep from * to last
7(9,7,9) sts, p4, k3(4,3,4), then *for 2nd and
4th sizes only* p1.
Row 7 *For 2nd and 4th sizes only* k1, *for all
sizes* p3(4,3,4), * k4, p4, rep from * to last
7(9,7,9) sts, k4, p3(4,3,4), then *for 2nd and
4th sizes only* k1.
Row 8 As row 6.
Continuing in patt, inc and work into patt
1 st each end of next and every foll 4th row
until there are 96(100,104,108) sts.
Work straight until sleeve measures 46cm/
18in from cast-on edge, ending with a WS
row.
Cast off.

To make up
Join shoulder seams for approx
9(10.5,12,13.5)cm/3½(4,4¾,5¼)in, leaving
rem 30(31,32,33)cm/12(12½,12½,13)in for
neck opening. Fold sleeves in half
lengthwise, then placing folds to shoulder
seams, sew into place. Join side and
sleeve seams.

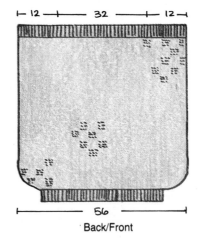

Back/Front

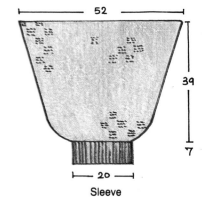

Sleeve

Measurements given in cm for third size

SCOOP NECK
LACY COTTON JERSEY

✳✳✳
An open
lacy stitch is
used on this cool
cotton jersey.

Materials

8(9,10)×50g balls of Rowan Cotton Glace (4 ply)
A pair each of 3¼mm/No10 and 4mm/No8 knitting needles

Measurements

To fit bust 86(91-96,102)cm/34(36-38,40)in
Actual measurements
Bust 97(109,121)cm/38(43,47¾)in
Length to shoulders 51(53.5,56)cm/20(21,22)in
Sleeve seam 41(43,46)cm/16(17,18)in

Tension

20 sts and 25 rows to 10cm/4in measured over patt worked on 4mm needles

Back

Using 3¼mm needles cast on 74(82,94) sts.
Rib row 1 K2, * p2, k2, rep from * to end.
Rib row 2 P2, * k2, p2, rep from * to end.
Rep these 2 rows for 8.5cm/3½in, ending with rib row 1.
Inc row Rib 4(2,8), * M1, rib 3, rep from * to last 4(2,8) sts, M1, rib to end.
97(109,121) sts.
Change to 4mm needles.
Work in patt as follows:
Row 1 (RS) K1, * yf, k4, p3 tog, k4, yf, k1, rep from * to end.
Row 2 and every foll alt row P6, * k1, p11, rep from * to last 7 sts, k1, p6.
Row 3 K2, * yf, k3, p3 tog, k3, yf, k3, rep from * to last 11 sts, yf, k3, p3 tog, k3, yf, k2.
Row 5 K3, * yf, k2, p3 tog, k2, yf, k2, yfon, skpo, k1, rep from * to last 10 sts, yf, k2, p3 tog, k2, yf, k3.
Row 7 K1, * k2 tog, [yf, k1] twice, p3 tog, k1, yf, k1, yfon, skpo, k1, rep from * to end.

Row 9 K2 tog, * yf, k3, yrn, p3 tog, yon, k3, yfon, sl 1, k2 tog, psso, rep from * to last 10 sts, yf, k3, yrn, p3 tog, yon, k3, yfon, skpo.
Row 10 As row 2.
These 10 rows form the patt.
Cont in patt until back measures 30(32.5,35)cm/12(13,14)in from cast-on edge, ending with a WS row.
Shape armholes
Cast off 3 sts at beg of next 2 rows.
91(103,115) sts.
Dec 1 st each end of next and every foll alt row until 77(89,101) sts rem, ending with a WS row.
Work straight until back measures 51(53.5,56)cm/20(21,22)in from cast-on edge, ending with a WS row.
Shape shoulders
Cast off 20(24,28) sts at beg of next 2 rows.
Cut off yarn and leave rem 37(41,45) sts on a holder.

Front

Work as given for back until front measures 42(44.5,47)cm/16½(17½,18½)in from cast-on edge, ending with a WS row.
Shape neck
Next row Patt 30(34,38), turn and leave rem sts on a spare needle.
Keeping patt correct, cast off 2 sts at beg of next and foll alt row. 26(30,34) sts.
Dec 1 st at neck edge on next and every foll alt row until 20(24,28) sts rem.
Work straight until front measures same as back to shoulder, ending with a WS row.
Cast off.
Return to sts on spare needle.
With RS facing, slip first 17(21,25) sts on to a holder, join on yarn and patt to end.
30(34,38) sts.

Patt 1 row, then complete to match first side of neck.

Sleeves

Using 3¼mm needles cast on 46 sts.
Work 7cm/2¾in rib as given for back, ending with rib row 1.
Inc row Rib 2, * M1, rib 3, rep from * to last 2 sts, M1, rib to end. 61 sts.
Change to 4mm needles.
Working in patt as given for back, inc and work into patt 1 st each end of 3rd(5th,7th) and every foll 10th row until there are 77 sts.
Work straight until sleeve measures 41(43,46)cm/16(17,18)in from cast-on edge, ending with a WS row.
Shape top
Cast off 3 sts at beg of next 2 rows. 71 sts.
Dec 1 st each end of next and every foll alt row until 61 sts rem, ending with a WS row.
Cast off 2 sts at beg of every row until 17 sts rem, ending with a WS row.
Cast off.

Neckband

Join right shoulder seam.
With RS facing and using 3¼mm needles, pick up and k20 sts down left side of front neck, k17(21,25) sts from front neck holder, pick up and k20 sts up right side of front neck, then k37(41,45) sts from back neck holder. 94(102,110) sts.
Beg with rib row 2, work 8 rows rib as given for back.
Cast off in rib.

To make up

Join left shoulder and neckband seam.
Set in sleeves, then join side and sleeve seams.

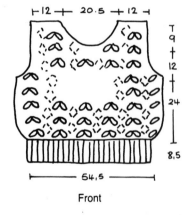

Front

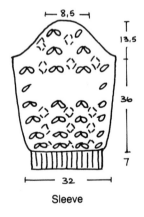

Sleeve

Measurements given in cm for second size

CABLE AND TWIST STITCH RIB JERSEY

* *

The twisted stitches give the b a more defined texture on this simple jersey.

Materials

17(18,19)×50g balls of Sunbeam Aran Knit
A pair each of 4mm/No8 and 5mm/No6
   knitting needles
Cable needle

Measurements

To fit bust 81-86(91-97,102-107)cm/
32-34(36-38,40-42)in
Actual measurements
Bust 96(104,112)cm/37¾(41,44)in
Length to shoulders 60(64,64)cm/
23¾(25¼,25¼)in
Sleeve seam 47cm/18½in

Tension

21 sts and 26 rows to l0cm/4in measured
over rib patt worked on 5mm needles
1 cable panel (28 sts) measures 12cm/
4¾in worked on 5mm needles

Special abbreviation

Tw2 Twist 2 as follows: k into front of
second st on left-hand needle, then p into
first st, slipping both sts off needle tog

Back

Using 4mm needles cast on
97(105,113) sts.
Rib row 1 K1, * p1, k1, rep from * to end.
Rib row 2 P1, * k1, p1, rep from * to end.
Rep these 2 rows for 8cm/3¼in, ending
with rib row 1.
Inc row Rib 16(20,24), * M1, rib 6, [M1 pw,
rib 2] twice, M1 pw, rib 5, M1 *, rib 35, rep
from * to * once, rib 16(20,24).
107(115,123) sts.
Change to 5mm needles.
Work in patt as follows:
Row 1 (RS) [P1, k3] 3(4,5) times, * p3,
Tw2, p4, k10, p4, Tw2, p3 *, [k3, p1]
6 times, k3, rep from * to * once, [k3, p1]
3(4,5) times.
Row 2 K2, p1, [k3, p1] 2(3,4) times, * k4,
p2, k4, p10, k4, p2, k4 *, p1, [k3, p1]
6 times, rep from * to * once, [p1, k3]
2(3,4) times, p1, k2.
Rows 3 to 8 Rep rows 1 and 2 three times
more.
Row 9 [P1, k3] 3(4,5) times, * p3, Tw2, p4,
slip next 5 sts on to cable needle and leave
at front of work, k5, then k5 from cable
needle, p4, Tw2, p3 *, [k3, p1] 6 times, k3,
rep from * to * once, [k3, p1] 3(4,5) times.
Row 10 As row 2.
These 10 rows form the patt.
Cont in patt until work measures approx
60(64,64)cm/23¾(25¼,25¼)in from cast-on
edge, ending with row 6.

Shape shoulders

Cast off 34(38,42) sts, patt to last
34(38,42) sts, cast off rem sts.
Cut off yarn and leave rem 39 sts on a
holder.

Front

Work as given for back until front measures
54(58,58)cm/21¼(22¾,22¾)in from cast-on
edge, ending with a WS row.
Shape neck
Next row Patt 38(42,46), work 2 tog, turn
and leave rem sts on a spare needle.
★ **Next row** Patt to end.
Dec 1 st at neck edge on next and every
foll alt row until 34(38,42) sts rem.
Work straight until front measures same as
back to shoulders, ending with the same
patt row.
Cast off. ★
Return to sts on spare needle.
With RS facing, slip first 27 sts on to a
holder, join on yarn and work 2 tog, then
patt to end.
Now complete as given for first side of
neck from ★ to ★.

Sleeves

Using 4mm needles cast on 45(49,53) sts.
Work 8cm/3¼in rib as given for back,
ending with rib row 2.
Change to 5mm needles.
Work in patt as follows:
Row 1 (RS) P1, * k3, p1, rep from * to end.
Row 2 K2, * p1, k3, rep from * to last 3 sts,
p1, k2.
These 2 rows form the patt.
Continuing in patt, inc and work into patt
1 st each end of next and every foll 5th row
until there are 85(89,93) sts.
Work straight until sleeve measures
47cm/18½in from cast-on edge, ending
with a WS row.   Cast off.

Neckband

Join right shoulder seam.
With RS facing and using 4mm needles,
pick up and k16 sts down left side of front
neck, k27 from front neck holder, pick up
and k16 sts up right side of front neck, then
k39 from back neck holder. 98 sts.
Work 2.5cm/1in k1, p1 rib.
Cast off in rib.

To make up

Join left shoulder and neckband seam.
Fold sleeves in half lengthwise, then
placing folds to shoulder seams, sew into
place. Join side and sleeve seams.

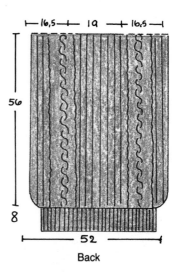

Back

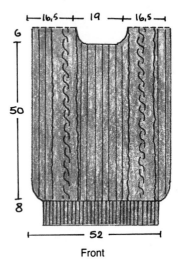

Front

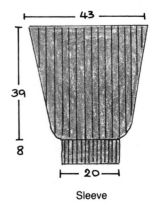

Sleeve

Measurements given in cm for second size

FULLY FASHIONED CARDIGAN

✳✳

A single purl
stitch worked on
knit row, moving
outwards
with
stitches
made and lost
each side, defines
the shaping
of this neat
fitted cardigan.

Materials

8(9,10)×50g balls of Emu Superwash 4 ply
A pair each of 2¾mm/No12 and 3¼mm/
No10 knitting needles
9 buttons

Measurements

To fit bust 81(86,91)cm/32(34,36)in
Actual measurements
Bust 89(94,99)cm/35(37,39)in
Length to shoulders 55(57,59)cm/
21¾(22½,23¼)in
Sleeve seam 50.5cm/20in

Tension

28 sts and 36 rows to 10cm/4in measured
over st st worked on 3¼mm needles

Back

Using 2¾mm needles cast on
107(115,121) sts.
Rib row 1 K1 tbl, * p1, k1 tbl, rep from * to
end.
Rib row 2 P1, * k1 tbl, p1, rep from * to
end.
Rep these 2 rows for 3cm/1¼in, ending
with rib row 1.
Inc row Rib 5(9,4), * inc in next st, rib
5(5,6), rep from * to last 6(10,5) sts, inc in
next st, rib 5(9,4). 124(132,138) sts.
Change to 3¼mm needles.
Work in st st with purl st mock seams as
follows:
Row 1 (RS) K33(35,37), p1, k56(60,62), p1,
k33(35,37).
Row 2 P33(35,37), k1, p56(60,62), k1,
p33(35,37).
Rep these 2 rows until work measures
32(33,34)cm/12½(13,13½)in from cast-on
edge, ending with a WS row.
Now move the purl st mock seam towards
outer edges as follows:
Next row K28(30,32), skpo, k3, p1, k5, M1,
k46(50,52), M1, k5, p1, k3, k2 tog,
k28(30,32).
Next row P32(34,36), k1, p58(62,64), k1,
p32(34,36).
Work 2 rows straight.
Shape armholes
Next row Cast off 6 sts, k until there are
21(23,25) sts on right-hand needle, skpo,
k3, p1, k5, M1, k48(52,54), M1, k5, p1, k3,
k2 tog, k to end.
Next row Cast off 6 sts, p until there are
25(27,29) sts on right-hand needle, k1,
p60(64,66), k1, p to end.
Next 2 rows Cast off 2 sts, work to end.
Continuing to move the purl sts towards
outer edges on next and every foll alt 4th
row, dec 1 st at each end of next and every
foll alt row until 104(110,116) sts rem.
Continuing to move the purl sts as before,
work straight until a row has been worked
as follows: k1, skpo, k3, p1, k5, M1,
k80(86,92), M1, k5, p1, k3, k2 tog, k1.
Next row P5, k1, p92(98,104), k1, p5.
Keeping purl sts as set, work straight until
armholes measure 22(23,24)cm/8¾(9,9½)in
from beg of shaping, ending with a WS row.
Shape neck and shoulders
Next row Cast off 8 sts, k until there are
32(34,36) sts on right-hand needle, turn and
leave rem sts on a spare needle.
Next row Cast off 5 sts, p to end.
Next row Cast off 8 sts, k to end.
Next row Cast off 5 sts, p to end.
Cast off 7(8,9) sts at beg of next row.
Work 1 row. Cast off.
Return to sts on spare needle.
With RS facing, join on yarn and cast off first
24(26,28) sts, patt to end.
40(42,44) sts.
Next row Cast off 8 sts, p to end.
Next row Cast off 5 sts, k to end.

Rep the last 2 rows once more.
Cast off 7(8,9) sts at beg of next row.
Work 1 row. Cast off.

Left front

★ Using 2¾mm needles cast on
53(57,61) sts.
Rib row 1 K1 tbl, * p1, k1 tbl, rep from * to
end.
Rib row 2 P1, * k1 tbl, p1, rep from * to end.
Rep these 2 rows for 3cm/1¼in from cast-on
edge, ending with rib row 1.
Inc row Rib 1(4,6), * inc in next st,
rib 9(11,11), rep from * to last 2(5,7) sts, inc
in next st, rib 1(4,6). 59(62,66) sts. ★
Change to 3¼mm needles.
Work in st st with purl st mock seam as
follows:
Row 1 (RS) K33(35,37), p1, k25(26,28).
Row 2 P25(26,28), k1, p33(35,37).
Rep these 2 rows until work measures
32(33,34)cm/12½(13,13½)in from cast-on
edge, ending with a WS row.
Now move the purl st towards outer edge as
follows:
Next row K28(30,32), skpo, k3, p1, k5, M1,
k20(21,23).
Next row P26(27,29), k1, p32(34,36).
Work 2 rows straight.
Shape armhole
Next row Cast off 6 sts, k until there are
21(23,25) sts on right-hand needle, skpo, k3,
p1, k5, M1, k to end.
Next row P27(28,30), k1, p to end.
Next row Cast off 2 sts, work to end.
Work 1 row.
Continuing to move the purl st towards outer
edge on next and every foll 4th row, dec 1 st
at armhole edge on next and every foll alt
row until 49(51,55) sts rem.
Continuing to move the purl st as before,
work straight until a row has been worked as
follows: k4(5,6), skpo, k3, p1, k5, M1,
k34(35,38), so ending at front edge.
★★ Shape neck
Continuing to move the purl st as before,
cast off 6 sts at beg of next row and 2 sts at
beg of foll 5 alt rows.
Continuing to move the purl st until there are
5 knit sts left at outer edge, dec 1 st at neck
edge on next and every foll alt row until
30(32,34) sts rem.
Work straight until front measures same as
back to beg of shoulder shaping, ending at
armhole edge.
Shape shoulder
Cast off 8 sts at beg of next and foll alt row
and 7(8,9) sts at beg of foll alt row.
Work 1 row. Cast off. ★★

Right front

Work as given for left front from ★ to ★.
Change to 3¼mm needles.
Work in st st with purl st mock seam as
follows:
Row 1 (RS) K25(26,28), p1, k33(35,37).
Row 2 P33(35,37), k1, p25(26,28).
Rep these 2 rows until work measures
32(33,34)cm/12½(13,13½)in from cast-on
edge, ending with a WS row.
Now move the purl st towards outer edge as
follows:
Next row K20(21,23), M1, k5, p1, k3, k2 tog,
k28(30,32).
Next row P32(34,36), k1, p26(27,29).
Work 2 rows straight.
Next row K21(22,24), M1, k5, p1, k3, k2 tog,
k27(29,31).
Shape armhole
Next row Cast off 6 sts, p until there are
25(27,29) sts on right-hand needle, k1, p to
end. Work 1 row.
Next row Cast off 2 sts, p until there are
23(25,27) sts on right-hand needle, k1, p to

end.
Continuing to move the purl st towards outer
edge on next and foll 4th rows, dec
1 st at armhole edge on next and foll alt rows
until 49(51,55) sts rem.
Continuing to move the purl st as before,
work straight until a row has been worked as
follows: p9(10,11), k1, p39(40,43), so ending
at front edge.
Now work as given for left front from ★★ to
★★.

Sleeves

Using 2¾mm needles cast on 49(53,57) sts.
Work 6cm/2½in rib as given for back, ending
with rib row 1.
Inc row Rib 6(2,4), * inc in next st, rib 2(3,2),
rep from * to last 7(3,5) sts, inc in next st, rib
6(2,4). 62(66,74) sts.
Change to 3¼mm needles.
Working in st st, inc 1 st each end of 9th
and every foll 8th row until there are
100(104,112) sts.
Work straight until sleeve measures
50.5cm/20in from cast-on edge, ending with
a WS row.
Shape top
Cast off 4 sts at beg of every row until
12(16,16) sts rem. Cast off.

Buttonhole border

With RS facing and using 2mm needles,
pick up and k161(169,177) sts evenly up
right front edge.
K 1 row.
Beg with rib row 1, rib 4 rows as given for
back.

Measurements given in cm for smallest
size

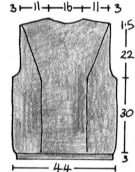

Back

Buttonhole row 1 (RS) Rib 4, [cast off 2, rib
until there are 17(18,19) sts on right-hand
needle after cast-off] 8 times, cast off 2, rib
to end.
Buttonhole row 2 Rib to end casting on 2 sts
over those cast off in previous row.
Rib 4 more rows. Cast off in rib.

Button border

With RS facing and using 2¾mm needles,
pick up and k161(169,177) sts evenly down
left front edge. K 1 row.
Beg with rib row 1, rib 10 rows as given for
back. Cast off in rib.

Neckband

Join shoulder seams.
With RS facing, and using 2¾mm needles,
join yarn to cast-off edge of buttonhole
border at neck edge and pick up and
k34(35,36) sts up right front neck, 43(45,47)
sts across back neck and 34(35,36) sts
down left front neck, ending at cast-off edge
of button border. 111(115,119) sts. K 1 row.
Beg with rib row 1, rib 10 rows as given for
back. Cast off in rib.

To make up

Set in sleeves, then join side and sleeve
seams. Sew on buttons.

V NECK TOP IN LACE FLOWER STITCH

***

Rows of lace stitch flowers are worked on the front alone of this summer top.

Materials

6(6,7,8,9)×50g balls of Wendy Miami (DK cotton)
A pair each of 3¼/No10 and 4mm/No8 knitting needles

Measurements

To fit bust 81(86,91,97,102)cm/
32(34,36,38,40)in

Actual measurements
Bust 90(95,100,106,110)cm/
35½(37¾,39½, 41¾,43¼)in
Length to shoulders 60.5cm/23¾in
Sleeve seam 13cm/5in

Tension

22 sts and 31 rows to 10cm/4in measured over patt worked on 4mm needles

Front

★ Using 3¼mm needles cast on 94(100,104,110,116) sts.
Work 8cm/3in k1, p1 rib.
Inc row Rib 11(12,9,10,12), * M1, rib 18(19,17,18,23), rep from * to last 11(12,10,10,12) sts, M1, rib to end. 99(105,110,116,121) sts. ★
Change to 4mm needles
Work in patt as follows:
Row 1 (RS) K to end.
Row 2 and every foll alt row P to end.
Row 3 K to end.
Row 5 K3(6,3,6,3), * yfon, skpo, k9, rep from * to last 8(11,8,11,8) sts, yfon, skpo, k6(9,6,9,6).
Row 7 K4(7,4,7,4), * yfon, skpo, k9, rep from * to last 7(10,7,10,7) sts, yfon, skpo, k5(8,5,8,5).
Row 9 K5(8,5,8,5), * yfon, skpo, k9, rep from * to last 6(9,6,9,6) sts, yfon , skpo, k4(7,4,7,4).
Row 11 K3(6,3,6,3), * k2 tog, yf, k1, yfon, skpo, k6, rep from * to last 8(11,8,11,8) sts, k2 tog, yf, k1, yfon, skpo, k3(6,3,6,3).
Row 13 K2(5,2,5,2), * k2 tog, yf, k3, yfon, skpo, k4, rep from * to last 9(12,9,12,9) sts, k2 tog, yf, k3, yfon, skpo, k2(5,2,5,2).
Row 15 As row 11.
Row 17 As row 13.
Row 19 K4(7,4,7,4), * yfon, sl 1, k2 tog, psso, yf, k8, rep from * to last 7(10,7,10,7) sts, yfon , sl 1, k2 tog, psso, yf, k4(7,4,7,4).
Row 21 K to end.
Row 23 K to end.
Row 25 K10(13,10,13,10), * yfon, skpo, k9, rep from * to last 12(15,12,15,12) sts, yfon, skpo, k10(13,10,13,10).
Row 27 K11(14,11,14,11), * yfon, skpo, k9, rep from * to last 11(14,11,14,11) sts, yfon, skpo, k9(12,9,12,9).
Row 29 K12(15,12,15,12), * yfon, skpo, k9, rep from * to last 10(13,10,13,10) sts, yfon, skpo, k8(11,8,11,8).
Row 31 K10(13,10,13,10), * k2 tog, yf, k1, yfon, skpo, k6, rep from * to last 12(15,12,15,12) sts, k2 tog, yf, k1, yfon, skpo, k7(10,7,10,7).
Row 33 K9(12,9,12,9), * k2 tog, yf, k3, yfon, skpo, k4, rep from * to last 13(16,13,16,13) sts, k2 tog, yf, k3, yfon, skpo, k6(9,6,9,6).
Row 35 As row 31.
Row 37 As row 33.
Row 39 K11(14,11,14,11), * yfon, sl 1, k2 tog, psso, yf, k8, rep from * to last

11(14,11,14,11) sts, yfon, sl 1, k2 tog, psso, yf, k8(11,8,11,8).
Row 40 P to end.
These 40 rows form the patt.
Rep these 40 rows once more, then work rows 1 to 4 again.
Divide for neck
Next row Patt 49(52,55,58,60), turn and leave rem sts on a spare needle.
★★ Keeping patt correct, dec 1 st at neck edge on every foll alt row until 41(46,49,53,56) sts rem, ending with a p row. ★★
Place a marker at end of last row.
Shape for sleeve
Next row Inc in first st, patt to last 2 sts, k2 tog.
Next row P to last 2 sts, inc in last st.
Rep these 2 rows four times more. 46(51,54,58,61) sts.
Next row Cast on 8 sts, patt to last 2 sts, k2 tog.
Keeping sleeve edge straight, cont to dec 1 st at neck edge on every foll alt row until 45(48,49,50,52) sts rem.
Dec 1 st at neck edge on every foll 4th row until 37(40,42,44,46) sts rem.
Patt 3 rows straight, so ending with a p row.
Cast off.
Return to sts on spare needle.
With RS facing, join on yarn and *for 1st, 2nd and 5th sizes only* k2 tog, then *for all sizes* patt to end. 49(52,55,58,60) sts.
Work as given for first side of neck from ★★ to ★★.
Place a marker at beg of last row.
Shape underarm and neck
Next row K2 tog, patt to last st, inc in last st.
Next row Inc in first st, p to end.
Rep the last 2 rows four times more.
Next row K2 tog, patt to end. 45(50,53,57) sts.
Next row Cast on 8 sts, p to end.
Keeping sleeve edge straight, cont to dec 1 st at neck edge on next and every foll alt row until 45(48,49,50,52) sts rem.
Dec 1 st at neck edge on every foll 4th row until 37(40,42,44,46) sts rem.
Patt 3 rows straight, so ending with a p row.
Cast off.

Back

Work as given for front from ★ to ★.
Change to 4mm needles.
Work in st st until back measures same as front to markers, ending with a p row.
Shape for sleeves
Inc 1 st each end of every row until there are 119(125,130,136,141) sts.

Cast on 8 sts at beg of next 2 rows. 135(141,146,152,157) sts.
Work straight until back measures 16 rows less than front to shoulders, ending with a p row.
Shape neck
Next row K51(54,56,58,60), turn and leave rem sts on a spare needle.
Cast off 2 sts at beg of next and every foll alt row until 37(40,42,44,46) sts rem.
K 1 row and p 1 row.
Cast off.
Return to sts on spare needle.
With RS facing, join on yarn and cast off first 33(33,34,36,37) sts then k to end. 51(54,56,58,60) sts.
P 1 row.
Cast off 2 sts at beg of next and every foll alt row until 37(40,42,44,46) sts rem.
P 1 row.
Cast off.

Neckband

Join right shoulder and upper sleeve seam.
With RS facing and using 3¼mm needles, pick up and k70 sts down left side of front neck, pick up the horizontal bar at base of V and k into back of it, then mark this st with a coloured thread, pick up and k70 sts up right side of front neck, 15 sts down right side of back neck, 32(32,34,36,36) sts across back neck and 15 sts up left side of back neck. 203(203,205,207,207) sts.
Rib row 1 [K1, p1] to within 2 sts of marked st, skpo, p marked st, k2 tog, [p1, k1] to end.
Rib row 2 Rib to within 2 sts of marked st, skpo, k marked st, k2 tog, rib to end.
Rep these 2 rows for 5cm/2in.
Cast off in rib, decreasing 1 st each side of marked st as before.

Sleeve borders

Join neckband, left shoulder and upper sleeve seam.
With RS facing and using 3¼mm needles, pick up and k80(84,88,92,96) sts along sleeve edge.
Work 5cm/2in k1, p1 rib.
Cast off in rib.

To make up

Join side and sleeve seams.

Measurements given in cm for third size

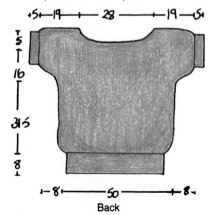

Back

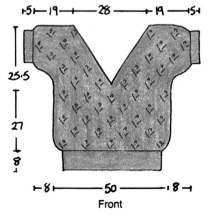

Front

STOCKING STITCH JERSEY WITH RIB-TOPPED POCKETS

*

This classic styled jersey has a deep button opening down the front. The pocket tops, button borders and neck edging are worked in a bold two by two rib.

Materials
12(13,13,14,15)×50g balls of Hayfield
  Grampian
A pair each of 3¾mm/No9 and 4½mm/No7
  knitting needles
4 buttons

Measurements
To fit bust 81(86,91,97,102)cm/
32(34, 36,38,40)in
Actual measurements
Bust 98(102,108,110,116)cm/
38½(40¼, 42½, 43¼, 45¾)in
Length to shoulders 53(54,54,54.5,54.5)cm/
21(21¼, 21¼, 21½, 21½)in
Sleeve seam 47(47,48,48,48)cm/
18½ (18½, 19,19,19)in.

Tension
20 sts and 25 rows to 10cm/4in measured
over st st worked on 4½mm needles

Pocket linings (make 2)
Using 4½mm needles cast on
19(19,21,21,21) sts.
Work 6cm/2½in st st, ending with a p row.
Cut off yarn and leave sts on a holder.

Front
Using 3¾mm needles cast on
92(96,102,104,110) sts.
Work 2.5cm/1in k1, p1 rib.
Change to 4½mm needles.
Continuing in st st, inc 1 st each end of 9th
and every foll 14th row until there are
98(102,108,110,116) sts.
Work straight until front measures 19cm/7½in
from cast-on edge, ending with a p row.
Divide for front opening
Next row K44(46,49,50,53), turn and leave
rem sts on a spare needle.
Work straight until front measures 12cm/4¾in
from base of opening, ending with a p row.
Shape armhole
Cast off 6(6,7,7,8) sts at beg of next row and
3 sts at beg of foll alt row.
P 1 row.
Dec 1 st at armhole edge on next 4 rows, so
ending at armhole edge. 31(33,35,36,38) sts.
Place pocket
Next row K8(9,8,9,11), slip next
19(19,21,21,21) sts on to a holder and in
their place k the sts from one pocket lining,
then k to end. 31(33,35,36,38) sts.
Cont in st st until armhole measures
14(15,15,15.5,15.5)cm/5½(6,6,6¼,6¼)in from
beg of shaping, ending at front edge.
Shape neck
Cast off 5(5,6,6,6) sts at beg of next and
3 sts at beg of foll 2 alt rows.
Dec 1 st at neck edge on every row until
17(19,20,21,23) sts rem.
Dec 1 st at neck edge on every foll alt row
until 14(16,17,18,20) sts rem.
Work straight until armhole measures
22(23,23,23.5,23.5)cm/8¾(9,9,9¼,9¼)in from
beg of shaping, ending with a p row.
Cast off.
Return to sts on spare needle.
With RS facing, join on yarn and cast off first
10 sts, then k to end. 44(46,49,50,53) sts.
Work straight until front measures 12cm/4¾in
from base of opening, ending with a k row.
Shape armhole
Cast off 6(6,7,7,8) sts at beg of next row and
3 sts at beg of foll alt row.
Dec 1 st at armhole edge on next 4 rows, so
ending at armhole edge. 31(33,35,36,38) sts.
Place pocket
Next row K4(5,6,6,6), slip next
19(19,21,21,21) sts on to a holder and in
their place k the sts from 2nd pocket lining,

then k to end. 31(33,35,36,38) sts.
Now complete to match first side of neck.

Back
Using 3¾mm needles cast on
92(96,102,104,110) sts.
Work 2.5cm/1in k1, p1 rib.
Change to 4½mm needles.
Continuing in st st, inc 1 st each end of 9th
and every foll 14th row until there are
98(102,108,110,116) sts.
Work straight until back measures same as
front to beg of armhole shaping, ending with
a p row.
Shape armholes
Cast off 6(6,7,7,8) sts at beg of next 2 rows
and 3 sts at beg of foll 2 rows.
Dec 1 st each end of every row until
72(76,80,82,86) sts rem.
Work straight until back measures same as
front to shoulders, ending with a p row.
Cast off.

Sleeves
Using 3¾mm needles cast on 38(38,38,42,42)
sts.
Work 8cm/3in k1, p1 rib.
Inc row Rib 2(2,2,4,4), * M1, rib 3, rep from *
to last 3(3,3,5,5) sts, M1, rib to end.
50(50,50,54,54) sts.
Change to 4½mm needles.
Continuing in st st, inc 1 st each end of
5th(5th,3rd,5th,5th) and every foll
8th(6th,6th,6th,6th) row until there are
58(60,62,62,64) sts.
Inc 1 st each end of every foll 6th row until
there are 78(80,82,84,84) sts.
Work straight until sleeve measures
47(47,48,48,48)cm/18½(18½,19,19,19)in from
cast-on edge, ending with a p row.
Shape top
Cast off 6(6,7,7,7) sts at beg of next 2 rows
and 3 sts at beg of foll 4 rows.
Dec 1 st each end of next 10 rows.
34(36,36,38,38) sts.
Cast off 4 sts at beg of foll 4 rows.
Cast off.

Button border
With RS facing and using 3¾mm needles,
pick up and k58(62,62,66,66) sts down left
side of front opening.
Rib row 1 P2, * k2, p2, rep from * to end.
Rib row 2 K2, * p2, k2, rep from * to end.
Rep these 2 rows 5 times more, then work
rib row 1 again.
Cast off in rib.

Buttonhole border
With RS facing and using 3¾mm needles,
pick up and k58(62,62,66,66) sts up right
side of front opening.
Work rib rows 1 and 2 twice, then work rib
row 1 again.
Buttonhole row 1 (RS) Rib 12, [cast off 2 sts,
rib 16(18,18,20,20) including st left on needle
after cast off] twice, cast off 2 sts, rib to end.
Buttonhole row 2 Rib to end, casting on 2 sts
over those cast off in previous row.
Rib 6 rows.
Cast off in rib.

Neckband
Join shoulder seams.
With RS facing and using 3¾mm needles,
pick up and k42(42,43,43,43) sts across
buttonhole border and up right front neck,
44(44,44,46,46) sts across back neck and
42(42,43,43,43) sts down left front neck and
across button border.
128(128,132,132,132) sts.
Rep rib rows 1 and 2 twice, then work rib

row 1 again.
Buttonhole row 1 (RS) Rib 5, cast off 2 sts,
rib to end.
Buttonhole row 2 Rib to end, casting on 2 sts
over those cast off in previous row.
Rib 6 rows.
Cast off in rib.

Pocket tops
With RS facing and using 3¾mm, work across
sts from holder as follows: k3(3,2,2,2), [M1,
k6(6,4,4,4) sts] 2(2,4,4,4) times, M1, k to
end. 22(22,26,26,26) sts.
Beg with rib row 2, rep the 2 rib rows for
4cm/1½ in.
Cast off in rib.

To make up
Sew in sleeves, then join side and sleeve
seams. Sew row ends of borders to cast-off
edge at base of opening. Sew pocket linings
and row ends of pocket tops into position.
Sew on buttons.

Measurements given in cm for third size

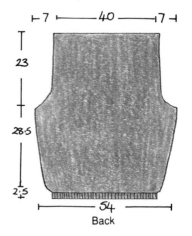

Back

Front

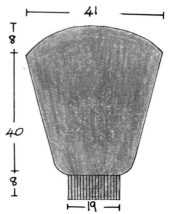

Sleeve

PLAIN AND PATTERNED PANELLED CARDIGAN

***

There
are no
buttons
on this
long line cardigan
but you could work
buttonholes up the
right front border
if you wish to.

Materials
14(15,16) x 50g balls of Jaeger Pure Cotton DK
A pair each of 3¼mm/No10 and 4mm/No8 knitting needles

Measurements
To fit bust 91(97,102)cm/36(38,40)in
Actual measurements
Bust 109(115,123)cm/43(45¼,48½)in
Length to shoulders 67cm/26½in
Sleeve seam 43cm/17in

Tension
Loop st panel (24 sts) measures 10cm/4in worked on 4mm needles
22 sts and 30 rows to 10cm/4in measured over rev st st worked on 4mm needles

Special abbreviation
loop 4 as follows: insert right-hand needle knitwise through front loop of 4th st on left-hand needle and knit in the usual way, leaving st on needle, k first st on left-hand needle and p next 2 sts, then let loop of 4th st drop off needle

Back
Using 3¼mm needles cast on 101(107,113) sts.
Rib row 1 K1, * p1, k1, rep from * to end.
Rib row 2 P1, * k1, p1, rep from * to end.
Rep these 2 rows for 4cm/1½in, ending with rib row 1.
Inc row Rib 8, * M1, rib 3, rep from * to last 9 sts, M1, rib to end. 130(138,146) sts.
Change to 4mm needles.
Work in patt as follows:
Row 1 (RS) P5(6,7), * k24, p8(10,12), rep from * twice more, k24, p5(6,7).
Row 2 K5(6,7), * [loop 4] 6 times, k8(10,12), rep from * twice more, [loop 4] 6 times, k5(6,7).
Row 3 P7(8,9), * k2, [p2, k2] 5 times, p10(12,14), rep from * twice more, k2, [p2, k2] 5 times, p5(6,7).
Row 4 K7(8,9), * p2, [k2, p2] 5 times, k10(12,14), rep from * twice more, p2, [k2, p2] 5 times, k5(6,7).
These 4 rows form the patt.
Cont in patt until back measures 44cm/17¼in from cast-on edge, ending with a WS row.
Shape armholes
Cast off 13(14,15) sts at beg of next 2 rows. 104(110,116) sts.
Cont in patt until back measures 67cm/26½in from cast-on edge, ending with a WS row.
Shape shoulders
Cast off 36(38,40) sts at beg of next 2 rows.
Cast off rem 32(34,36) sts.

Pocket linings (make 2)
Using 4mm needles cast on 24(26,28) sts.
Work 14cm/5½in st st, ending with a p row.
Cut off yarn and leave sts on a holder.

Left front
Using 3¼mm needles cast on 51(55,59) sts.
Work 4cm/1½in rib as given for back, ending with rib row 1.
Inc row Rib 4(2,2), * M1, rib 4(5,6), rep from * to last 3 sts, M1, rib to end. 63(66,69) sts.
Change to 4mm needles.
Work in patt as follows:
Row 1 P5(6,7), k24, p8(10,12), k24, p2.
Row 2 K2, [loop 4] 6 times, k8(10,12), [loop 4] 6 times, k5(6,7).
Row 3 P7(8,9), k2, [p2, k2] 5 times, p10(12,14), k2, [p2, k2] 5 times, p2.
Row 4 K4, p2, [k2, p2] 5 times, k10(12,14), p2, [k2, p2] 5 times, k5(6,7).

These 4 rows form the patt.
Cont in patt until front measures 19cm/7½in from cast-on edge, ending with a WS row.
Place pocket
Next row Patt 25(26,27), slip next 24(26,28) sts on to a holder and in their place patt across sts of first pocket lining, then patt to end.
Cont in patt until front measures 44cm/17¼in from cast-on edge, ending with a WS row.
Shape armhole
Cast off 13(14,15) sts at beg of next row.
Shape neck edge
Dec 1 st at beg of next and every foll 4th row until 36(38,40) sts rem.
Work straight until front measures same as back to shoulder, ending with a WS row.
Cast off.

Right front
Using 3¼mm needles cast on 51(55,59) sts.
Work 4cm/1½in rib as given for back, ending with rib row 1.
Inc row Rib 4(2,2), * M1, rib 4(5,6), rep from * to last 3 sts, M1, rib to end. 63(66,69) sts.
Change to 4mm needles.
Work in patt as follows:
Row 1 P2, k24, p8(10,12), k24, p5(6,7).
Row 2 K5(6,7), [loop 4] 6 times, k8(10,12), [loop 4] 6 times, k2.
Row 3 P4, k2, [p2, k2] 5 times, p10(12,14), k2, [p2, k2] 5 times, p5(6,7).
Row 4 K7(8,9), p2, [k2, p2] 5 times, k10(12,14), p2, [k2, p2] 5 times, k2.
These 4 rows form the patt.
Cont in patt until front measures 19cm/7½in from cast-on edge, ending with a WS row.
Place pocket
Next row Patt 14, slip next 24(26,28) sts on to a holder and in their place patt across sts of 2nd pocket lining, then patt to end.
Cont in patt until front measures 44cm/17¼in from cast-on edge, ending with a RS row.
Shape armhole
Cast off 13(14,15) sts at beg of next row.
Shape neck edge
Dec 1 st at beg of next and every foll 4th row until 36(38,40) sts rem.
Work straight until front measures same as back to shoulder, ending with a WS row.
Cast off.

Sleeves
Using 3¼mm needles cast on 47(51,55) sts.
Work 4cm/1½in rib as given for back, ending

with rib row 1.
Inc row Rib 4(2,4), * M1, rib 5(6,6), rep from * to last 3(1,3) sts, M1, rib to end. 56(60,64) sts.
Change to 4mm needles.
Work in patt as follows:
Row 1 K8, p8(10,12), k24, p8(10,12), k8.
Row 2 [Loop 4] twice, k8(10,12), [loop 4] 6 times, k8(10,12), [loop 4] twice.
Row 3 [P2, k2] twice, p10(12,14), k2, [p2, k2] 5 times, p10(12,14), k2, p2, k2.
Row 4 [K2, p2] twice, k10(12,14), p2, [k2, p2] 5 times, k10(12,14), p2, k2, p2.
These 4 rows form the patt.
Continuing in patt, inc and work into patt 1 st each end of next and every foll 4th row until there are 104(112,120) sts.
Work straight until sleeve measures 48.5(49,49.5)cm/19(19¼,19½)in from cast-on edge, ending with a WS row.
Cast off.

Neck border
Join shoulder seams.
With RS facing, using 3¼mm needles and beginning at centre back neck, pick up and k15(17,19) sts to shoulder, 51 sts down front neck shaping and 99 sts down left front to lower edge. 165(167,169) sts.
Work 3cm/1¼in rib as given for back.
Cast off in rib.
With RS facing and using 3¼mm needles, pick up and k99 sts up right front to beg of shaping, 51 sts to shoulder and 15(17,19) sts to centre back neck. 165(167,169) sts.
Work 3cm/1¼in rib as given for back.
Cast off in rib.

Pocket tops
With RS facing, slip 24(26,28) sts from holder on to a 3¼mm needle.
Join on yarn, then increasing 1 st at centre of first row, work 3cm/1¼in rib as given for back.
Cast off in rib.

To make up
Sew down row ends of pocket tops and slipstitch pocket linings into place. Fold sleeves in half lengthwise, then placing folds to shoulder seams, sew into place joining row ends at tops of sleeves to cast-off sts at armholes. Join side and sleeve seams.

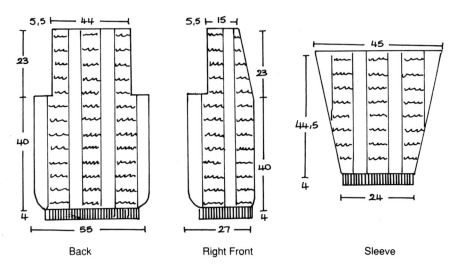

Back   Right Front   Sleeve

Measurements given in cm for first size

BOLDLY STRIPED CARDIGAN IN A FINE ALPACA YARN

*

A luxury 4 ply
rn has been used
to knit this
classic cardigan.

Materials

5(5,6,7) x 25g balls of Jaeger Alpaca (4 ply) in main colour A

4(4,5,6) balls of same in contrast colour B

A pair each of 2¾mm/No12 and 3¾mm/No9 knitting needles

5 buttons

Measurements

To fit bust 86(91,97,102)cm/34(36,38,40)in

Actual measurements

Bust 101(106,112,117)cm/39¾(41¾,44,46)in

Length to shoulders 63cm/24¾in

Sleeve seam 46cm/18in

Tension

26 sts and 36 rows to 10cm/4in measured over st st worked on 3¾mm needles

Back

Using 2¾mm needles and B, cast on 112(118,126,132) sts.

Work 8cm/3in k1, p1 rib, ending with a RS row.

Inc row Rib 8(2,6,9), * M1, rib 5(6,6,6), rep from * to last 9(2,6,9) sts, M1, rib 9(2,6,9). 132(138,146,152) sts.

Cut off B.

Change to 3¾mm needles.

Joining on and cutting off colours as required, work in st st striped of 32 rows A and 14 rows B until back measures 60cm/23½in from cast-on edge, ending with a p row.

Shape neck

Next row K51(53,55,57), turn and leave rem sts on a spare needle.

Keeping stripe patt correct, dec 1 st at neck edge on next 6 rows. 45(47,49,51) sts.

Patt 3 rows.

Cast off.

Return to sts on spare needle.

With RS facing, slip first 30(32,36,38) sts on to a holder, join on yarn and k to end.

Dec 1 st at neck edge on next 6 rows.

Patt 3 rows.

Cast off.

Left front

Using 2¾mm needles and B, cast on 56(58,62,66) sts

Work 8cm/3in k1, p1 rib, ending with a RS row.

Inc row Rib 6(4,6,6), * M1, rib 5(5,5,6), rep from * to last 5(4,6,6) sts, M1, rib 5(4,6,6) 66(69,73,76) sts.

Change to 3¾mm needles.

Work in striped patt as given for back until front measures 56cm/22in from cast-on edge, ending with a k row. (For right front end with a p row.)

Shape neck

Cast off 8(9,10,11) sts at beg of next row and 4(5,6,7) sts at beg of foll alt row.

Dec 1 st at neck edge on every foll alt row until 45(47,49,51) sts rem.

Work straight until front measures same as back to shoulder, ending with a p row.

Cast off.

Right front

Work as given for left front, noting the exception given in brackets.

Sleeves

Using 2¾mm needles and B, cast on 48(50,52,54) sts.

Work 5cm/2in k1, p1 rib, ending with a RS row.

Inc row Rib 5(4,3,2), * M1, rib 2, rep from * to last 5(4,3,2) sts, M1, rib 5(4,3,2). 68(72,76,80) sts.

Change to 3¾mm needles.

Working in striped patt as given for back, inc 1 st each end of every 5th row until there are 118(122,126,130) sts.

Work straight until sleeve measures 46cm/18in from cast-on edge, ending with a p row.

Cast off.

Neckband

Join shoulder seams.

With RS facing, using 2¾mm needles and B, pick up and k45 sts up right side of front neck and 10 sts down right side of back neck, k30(32,36,38) sts from back neck holder, then pick up and k10 sts up left side of back neck and 45 sts down left side of front neck. 140(142,146,148) sts.

Work 12 rows k1, p1 rib.

Cast off in rib.

Buttonhole border

With RS facing, using 2¾mm needles and B, pick up and k174 sts evenly up right front.

Work 5 rows k1, p1 rib.

Buttonhole row 1 Rib 7, * cast off 2 sts, rib next 37 sts, rep from * 3 times more, cast off 2 sts, rib to end.

Buttonhole row 2 Rib to end, casting on 2 sts over those cast off in previous row.

Rib 5 rows.

Cast off in rib.

Button border

Work to match buttonhole border omitting buttonholes.

To make up

Fold sleeves in half lengthwise, then placing folds to shoulder seams, sew into place. Join side and sleeve seams. Sew on buttons.

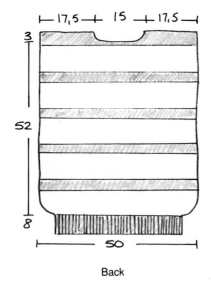

Back

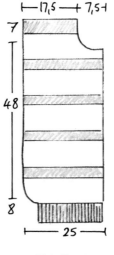

Right Front

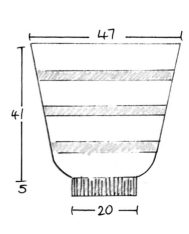

Sleeve

Measurements given in cm for second size

RICHLY COLOURED FAIR ISLE JERSEY

***

A selection of
rich autumn
colours
has been
used to
knit this jersey.
A lighter, pastel
selection would
give a completely
different look.

Materials
4(5,5)×50g balls of Wendy Family Choice DK in main colour A
1(2,2) balls of same in contrast colour D
1(1,2) balls of same in each of contrast colours B and C
A pair each of 3¼mm/No10 and 4mm/No8 knitting needles

Measurements
To fit bust 86(91,96)cm/34(36,38)in
Actual measurements
Bust 100(106,111)cm/39½(41¾, 43¾)in
Length to shoulders 54(55,57)cm/21¼(21¾, 22½)in
Sleeve seam 45(46,47)cm/17¾(18,18½)in

Tension
22 sts and 26 rows to 10cm/4in measured over patt worked on 4mm needles

Back
Using 3¼mm needles and A, cast on 100(106,112) sts.
Work 6cm/2¼in k1, p1 rib, ending with a RS row.
Inc row Rib 9(3,2), * M1, rib 9(11,12), rep from * to last 10(4,2) sts, M1, rib to end. 110(116,122) sts.
Change to 4mm needles.
Beg with a k row, work 8(12,16) rows st st.
Join on and cut off colours as required and carry yarn not in use loosely across WS of work.
Reading odd numbered (k) rows from right to left and even numbered (p) rows from left to right, work from chart as follows:
Row 1 (RS) *For 2nd size only* k2D, *for 3rd size only* k3A, 2D, then *for all sizes* k4(5,5)A, * 2D, 9A, 2D, 5A, rep from * to last 16(19,4) sts, k2D, 9(9,2)A, *for 1st and 2nd sizes only* k2D, 3(5)A, then *for 2nd size only* k1D.
Row 2 *For 2nd and 3rd sizes only* [p1A, 1D, 1A] 1(2) times, then *for all sizes* [p2A, 1D] twice, * 7A, 1D, 2A, 1D, 3A, 1D, 2A, 1D, rep from * to last 14(17,2) sts, p7(7,2)A, then *for 1st size only* p1D, 2A, 1D, 3A, and *for 2nd size only* p1D, 2A, 1D, 3A, 1D, 2A.
Beg with row 3, cont in patt from chart until row 58 has been completed.
Shape armholes
Cast off 12(13,14) sts at beg of next 2 rows. 86(90,94) sts.
Cont in patt from chart until row 116 has been completed.
Shape shoulders
Using A, cast off 24(26,28) sts at beg of next 2 rows.
Cut off yarn and leave rem 38 sts on a holder.

Front
Work as given for back until row 98 has been completed.
Shape neck
Next row Patt 24(26,28), turn and leave rem sts on a spare needle.
Work straight until row 116 has been completed
Cast off.
Return to sts on spare needle.
With RS facing, slip the first 38 sts on to a holder, join on yarn and k to end. 24(26,28) sts.
Now complete to match first side of neck.

Sleeves
Using 3¼mm needles and A, cast on 40 sts.
Work 6cm/2¼in k1, p1 rib, ending with a RS row.
Inc row Rib 3, * M1, rib 2, rep from * to last 3 sts, M1, rib to end. 58 sts.
Change to 4mm needles.
Beg with a k row, work 2(4,6) rows st st.
Next row Inc in first st, k to last st, inc in last st. 60 sts.
Beg with a p row, work 3 rows st st.
Beg with row 1, work from chart as follows:
Row 1 Inc in first st, k7A, [2D, 5A, 2D, 9A] twice, k2D, 5A, 2D, 6A, inc in last st. 62 sts.
Row 2 P7A, [1D, 2A, 1D, 3A, 1D, 2A, 1D, 7A] 3 times, p1D.
Beginning with row 3 and continuing in patt from chart, inc 1 st each end of row 5 and every foll 4th row until there are 108 sts.
Work straight until row 110 has been completed.
Cast off.

Neckband
Join right shoulder seam.
With RS facing, using 3¼mm needles and A, pick up and k18 sts down left side of front neck, k38 sts from front neck holder, pick up and k18 sts up right side of front neck, then k38 sts from back neck holder. 112 sts.
Work 6cm/2¼in k1, p1 rib.
Cast off in rib.

To make up
Join left shoulder and neckband seam.
Fold sleeves in half lengthwise, then placing folds to shoulder seams, sew into place. Join side and sleeve seams.

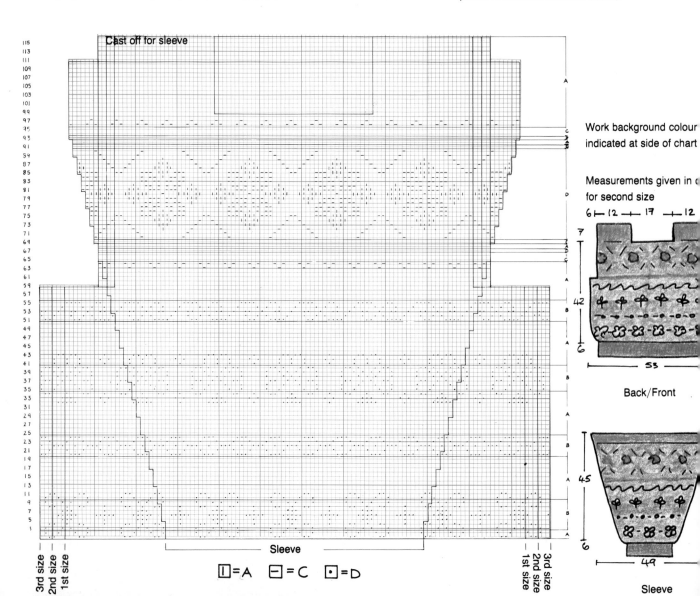

Work background colour as indicated at side of chart

Measurements given in cm for second size

Back/Front

Sleeve

Sleeve

☐=A ⊟ = C ☐·= D

TWIST STITCH CARDIGAN

**

Columns of
alternating twist
stitches form the
all-over pattern
on this slim-line
cardigan.

Materials
11(12,13)×50g balls of Emu Superwash Chunky
A pair each of 4½mm/No7 and 5½mm/No5 knitting needles
5 buttons

Measurements
To fit bust 81-86(91-97,102-107)cm/ 32-34(36-38,40-42)in
Actual measurements
Bust 98(108,117)cm/38½(42½,46)in
Length to shoulders 64cm/25¼in
Sleeve seam 43cm/17in

Tension
21 sts and 21 rows to 10cm/4in measured over patt worked on 5½mm needles

Special abbreviation
Tw2R Twist 2 right as follows: k into front of 2nd st on left-hand needle, then k first st, dropping both sts off needle tog

Left front
Using 4½mm needles cast on 42(46,50) sts.
Rib row 1 *K1, p1, rep from * to last 2 sts, k2.
Rib row 2 * K1, p1, rep from * to end.
Rep these 2 rows for 5cm/2in, ending with rib row 1.
Inc row Rib 6 and slip these 6 sts on to a safety-pin, then rib 4(5,6), * M1, rib 2, rep from * to last 4(5,6) sts, M1, rib to end. 51(56,61) sts.
Change to 5½mm needles.
Work in patt as follows:
Row 1 (RS) * P2, Tw2R, p2, k4, rep from * to last 1(6,1) sts, p1(2,1), then *for 2nd size only* Tw2R, p2.
Row 2 For 2nd size only k2, p2, then *for all sizes* k1(2,1), * p4, k2, p2, k2, rep from * to end.
Rows 3 to 8 Rep rows 1 and 2 three times.
Row 9 P1, * k4, p2, Tw2R, p2, rep from * to last 10(5,10) sts, k4, p2(1,2), then *for 1st and 3rd sizes only* Tw2R, p2.
Row 10 For 1st and 3rd sizes only k2, p2, then *for all sizes* k2(1,2), p4, * k2, p2, k2, p4, rep from * to last st, k1.
Rows 11 to 16 Rep rows 9 and 10 three times.
These 16 rows form the patt.
Cont in patt until front measures 22cm/8¾in from cast-on edge, ending with a WS row.
Shape front edge
Dec 1 st at end of next and every foll 4th row until 40(45,50) sts rem.
Patt 1 row, so ending with a WS row.
Shape armhole
Cast off 3 sts at beg of next row.
Patt 1 row.
★ Continuing to dec 1 st at front edge on next and every foll 4th row, dec 1 st at armhole edge on next 7 rows.
Keeping armhole edge straight, cont decreasing at front edge as before until 21(26,31) sts rem. ★
Work straight until armhole measures 22cm/8¾in from beg of shaping, ending

with a WS row.
Shape shoulder
Cast off 11(13,16) sts at beg of next row.
Patt 1 row.
Cast off rem 10(13,15) sts.

Right front
Using 4½mm needles cast on 42(46,50) sts.
Rib row 1 K2, * p1, k1, rep from * to end.
Rib row 2 * P1, k1, rep from * to end.
Buttonhole row Rib 2, p2 tog, yrn, rib to end. Cont in rib as set for 5cm/2in, ending with rib row 1.
Inc row Rib 4(5,6), * M1, rib 2, rep from * to last 10(11,12) sts, M1, rib 4(5,6), turn and leave rem 6 sts on a safety-pin. 51(56,61) sts.
Change to 5½mm needles.
Work in patt as follows:
Row 1 (RS) For 2nd size only p2, Tw2R, then *for all sizes* p1(2,1), * k4, p2, Tw2R, p2, rep from * to end.
Row 2 * K2, p2, k2, p4, rep from * to last 1(6,1) sts, k1(2,1), then *for 2nd size only* p2, k2.
Rows 3 to 8 Rep rows 1 and 2 three times.
Row 9 For 1st and 3rd sizes only p2, Tw2R, then *for all sizes* p2(1,2), k4, * p2, Tw2R, p2, k4, rep from * to last st, p1.
Row 10 K1, * p4, k2, p2, k2, rep from * to last 10(5,10) sts, p4, k2(1,2), then *for 1st and 3rd sizes only* p2, k2.
Rows 11 to 16 Rep rows 9 and 10 three times.
These 16 rows form the patt.
Cont in patt until front measures 22cm/8¾in from cast-on edge, ending with a WS row.
Shape front edge
Dec 1 st at beg of next and every foll 4th row until 40(45,50) sts rem.
Patt 2 rows, so ending with a RS row.
Shape armhole
Cast off 3 sts at beg of next row.
Work as given for left front from ★ to ★.
Work straight until armhole measures 22cm/8¾in from beg of shaping, ending with a RS row.
Shape shoulder
Cast off 11(13,16) sts at beg of next row.
Patt 1 row.
Cast off rem 10(13,15) sts.

Back
Using 4½mm needles cast on 69(77,83) sts.
Rib row 1 K1, * p1, k1, rep from * to end.
Rib row 2 P1, * k1, p1, rep from * to end.
Rep these 2 rows for 5cm/2in, ending with rib row 1.
Inc row Rib 2(3,1), * M1, rib 2, M1, rib 3, rep from * to last 2(4,2) sts, M1, rib to end. 96(106,116) sts.
Change to 5½mm needles.
Work in patt as follows:
Row 1 (RS) P1, k4, * p2, Tw2R, p2, k4, rep from * to last st, p1.
Row 2 K1, p4, * k2, p2, k2, p4, rep from * to last st, k1.
Rows 3 to 8 Rep rows 1 and 2 three times.
Row 9 P2, Tw2R, p2, * k4, p2, Tw2R, p2,

rep from * to end.
Row 10 K2, p2, k2, * p4, k2, p2, k2, rep from * to end.
Rows 11 to 16 Rep rows 9 and 10 three times.
These 16 rows form the patt.
Cont in patt until back measures same as left front to beg of armhole shaping, ending with same patt row.
Shape armholes
Cast off 3 sts at beg of next 2 rows.
Dec 1 st each end of foll 7 rows.
76(86,96) sts.
Work straight until back measures same as left front to beg of shoulder shaping, ending with same patt row.
Shape shoulders
Cast off 11(13,16) sts at beg of next 2 rows and 10(13,15) sts at beg of foll 2 rows.
34 sts.
Cast off rem sts.

Sleeves
Join shoulder seams.
With RS facing and using 5½mm needles, pick up and k96 sts evenly round armhole edge.
P 1 row.
Beginning with row 1, work 8 rows patt as given for back.
Keeping patt correct, dec 1 st each end of next and every foll 4th row until 62 sts rem.
Patt 7 rows.
Dec row * K2 tog, rep from * to end.
31 sts.
Change to 4½mm needles.
Beg with rib row 2, work 5cm/2in rib as given for back.
Cast off in rib.

Button border
With RS facing and using 4½mm needles, join on yarn and work across 6 sts from safety-pin on left front as follows: inc in first st, rib to end. 7 sts.
Work in rib as set until border, slightly stretched, fits up front and round to centre back neck.
Cast off in rib.
Sew on the button border.
Mark 5 button positions on this border, the first 1.5cm/½in below beg of front shaping, the last to match buttonhole already made on right front welt and the others spaced evenly between.

Buttonhole border
With WS facing and using 4½mm needles, join on yarn and work across 6 sts from safety-pin on right front as follows: inc in first st, rib to last st. 7 sts.
Work as given for button border, making buttonholes to correspond with markers as follows:
Buttonhole row (RS) Rib 2, p2 tog, yrn, rib 3.

To make up
Sew on buttonhole border, joining seam at centre back neck. Join side and sleeve seams. Sew on buttons.

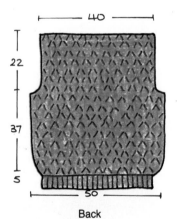

Back

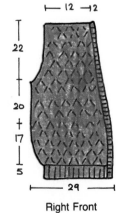

Right Front

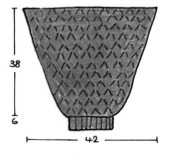

Sleeve

Measurements given in cm for second size

LOOSE FITTING FAN AND CABLE COTTON TOP

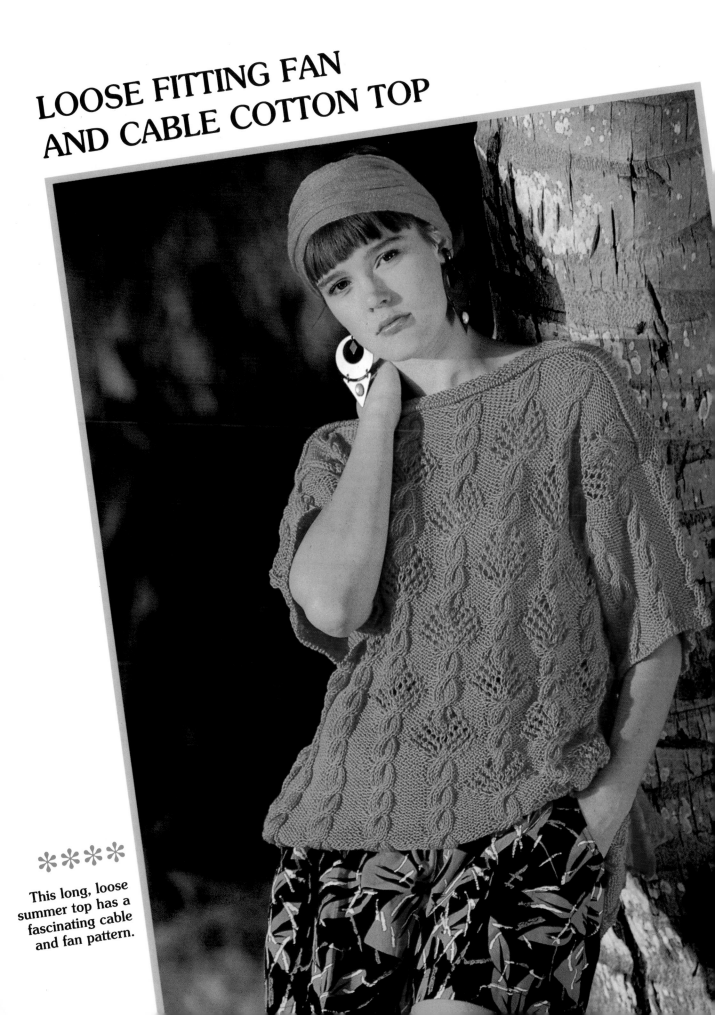

✳✳✳✳

This long, loose summer top has a fascinating cable and fan pattern.

Materials
15×50g balls of Mayflower Helarsgarn
A pair each of 3¼mm/No10 and 4mm/No8 knitting needles
Cable needle

Measurements
To fit bust 86–91cm/34–36in
Actual measurements
Bust 106cm/41¾in
Length to shoulders 73.5cm/29in
Sleeve seam 17cm/6¾in

Tension
24 sts and 25 rows to 10cm/4in measured over patt worked on 4mm needles

Special abbreviation
C7 Cable 7 as follows: slip next 4 sts on to cable needle and leave at back of work, k3, then k4 from cable needle

Back and front (alike)
Using 3¼mm needles cast on 121 sts.
Rib row 1 K1, * p1, k1, rep from * to end.
Rib row 2 P1, * k1, p1, rep from * to end.
Rep rib row 1 once more.
Inc row Rib 19, * M1, rib 14, rep from * to last 18 sts, M1, rib to end. 128 sts.
Change to 4mm needles.
Cont in cable patt as follows:
Row 1 (RS) P8, * k7, p8, rep from * to end.
Row 2 K8, * p7, k8, rep from * to end.
Row 3 P8, * C7, p8, rep from * to end.
Row 4 As row 2.
Rows 5 to 8 Rep rows 1 and 2 twice.
These 8 rows form the cable patt.
Rows 9 to 16 As rows 1 to 8.
Rows 17 to 20 As rows 1 to 4.
Cont in fan and cable patt as follows:
Row 21 P6, k3 tog, yf, k1, yf, skpo, [yf, k1] twice, yf, k3 tog tbl, p6, [k7, p8] 7 times.
Row 22 [K8, p7] 7 times, k6, p11, k6.
Row 23 P5, ytb, [skpo, yf] 3 times, k1 tbl, [yf, k2 tog] 3 times, p5, [k7, p8] 7 times.
Row 24 [K8, p7] 7 times, k5, p13, k5.
Row 25 P3, k3 tog, [yf, skpo] twice, yf, k1 tbl, yf, k1, yf, k1 tbl, [yf, k2 tog] twice, yf, k3 tog tbl, p3, [k7, p8] 7 times.
Row 26 [K8, p7] 7 times, k3, p17, k3.
Row 27 P4, ytb, [skpo, yf] 3 times, k1 tbl, k1, k1 tbl, [yf, k2 tog] 3 times, p4, [C7, p8] 7 times.
Row 28 [K8, p7] 7 times, k4, p15, k4.
Row 29 P5, ytb, [skpo, yf] twice, k1 tbl, k3, k1 tbl, [yf, k2 tog] twice, p5, [k7, p8] 7 times.
Row 30 As row 24.
Row 31 P6, ytb, skpo, yf, k1 tbl, k5, k1 tbl, yf, k2 tog, p6, [k7, p8] 7 times.
Row 32 As row 22.
Rows 33 to 36 As rows 1 to 4.
The last 16 rows (rows 21 to 36) set the position for the first fan.
Row 37 P8, k7, p6, k3 tog, yf, k1, yf, skpo, [yf, k1] twice, yf, k3 tog tbl, p6, [k7, p8] 6 times.
Row 38 [K8, p7] 6 times, k6, p11, k6, p7, k8.
Row 39 P8, k7, p5, ytb, [skpo, yf] 3 times, k1 tbl, [yf, k2 tog] 3 times, p5, [k7, p8] 6 times.
Row 40 [K8, p7] 6 times, k5, p13, k5, p7, k8.

Row 41 P8, k7, p3, k3 tog, yf, [skpo, yf] twice, k1 tbl, yf, k1, yf, k1 tbl, [yf, k2 tog] twice, yf, k3 tog tbl, p3, [k7, p8] 6 times.
Row 42 [K8, p7] 6 times, k3, p17, k3, p7, k8.
Row 43 P8, C7, p4, ytb, [skpo, yf] 3 times, k1 tbl, k1, k1 tbl, [yf, k2 tog] 3 times, p4, [C7, p8] 6 times.
Row 44 [K8, p7] 6 times, k4, p15, k4, p7, k8.
Row 45 P8, k7, p5, ytb, [skpo, yf] twice, k1 tbl, k3, k1 tbl, [yf, k2 tog] twice, p5, [k7, p8] 6 times.
Row 46 As row 40.
Row 47 P8, k7, p6, ytb, skpo, yf, k1 tbl, k5, k1 tbl, yf, k2 tog, p6, [k7, p8] 6 times.
Row 48 As row 38.
Rows 49 to 52 As rows 1 to 4.
The last 16 rows (rows 37 to 52) set the position for the second fan.
Row 53 * P6, k3 tog, yf, k1, yf, skpo, [yf, k1] twice, yf, k3 tog tbl, p6, k7 *, rep from * to * once more, p8, [k7, p8] 4 times.
Row 54 [K8, p7] 4 times, k8, [p7, k6, p11, k6] twice.
Row 55 * P5, ytb, [skpo, yf] 3 times, k1 tbl, [yf, k2 tog] 3 times, p5, k7 *, rep from * to * once more, p8, [k7, p8] 4 times.
Row 56 [K8, p7] 4 times, k8, [p7, k5, p13, k5] twice.
Row 57 * P3, k3 tog, [yf, skpo] twice, yf, k1 tbl, yf, k1, yf, k1 tbl, [yf, k2 tog] twice, yf, k3 tog tbl, p3, k7 *, rep from * to * once more, p8, [k7, p8] 4 times.
Row 58 [K8, p7] 4 times, k8, [p7, k3, p17, k3] twice.
Row 59 * P4, ytb, [skpo, yf] 3 times, k1 tbl, k1, k1 tbl, [yf, k2 tog] 3 times, p4, C7 *, rep from * to * once more, p8, [C7, p8] 4 times.
Row 60 [K8, p7] 4 times, k8, [p7, k4, p15, k4] twice.

Row 61 * P5, ytb, [skpo, yf] twice, k1 tbl, k3, k1 tbl, [yf, k2 tog] twice, p5, k7 *, rep from * to * once more, p8, [k7, p8] 4 times.
Row 62 [K8, p7] 4 times, k8, [p7, k5, p13, k5] twice.
Row 63 * P6, ytb, skpo, yf, k1 tbl, k5, k1 tbl, yf, k2 tog, p6, k7 *, rep from * to * once more, p8, [k7, p8] 4 times.
Row 64 [K8, p7] 4 times, k8, [p7, k6, p11, k6] twice.
Rows 65 to 68 As rows 1 to 4.
The last 16 rows (rows 53 to 68) set the position for the 3rd row of fans.
Cont in patt in this way, working 1 more fan at the left on every foll 16 rows until the 15th row on the 2nd band of four fans has been worked as follows:
Next row K6, p11, k6, p7, rep from * to last 8 sts, k8.
Keeping patt correct, work a further 16 rows, so completing the 3rd band of four fans.
Now working in cable patt only, rep row 1 to 12.
Change to 3¼mm needles.
Beg with a k row, work 7 rows in st st.
Next row * Pick up loop of next st 5 rows below and place on left-hand needle, p this loop tog with next st on left-hand needle, rep from * to end.
K 12 rows.
Cast off.

Sleeves
Using 4mm needles cast on 99 sts.
Rib row 1 K1, * p1, k1, rep from * to end.
Rib row 2 P1, * k1, p1, rep from * to end.
Rep rib row 1 once more.
Inc row Rib 15, * M1, rib 14, rep from * to end. 105 sts.
Cont in cable patt as follows:
Row 1 (RS) P4, k7, * p8, k7, rep from * to last 4 sts, p4.
Row 2 K4, p7, * k8, p7, rep from * to last 4 sts, k4.
Row 3 P4, C7, * p8, C7, rep from * to last 4 sts, p4.
Row 4 As row 2.
Rows 5 to 8 Rep rows 1 and 2 twice more.
These 8 rows form the patt.
Rep these 8 rows 4 times more.
Cast off.

To make up
Join shoulder seams for 15cm/6in. Fold sleeves in half lengthwise, then placing folds to shoulder seams, sew into place. Join side and sleeve seams.

Measurements given in cm

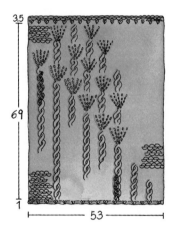

3.5

69

1

53

Back/Front

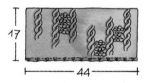

17

44

Sleeve

CARDIGAN WITH A FAIR ISLE YOKE

✳✳✳

The Fair Isle yoke is worked in one piece after the fronts and back have been knitted.

Materials

9(10,11)×50g balls of Patons Beehive Soft Blend Chunky in main colour A
1 ball of same in each of contrast colours B and E
1(1,2) balls of same in contrast colour C
1 ball of Patons Fashion Mohair in contrast colour D
A pair each of 5mm/No6, 6mm/No4 and 6½mm/No3 knitting needles
8 buttons

Measurements

To fit bust 81-86(91-97,102-107)cm/ 32-34(36-38,40-42)in
Actual measurements
Bust 94.5(104.5,115)cm/37¼(41,45¼)in
Length to shoulders 60cm/23½in
Sleeve seam 44(44,45)cm/17¼(17¼,17¾)in

Tension

15 sts and 20 rows to 10cm/4in measured over st st worked on 6mm needles

Back

Using 5mm needles and A, cast on 63(71,79)sts.
Rib row 1 K1, * p1, k1, rep from * to end.
Rib row 2 P1, * k1, p1, rep from * to end.
Rep these 2 rows for 6cm/2½in, ending with rib row 1.
Inc row Rib 7(7,8), * M1, rib 7(8,9), rep from * to last 7(8,8) sts, M1, rib to end. 71(79,87) sts.
Change to 6½mm needles.
Join on and cut off colours as required.
Carrying yarns in use loosely across WS of work and weaving them in when passing across more than 5 sts, work in patt as follows:
Row 1 (RS) With A, k to end.
Row 2 With A, p to end.
Row 3 With B, k to end.
Row 4 With C, p to end.
Row 5 K1D, * 1C, 1D, rep from * to end.
Row 6 P1D, * 1C, 1D, rep from * to end.
Row 7 With D, k to end.
Row 8 With A, p to end.
Row 9 With D, k to end.
Row 10 P1D, * 1A, 1D, rep from * to end.
Row 11 K1D, * 1A, 1D, rep from * to end.
Row 12 P1A, * 1B, 3A, rep from * to last 2 sts, 1B, 1A.
Row 13 K1A, 1C, 1A, * 1E, 1A, 1C, 1A, rep from * to end.
Row 14 P1A, * 1C, 3A, rep from * to last 2 sts, 1C, 1A.
Row 15 K3C, *1A, 3C, rep from * to end.
Change to 6mm needles.
Using A only and beginning with a p row, work in st st until back measures 44cm/17¼in from cast-on edge, ending with a p row.
Shape armholes
Cast off 3(4,5) sts at beg of next 2 rows. 65(71,77) sts.
Dec 1 st each end of next and foll 2 alt rows, ending with a p row. 59(65,71) sts.
Cut off yarn and leave rem sts on a holder.

Left front

Using 5mm needles and A, cast on 31(35,39) sts.
Rib row 1 K1, * p1, k1, rep from * to end.
Rib row 2 P1, * k1, p1, rep from * to end.
Rep these 2 rows for 6cm/2½in, ending with rib row 1.
Inc row Rib 5(5,6), * M1, rib 7(8,9), rep from * to last 5(6,6) sts, M1, rib to end. 35(39,43) sts.
Change to 6½mm needles.
Work in patt as follows:
Row 1 (RS) With A, k to end.
Row 2 With A, p to end.
Row 3 With B, k to end.
Row 4 With C, p to end.
Row 5 K1D, * 1C, 1D, rep from * to end.
Row 6 P1D, * 1C, 1D, rep from * to end.
Row 7 With D, k to end.
Row 8 With A, p to end.
Row 9 With D, k to end.
Row 10 P1D, * 1A, 1D, rep from * to end.
Row 11 K1D, * 1A, 1D, rep from * to end.
Row 12 P1A, * 1B, 3A, rep from * to last 2 sts,

1B, 1A.
Row 13 K1A, 1C, 1A, * 1E, 1A, 1C, 1A, rep from * to end.
Row 14 P1A, * 1C, 3A, rep from * to last 2 sts, 1C, 1A.
Row 15 K3C, * 1A, 3C, rep from * to end.
Change to 6mm needles.
Using A only and beginning with a p row, work in st st until left front measures same as back to beg of armhole shaping, ending with a p row.
Shape armhole
Cast off 3(4,5) sts at beg of next row. 32(35,38) sts.
Dec 1 st at armhole edge on foll 3 alt rows, ending with a p row. 29(32,35) sts.
Cut off yarn and leave rem sts on a holder.

Right front

Work as given for left front to beg of armhole shaping, ending with a k row.
Shape armhole
Cast off 3(4,5) sts at beg of next row. 32(35,38) sts.
Dec 1 st at armhole edge on next and foll 2 alt rows, ending with a p row. 29(32,35) sts.
Cut off yarn and leave rem sts on a holder.

Sleeves

Using 5mm needles and A, cast on 30(32,34) sts.
Work 6cm/2½in k1, p1 rib.
Inc row Rib 3(2,5), * M1, rib 2, rep from * to last 3(2,5) sts, M1, rib to end. 43(47,47) sts.
Change to 6½mm needles.
Work in patt as follows:
Row 1 (RS) With A, k to end.
Row 2 With A, p to end.
Row 3 With B, inc in first st, k to last st, inc in last st. 45(49,49) sts.
Row 4 With C, p to end.
Row 5 K1C, * 1D, 1C, rep from * to end.
Row 6 P1C, * 1D, 1C, rep from * to end.
Row 7 With D, k to end.
Row 8 With A, p to end.
Row 9 With D, k to end.
Row 10 P1A, * 1D, 1A, rep from * to end.
Row 11 K1A, * 1D, 1A, rep from * to end.
Row 12 P2A, * 1B, 3A, rep from * to last 3 sts, 1B, 2A.
Row 13 With A inc in first st, k1A, 1C, 1A, * k1E, 1A, 1C, 1A, rep from * to last st, with A inc in last st. 47(51,51) sts.
Row 14 P3A, * 1C, 3A, rep from * to end.
Row 15 K2A, * 3C, 1A, rep from * to last 5 sts, 3C, 2A.
Change to 6mm needles.
Using A only, beginning with a p row and working in st st, inc 1 st each end of 10th and every foll 10th(14th,10th) row until there are 57(59,61) sts.
Work straight until sleeve measures 44(44,45)cm/17¼(17¼,17¾)in from cast-on edge, ending with a p row.
Shape top
Cast off 3(4,5) sts at beg of next 2 rows. 51 sts.
Dec 1 st each end of next and foll 2 alt rows, ending with a p row. 45 sts.
Cut off yarn and leave rem sts on a holder.

Yoke

With RS facing, using 6½mm needles and A, k29(32,35) sts from right front holder, work across the 45 sts from right sleeve holder as follows: inc in first st, k44, k59(65,71) sts from back holder, work across the 45 sts from left sleeve holder as follows: k44, inc in last st, then k29(32,35) sts from left front holder. 209(221,233) sts.
Next row P to end.
Work in patt as follows:
Row 1 (RS) K1B, * 3C, 1B, rep from * to end.
Row 2 P2B, * 1C, 3B, rep from * to last 3 sts, 1C, 2B.
Row 3 K2A, * 1C, 3A, rep from * to last 3 sts, 1C, 2A.
Row 4 With A, p to end.
Row 5 With C, k to end.
Row 6 With D, p to end.
Row 7 With E, k to end.
Row 8 With D, p to end.
Row 9 With A, k to end.
Row 10 With B, p to end.

Row 11 (Dec row) With A, k12(6,12), * k2 tog, k6(7,7), rep from * to last 13(8,14) sts, k2 tog, k to end. 185(197,209) sts.
Row 12 P1A, * 1D, 1A, rep from * to end.
Row 13 K1A, * 1D, 1A, rep from * to end.
Row 14 (Dec row) With D, p11(3,9), * p2 tog, p4(5,5), rep from * to last 12(5,11) sts, p2 tog, p to end. 157(169,181) sts.
Row 15 K1D, * 3A, 1D, rep from * to end.
Row 16 With C, p to end.
Row 17 (Dec row) With C, k9(3,9), * k2 tog, k4, rep from * to last 10(4,10) sts, k2 tog, k to end. 133(141,153) sts.
Row 18 P1C, * 3A, 1C, rep from * to end.
Row 19 K1E, * 3A, 1E, rep from * to end.
Row 20 (Dec row) With E, k12(8,14), * p2 tog, p2, rep from * to last 13(9,15) sts, p2 tog, p to end. 105(109,121) sts.
Row 21 K1D, * 3C, 1D, rep from * to end.
Row 22 With D, p to end.
Row 23 K1C, * 3D, 1C, rep from * to end.
Row 24 (Dec row) With C, p8(4,1), * p2 tog, p1, rep from * to last 10(6,3) sts, p2 tog, p to end. 75(75,81) sts.
Row 25 K4C, * 1A, 5C, rep from * to last 5 sts, 1A, 4C.
Row 26 P3C, * 1A, 1B, 1A, 3C, rep from * to end.
Row 27 K1A, * 1C, 5A, rep from * to last 2 sts, 1C, 1A.
Row 28 P1A, * 1D, 5A, rep from * to last 2 sts, 1D, 1A.
Row 29 K3D, * 3A, 3D, rep from * to end.
Row 30 P3D, * 3A, 3D, rep from * to end.
Row 31 As row 29.
Row 32 As row 28.
Change to 5mm needles.
Next row With A, k to end
Using A only and beginning with rib row 2 work 4cm/1½in rib as given for back.
Cast off in rib.

Button border

Using 5mm needles and A, cast on 13 sts.
Rib row 1 (RS) K1, * p1, k1, rep from * to end
Rib row 2 P1, * k1, p1, rep from * to end.
Rep these 2 rows until border, slightly stretched, fits up front to top of neckband.
Cast off in rib.
Sew on border.
Mark 8 button positions on this border, the first 1.5cm/¾in from cast-on edge, the last 1.5cm/¾in from cast-off edge and the others evenly spaced between.

Buttonhole border

Work as given for button border, making buttonholes to correspond with markers as follows:
Buttonhole row 1 (RS) Rib 5, cast off 2 sts, rib to end.
Buttonhole row 2 Rib to end, casting on 2 sts over those cast off in previous row.

To make up

Join raglan seams. Join side and sleeve seams. Sew on buttonhole border. Sew on buttons.

Measurements given in cm for second size

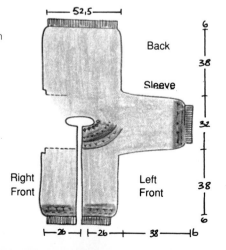

JERSEY USING CHURCH WINDOW STITCH

✳✳✳

This lace and cable pattern has an unusual cable twist which gives the stitch the appearance of arched windows.

Materials
6×50g balls of Scheepjeswol Voluma
A pair each of 4½mm/No7 and 6mm/No4 knitting needles
Cable needle

Measurements
To fit bust 86–91cm/34–36in
Actual measurements
Bust 118cm/46½in
Length to shoulders 62cm/24½in
Sleeve seam 42cm/16½in

Tension
17 sts and 24 rows to 10cm/4in measured over patt worked on 6mm needles

Special abbreviations
C6 Cable 6 as follows: slip next 3 sts on to cable needle and leave at front of work, yon, k next 2 sts tog, k1, slip 3 sts from cable needle back on to left-hand needle, then skpo, k1, yrn
C4F Cable 4 front as follows: slip next 2 sts on to cable needle and leave at front of work, k2, then k2 from cable needle

Back and front (alike)
Using 4½mm needles cast on 81 sts.
Rib row 1 (RS) K1, * p1, k1, rep from * to end.
Rib row 2 P1, * k1, p1, rep from * to end.
Rep these 2 rows for 6cm/2¼in, ending with a RS row.
Inc row Rib 3, * M1, rib 4, rep from * to last 2 sts, M1, rib 2. 101 sts.
Change to 6mm needles.
Work in patt as follows:
Row 1 K1, * yf, k1, skpo, p6, k2, rep from * to last st, k1.
Row 2 K1, * p2, k6, p2, k1, rep from * to last st, k1.
Row 3 K1, * p1, yon, k1, skpo, p4, k2 tog, k1, yrn, rep from * to last 12 sts, p1, yon, k1, skpo, p4, k2 tog, k1, yon, k1.
Row 4 K2, * p2, k4, p2, k3, rep from * to last 11 sts, p2, k4, p2, k3.
Row 5 K1, p2, * yon, k1, skpo, p2, k2 tog, k1, yrn, p3, rep from * to last 10 sts, yon, k1, skpo, p2, k2 tog, k1, yrn, p1, k1.
Row 6 K3, * p2, k2, p2, k5, rep from * to last 10 sts, p2, k2, p2, k4.
Row 7 K1, p3, * C6, p5, rep from * to last 9 sts, C6, p2, k1.
Row 8 K4, * p4, k7, rep from * to last 9 sts, p4, k5.
Row 9 K1, p4, * C4F, p7, rep from * to last 8 sts, C4F, p3, k1.
Row 10 As row 8.
Row 11 K2, * yf, skpo, p1, k4, p1, k2 tog, yf, k1, rep from * to end.
Row 12 K4, * p4, k3, p1, k3, rep from * to last 9 sts, p4, k3, p1, k1.
Row 13 K1, skpo, yrn, p2, * k4, p2, yon, slip 1, k2 tog, psso, yrn, p2, rep from * to last 8 sts, k4, p3, k1.
Row 14 As row 12.
Row 15 K1, p4, * k4, p2, k2 tog, yrn, p3, rep from * to last 8 sts, k4, p3, k1.
Row 16 As row 8.

Row 17 K1, p4, * k4, p7, rep from * to last 8 sts, k4, p3, k1.
Row 18 As row 8.
Row 19 K1, p3, * k2 tog, k1, yf, k2, p6, rep from * to last 9 sts, k2 tog, k1, yf, k2, p3, k1.
Row 20 K4, p2, k1, p2, * k6, p2, k1, p2, rep from * to last 4 sts, k4.
Row 21 K1, p2, * k2 tog, k1, yrn, p1, yon, k1, skpo, p4, rep from * to last 10 sts, k2 tog, k1, yrn, p1, yon, k1, skpo, p2, k1.
Row 22 K3, * p2, k3, p2, k4, rep from * ending last rep k3 instead of k4.
Row 23 K1, p1, * k2 tog, k1, yrn, p3, yon, k1, skpo, p2, rep from * ending last rep p1, k1 instead of p2.
Row 24 K2, * p2, k5, p2, k2, rep from * to end.
Row 25 K1, k2 tog, k1, yrn, * p5, C6, rep from * to last 9 sts, p5, yon, k1, skpo, k1.
Row 26 K1, p2, * k7, p4, rep from * to last 10 sts, k7, p2, k1.
Row 27 K3, * p7, C4F, rep from * to last 10 sts, p7, k3.
Row 28 As row 26.
Row 29 K3, * p1, k2 tog, yf, k1, yf, skpo, p1, k4, rep from * ending last rep k3 instead of k4.
Row 30 K1, p2, * k3, p1, k3, p4, rep from * ending last rep p2, k1 instead of p4.
Row 31 K3, * p2, yon, sl 1, k2 tog, psso, yrn, p2, k4, rep from * ending last rep k3 instead of k4.
Row 32 As row 30.
Row 33 K3, * p2, k2 tog, yrn, p3, k4, rep from * ending last rep k3 instead of k4.
Row 34 K1, p2, * k7, p4, rep from * to last 10 sts, k7, p2, k1.
Row 35 K3, * p7, k4, rep from * to last 10 sts, p7, k3.
Row 36 As row 34.
Rows 1 to 36 form the patt.
Rows 37 to 94 Rep rows 1 to 36 once more, then rows 1 to 22 again.
Keeping patt correct, beg rib V inset as follows:
Row 95 Patt 50, k1, patt 50.
Row 96 Patt 49, k1, p1, k1, patt 49.
Row 97 Patt 49, p1, k1, p1, patt 49.
Row 98 Patt 48, [p1, k1] twice, p1, patt 48.
Row 99 Patt 47, [p1, k1] 3 times, p1, patt 47.
Row 100 Patt 47, [k1, p1] 3 times, k1, patt 47.
Row 101 Patt 46, [k1, p1] 4 times, k1, patt 46.
Row 102 Patt 45, [k1, p1] 5 times, k1, patt 45.
Row 103 Patt 45, [p1, k1] 5 times, p1, patt 45.
Row 104 Patt 44, [p1, k1] 6 times, p1, patt 44.
Row 105 Patt 43, [p1, k1] 7 times, p1, patt 43.
Cont in this way, taking 1 st into rib inset on each side of every 2nd and 3rd row until there are 51 sts in rib.
Work 2 rows straight.
Cast off in patt.

Sleeves
Using 4½mm needles cast on 34 sts.
Work 6cm/2¼in k1, p1 rib ending with a RS row.
Inc row Inc in every st. 68 sts.
Change to 6mm needles.
Work in patt as given for back and front, increasing and working into patt 1 st each end of 13th and every foll 6th row until there are 88 sts.
Work straight until sleeve measures 42cm/16½in from cast-on edge, ending with a WS row.
Cast off.

To make up
Join shoulder seams, leaving rib V inset open for neck. Fold sleeves in half lengthwise, then placing folds to shoulder seams, sew in place. Join side and sleeve seams.

Measurements given in cm

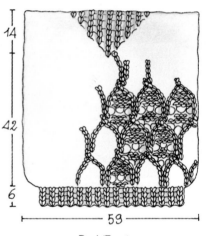

Back/Front

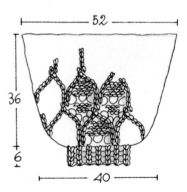

Sleeve

CHURCH WINDOW PATTERN

skpo

Slip the next stitch from the left-hand needle on to right-hand needle, knit 1, then pass slipped stitch over.

C6, a six stitch cable

1 Slip the next 3 sts on to a cable needle and leave at front of work, take yarn over needle to make a stitch and knit the next 2 sts tog, then k1.

2 Slip the stitches from the cable needle back on to the left-hand needle, slip 1, knit 1, pass slipped stitch over, then knit 1 and wind yarn round needle to make a stitch.

The pattern

Cast on a multiple of 11 sts plus 2 edge sts.
Row 1 K1 edge st, * yf, k1, skpo, p6, k2, rep from * to last st, k1 edge st.
Row 2 K1 edge st, * p2, k6, p2, k1, rep from * to last st, k1 edge st.
Row 3 K1, * p1, yon, k1, skpo, p4, k2 tog, k1, yrn, rep from * to last 12 sts, p1, yon, k1, skpo, p4, k2 tog, k1, yon, k1.
Row 4 K1 edge st, k1, * p2, k4, p2, k3, rep from * to last 11 sts, p2, k4, p2, k2, k1 edge st.
Row 5 K1, p2, * yon, k1, skpo, p2, k2 tog, k1, yrn, p3, rep from * to last 10 sts, yon, k1, skpo, p2, k2 tog, k1, yrn, p1, k1.
Row 6 K3, * p2, k2, p2, k5, rep from * to last 10 sts, p2, k2, p2, k4.
Row 7 K1, p3, * C6, p5, rep from * to last 9 sts, C6, p2, k1.
Row 8 K4, * p4, k7, rep from * to last 9 sts, p4, k5.
Row 9 K1, p4, * C4F, p7, rep from * to last 8 sts, C4F, p3, k1.
Row 10 As row 8.
Row 11 K2, * yf, skpo, p1, k4, p1, k2 tog, yf, k1, rep from * to end.
Row 12 K4, * p4, k3, p1, k3, rep from * to last 9 sts, p4, k3, p1, k1.
Row 13 K1, skpo, yrn, p2, * k4, p2, yon, slip 1, k2 tog, psso, yrn, p2, rep from * to last 8 sts, k4, p3, k1.
Row 14 As row 12.
Row 15 K1, p4, * k4, p2, k2 tog, yrn, p3, rep from * to last 8 sts, k4, p3, k1.
Row 16 As row 8.
Row 17 K1, p4, * k4, p7, rep from * to last 8 sts, k4, p3, k1.
Row 18 As row 8.
Row 19 K1, p3, * k2 tog, k1, yf, k2, p6, rep from * to last 9 sts, k2 tog, k1, yf, k2, p3, k1.
Row 20 K4, p2, k1, p2, * k6, p2, k1, p2, rep from * to last 4 sts, k4.
Row 21 K1, p2, * k2 tog, k1, yrn, p1, yon, k1, skpo, p4, rep from * to last 10 sts, k2 tog, k1, yrn, p1, yon, k1, skpo, p2, k1.
Row 22 K3, * p2, k3, p2, k4, rep from * ending last rep k3 instead of k4.
Row 23 K1, p1, * k2 tog, k1, yrn, p3, yon, k1, skpo, p2, rep from * ending last rep p1, k1

instead of p2.
Row 24 K2, * p2, k5, p2, k2, rep from * to end.
Row 25 K1, k2 tog, k1, yrn, * p5, C6, rep from * to last 9 sts, p5, yon, k1, skpo, k1.
Row 26 K1, p2, * k7, p4, rep from * to last 10 sts, k7, p2, k1.
Row 27 K3, * p7, C4F, rep from * to last 10 sts, p7, k3.
Row 28 As row 26.
Row 29 K3, * p1, k2 tog, yf, k1, yf, skpo, p1, k4, rep from * ending last rep k3 instead of k4.
Row 30 K1, p2, * k3, p1, k3, p4, rep from * ending last rep p2, k1 instead of p4.
Row 31 K3, * p2, yon, sl 1, k2 tog, psso, yrn, p2, k4, rep from * ending last rep k3 instead of k4.
Row 32 As row 30.
Row 33 K3, * p2, k2 tog, yrn, p3, k4, rep from * ending last rep k3 instead of k4.
Row 34 K1, p2, * k7, p4, rep from * to last 10 sts, k7, p2, k1.
Row 35 K3, * p7, k4, rep from * to last 10 sts, p7, k3.
Row 36 As row 34.
Rep rows 1 to 36 to form patt.

C4F, a four stitch cable

Slip next 2 sts from left-hand needle on to cable needle and leave at front of work, knit 2, then knit 2 from cable needle.

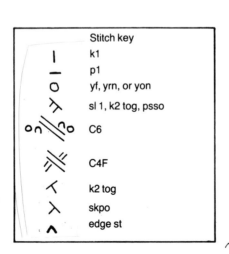

	Stitch key
$\vert$	k1
—	p1
o	yf, yrn, or yon
⅄	sl 1, k2 tog, psso
ᵒⁿ⫽⫽ᵒⁿ	C6
⫽⫽	C4F
⼊	k2 tog
⼞	skpo
⌃	edge st

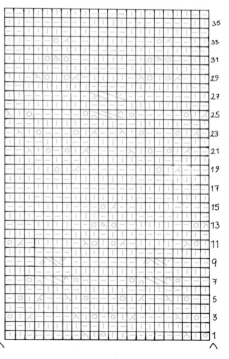

MEN'S PATTERNS

CABLE JERSEY IN A FINE YARN

✳✳
This cabled jersey has an unusual raglan detail. Knitted in 4-ply wool, it makes a garment which is warm without being bulky.

Materials

9(12)×50g balls of Patons Diploma Gold 4 ply
A pair each of 2¾mm/No12 and 3¾mm/No9 knitting needles

Measurements

To fit chest 91(107)cm/36(42)in
Actual measurements
Chest 100(126)cm/39½(49½)in
Length to shoulders 64(70)cm/25¼(27½)in
Sleeve seam 50cm/19¾in

Tension

30 sts and 32 rows to 10cm/4in measured over cable patt, slightly opened out, worked on 3¾mm needles

Special abbreviations

C6B Cable 6 as follows: slip next 3 sts on to cable needle and leave at back of work, k3, then k3 from cable needle.

Note

Two sizes are given for this jersey. The smaller size is suitable for a teenager.

Back

Using 2¾mm needles cast on 150(190) sts.
Rib row 1 K2, * p2, k2, rep from * to end.
Rib row 2 P2, * k2, p2, rep from * to end.
Rep these 2 rows for 9cm/3½in, ending with rib row 2.
Change to 3¾mm needles.
Work in cable and rib patt as follows:
Row 1 P4, * k2, p6, k6, p6, rep from * to last 6 sts, k2, p4.
Row 2 K4, * p2, k6, p6, k6, rep from * to last 6 sts, p2, k4.
Row 3 P4, * k2, p6, C6B, p6, rep from * to last 6 sts, k2, p4.
Row 4 As row 2.
Rows 5 to 10 Rep rows 1 and 2 three times.
These 10 rows form the patt.
Cont in patt until back measures 39cm/15½in from cast-on edge, ending with a WS row.
Now work in rib patt as follows:
Row 1 P4, * k2, p6, k6, p6, rep from * to last 6 sts, k2, p4.
Row 2 K4, * p2, k6, p6, k6, rep from * to last 6 sts, p2, k4.
Rep these two rows until back measures 42cm/16½in from cast-on edge, ending with a WS row.
Shape raglans
Next row P4, skpo, patt to last 6 sts, k2 tog, p4.
Next row K4, p2 tog, patt to last 6 sts, p2 tog tbl, k4.
Rep these 2 rows until 86 sts rem.
Next row P4, skpo, patt to last 6 sts, k2 tog, p4.
Next row K4, p1, patt to last 5 sts, p1, k4.
Rep these two rows until 48 sts rem, ending with a WS row.
Cut off yarn and leave sts on a holder.

Front

Work as given for back until 110 sts rem when shaping raglans.
Divide for neck
Next row P4, skpo, patt 49, turn and leave rem sts on spare needle.
Next row Cast on 3 sts, k3, patt to last 6 sts, p2 tog tbl, k4.

Next row P4, skpo, patt to last 3 sts, p1, k2.
Next row K3, patt to last 6 sts, p2 tog tbl, k4.
Rep the last 2 rows until 45 sts rem.
Keeping neck border and patt correct, cont dec at raglan edge on every foll alt row until 34 sts rem, ending at armhole edge.
Next row P4, skpo, patt to last 12 sts, turn and leave rem sts on a safety-pin.
Continuing to shape raglan edge as before, dec 1 st at neck edge on every row until 2 sts rem, decreasing in the rev st st border when only 5 sts rem.
Work 1 row.
Cast off.
Return to sts on spare needle.
With RS facing, join on yarn and cast on 3 sts, k2, p1, patt to last 6 sts, k2 tog, p4.
Next row K4, p2 tog, patt to last 3 sts, k3.
Next row K2, p1, patt to last 6 sts, k2 tog, p4.
Rep these 2 rows until 45 sts rem.
Keeping neck border and patt correct, cont dec at raglan edge on every foll alt row until 34 sts rem, ending at raglan edge.
Next row K4, p1, patt to last 12 sts, turn and leave rem sts on a safety-pin.
Continuing to shape raglan edge as before,

dec 1 st at neck edge on every row until 2 sts rem, decreasing on the rev st st border when only 5 sts rem.
Work 1 row.
Cast off.

Sleeve

Using 2¾mm needles cast on 70 sts.
Rib row 1 (RS) K2, * p2, k2, rep from * to end.
Rib row 2 P2, * k2, p2, rep from * to end.
Rep these 2 rows for 7cm/3in, ending with a RS row.
Inc row P2, M1, k2, M1, rib to last 4 sts, M1, k2, M1, p2. 74 sts.
Change to 3¾mm needles.
Work in cable and rib patt as follows:
Row 1 P6, * k2, p6, k6, p6, rep from * to last 8 sts, k2, p6.
Row 2 K6, * p2, k6, p6, k6, rep from * to last 8 sts, p2, k6.
Row 3 P6, * k2, p6, C6B, p6, rep from * to last 8 sts, k2, p6.
Row 4 As row 2.
This establishes the cable and rib patt.
Continuing in patt, inc and work into patt 1 st at each end of next and every foll 6th(3rd) row until there are 116(156) sts, ending with a WS row.
Next row K1, p6, * k2, p6, k6, p6, rep from * to last 9 sts, k2, p6, k1.
Next row P1, k6, * p2, k6, p6, k6, rep from * to last 9 sts, p2, k6, p1.
Rep these 2 rows once more, increasing 1 st at each end of 2nd row. 118(158) sts.
Work in rib patt as follows:
Row 1 K2, p6, * k2, p6, k6, p6, rep from * to last 10 sts, k2, p6, k2.
Row 2 P2, k6, * p2, k6, p6, k6, rep from * to last 10 sts, p2, k6, p2.
Rep these 2 rows 3 times more.
Shape raglans
Next row P4, skpo, patt to last 6 sts, k2 tog, p4.
Next row K4, p2 tog, patt to last 6 sts, p2 tog tbl, k4.
Rep these 2 rows until 54 sts rem.
Next row P4, skpo, patt to last 6 sts, k2 tog, p4.
Next row K4, p1, patt to last 5 sts, p1, k4.
Rep these two rows until 16 sts rem, ending with a WS row.
Cut off yarn and leave sts on a holder.

Collar

Join raglan seams.
With RS facing and using 2¾mm needles, k across 12 sts from safety-pin at right front neck, pick up and k19 sts up right front neck, k16 sts from top of right sleeve, 48 sts from back neck holder and 16 sts from top of left sleeve, pick up and k19 sts down left side of neck, then k across 12 sts from safety-pin. 142 sts.
Rib row 1 K2, * p2, k2, rep from * to end.
Rib row 2 P2, * k2, p2, rep from * to end.
Rep these 2 rows for 9cm/3½in, ending with a WS row.
Cast off loosely in rib.

To make up

Join side and sleeve seams. Overlapping left over right sew cast-on edges of neck borders neatly into place.

Measurements given in cm for smaller size

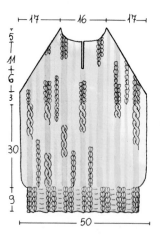

Front

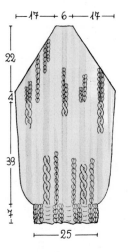

Sleeve

SUMMER JERSEY WITH BUTTONED NECK OPENING

***

This casual
round-necked
jersey with a
buttoned
opening, knitted
in a cool cotton
yarn will be a
summer
favourite

Materials
14×50g balls of Pingouin Fil D'ecosse No4
A pair each of 4mm/No8 and 4½mm/No7 knitting needles
Cable needle   2 buttons

Measurements
Chest 91–102cm/36–40in
Actual measurements
Chest 112cm/44in
Length to shoulders 66cm/26in
Sleeve seam 50cm/19½in

Tension
18 sts and 23 rows to 10cm/4in measured over moss st worked on 4½mm needles

Special abbreviations
Tw2L Twist 2 left as follows: knit into back of second st on left-hand needle, then knit into front of first st, letting both sts drop off left-hand needle together.
Cr3BK Cross 3 back knitwise as follows: slip next st on to a cable needle and leave at back of work, k2, then k1 from cable needle
Cr3FK Cross 3 front knitwise as follows: slip next 2 sts on to a cable needle and leave at front of work, k1, then k2 from cable needle
Cr3FP Cross 3 front purlwise as follows: slip next 2 sts on to a cable needle and leave at front of work, p1, then k2 from cable needle
Cr3BP Cross 3 back purlwise as follows: slip next st on to a cable needle and leave at back of work, k2, then p1 from cable needle
C4F Cable 4 front as follows: slip next 2 sts on to cable needle and leave at front of work, k2, then k2 from cable needle
C6F Cable 6 front as follows: slip next 3 sts on to cable needle and leave at front of work, k3, then k3 from cable needle
C6B Cable 6 back as follows: work as C6F but leaving sts at back of work.

Back
★ Using 4mm needles cast on 104 sts.
Work 5cm/2in k1, p1 rib.
Inc row Rib 6, * M1, rib 7, rep from * to end. 118 sts. ★
Change to 4½mm needles.
Work in patt as follows:
Row 1 K1, [p1, k1] 7 times for moss st (moss), p1, k1, p2, k6, p2, k1, p1 for left cable, k1, [p1, k1] 7 times for Irish moss st (Irish), [p2, k2] twice for twisted braids, p5, k4, p5 for centre panel, [k2, p2] twice for twisted braids, k1, [p1, k1] 7 times for Irish, p1, k1, p2, k6, p2, k1, p1 for right cable, k1, [p1, k1] 7 times for moss.
Row 2 K1, [p1, k1] 7 times (moss), k1, p1, k2, p6, k2, p1, k1 (right cable), p1, [k1, p1] 7 times (Irish), [k2, p2] twice (braid), k5, p4, k5 (panel), [p2, k2] twice (braid), p1, [k1, p1] 7 times (Irish), k1, p1, k2, p6, k2, p1, k1 (left cable), k1, [p1, k1] 7 times (moss).
Rows 1 and 2 form the moss st patt over 15 sts; cont as follows:
Row 3 Moss 15, p1, k1, p2, k6, p2, k1, p1 (left cable), p1, [k1, p1] 7 times (Irish), [p2, Tw2L] twice (braid), p4, Cr3BK, Cr3FP, p4 (panel), [Tw2L, p2] twice (braid), p1, [k1, p1] 7 times (Irish), k1, p1, k2, p6, k2, p1, k1 (right cable), moss 15.
Row 4 Moss 15, k1, p1, k2, p6, k2, p1, k1 (right cable), k1, [p1, k1] 7 times (Irish), [k2, p2] twice (braid), k4, p3, k1, p2, k4, (panel), [p2, k2] twice (braid), k1, [p1, k1] 7 times (Irish), k1, p1, k2, p6, k2, p1, k1 (left cable), moss 15.
Rows 1 to 4 form the Irish moss patt over 15 sts and the twisted braid over 8 sts; cont as follows:
Row 5 Moss 15, p1, k1, p2, C6B, p2, k1, p1 (left cable), Irish 15, braid 8, p3, Cr3BP, k1,

p1, Cr3FK, p3 (panel), braid 8, Irish 15, p1, k1, p2, C6F, p2, k1, p1 (right cable), moss 15.
Row 6 Moss 15, k1, p1, k2, p6, k2, p1, k1 (right cable), Irish 15, braid 8, k3, p2, k1, p1, k1, p3, k3 (panel), braid 8, Irish 15, k1, p1, k2, p6, k2, p1, k1 (right cable), moss 15.
Rows 1 to 6 form the cable panels over 14 sts; cont as follows:
Row 7 Moss 15, cable 14, Irish 15, braid 8, p2, Cr3BK, [p1, k1] twice, Cr3FP, p2 (panel), braid 8, Irish 15, cable 14, moss 15.
Row 8 Moss 15, cable 14, Irish 15, braid 8, k2, p3, [k1, p1] twice, k1, p2, k2 (panel), braid 8, Irish 15, cable 14, moss 15.
Row 9 Moss 15, cable 14, Irish 15, braid 8, p1, Cr3BP, [k1, p1] 3 times, Cr3FK, p1 (panel), braid 8, Irish 15, cable 14, moss 15.
Row 10 Moss 15, cable 14, Irish 15, braid 8, k1, p2, [k1, p1] 3 times, k1, p3, k1 (panel), braid 8, Irish 15, cable 14, moss 15.
Row 11 Moss 15, cable 14, Irish 15, braid 8, Cr3BK, [p1, k1] 4 times, Cr3FP (panel), braid 8, Irish 15, cable 14, moss 15.
Row 12 Moss 15, cable 14, Irish 15, braid 8, p3, [k1, p1] 4 times, k1, p2 (panel), braid 8, Irish 15, cable 14, moss 15.
Row 13 Moss 15, cable 14, Irish 15, braid 8, Cr3FP, [p1, k1] 4 times, Cr3BP (panel), braid 8, Irish 15, cable 14, moss 15.
Row 14 As row 10.
Row 15 Moss 15, cable 14, Irish 15, braid 8, p1, Cr3FP, [k1, p1] 3 times, Cr3BP, p1 (panel), braid 8, Irish 15, cable 14, moss 15.
Row 16 As row 8.
Row 17 Moss 15, cable 14, Irish 15, braid 8, p2, Cr3FP, [p1, k1] twice, Cr3BP, p2 (panel), braid 8, Irish 15, cable 14, moss 15.
Row 18 As row 6.
Row 19 Moss 15, cable 14, Irish 15, braid 8, p3, Cr3FP, k1, p1, Cr3BP, p3 (panel), braid 8, Irish 15, cable 14, moss 15.
Row 20 As row 4.
Row 21 Moss 15, cable 14, Irish 15, braid 8, p4, Cr3FP, Cr3BP, p4 (panel), braid 8, Irish 15, cable 14, moss 15.
Row 22 As row 2.
Row 23 Moss 15, cable 14, Irish 15, braid 8, p5, C4F, p5 (panel), braid 8, Irish 15, cable 14, moss 15.
Row 24 Moss 15, cable 14, Irish 15, braid 8, k5, p4, k5 (panel), braid 8, Irish 15, cable 14, moss 15.
These 24 rows form the patt. Cont in patt until back measures 66cm/26in from cast-on edge, ending with a WS row.
Shape shoulders
Cast off 37 sts at beg of next 2 rows. Cut off yarn and leave rem 44 sts on a holder.

Front
Work as given for back from ★ to ★.
Beg with row 13, work in patt as given for back until front measures approx 48cm/19in from cast-on edge, ending with row 24 of patt.
Divide for neck opening
Patt 56, [p1, k1] 3 times for rib border, turn and leave rem sts on spare needle. 62 sts. Keeping 6 st rib border and patt correct, work 4 rows.
Buttonhole row P1, k1, yf, k2 tog, p1, k1, patt to end.
Keeping rib border and patt correct, work until left front measures 58cm/22¾in from cast-on edge, ending at side edge.
Shape neck
Next row Patt 50, turn and leave rem sts on a spare needle.
Keeping patt correct, cast off 2 sts at neck edge at beg of next and every foll alt row until there are 40 sts, then dec 1 st at neck edge on foll 3 alt rows. 37 sts.
Work straight until left front measures same as back to shoulder, ending with a WS row.

Cast off. Return to sts on spare needle. With RS facing, join on yarn and cast on 6 sts, [k1, p1] 3 times over these 6 sts, then patt to end.
Now complete to match left side of neck, omitting buttonholes.

Left sleeve
Using 4mm needles cast on 42 sts.
Work 6cm/2½in k1, p1 rib.
Inc row Rib 1, M1, rib 1, * M1, rib 2, rep from * to last 2 sts [M1, rib 1] twice. 64 sts.
Change to 4½mm needles.
Work in patt as follows:
Row 1 K1, [p1, k1] 12 times for Irish, p1, k1, p2, k6, p2, k1, p1 for cable, k1, [p1, k1] 12 times for Irish.
Row 2 P1, [k1, p1] 12 times (Irish), k1, p1, k2, p6, k2, p1, k1 (cable), p1, [k1, p1] 12 times (Irish).
Measurements given in cm

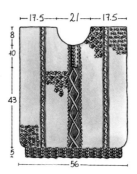

Back/Front   Sleeve

Row 3 P1, [k1, p1] 12 times (Irish), p1, k1, p2, k6, p2, k1, p1 (cable), p1, [k1, p1] 12 times (Irish).
Row 4 K1, [p1, k1] 12 times (Irish), k1, p1, k2, p6, k2, p1, k1 (cable), k1, [p1, k1] 12 times (Irish).
Row 5 K1, [p1, k1] 12 times (Irish), p1, k1, p2, C6B, p2, k1, p1 (cable) k1, [p1, k1] 12 times (Irish).
Row 6 As row 2.
These 6 rows establish the patt.
Cont in patt, increasing and working into Irish moss 1 st each end of next and every foll 6th row until there are 96 sts.
Work straight until sleeve measures 50cm/19½in from cast-on edge, ending with a WS row. Cast off.

Right sleeve
Work as given for left sleeve, working C6F instead of C6B.

Neckband
Join shoulder seams.
With RS facing and using 4mm needles, rib across 12 sts from right front holder, pick up and k15 sts up right side of neck, increasing 1 st at centre k across sts from back neck holder, pick up and k15 sts down left side of neck, then rib across 12 sts from left front holder. 99 sts.
Rib row 1 P1, * k1, p1, rep from * to end.
Rib row 2 K1, * p1, k1, rep from * to end.
Buttonhole row P1, k1, yf, k2 tog, p1, k1, rib to end.
Work 3 more rows in rib. Cast off in rib.

To make up
Fold sleeves in half lengthwise, then placing folds to shoulder seams, sew into place. Join side and sleeve seams. Overlapping buttonhole band over button band, slipstitch row ends of borders into place. Sew on buttons to correspond with buttonholes.

ZIG ZAG PATTERN COTTON SUMMER JERSEY

***

This attractive
summer
jersey is an
introduction
to simple Fair
Isle knitting
from a chart.

Materials

10(11,12)×50g balls of Pingouin Corrida 4 in main colour A
2 balls of same in contrast colour B
1 ball of same in contrast colour C
A pair each of 4mm/No8 and 5mm/No6 knitting needles

Measurements

To fit chest 91(102,112)cm/36(40,44)in
Actual measurements
Chest 102(112,124)cm/40(44,49)in
Length to shoulders 69cm/27in
Sleeve seam 47cm/18½in

Tension

21 sts and 23 rows to 10cm/4in measured over jacquard patt worked on 5mm needles

Back

Using 4mm needles and A, cast on 87(99,111) sts.
Rib row 1 K1, * p1, k1, rep from * to end.
Rib row 2 P1, * k1, p1, rep from * to end.
Rep these 2 rows for 4cm/1½in, ending with rib row 1.
Inc row Rib 6(12,18), * M1, rib 4, rep from * to last 5(11, 17) sts, M1, rib 5(11,17). 107(119,131) sts.
Change to 5mm needles.
Join on and cut off colours as required and carry yarns not in use loosely across wrong side of work.
Begin all rows by reading chart from right to left, then knit centre st once, and complete the row by reading chart from left to right. Working odd numbered rows as knit rows and even numbered rows as purl rows, work in patt from chart as follows:
Rows 1 to 12 Work 12 rows st st.
Row 13 K 2A, * 1B, 5A, rep from * to last 3 sts, 1B, 2A.
Row 14 P 1A, * 3B, 3A, rep from * to last 4 sts, 3B, 1A.
Beg at row 15 of chart, cont in patt until row 152 has been completed.
Shape shoulders
Cast off 31(37, 43) sts at beg of next 2 rows.
Cut off yarn and leave rem sts on a holder.

Front

Work as given for back until row 132 has been completed.
Shape neck
Next row K40(46, 52), turn and leave rem sts on a holder.
Next row Patt to end.
Next row Patt to last 4 sts, k2 tog, k2A.
Next row P2A, patt to end.
Rep in last 2 rows until 31(37, 43) sts rem.
Patt 1 row. Cast off.
Return to sts on spare needle.

With RS facing, slip first 27 sts on to a holder, join on yarn and patt to end. Work 1 row.
Next row K2A, skpo, patt to end.
Next row Patt to last 2 sts, p2A.
Now complete to match first side of neck.

Sleeve

Using 4½mm needles, cast on 44 sts.
Work 4cm/1½in k1, p1 rib.
Inc row Rib 6, * M1, rib 2, rep from * to last 6 sts, M1, rib 6. 61 sts.
Change to 5mm needles.
Work in patt from chart as follows:
Rows 1 to 12 Work 12 rows st st, inc 1 st at each end of 3rd and every foll 4th row.
Row 13 * K 1B, 5A, rep from * to last st, 1B.
Row 14 P 2B, * 3A, 3B, rep from * to last 2 sts, 2B.
Keeping patt correct, inc 1 st each end of next and every foll 4th row until there are

107 sts.
Work straight until row 104 has been completed.
Cast off.

Neckband

Join right shoulder seam.
With RS facing, using 4½mm needles and A, pick up and k18 sts down left side of front neck, k27 sts from front neck holder, pick up and k18 sts up right side of front neck, then k45 sts from back neck holder. 108 sts.
Work 5 rows k1, p1 rib.
Cast off in rib.

To make up

Join left shoulder and neckband seam.
Fold sleeves in half lengthwise, then placing folds to shoulder seams, sew into place.
Join side and sleeve seams.

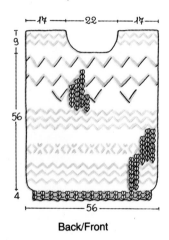

Back/Front

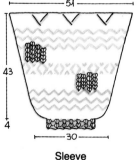

Sleeve

Measurements given in cm for second size

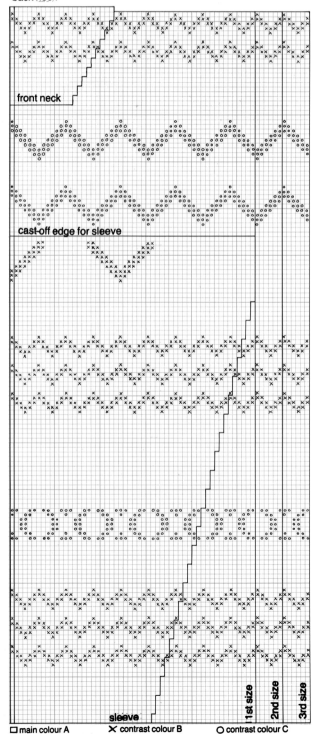

back neck

front neck

cast-off edge for sleeve

sleeve

□ main colour A   ✕ contrast colour B   ○ contrast colour C

CHEQUERED CABLE JERSEY

**

This man's jersey in a soft chunky yarn has a plain stocking stitch back and a single cable set in stocking stitch on the sleeves.

Materials
11(12,13,14)×50g balls of Sunbeam Scoop Chunky
A pair each of 5mm/No6 and 6½mm/No3 knitting needles
Cable needle

Measurements
To fit chest 86–91(97–102, 107–112, 117–122)cm/34–36(38–40, 42–44, 46–48)in

Actual measurements
Chest 97(109,121,133)cm/
38¼(43,47¾,52½)in
Length to shoulders 68cm/27in
Sleeve seam 50cm/19¾in

Tension
15 sts and 19 rows to 10cm/4in measured over patt worked on 6½mm needles
13 sts and 19 rows to 10cm/4in measured over st st worked on 6½mm needles

Special abbreviation
C6B Cable 6 back as follows: slip next 3 sts on to cable needle and leave at back of work, k3, then k3 from cable needle

Front
Using 5mm needles cast on 57(63,71,77) sts.
Rib row 1 K1, * p1, k1, rep from * to end.
Rib row 2 P1, * k1, p1, rep from * to end.
Rep these 2 rows for 5cm/2in, ending with rib row 1.
Inc row For 2nd and 4th sizes only rib 2, M1, rib 1, M1, rib 2, M1, rib 1, then for all sizes * rib 4, M1, rib 6, [M1, rib 1] twice, M1, rib 2, rep from * to last st, rib 1. 73(82,91,100) sts.
Change to 6½mm needles.
Work in patt as follows:
Row 1 (RS) * K1, p8, k1, p1, k6, p1, rep from * to last 1(10,1,10) sts, k1 then for 2nd and 4th sizes only p8, k1.
Row 2 For 2nd and 4th sizes only p1, k8, then for all sizes p1, * k1, p6, k1, p1, k8, p1, rep from * to end.
Row 3 * K2, p6, k2, p1, C6B, p1, rep from * to last 1(10,1,10) sts, k1(2,1,2), then for 2nd and 4th sizes only p6, k2.
Row 4 For 2nd and 4th sizes only p2, k6, then for all sizes p1(2,1,2), * k1, p6, k1, p2, k6, p2, rep from * to end.
Row 5 * K3, p4, k3, p1, k6, p1, rep from * to last 1(10,1,10) sts, k1(3,1,3), then for 2nd and 4th sizes only p4, k3.
Row 6 For 2nd and 4th sizes only p3, k4, then for all sizes p1(3,1,3), * k1, p6, k1, p3, k4, p3, rep from * to end.
Row 7 * K4, p2, k4, p1, k6, p1, rep from * to last 1(10,1,10) sts, k1(4,1,4), then for 2nd and 4th sizes only p2, k4.
Row 8 For 2nd and 4th sizes only p4, k2, then for all sizes p1(4,1,4), * k1, p6, k1, p4, k2, p4, rep from * to end.
Row 9 * K10, p1, C6B, p1, rep from * to last 1(10,1,10) sts, k1(10,1,10).
Row 10 P1(10,1,10), * k1, p6, k1, p10, rep from * to end.
Rows 11 and 12 As rows 7 and 8.
Rows 13 and 14 As rows 5 and 6.
Rows 15 and 16 As rows 3 and 4.
Rows 17 and 18 As rows 1 and 2.
Row 19 * K1, p1, k6, p1, k1, p8, rep from * to last 1(10,1,10) sts, k1, then for 2nd and 4th sizes only p1, k6, p1, k1.

Row 20 For 2nd and 4th sizes only p1, k1, p6, k1, then for all sizes p1, * k8, p1, k1, p6, k1, p1, rep from * to end.
Row 21 K1, * p1, C6B, p1, k2, p6, k2, rep from * to last 18(27,18,27) sts, p1, C6B, p1, k2, p6, k2, then for 2nd and 4th sizes only p1, C6B, p1, k1.
Row 22 For 2nd and 4th sizes only p1, k1, p6, k1, then for all sizes * p2, k6, p2, k1, p6, k1, rep from * to last st, p1.
Row 23 K1, * p1, k6, p1, k3, p4, k3, rep from * to last 18(27,18,27) sts, p1, k6, p1, k3, p4, k3, then for 2nd and 4th sizes only p1, k6, p1, k1.
Row 24 For 2nd and 4th sizes only p1, k1, p6, k1, then for all sizes * p3, k4, p3, k1, p6, k1, rep from * to last st, p1.
Row 25 K1, * p1, k6, p1, k4, p2, k4, rep from * to last 18(27,18,27) sts, p1, k6, p1, k4, p2, k4, then for 2nd and 4th sizes only p1, k6, p1, k1.
Row 26 For 2nd and 4th sizes only p1, k1, p6, k1, then for all sizes * p4, k2, p4, k1, p6, k1, rep from * to last st, p1.
Row 27 K1, * p1, C6B, p1, k10, rep from * to last 18(27,18,27) sts, p1, C6B, p1, k10, then for 2nd and 4th sizes only p1, C6B, p1, k1.
Row 28 For 2nd and 4th sizes only p1, k1, p6, k1, then for all sizes * p10, k1, p6, k1, rep from * to last st, p1.
Rows 29 and 30 As rows 25 and 26.
Rows 31 and 32 As rows 23 and 24.
Rows 33 and 34 As rows 21 and 22.
Rows 35 and 36 As rows 19 and 20.
These 36 rows form the patt.
Cont in patt until front measures 58cm/23in from cast-on edge, ending with a WS row.
Shape neck
Next row Patt 29(33,37,41), turn and leave rem sts on a spare needle.
Dec 1 st at neck edge on next and every foll alt row until 23(27,31,35) sts rem.
Work straight until front measures 68cm/27in from cast-on edge, ending with a WS row.
Cast off.
Return to sts on spare needle.
With RS facing, slip first 15(16,17,18) sts on to a holder, join on yarn and patt to end.
Now complete to match first side of neck.

Back
Using 5mm needles cast on 57(63,71,77) sts. Work 5cm/2in rib as given for front, ending with rib row 1.
Inc row Rib 8(4,4,2), * M1, rib 8(8,9,8), rep from * to last 9(3,4,3) sts, M1, rib to end.

63(71,79,87) sts.
Change to 6½mm needles.
Beg with a k row, work in st st until back measures same as front to shoulders, ending with a p row.
Shape shoulders
Cast off 20(23,26,30) sts at beg of next 2 rows.
Cut off yarn and leave rem 23(25,27,27) sts on a holder.

Sleeves
Using 5mm needles cast on 33(35,37,39) sts.
Work 5cm/2in rib as given for front, ending with rib row 1.
Inc row Rib 4(6,6,8), * M1, rib 3, rep from * to last 5(5,7,7) sts, M1, rib 5(5,7,7).
42(44,46,48) sts.
Change to 6½mm needles.
Work in patt as follows:
Row 1 (RS) K17(18,19,20), p1, k6, p1, k17(18,19,20).
Row 2 P17(18,19,20), k1, p6, k1, p17(18,19,20).
Rows 3 and 4 As rows 1 and 2.
Row 5 K17(18,19,20), p1, C6B, p1, k17(18,19,20).
Row 6 As row 2.
These 6 rows form the patt.
Continuing in patt, inc and work into st st 1 st each end of next and every foll 4th row until there are 68(70,72,74) sts.
Work straight until sleeve measures 50cm/19¾in from cast-on edge, ending with a WS row.
Cast off.

Neckband
Join right shoulder seam.
With RS facing and using 5mm needles, pick up and k15 sts down left side of front neck, k15(16,17,18) sts from front neck holder, pick up and k15 sts up right side of front neck then increasing 1 st at centre of 1st and 3rd sizes only k the back neck sts from holder. 69(71,75,75) sts.
Work 5cm/2in rib as given for front.
Cast off in rib.

To make up
Join left shoulder and neckband seam. Fold neckband in half to WS and slipstitch into place. Fold sleeves in half lengthwise, then placing folds to shoulder seams, sew into place. Join side and sleeve seams.

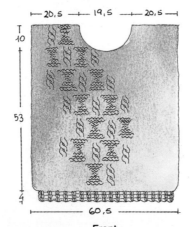

Front

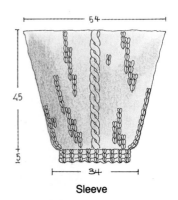

Measurements given in cm for third size

Sleeve

CARDIGAN IN A PLAID STITCH PATTERN

✳✳

The reverse
stocking stitch
bands weave
over and
under each
other where they
meet at the
corners of this
plaid stitch
pattern.

Materials
12 × 50g balls of Patons Waverley DK
    Tweeds
A pair each of 4½mm/No7 and 5mm/No6
    knitting needles
A 4½mm/No7 circular knitting needle 45cm/
    18in long
6 buttons

Measurements
One size only to fit chest 102-112cm/
40-44in
Actual measurements
Chest 124cm/48¾in
Length to shoulders 70cm/27½in
Sleeve seam 43cm/17in

Tension
18 sts and 25 rows to 10cm/4in measured
over patt worked on 5mm needles

Right front
Using 4½mm needles cast on 38 sts.
Rib row 1 K2, * p2, k2, rep from * to end.
Rib row 2 P2, * k2, p2, rep from * to end.
Rep these 2 rows for 8cm/3in, ending with
rib row 1.
Inc row Rib 2, * M1, rib 2, rep from * to end.
56 sts.
Change to 5mm needles.
Work in patt as follows:
Row 1 * K13, p1, rep from * to end.
Row 2 K1, * p2, k12, rep from * to last
13 sts, p2, k11.
Row 3 P11, * k2, p12, rep from * to last
3 sts, k2, p1.
Row 4 As row 2.
Row 5 As row 1.
Row 6 * K12, p2, rep from * to end.
Row 7 K2, p12, rep from * to end.
Row 8 * K12, p2, rep from * to end.
Row 9 As row 1.
Row 10 K1, p3, * [k1, p1] 3 times, [k1, p3]
twice, rep from * to last 10 sts, [k1, p1]
3 times, k1, p3.
Row 11 K2, *[p1, k1] 4 times, [p1, k2] twice,
rep from * to last 12 sts, [p1, k1] 4 times, p1,
k2, p1.
Rows 12 to 19 Rep rows 10 and 11 four
times.
Row 20 * K1, p13, rep from * to end.
Row 21 As row 3.
Row 22 As row 2.
Row 23 As row 3.
Row 24 * K1, p13, rep from * to end.
Rows 25 to 26 Rep rows 7 and 8.
Row 27 As row 7.
Row 28 * K1, p13, rep from * to end.
Row 29 As row 11.
Rows 30 to 37 Rep rows 10 and 11 four
times.
Row 38 As row 10.
These 38 rows form the patt.
Cont in patt until front measures 38cm/15in
from cast-on edge, ending with a WS row.
(For left front end with a RS row.)
Shape neck
Keeping patt correct dec 1 st at beg of next
and every alt row until there are 50 sts.
Patt 5 rows.
Dec 1 st at beg of next row. 49 sts.
Patt 4 rows, so ending with a RS row. (For
left front end with a WS row.)
Shape armhole
Cast off 11 sts, patt to end. 38 sts.
Keeping armhole edge straight, dec 1 st at
neck edge at beg of next and every foll 6th
row until there are 32 sts, ending with a WS
row.
Work straight until front measures 70cm/
27½in from cast-on edge, ending at
armhole edge.
Cast off.

Left front
Work as given for right front noting
exceptions in brackets.

Back
Using 4½mm needles cast on 82 sts.
Work 8cm/3in rib as given for right front,
ending with rib row 1.
Inc row Rib 5, * M1, rib 2, M1, rib 3, rep from
* to last 2 sts, rib 2. 112 sts.

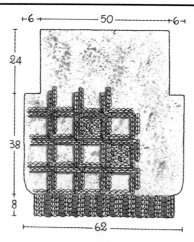

Back

Change to 5mm needles.
Work in patt as given for right front until back
measures same as fronts to armhole,
ending with a WS row.
Shape armhole
Keeping patt correct, cast off 11 sts at beg
of next 2 rows. 90 sts.
Work straight until back measures same as
fronts to shoulders, ending with a WS row.
Cast off 32 sts at beg of next 2 rows.
Cut off yarn and leave rem 26 sts on a
holder.

Sleeves
Using 4½mm needles cast on 42 sts.
Work in rib as given for back for 8cm/3in
ending with rib row 1.
Inc row Rib 1, * M1, rib 3, rep from * to last
2 sts, M1, rib 2. 56 sts.
Change to 5mm needles.
Work in patt as follows:
Row 1 * K13, p1, rep from * to end.
Row 2 K1, * p2, k12, rep from * to last
13 sts, p2, k11.
Row 3 P11, * k2, p12, rep from * to last
3 sts, k2, p1.
Row 4 As row 2.
Row 5 Inc in first st, k12, * p1, k13, rep from
* to last st, inc in last st. 58 sts.
Row 6 P1, * k12, p2, rep from * to last st, k1.
Row 7 P1, * k2, p12, rep from * to last st, k1.
Row 8 As row 6.
Row 9 * P1, k13, rep from * to last 2 sts, p1,
k1.
Row 10 P1, k1, p3, * [k1, p1] 3 times, [k1,
p3] twice, rep from * to last 11 sts, [k1, p1]
3 times, k1, p3, k1.
Row 11 Inc in first st, k2, * [p1, k1] 4 times,
[p1, k2] twice, rep from * to last 13 sts, [p1,
k1] 4 times, p1, k2, p1, inc in last st. 60 sts.
Row 12 P2, k1, p3, * [k1, p1] 3 times, [k1,
p3] twice, rep from * to last 12 sts, [k1, p1]
3 times, k1, p3, k1, p1.
Row 13 K1, p1, k2, * [p1, k1] 4 times, [p1,
k2] twice, rep from * to end.
Rows 14 and 15 As rows 12 and 13.
Row 16 As row 12.
Row 17 Inc in first st, p1, k2, * [p1, k1]
4 times, [p1, k2] twice, rep from * to last
13 sts, [p1, k1] 4 times, p1, k2, p1, k1, inc in
last st. 62 sts.
Row 18 P3, k1, p3, * [k1, p1] 3 times, [k1,
p3] twice, rep from * to last 13 sts, [k1, p1]
3 times, k1, p3, k1, p2.
Row 19 * [K2, p1] twice, [k1, p1] 4 times,
rep from * to last 6 sts, [k2, p1] twice.
Row 20 P3, * k1, p13, rep from * to last
3 sts, k1, p2.
Row 21 K2, * p12, k2, rep from * to last
4 sts, p4.
Row 22 K4, * p2, k12, rep from * to last
2 sts, p2.
Row 23 Inc in first st, k1, * p12, k2, rep from
* to last 4 sts, p3, inc in last st. 64 sts.
Row 24 P4, * k1, p13, rep from * to last
4 sts, k1, p3.
Row 25 P4, * k2, p12, rep from * to last
4 sts, k2, p2.
Row 26 K2, p2, * k12, p2, rep from * to last
4 sts, k4.
Row 27 As row 25.
Row 28 P4, * k1, p13, rep from * to last

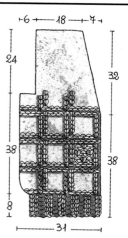

Right Front

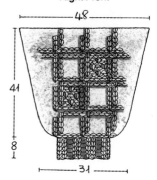

Sleeve

Measurements given in cm

4 sts, k1, p3.
Row 29 Inc in first st, * [k2, p1] twice, [k1,
p1] 4 times, rep from * to last 7 sts, [k2, p1]
twice, inc in last st. 66 sts.
Row 30 P1, * [k1, p3] twice, [k1, p1] 3 times,
rep from * to last 9 sts, [k1, p3] twice, k1.
Row 31 K1, p1, * [k2, p1] twice, [k1, p1]
4 times, rep from * to last 8 sts, [k2, p1]
twice, k1, p1.
Rows 32 and 33 As rows 30 and 31.
Row 34 As row 30.
Row 35 Inc in first st, p1, * [k2, p1] twice,
[k1, p1] 4 times, rep from * to last 8 sts, [k2,
p1] twice, k1, inc in last st. 68 sts.
Row 36 K1, p1, * [k1, p3] twice, [k1, p1]
3 times, rep from * to last 10 sts, [k1, p3]
twice, k1, p1.
Row 37 P1, k1, p1, * [k2, p1] twice, [k1, p1]
4 times, rep from * to last 9 sts, [k2, p1]
twice, k1, p1, k1.
Row 38 As row 36.
Keeping patt correct, cont to inc 1 st each
end of every 6th row until there are 86 sts.
Work straight until sleeve measures 49cm/
19¼in from cast-on edge, ending with a WS
row.
Cast off.

Border
Join shoulder seams.
With RS facing and using the 4½mm
circular needle, pick up and k81 sts up right
front edge, 81 sts along right front shaping,
k26 sts from back neck holder, pick up and
k81 sts down left front shaping then 81 sts
down left front edge. 350 sts.
Working backwards and forwards in rows
and beg with rib row 1, work 2 rows in rib as
given for back.
Buttonhole row 1 Rib 4, [cast off 2 sts, rib
14] 5 times, cast off 2 sts, rib to end.
Buttonhole row 2 Rib to end, casting on 2 sts
over those cast off in previous row.
Rib 2 more rows.
Cast off in rib.

To make up
Sew in sleeves, then join side and sleeve
seams. Sew on buttons.

CHUNKY CABLED CARDIGAN

***

This
classic
cardigan
has a plain
stocking stitch
back and a single
cable running
up each sleeve.

Materials

13(14,15,16)×50g balls of Patons Beehive
   Soft Blend Chunky
A pair each of 4mm/No8 and 5mm/No6
   knitting needles
Cable needle
4 buttons

Measurements

To fit chest 91–97(97–102,102–107,107–
112)cm/36–38(38–40,40–42,42–44)in
Actual measurements
Chest 105(110,117,121)cm/
41½(43½,46,47¾)in
Length to shoulders 69(71,72,73)cm/
27¼(28,28¼,28¾)in
Sleeve seam 48(49,49,50)cm/
19(19¼,19¼,19¾)in

Tension

14 sts and 19 rows to 10cm/4in measured
over st st worked on 5mm needles
24 st cable panel measures 12cm/4¾in

Special abbreviations

C8B Cable 8 back as follows: slip next 4 sts
on to cable needle and leave at back of
work, k1, p2, k1, then k1, p2, k1 from cable
needle
C8F Cable 8 front as follows: slip next 4 sts
on to cable needle and leave at front of
work, k1, p2, k1, then k1, p2, k1 from cable
needle

Left front

★ Using 4mm needles cast on
37(39,41,43) sts.
Rib row 1 K1, * p1, k1, rep from * to end.
Rib row 2 P1, * k1, p1, rep from * to end.
Rep these 2 rows for 7cm/2¾in, ending with
rib row 1.
Inc row Rib 10(11,12,13), M1, rib 3, M1, rib 5,
M1, rib 6, M1, rib 3, M1, rib 10(11,12,13).
42(44,46,48) sts.
Change to 5mm needles.
Work in patt as follows:
Row 1 (RS) K9(10,11,12), p4, [k1 tbl, p2,
k1 tbl] 4 times, p4, k9(10,11,12).
Row 2 P9(10,11,12), k4, [p1 tbl, k2, p1 tbl]
4 times, k4, p9(10,11,12).
Rows 3 to 10 Rep rows 1 and 2 four times.
Row 11 K9(10,11,12), p4, C8B, C8F, p4,
k9(10,11,12).
Row 12 P9(10,11,12), k4, [p1 tbl, k2, p1 tbl]
4 times, k4, p9(10,11,12).
These 12 rows form the patt.
Cont in patt until work measures
37(37,38,38)cm/14½(14½,15,15)in from
cast-on edge, ending with a WS row. ★
Shape front edge
Next row Patt to last 3 sts, k2 tog, k1.
Next 3 rows Patt to end.
Rep last 4 rows 2(3,3,3) times more.
Next row Patt to last 3 sts, k2 tog, k1.
38(39,41,43) sts.
Patt 1 row.
Shape armhole
Cast off 5(6,6,7) sts, patt to end.
Now decreasing 1 st at armhole edge on
foll 2 alt rows, cont to dec at front edge on
every 4th row, as before, until
28(28,30,30) sts rem.
Work straight until front measures
69(71,72,73)cm/27(28,28¼,28¾)in from

cast-on edge, ending with a WS row.
Cast off in patt.

Right front

Work as given for left front from ★ to ★.
Shape front edge
Next row K1, skpo, patt to end.
Next 3 rows Patt to end.
Rep last 4 rows 2(3,3,3) times.
Next row K1, skpo, patt to end.
Patt 2 rows,
Shape armhole
Cast off 5(6,6,7) sts, patt to end.
Now decreasing 1 st at armhole edge on
next and foll alt row, cont to dec at front
edge on every 4th row, as before, until
28(28,30,30) sts rem.
Work straight until front measures
69(71,72,73)cm/27(28,28¼,28¾)in from
cast-on edge, ending with a WS row.
Cast off in patt.

Back

Using 4mm needles cast on
77(81, 85, 89) sts.
Rib row 1 (RS) K1, * p1, k1, rep from * to
end.
Rib row 2 P1, * k1, p1, rep from * to end.
Rep these 2 rows for 7cm/2¾in, ending with
rib row 2.
Change to 5mm needles.
Work in st st until back measures same as
fronts to beg of armhole shaping, ending
with a p row.
Shape armholes
Cast off 5(6,6,7) sts at beg of next 2 rows.
Dec 1 st each end of next and foll alt row.
63(65,69,71) sts.
Cont in st st until back measures same as
fronts to shoulders, ending with a p row.
Cast off.

Sleeves

Using 4mm needles cast on
43(45,47,49) sts.
Work 7cm/2¾in rib as given for back,
ending with rib row 1.
Inc row Rib 13(14,15,16), M1, rib 3, M1,
rib 5, M1, rib 6, M1, rib 3, M1, rib 13
(14,15,16). 48(50,52,54) sts.
Change to 5mm needles.
Work in patt as follows:
Row 1 (RS) K12(13,14,15), p4, [k1 tbl, p2,
k1 tbl] 4 times, p4, k12(13,14,15).
Row 2 P12(13,14,15), k4, [p1 tbl, k2, p1 tbl]
4 times, k4, p12(13,14,15).
Rows 3 to 6 Rep rows 1 and 2 twice.
Row 7 K12(13,14,15), p4, [k1 tbl, p2, k1 tbl]
4 times, p4, k12(13,14,15), inc into last st.
Row 8 P12(13,14,15), k4, [p1 tbl, k2, p1 tbl]

4 times, k4, p12(13,14,15).
Row 9 K12(13,14,15), p4, [k1 tbl, p2, k1 tbl]
4 times, p4, k12(13,14,15).
Row 10 P12(13,14,15), k4, [p1 tbl, k2,
p1 tbl] 4 times, k4, p12(13,14,15).
Row 11 K12(13,14,15), p4, C8B, C8F, p4,
k12(13,14,15).
Row 12 P12(13,14,15), k4, [p1 tbl, k2,
p1 tbl] 4 times, k4, p12(13,14,15).
Continuing in patt as set, inc and work into
st st 1 st each end of next and every foll 4th
row until there are 76(78,80,82) sts.
Work straight until sleeve measures
48(49,49,50)cm/19(19¼,19¼,19¾)in from
cast-on edge, ending with a WS row.
Shape top
Cast off 5(6,6,7) sts at beg of next 2 rows.
Dec 1 st each end of next and every foll alt
row until 38(36,38,36) sts rem, ending with a
WS row.
Cast off 6 sts at beg of next 4 rows.
Cast off rem 14(12,14,12) sts.

Button border

Join shoulder seams.
With RS facing and using 4mm needles,
pick up and k81(81,83,83) sts up right front
to beg of front shaping, 70(74,74,76) sts up
right front shaping to shoulder and
22(24,26,28) sts to centre back neck.
173(179,183,187) sts.
Rib row 1 P1, * k1, p1, rep from * to end.
Rib row 2 K1, * p1, k1, rep from * to end.
Rep these 2 rows 3 times more, then rib row
1 again.
Cast off in rib.

Buttonhole border

With RS facing and using 4mm needles,
pick up and k22(24,26,28) sts across centre
back neck to shoulder, 70(74,74,76) sts
down left side of front shaping to beg of
front shaping and 81(81,83,83) sts down left
front to cast-on edge. 173(179,183,187) sts.
Work 4 rows in rib as given for button
border.
Next row Rib 5, * cast off 2 sts, rib next
21(21,22,22) sts, rep from * twice more,
cast off 2, rib to end.
Next row Rib to end, casting on 2 sts over
those cast off in previous row.
Rib 3 rows.
Cast off in rib.

To make up

Sew in sleeves. Join side and sleeve seams.
Join back neck border seam. Sew on the
buttons.
**Measurements given in cm
for second size**

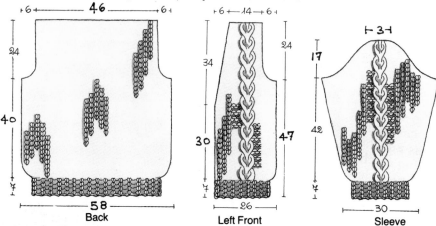

Back   Left Front   Sleeve

FLECKED CREW NECK JERSEY

*

You can easily
obtain
a subtle
flecked
effect by knitting
two different
coloured yarns
together as on
this jersey.

Materials
9(10,10,11,12,13)×50g balls of Rowan
   Cotton Glacé DK in colour A
9(10,10,11,12,13) balls of the same in
   colour B
A pair each of 4½mm/No7 and 5½mm/No5
   knitting needles

Measurements
To fit chest 91(97,102,107,112,117)cm/
36(38,40,42,44,46)in
Actual measurements
Chest 102(107,112,117,122,127)cm/
40(42,44,46,48,50)in
Length to shoulders 65(65,66,66,67,68)cm/
25½(25½,26,26,26¼,26¾)in
Sleeve seam 46(46,47,47,48,49)cm/
18(18,18½,18½,18¾,19¼)in

Tension
15 sts and 19 rows to 10cm/4in measured
over st st worked on 5½mm needles, using
1 strand of A and 1 strand of B together

Note
1 strand of A and 1 strand of B are used
together throughout.

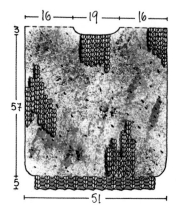

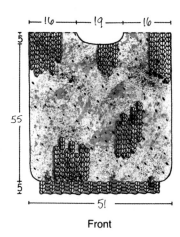

Front

Back
Using 4½mm needles and 1 strand of A and
1 strand of B together, cast on
69(73,77,81,85,89) sts.
Rib row 1 (RS) K1, * p1, k1, rep from * to
end.
Rib row 2 P1, * k1, p1, rep from * to end.
Rep these 2 rows for 5cm/2in, ending with
rib row 1.
Inc row Rib 4(6,8,10,12,14), * M1, rib 10, rep
from * to last 5(7,9,11,13,15) sts, M1, rib to
end. 76(80,84,88,92,96) sts.
Change to 5½mm needles.
Beg with a k row, work in st st until back
measures 62(62,63,63,64,65)cm/
24½(24½, 25,25,25¼,25½)in from cast-on
edge, ending with a p row.
Shape neck
Next row K29(31,33,34,36,38), turn and
leave rem sts on a spare needle.
Cast off 3(3,4,4,4,4) sts at beg of next row
and 2(2,2,2,3,3) sts at beg of foll alt row.
24(26,27,28,29,31) sts.
Work 2 rows straight.
Cast off.
Return to sts on spare needle.
With RS facing, slip first
18(18,18,20,20,20) sts on to a holder, join
on yarns and k to end of row.
29(31,33,34,36,38) sts.
P 1 row.
Now complete to match first side of neck.

Front
Work as given for back until front measures
60(60,61,61,62,63)cm/
23½(23½,24,24,24½,25)in from cast-on
edge, ending with a p row.
Shape neck
Next row K31(33,34,36,37,39), turn and
leave rem sts on a spare needle.

Measurements given in cm
for smallest size

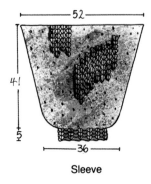

Sleeve

Cast off 2(2,2,3,3,3) sts at beg of next and
foll alt row.
Dec 1 st at neck edge on every row until
24(26,27,28,29,31) sts rem.
Work straight until front measures same as
back to shoulder, ending with a p row.
Cast off.
Return to sts on spare needle.
With RS facing, slip first
14(14,16,16,18,18) sts on to a holder, join
on yarns and k to end of row.
31(33,34,36,37,39) sts.
P 1 row.
Now complete to match first side of neck.

Sleeves
Using 4½mm needles and 1 strand of A and
1 strand of B together, cast on
41(41,43,43,45,47) sts.
Rib row 1 (RS), K1, * p1, k1, rep from * to
end.
Rib row 2 P1, * k1, p1, rep from * to end.
Rep these 2 rows for 5cm/2in, ending with
rib row 1.
Inc row Rib 5(5,6,6,6,3), * M1, rib
3(3,3,3,4,5), rep from * to last
6(6,7,7,7,4) sts, M1, rib to end.
52(52,54,54,54,56) sts.
Change to 5½mm needles.
Working in st st, inc 1 st each end of 3rd and
every foll 6th row to 72(72,74,74,74,74) sts,
then every foll alt row until there are
78(78,80,80,82,84) sts.
Work straight until sleeve measures
46(46,47,47,48,49)cm/
18(18,18½,18½,18¾,19¼)in from cast-on
edge, ending with a p row.
Cast off.

Roll neckband
Join right shoulder seam.
With RS facing, using 4½mm needles and 2
strands of A together, pick up and k12 sts
down left side of front neck, k across front
neck sts from holder, pick up and k12 sts up
right side of front neck and 9 sts down right
side of back neck, decreasing 1 st at centre
k across back neck sts from holder, then
pick up and k9 sts up left side of back neck.
73(73,75,77,79,79) sts.
Beg with a p row, work 2.5cm/1in st st,
ending with a p row.
Cast off loosely knitwise.

Inner neckband
With RS facing, using 4½mm needles and
1 strand of A and 1 strand of B together, join
yarn to inner edge of first neckband, then,
through same sts as roll neckband, pick up
and k73(73,75,77,79,79) sts round neck.
Beg with rib row 2, work 2.5cm/1in rib.
Cast off loosely in rib.

To make up
Join left shoulder and inner neckband
seam. Join roll neckband seam, reversing
seam on last few rows. Fold sleeves in half
lengthwise, then placing folds to shoulder
seams, sew into place. Join side and sleeve
seams.

DIAGONAL TEXTURED JERSEY

**

A classic round
necked jersey with
a subtle textured
pattern to add a
little interest.

Materials

14(15,16,17)×50g balls of Emu Superwash Chunky
A pair each of 4½mm/No7 and 5½mm/No5 knitting needles

Measurements

To fit chest 97(102,107,112)cm/ 38(40,42,44)in
Actual measurements
Chest 112(117,122,127)cm/44(46,48,50)in
Length to shoulders 66(67,68,69)cm/ 26(26¼,26¾,27¼)in
Sleeve seam 47(48,48,49)cm/ 18½(19,19,19¼)in

Tension

16 sts and 22 rows to 10cm/4in measured over st st worked on 5½mm needles

Front

★ Using 4½mm needles cast on 82(86,90,94) sts.
Rib row 1 K2, * p2, k2, rep from * to end.
Rib row 2 P2, * k2, p2, rep from * to end.
Rep these 2 rows for 9cm/3½in, ending with rib row 1.
Inc row Rib 6(8,6,8), * M1, rib 10(10,11,11), rep from * to last 6(8,7,9) sts, M1, rib to end. 90(94,98,102) sts. ★
Change to 5½mm needles.
Work in diagonal patt as follows:
Row 1 (RS) P12(14,16,18) sts, [k3, p16] 4 times, k2(4,6,8).
Row 2 P2(4,6,8) sts, [k16, p3] 4 times, k12(14,16,18).
Row 3 P11(13,15,17) sts, [k3, p16] 4 times, k3(5,7,9).
Row 4 P3(5,7,9) sts, [k16, p3] 4 times, k11(13,15,17).
Row 5 P10(12,14,16) sts, [k3, p16] 4 times, k4(6,8,10).
Row 6 P4(6,8,10) sts, [k16, p3] 4 times, k10(12,14,16).
Cont in this way, moving the rev st st diagonal stripes 1 st to the right on every RS row and working 1 st more into the st st side panel on every RS row, until a row has been worked as follows: p26(28,30,32) sts, [k16, p3] 3 times, k7(9,11,13).

Next row P6(8,10,12) sts, [k3, p16] 3 times, k1 for moss st panel, then k26(28,30,32).
Next row P26(28,30,32), k1 for moss st panel, [k16, p3] 3 times, k6(8,10,12).
Next row P5(7,9,11) sts, [k3, p16] 3 times, p1, k1, for moss st panel, then k26(28,30,32).
Next row P26(28,30,32), k1, p1, for moss st panel, [k16, p3] 3 times, k5(7,9,11).
Next row P4(6,8,10) sts, [k3, p16] 3 times, k1, p1, k1, for moss st panel, then k26(28,30,32).
Next row P26(28,30,32), k1, p1, k1, for moss st panel, [k16, p3] 3 times, k4(6,8,10).
Cont in this way, moving the rev st st diagonal stripes 1 st to the right on every RS row and working 1 st more into the moss st panel on every RS row, until a row has been worked as follows: p26(28,30,32) sts, [k1, p1] 13 times, k17, then patt to end of row.
Cont in diagonal stripes and st st only, moving the rev st st diagonal stripes 1 st to the right on every RS row and working 1 st more into the st st panel on every RS row, until a row has been worked as follows: p57(60,63,66), k16, p3, k14(15,16,17).
Shape neck
Next row Continuing to move the rev st st diagonal stripes 1 st to the right on every RS row as before, patt 39(41,42,44), turn and leave rem sts on a spare needle.
Keeping patt correct, dec 1 st at neck edge on every row until 30(32,33,35) sts rem.
Patt 6 rows, so ending with a WS row.
Shape shoulder
Cast off in patt 10(11,11,12) sts at beg of next and foll alt row.
Patt 1 row.
Cast off in patt.
Return to sts on spare needle.
With RS facing, slip first 12(12,14,14) sts on to a holder, join on yarn and k to end. 39(41,42,44) sts.
Dec 1 st at neck edge on every row until 30(32,33,35) sts rem.
Patt 7 rows, so ending with a RS row.
Shape shoulder
Cast off 10(11,11,12) sts at beg of next and foll alt row.
Work 1 row. Cast off.

Back

Work as given for front from ★ to ★.
Change to 5½mm needles.
Work in st st until back measures same as front to beg of shoulder shaping, ending with a p row.
Shape shoulders
Cast off 10(11,11,12) sts at beg of next 4 rows and 10(10,11,11) sts at beg of foll 2 rows.
Cut off yarn and leave rem 30(30,32,32) sts on a holder.

Sleeves

Using 4½mm needles cast on 42(42,46,46) sts.
Work 8cm/3in rib as given for back, ending with rib row 1.
Inc row Rib 3(3,5,5), * M1, rib 5(4,5,4), rep from * to last 4(3,6,5) sts, M1, rib to end. 50(52,54,56) sts.
Change to 5½mm needles.
Working in st st, inc 1 st each end of 3rd and every foll 4th row to 58(58,60,62) sts, then each end of every foll 6th row until there are 78(80,82,82) sts.
Work straight until sleeve measures 47(48,48,49)cm/18½(19,19,19¼)in from cast-on edge, ending with a p row. Cast off.

Neckband

Join right shoulder seam.
With RS facing and using 4½mm needles, pick up and k16 sts down left side of front neck, k the front neck sts from holder, pick up and k16 sts up right side of front neck, then k the back neck sts from holder. 74(74,78,78) sts.
Beg with rib row 2, work 4cm/1½in rib. Cast off in rib.

To make up

Join left shoulder and neckband seam. Fold sleeves in half lengthwise, then placing folds to shoulder seams, sew into place. Join side and sleeve seams. Fold neckband in half to WS and slipstitch into position.

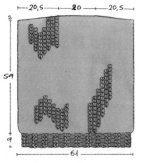

Back

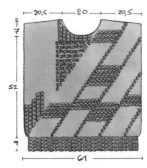

Front

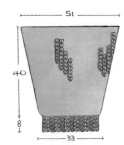

Sleeve

Measurements given in cm for third size

JERSEY WITH BOLD FAIR ISLE BAND

**

The Fair Isle bands stand out against the lighter coloured background. A completely different effect is gained by using a stronger main colour.

Materials
3(4,4)×100g balls of Water Wheel Concorde DK in main colour A
1 ball of same in each of contrast colours B, C and D
A pair each of 3¼mm/No10, 4mm/No8 and 4½mm/No7 knitting needles

Measurements
To fit chest 97(102,107)cm/38(40,42)in
Actual measurements
Chest 102(107,113)cm/40(42,44½)in
Length to back neck 71.5cm/28¼in
Sleeve seam 47cm/18½in

Tension
22 sts and 30 rows to 10cm/4in measured over st st worked on 4mm needles.

Back
★ Using 3¼mm needles and A, cast on 105(111,117) sts.
Rib row 1 K1, * p1, k1, rep from * to end.
Rib row 2 P1, * k1, p1, rep from * to end.
Rep these 2 rows for 4.5cm/1¾in, ending with rib row 1.
Inc row Rib 7, * M1, rib 15(16,17), rep from * to last 8 sts, M1, rib to end.
112(118,124) sts. Change to 4mm needles.
Work in st st until back measures 14.5cm/5¾in, ending with a p row.
Change to 4½mm needles. Carrying yarn not in use loosely across WS of work and weaving yarn in when passing across more than 5 sts, work in patt from chart:
Row 1 (RS) for 3rd size only k1D, for 2nd and 3rd sizes only k1(3)A, 2B, then for all sizes k2C, 2D, 1A, * k1A, 2B, 2C, 2D, 3A, 2B, 2C, 2D, 1A, rep from * 5 times more, 1A, 2B, 2C, for 2nd and 3rd sizes only k2D, 1(3)A, then for 3rd size only k1B.
Row 2 For 3rd size only p2B, 1A, for 2nd and.3rd sizes only p2D, then for all sizes p1(2,2)C, 2B, 2A, * p2A, 2D, 2C, 2B, 1A, 2D, 2C, 2B, 2A, rep from * 5 times more, 2A, 2D, 1(2,2)C, for 2nd and 3rd sizes only p2D, then for 3rd size only p1A, 2D.
Now beg with row 3, cont in patt from chart until row 21 has been completed. Change to 4mm needles. With A, work 5 rows st st.
Change to 4½mm needles. Beg with row 1, work in patt from chart until row 21 has been completed.
Change to 4mm needles. With A, cont in st st until back measures 44.5cm/17½in from cast-on edge, ending with a p row. ★
Shape armholes
Cast off 4 sts at beg of next 2 rows.
Next row K1, skpo, k to last 3 sts, k2 tog, k1.
Next row P to end.
Rep last 2 rows 3 times more.
96(102,108) sts. Work straight until back measures 62.5cm/24½in from cast-on

edge, ending with a p row.
Shape shoulders
Cast off 2 sts at beg of next 28(22,16) rows. 40(58,76) sts.
2nd and 3rd sizes only
Cast off 3 sts at beg of next 6(12) rows. 40 sts.
All sizes
Cut off yarn and leave rem sts on a holder.

Front
Work as given for back from ★ to ★.
Shape armholes
Cast off 4 sts at beg of next 2 rows.
Divide for neck
Next row K1, skpo, k45(48,51), k2 tog, k2, turn and leave rem sts on a spare needle.
Next row P to end.
Next row K1, skpo, k to end.
Next row P to end.
Next row K1, skpo, k to last 4 sts, k2 tog, k2.
Next row P to end.
Next row K1, skpo, k to end. 46(49,52) sts.
Next row P to end.
Next row K to last 4 sts, k2 tog, k2.
Work 3 rows st st.
Rep last 4 rows until 29(32,35) sts rem.
Next row K to last 4 sts, k2 tog, k2.
Work 2 rows st st. Cast off.
Return to sts on spare needle. With RS facing, join on yarn and work as follows:
Next row K2, skpo, k to last 3 sts, k2 tog, k1.
Next row P to end.
Next row K to last 3 sts, k2 tog, k1.
Next row P to end.
Next row K2, skpo, k to last 3 sts, k2 tog, k1.
Next row P to end.
Next row K to last 3 sts, k2 tog, k1.
46(49,52) sts.
Next row P to end.
Next row K2, skpo, k to end.
Work 3 rows st st.
Rep last 4 rows until 29(32,35) sts rem.
Next row K2, skpo, k to end.
Work 2 rows st st. Cast off.

Sleeves
Using 3¼mm needles and A, cast on 49 sts.
Work 4.5cm/1¾in rib as given for back, ending with rib row 1.
Inc row Rib 6, * M1, rib 12, rep from * to last 7 sts, M1, rib to end. 53 sts.
Change to 4mm needles. Working in st st, inc 1 st each end of 11th and every foll 6th row until there are 61 sts.
Cont to inc each end of every 6th row as before, work as follows:
P 1 row. Change to 4½mm needles.
Beg with row 1, work 21 rows in patt from chart for first band on sleeves, taking extra sts into patt. 67 sts.
Change to 4mm needles. With A, p 1 row.
Increasing 1 st each end of first row, work 4

rows st st. 69 sts.
Change to 4½mm needles. Beg with row 1 and continuing to inc every 6th row, work 21 rows in patt from chart as indicated for second band on sleeves, taking extra sts into patt. 77 sts.
Change to 4mm needles. Continuing in A only, inc 1 st each end of every 6th row until there are 89 sts.
Work straight until sleeve measures 47cm/18½in from cast-on edge, ending with a p row.
Shape top
Cast off 4 sts at beg of next 2 rows.
Next row K1, skpo, k to last 3 sts, k2 tog, k1.
Next row P to end.
Rep the last 2 rows until 37 sts rem.
Next row K1, skpo, k to last 3 sts, k2 tog, k1.
Next row P1, p2 tog, p to last 3 sts, p2 tog tbl, p1.
Rep the last 2 rows 3 times more. 21 sts.
Cast off.

Neckband
Join right shoulder seam. With RS facing, using 3¼mm needles and A, pick up and k62 sts down left front neck, pick up and k into back of loop at centre of V, then mark this st with a coloured thread, pick up and k62 sts up right front neck, then k across 40 sts from back neck holder. 165 sts.
Rib row 1 (WS) [K1, p1] to within 2 sts of marked st, skpo, p centre st, k2 tog, [p1, k1] to end.
Rib row 2 Rib to within 2 sts of marked st, skpo, k centre st, k2 tog, rib to end.
Rep these 2 rows twice more, then row 1 again. Cast off in rib.

To make up
Join left shoulder and neckband seam. Set in the sleeves; join side and sleeve seams.

Measurements given in cm for smallest size

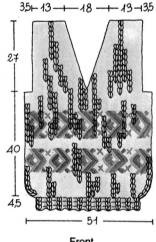

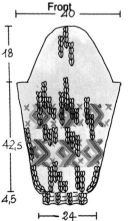

Sleeve

Chart

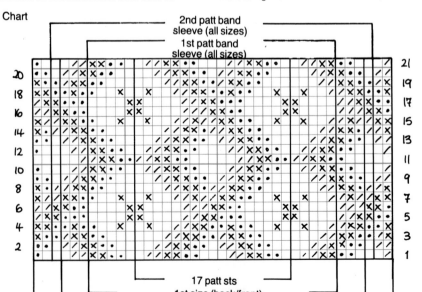

2nd patt band sleeve (all sizes)
1st patt band sleeve (all sizes)
17 patt sts
1st size (back/front)
2nd size (back/front)
3rd size (back/front)

DIAMOND PATTERNED JERSEY

***

Once you have
completed a
pattern
repeat
this regular
stitch is easy to
follow. The fold
back neckline is
unusual.

Materials

11×100g balls of Water Wheel Concorde Chunky

A pair each of 5½mm/No5 and 6½mm/No3 knitting needles

Measurements

One size only to fit chest 107–112cm/42–44in

Actual measurements

Chest 120cm/47¼in

Length to shoulders 72cm/28¼in

Sleeve seam 50cm/19½in

Tension

15 sts and 23 rows to 10cm/4in measured over patt worked on 6½mm needles

Back

Using 5½mm needles cast on 80 sts.

Work 6cm/2½in k1, p1 rib, ending with a RS row.

Inc row Rib 4, * M1, rib 8, rep from * to last 4 sts, M1, rib 4. 90 sts.

Change to 6½mm needles.

Work in patt as follows:

Row 1 (RS) P2, * k4, p6, k4, p22, rep from * once more, k4, p6, k4, p2.

Row 2 K2, p4, k6, p4, * k22, p4, k6, p4, rep from * once more, k2.

Row 3 K5, * p8, k28, rep from * once more, p8, k5.

Row 4 P4, * k10, p26, rep from * once more, k10, p4.

Row 5 K3, * p12, k5, p14, k5, rep from * once more, p12, k3.

Row 6 P2, * k6, p2, k6, p4, k14, p4, rep from * once more, [k6, p2] twice.

Row 7 K1, * p6, k4, p6, k20, rep from * once more, p6, k4, p6, k1.

Row 8 * K6, p6, k6, p18, rep from * once more, k6, p6, k6.

Row 9 P5, * k8, [p6, k5] twice, p6, rep from * once more, k8, p5.

Row 10 K4, * p10, [k6, p4] twice, k6, rep from * once more, p10, k4.

Row 11 P3, * k12, p6, rep from * 3 times more, k12, p3.

Row 12 K2, * [p4, k6] twice, p10, k6, rep from * once more, p4, k6, p4, k2.

Row 13 P1, * [k5, p6] twice, k8, p6, rep from * once more, k5, p6, k5, p1.

Row 14 * P18, k6, p6, k6, rep from * once more, p18.

Row 15 K19, p6, k4, p6, k20, p6, k4, p6, k19.

Row 16 P2, * k14, p4, k6, p2, k6, p4, rep from * once more, k14, p2.

Row 17 K2, * p14, k5, p12, k5, rep from * once more, p14, k2.

Row 18 P22, k10, p26, k10, p22.

Row 19 K23, p8, k28, p8, k23.

Row 20 K20, p4, k6, p4, k22, p4, k6, p4, k20.

Row 21 P20, k4, p6, k4, p22, k4, p6, k4, p20.

Row 22 P23, k8, p28, k8, p23.

Row 23 K22, p10, k26, p10, k22.

Row 24 P2, * k14, p5, k12, p5, rep from * once more, k14, p2.

Row 25 K2, * p14, k4, p6, k2, p6, k4, rep from * once more, p14, k2.

Row 26 P19, k6, p4, k6, p20, k6, p4, k6, p19.

Row 27 * K18, p6, k6, p6, rep from * once more, k18.

Row 28 K1, * [p5, k6] twice, p8, k6, rep from * once more, p5, k6, p5, k1.

Row 29 P2, * [k4, p6] twice, k10, p6, rep from * once more, k4, p6, k4, p2.

Row 30 K3, * p12, k6, rep from * 3 times more, p12, k3.

Row 31 P4, * k10, [p6, k4] twice, p6, rep from * once more, k10, p4.

Row 32 K5, * p8, [k6, p5] twice, k6, rep from * once more, p8, k5.

Row 33 * P6, k6, p6, k18, rep from * once more, p6, k6, p6.

Row 34 P1, * k6, p4, k6, p20, rep from * once more, k6, p4, k6, p1.

Row 35 K2, * p6, k2, p6, k4, p14, k4, rep from * once more, p6, k2, p6, k2.

Row 36 P3, * k12, p5, k14, p5, rep from * once more, k12, p3.

Row 37 K4, * p10, k26, rep from * once more, p10, k4.

Row 38 P5, * k8, p28, rep from * once more, k8, p5.

These 38 rows form the patt.

Cont in patt until back measures approx 66cm/26in from cast-on edge, ending with row 30.

Shape neck

Next row Patt 35, turn and leave rem sts on a spare needle.

★ Keeping patt correct, cast off 2 sts at beg of next and every foll alt row until 25 sts rem.

Work 2 rows straight.

Cast off in patt. ★

Return to sts on spare needle.

With RS facing, join on yarn and cast off 20 sts, then patt to end. 35 sts.

Patt 1 row.

Now complete to match first side of neck from ★ to ★.

Front

Work as given for back until front measures approx 64cm/25in from cast-on edge, ending with row 26.

Shape neck

Next row Patt 35, turn and leave rem sts on a spare needle.

★★ Keeping patt correct, cast off 2 sts at beg of next and every foll alt row until 29 sts rem.

Dec 1 st at neck edge on every foll alt row until 25 sts rem.

Work 2 rows straight.

Cast off in patt. ★★

Return to sts on spare needle.

With RS facing, join on yarn and cast off 20 sts, then patt to end. 35 sts.

Patt one row, then complete to match first side of neck from ★★ to ★★.

Sleeves

Using 5½mm needles cast on 44 sts.

Work 5cm/2in k1, p1 rib, ending with a RS row.

Inc row Rib 4, * M1, rib 4, rep from * to end. 54 sts.

Change to 6½mm needles.

Work in patt as follows:

Row 1 (RS) P2, k4, p6, k4, p22, k4, p6, k4, p2.

Row 2 K2, p4, k6, p4, k22, p4, k6, p4, k2.

Row 3 K5, p8, k28, p8, k5.

Row 4 P4, k10, p26, k10, p4.

Row 5 K3, p12, k5, p14, k5, p12, k3.

Row 6 Inc in first st, p1, k6, p2, k6, p4, k14, p4, k6, p2, k6, p1, inc in last st. 56 sts.

Row 7 K2, p6, k4, p6, k20, p6, k4, p6, k2.

Row 8 P1, k6, p6, k6, p18, k6, p6, k6, p1.

Row 9 P6, k8, [p6, k5] twice, p6, k8, p6.

Row 10 K5, p10, [k6, p4] twice, k6, p10, k5.

Row 11 P4, [k12, p6] twice, k12, p4.

Row 12 Inc in first st, k2, [p4, k6] twice, p10, [k6, p4] twice, k2, inc in last st. 58 sts.

The last 12 rows establish the 38 row patt as given for back.

Continuing in patt, inc and work into patt 1 st each end of every foll 6th row until there are 86 sts.

Work straight until sleeve measures 50cm/19½in from cast-on edge, ending with a WS row.

Cast off.

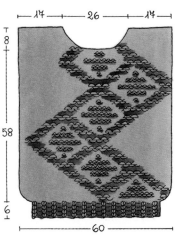

Back/Front

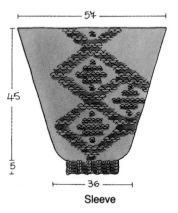

Sleeve

Measurements given in cm

Back neck border

With RS facing and using 5½mm needles, pick up and k54 sts evenly round back neck.

Beg with a p row, work 5 rows st st.

Cast off loosely.

Fold border in half to the WS and slipstitch into position.

Front neck border

With RS facing and using 5½mm needles, pick up and k62 sts evenly round front neck.

Now complete as given for back neck border.

Back neck rib insert

Using 5½mm needles cast on 60 sts.

Work 4 rows k1, p1 rib.

Continuing in rib, cast off 2 sts at beg of every row until 40 sts rem.

Cast off.

Sew shaped edge of rib insert to pick up row of neck border.

Front neck rib insert

Using 5½mm needles cast on 66 sts.

Work 4 rows k1, p1 rib.

Continuing in rib, cast off 2 sts at beg of every row until 46 sts rem.

Now complete as given for back rib insert.

To make up

Join shoulder, neck border and rib insert seams. Fold sleeves in half lengthwise, then placing folds to shoulder seams, sew in place. Join side and sleeve seams.

CARDIGAN WITH DIAMOND PATTERNED FRONTS

***

The back of this cardigan is plain with the diamond pattern, worked in a contrast tweedy yarn on the fronts. The same yarn is used for the ribs and borders.

Materials
8(8,9,10)×50g balls of Phildar Brisants (DK)
 in main colour A
2(3,3,3) balls of same in contrast colour B
A pair each of 3¼mm/No10 and 4½mm/
 No7 knitting needles
3¼mm/No10 circular knitting needle
5 buttons

Measurements
To fit chest 97(102,107,112)cm/
38(40,42,44)in
Actual measurements
Chest 110(116,121,127)cm/
43½(45½,47½,50)in
Length to shoulders 68cm/27in
Sleeve seam 54cm/21½in

Tension
19 sts and 26 rows to 10cm/4in measured
over st st worked on 4½mm needles

Left front
Using 3¼mm needles and B, cast on
46(50,52,54) sts.
Rib row 1 * K1, p1, rep from * to last 2 sts,
k2.
Rib row 2 * K1, p1, rep from * to end.
Rep these 2 rows for 4cm/1½in, ending with

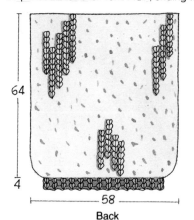

64

4

58

Back

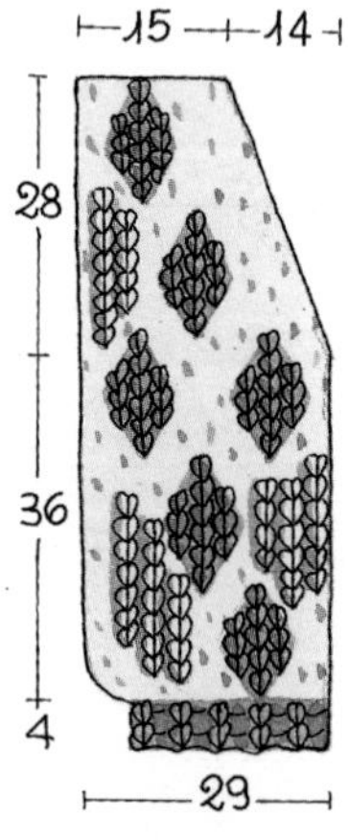

15 14

28

36

4

29

Right Front

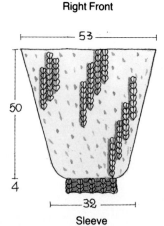

53

50

4

32

Sleeve

Measurements given in cm for second size

rib row 1.
Inc row Rib 3(5,6,2), * M1, rib 8(10,10,10),
rep from * to last 3(5,6,2) sts, M1, rib to end.
52(55,57,60) sts.
Change to 4½mm needles.
Carrying yarn not in use loosely across WS
of work and weaving yarn in at back of work
when passing across more than 5 sts, work
in patt from chart 1 as follows:
Row 1 (RS) *For 1st size only* k1A, 1B, *for 1st
and 4th sizes only* k3(3)A, *for 1st, 3rd and
4th sizes only* k2(2,2)A, then *for all sizes*
* k4A, 1B, 5A, rep from * 3(4,4,4) times
more, k5A.
Row 2 P5A, * p5A, 1B, 4A, rep from
* 3(4,4,4) times more, *for 1st, 3rd and 4th
sizes only* p2(2,2)A, *for 1st and 4th sizes
only* p3(3)A, then *for 1st size only* p1B, 1A.
Now beg with row 3, cont in patt from chart 1
until front measures approx 40cm/15½in
from cast-on edge, ending with row 22.
(Place a coloured marker at beg of last row.)
Shape front edge
Dec 1 st at end of next and every foll alt row
until 33(36,38,41) sts rem.
Work 3 rows.
Dec 1 st at end of next and every foll 4th row
until 25(28,30,33) sts rem.
Work 3 rows.
Cast off.

Right front
Using 3¼mm needles and B, cast on
46(50,52,54) sts.
Rib row 1 K2, * p1, k1, rep from * to end.
Rib row 2 * P1, k1, rep from * to end.
Rep these 2 rows for 4cm/1½in, ending with
rib row 1.
Inc row Rib 3(5,6,2), * M1, rib 8(10,10,10),
rep from * to last 3(5,6,2) sts, M1, rib to end.
52(55,57,60) sts.
Change to 4½mm needles.
Work in patt from chart 2 as follows:
Row 1 (RS) K5A, * k5A, 1B, 4A, rep from *
3(4,4,4) times more, *for 1st, 3rd and 4th
sizes only* k2(2,2)A, *for 1st and 4th sizes
only* k3(3)A, then *for 1st size only* k1B, 1A.
Row 2 *For 1st size only* p1A, 1B, *for 1st and
4th sizes only* p3(3)A, *for 1st, 3rd and 4th
sizes only* p2(2,2)A, then *for all sizes* * p4A,
1B, 5A, rep from * 3(4,4,4) times more, p5A.
Now beg with row 3, cont in patt from chart 2
until front measures approx 40cm/15½in
from cast-on edge, ending with row 22.
(Place a coloured marker at end of last row.)
Shape front edge
Dec 1 st at beg of next and every foll alt row
until 33(36,38,41) sts rem.
Work 3 rows.
Dec 1 st at beg of next and every foll 4th row
until 25(28,30,33) sts rem.
Work 3 rows.
Cast off.

Back
Using 3¼mm needles and B, cast on
95(101,105,111) sts.
Rib row 1 K1, * p1, k1, rep from * to end.
Rib row 2 P1, * k1, p1, rep from * to end.
Rep these 2 rows for 4cm/1½in, ending with
rib row 1.
Inc row Rib 7(5,7,6), * M1, rib 9(10,10,11),
rep from * to last 7(6,8,6) sts, M1, rib to end.
105(111,115,121) sts.
Change to 4½mm needles.
Cut off B, join on A.
Work in st st until back measures same as
front to shoulder, ending with a p row.
Shape shoulders
Cast off 25(28,30.33) sts at beg of next
2 rows. 55 sts.
Cast off.

Sleeves
Using 3¼mm needles and B, cast on 45 sts.
Work 4cm/1½in rib as given for back,
ending with rib row 1.
Inc row Rib 1, * M1, rib 3, rep from * to last
2 sts, M1, rib 2. 60 sts.
Change to 4½mm needles.
Cut off B, join on A.
Working in st st, inc 1 st each end of 7th and
every foll 6th row until there are 100 sts.
Work straight until sleeve measures 54cm/
21½in from cast-on edge, ending with a
p row.
Cast off.

Button and buttonhole border
Join shoulder seams.
With RS facing, using 3¼mm circular
needle and B and beg at hem, pick up and
k80 sts up right front edge to marker, 60 sts
up right front shaping, 57 sts across back
neck, 60 sts down left front shaping to
marker and 80 sts down left front to hem.
337 sts.
Rib row 1 (WS) K1, * p1, k1, rep from * to
end.
Rib row 2 K2, * p1, k1, rep from * to last st,
k1.
Rep these 2 rows once more, then rib row 1
again.
Buttonhole row Rib to last 78 sts, k2 tog, yf,
* rib 16, k2 tog, yf, rep from * 3 times more,
rib to end.
Rib 5 rows.
Cast off in rib.

To make up
Fold sleeves in half lengthwise, then placing
folds to shoulder seams, sew into place.
Join side and sleeve seams.
Sew on buttons.

Chart 1

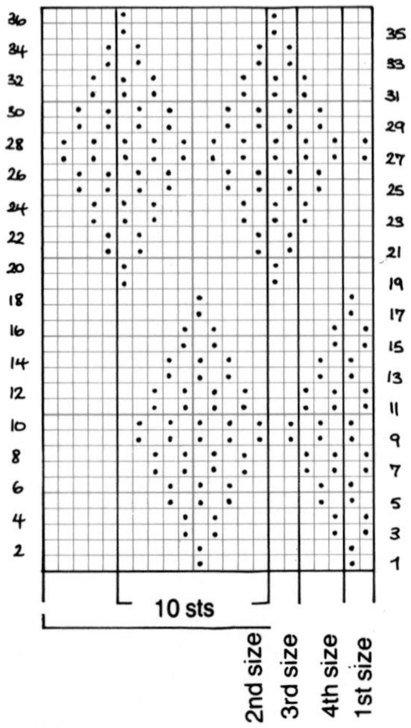

Chart 2

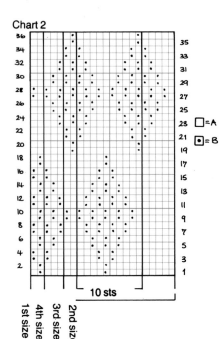

□ = A
▪ = B

10 sts

10 sts

2nd size
3rd size
4th size
1st size

RIBBED SQUARES V NECK JERSEY

**

A classic
V necked
jersey knitted in
a chunky yarn
with a contrast
colour worked
into the neckband.

Materials

13(14)×50g balls of Hayfield Grampian Chunky in main colour A
1 ball of same in contrast colour B
A pair each of 5mm/No6 and 6mm/No4 knitting needles

Measurements

To fit chest 91–97(102–112)cm/36–38 (40–44)in

Actual measurements

Chest 100(120)cm/39½(47)in
Length to shoulders 70(72)cm/27½(28¼)in
Sleeve seam 43cm/17in

Tension

15½ sts and 19 rows to 10cm/4in measured over patt (slightly opened out) worked on 6mm needles

Back

★ Using 5mm needles and A, cast on 64(76) sts.
Rib row 1 K2, * p1, k1, rep from * to end.
Rep this row for 8cm/3in, ending with a RS row.
Inc row P8(6) * M1, p4, rep from * to last 4(2) sts, p4(2). 77(93) sts.
Change to 6mm needles.
Work in patt as follows:
Row 1 K3, * p2, k3, p2, k1, p7, k1, rep from * to last 10 sts, [p2, k3] twice.
Row 2 [P3, k2] twice, * p1, k7, p1, k2, p3, k2, rep from * to last 3 sts, p3.
Rows 3 to 6 Rep rows 1 and 2 twice.
Row 7 As row 1.
Row 8 [P3, k2] twice, * p9, k2, p3, k2, rep from * to last 3 sts, p3.
Row 9 K3, * p2, k3, p2, k9, rep from * to last 10 sts, [p2, k3] twice.
Rows 10 and 11 As rows 8 and 9.
Row 12 As row 2.
Rows 13 to 16 Rep rows 1 and 2 twice.
Row 17 As row 1.
Row 18 K2, p1, k7, * p1, k2, p3, k2, p1, k7, rep from * to last 3 sts, p1, k2.
Row 19 P2, k1, * p7, k1, p2, k3, p2, k1, rep from * to last 10 sts, p7, k1, p2.
Row 20 As row 18.
Row 21 P2, k1, * p7, k1, p2, k3, p2, k1, rep from * to last 10 sts, p7, k1, p2.
Rows 22 and 23 As rows 18 and 19.
Row 24 As row 18.
Row 25 P2, k1, * k8, p2, k3, p2, k1, rep from * to last 10 sts, k8, p2.
Row 26 K2, p8, * p1, k2, p3, k2, p8, rep from * to last 3 sts, p1, k2.
Rows 27 and 28 As rows 25 and 26.
Row 29 As row 19.
Rows 30 to 33 Rep rows 18 and 19 twice.
Row 34 As row 18.
These 34 rows form the patt.
Cont in patt until back measures 44(46)cm/ 17¼(18)in from cast-on edge, ending with a WS row.

Shape armholes

Keeping patt correct, cast off 3 sts at beg of next 2 rows.
Dec 1 st each end of next and foll alt row.
Patt 1 row. 67(83) sts. ★
Work straight until armholes measure 26cm/ 10¼in from beg of shaping, ending with a WS row.

Shape shoulders

Cast off 22(29) sts at beg of next 2 rows.
Cut off yarn and leave rem 23(25) sts on a holder.

Front

Work as given for back from ★ to ★.
Shape neck
Next row Patt 33(41) sts, turn and leave rem sts on a spare needle.
Patt 1 row.
Keeping patt correct, dec 1 st at neck edge on next and every foll alt row until 22(29) sts rem.
Work straight until front measures same as back to shoulder, ending with a WS row.
Cast off.
Return to sts on spare needle.
With RS facing, slip next st on to a safety-pin, join on yarn, then patt to end. 33(41) sts.
Now complete to match first side of neck.

Sleeves

Using 5mm needles and A, cast on 36 sts.
Work 7cm/2¾in rib as given for back, ending with a RS row.
Inc row P6, * M1, p3, rep from * to last 3 sts, p3. 45 sts.
Change to 6mm needles.
Working in patt as given for back, inc and work into patt 1 st each end of 5th and every foll 4th row until there are 67 sts. Work straight until sleeve measures 43cm/17in, ending with a WS row.
Shape top
Keeping patt correct, cast off 3 sts at beg of

next 2 rows and 2 sts at beg of foll 2 rows.
Dec 1 st each end of next and foll alt row.
53 sts.
Patt 1 row.
Cast off.

Neckband

Join right shoulder seam.
With RS facing, using 5mm needles and B, pick up and k48(52) sts down left side of front neck, k the st from safety-pin and mark this st with a coloured thread, pick up and k48(52) sts up right side of front neck, then k across 23(25) sts from back neck holder. 120(130) sts.
Rib row 1 P1, [k1, p1] to within 2 sts of marked st, skpo, p centre st, k2 tog, [p1, k1] to end.
Rib row 2 Rib to within 2 sts of marked st, skpo, k centre st, k2 tog, rib to end.
Work rib row 1 once more.
Cut off B, join on A and k 1 row decreasing as before.
Rep rib rows 1 and 2 until neckband measures 5cm/2in, ending with a WS row.
Cast off in rib, decreasing as before.

To make up

Join left shoulder and neckband seam.
Set in sleeves, then join side and sleeve seams.

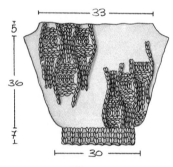

Sleeve

Measurements given in cm for larger size

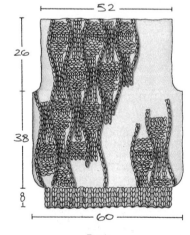

Back

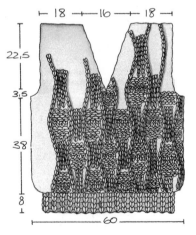

Front

STRIPED SHIRT NECKED JERSEY

**

The mock pocket edging can be omitted if you prefer on this brightly striped cotton jersey.

Materials

6(7,8)×50g balls of Scheepjeswol
   Mayflower Helarsgarn (Aran type cotton)
   in main colour A
3 balls of same in each of contrast colours
   C and E
2 balls of same in each of contrast colours
   B and D
A pair each of 4½mm/No7 and 5½mm/No5
   knitting needles
3 buttons

Measurements

To fit chest 102(107,112)cm/40(42,44)in
Actual measurements
Chest 110(115,120)cm/43¼(45¼,47¼)in
Length to shoulders 69cm/27in
Sleeve seam 46cm/18in

Tension

16 sts and 21 rows to 10cm/4in measured
over st st worked on 5½mm needles

Back

★ Using 4½mm needles and A, cast on
78(82,86) sts.
Work 6cm/2½in k1, p1 rib, ending with a RS
row.
Inc row Rib 7(9,11) * M1, rib 7, rep from * to
last 1(3,5) sts, rib to end. 88(92,96) sts.
Change to 5½mm needles.
Beg with a k row, work in st st and stripe patt
as follows:
3 rows A, 1 row B, 3 rows A, 2 rows E, 3 rows
A, 3 rows D, 2 rows A, 4 rows D, 2 rows A, 3
rows E, 3 rows A, 2 rows D, 3 rows A, 1 row
B, 2 rows A, 4 rows C, 2 rows A, 1 row B, 1
row A, 4 rows B, 1 row A, 1 row B, 2 rows A,
4 rows C, 2 rows A, 1 row E, 1 row A, 4 rows
E, 1 row A, 1 row E, 2 rows A, 1 row B, 3
rows A, 2 rows E, 3 rows A, 2 rows D ★, 1
row D, 2 rows A, 4 rows D, 2 rows A, 3 rows
E, 3 rows A, 2 rows D, 2 rows A, 3 rows B, 2
rows A, 4 rows C, 2 rows A, 1 row B, 1 row A,
4 rows B, 1 row A, 1 row B, 3 rows A, 4 rows
C, 3 rows A, 1 row E, 1 row A, and 2 rows E.
Shape shoulders
Using E, cast off 25(26,27) sts at beg of next
2 rows.
Cut off yarn and leave rem 38(40,42) sts on
a holder.

Front

Work as given for back from ★ to ★.
Divide for front neck opening
Next row Patt 41(44,45) sts, turn and leave
rem sts on a spare needle.
Work 38 rows more in stripe patt as given for
back, so ending with a RS row in A.
Shape neck
Keeping stripe patt correct, cast off 4 sts at
beg of next row and 3(4,4) sts at beg of foll
alt row.
Patt 1 row.
Cast off 3(3,4) sts at beg of next row and
3 sts at beg of foll 2 alt rows.
Patt 4 more rows, so ending with 2 rows E.
Using E, cast off.
Return to sts on spare needle.
With RS facing, join on D and cast off first
6 sts, then k to end. 41(44,45) sts.
Work 39 rows more in stripe patt as given for
back, so ending with a WS row in A.

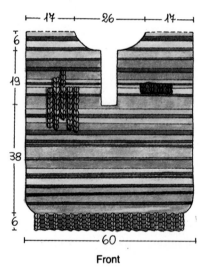

Back

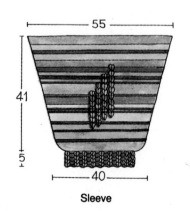

Front

Sleeve

Measurements given in cm for largest size

Now complete to match first side of neck,
ending with 2 rows in E.

Sleeves

Using 4½mm needles and A, cast on
40(44,48) sts.
Work 5cm/2in k1, p1 rib, ending with a RS
row.
Inc row Rib 6(1,8), * M1, rib 2(3,2), rep from
* to last 6(1,8) sts, rib to end. 54(58,64) sts.
Change to 5½mm needles.
Beg with a k row and increasing 1 st each
end of 5th and every foll 6th row until there
are 82(84,88) sts, work in st st and stripe
patt as follows:
2 rows A, 1 row B, 3 rows C, 2 rows E, 3 rows
C, 3 rows D, 2 rows C, 4 rows D, 2 rows C, 4
rows E, 2 rows C, 2 rows D, 2 rows C, 1 row
B, 3 rows A, 4 rows C, 2 rows A, 1 row B, 1
row A, 4 rows B, 1 row A, 1 row B, 2 rows A,
4 rows C, 2 rows A, 1 row E, 1 row C, 4 rows
E, 2 rows C, 1 row B, 3 rows C, 2 rows E, 3
rows C, 3 rows D, 2 rows C, 4 rows D, and 2
rows C.
Using C, cast off.

Buttonhole border

With RS facing, and using 4½mm needles
and A, pick up and k38 sts along left front
opening edge.
Work 2cm/¾in k1, p1 rib, ending with a WS
row.
Buttonhole row 1 Rib 3, * cast off 2 sts, rib
next 12 sts, rep from * once more, cast off
2 sts, rib to end.
Buttonhole row 2 Rib to end, casting on 2 sts
over those cast off in previous row.
Cont in rib until border measures 4cm/1½in
from beg, ending with a WS row.
Cast off in rib.

Button border

Work as given for buttonhole border,
omitting buttonholes.

Collar

Join shoulder seams.
With RS facing, using 4½mm needles and
A, beg at centre of button border and pick
up and k26(27,29) sts up right side of front
neck, k across 38(40,42) sts from back neck
holder, then pick up and k26(27,29) sts
down left side of front neck, ending at centre
of buttonhole border. 90(94,100) sts.
Work 6cm/2½in k1, p1 rib, ending with a WS
row.
Cast off in rib.

Mock pocket top

Using 4½mm needles and A, cast on 30 sts.
Work 3cm/1¼in k1, p1 rib.
Cast off in rib.

To make up

Lapping buttonhole border over button
border, slipstitch row ends to cast-off sts at
centre front. Fold sleeves in half lengthwise,
then placing folds to shoulder seams, sew
into place. Join side and sleeve seams. Sew
on buttons. Sew mock pocket top into place
on left front.

SIMPLE SLIPOVER IN A DROP STITCH PATTERN

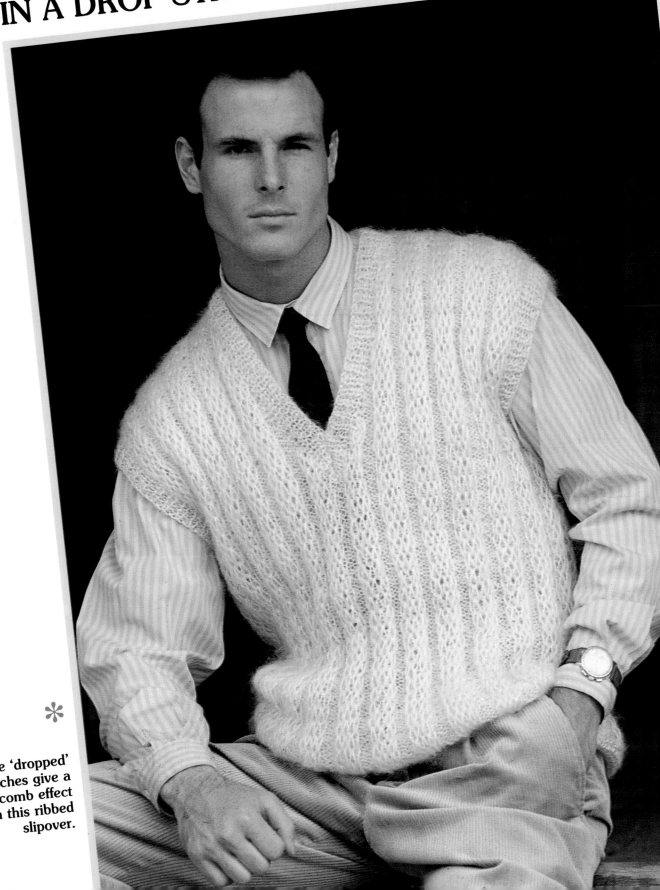

The 'dropped' stitches give a honeycomb effect on this ribbed slipover.

Materials

6(7,8)×50g balls of Neveda Cablee
A pair each of 4½mm/No7 and 5mm/No6
   knitting needles

Measurements

To fit chest 97(102,107)cm/38(40,42)in
Actual measurements
Chest 104(108,112)cm/41(42½,44)in
Length to shoulders 65(68,71)cm/
25½(27,28)in

Tension

20 sts and 23 rows to 10cm/4in measured
over patt worked on 5mm needles

Back

★ Using 4½mm needles, cast on
93(97,101) sts.
Rib row 1 K1, * p1, k1, rep from * to end.
Rib row 2 P1, * k1, p1, rep from * to end.
Rep these 2 rows for 5cm/2in, ending with
rib row 1.
Inc row Rib 6(9,10), M1, [rib 8, M1] 10 times,
rib 7(8,11). 104(108,112) sts.
Change to 5mm needles.
Carrying yarn loosely behind the slip
stitches, work in patt as follows:
Row 1 (RS) P6(8,10), * [winding yarn 3
times round needle, k next st] 4 times, p4,
rep from * 11 times, [winding yarn 3 times
round needle, k next st] 4 times, p6(8,10).
Row 2 K6(8,10), * ytf, [dropping extra loops
off needle, slip next st purlwise] 4 times, ytb,
k4, rep from * 11 times, ytf, [dropping extra
loops off needle, slip next st purlwise]
4 times, ytb, k6(8,10).
Row 3 P6(8,10), * ytb, sl 4 pw, ytf, p4, rep
from * 11 times, ytb, sl 4 pw, ytf, p6(8,10).
Row 4 K6(8,10), * ytf, sl 4 pw, ytb, k4, rep
from * 11 times, ytf, sl 4 pw, ytb, k6(8,10).
These 4 rows form the patt.
Cont in patt until back measures approx
39(41,43)cm/15½(16,17)in, ending with
row 4. ★
Shape armholes
Cast off in patt 4 sts at beg of next 2 rows.
Keeping patt correct and always knitting or
purling the st at each end of the row when
shaping, dec 1 st each end of next and
every foll alt row until 90(94,98) sts rem.
Cont in patt until armholes measure approx
26(27,28)cm/10¼(10½,11)in, ending with a
WS row.
Shape shoulders
Cast off in patt 10 sts at beg of next 6 rows.
Cut off yarn and leave rem 30(34,38) sts on
a holder.

Front

Work as given for back from ★ to ★.
Shape armholes and divide for neck
Next row Cast off 4 sts, patt until there are
48(50,52) sts on right-hand needle, turn and

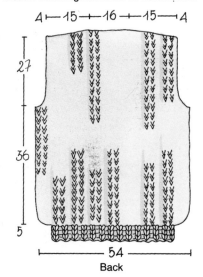

Measurements given in cm for second size

Back

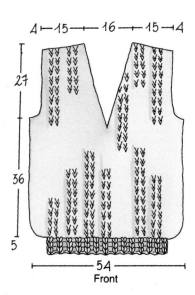

Front

leave rem sts on a spare needle.
★★ **Next row** Patt to end.
Next row Work 2 tog, patt to last 2 sts, work
2 tog.
Next row Patt to end.
Rep the last 2 rows twice more.
42(44,46) sts.
Keeping armhole edge straight, dec 1 st at
neck edge on next and every foll alt row to
39(38,36) sts, then on every foll 4th row until
30 sts rem.
Work straight until front measures same as
back to beg of shoulder shaping, ending
with a WS row.
Shape shoulder
Cast off in patt 10 sts at beg of next and foll
alt row.
Patt 1 row.
Cast off. ★★
Return to sts on spare needle.
With RS facing, join on yarn, then patt to
end. 52(54,56) sts.
Next row Cast off 4 sts, patt to end.
48(50,52) sts.
Now complete as given for first side of neck
from ★★ to ★★.

Left front neckband

Join right shoulder seam.
With RS facing and using 4½mm needles,
pick up and k57(59,61) sts down left side of
front neck.
Rib row P2 tog, k1, * p1, k1, rep from * to

end.
Continuing in rib as set and decreasing 1 st
at centre front on every row, work 8 rows rib.
Cast off in rib.

Back and right front neckband

With RS facing and beg at centre front, pick
up and k57(59,61) sts up right side of front
neck, then k30(34,38) sts from back neck
holder. 87(93,99) sts.
Rib row K1, * p1, k1, rep from * to last 2 sts,
p2 tog.
Continuing in rib as set and decreasing 1 st
at centre front on every row, work 8 rows rib.
Cast off in rib.

Armhole borders

Join left shoulder and neckband seam.
With RS facing, pick up and
k101(105,109) sts evenly along armhole
edge.
Work 8 rows rib as given for back.
Cast off in rib.

To make up

Join side and armhole border seams. Join
seam at centre front of neckband.

CLASSIC RICE STITCH CARDIGAN

**

Rice stitch
looks
a bit
like moss stitch
but is slightly
simpler to knit
as every other row
is a knit row.

Materials

15(16,17)×50g balls of Emu Superwash DK
A pair each of 3¼mm/No10 and 5mm/No6
  knitting needles
A 3¼mm/No10 circular needle 80–100cm/
  30–36in long
5 buttons

Measurements

To fit chest 91–97(102–107,112–117)cm/
36–38(40–42,44–46)in
Actual measurements
Chest 110(118.5,127)cm/43½(46¾,50)in
Length to shoulders 69(71,73)cm/
27(28,28¾)in
Sleeve seam 47(48,50)cm/18½(19,19½)in

Tension

21 sts and 28 rows to 10cm/4in measured
over rice st worked on 5mm needles

Back

Using 3¼mm needles, cast on
95(103,111) sts.
Rib row 1 P1, * k1, p1, rep from * to end.
Rib row 2 K1, * p1, k1, rep from * to end.
Rep these 2 rows for 5cm/2in, ending with
rib row 1.
Inc row K5(4,3), * M1, k5, rep from * to last
5(4,3) sts, M1, k5(4,3). 113(123,133) sts.
Change to 5mm needles.
Work in rice st as follows:
Row 1 (RS) P1, * k1 tbl, p1, rep from * to
end.
Row 2 K to end.
These 2 rows form the patt.
Cont in patt until work measures
69(71,73)cm/27(28,28¾)in from cast-on
edge, ending with a WS row.
Shape shoulders
Next row Cast off in patt 39(43,47) sts, patt
until there are 35(37,39) sts on the needle,
cast off rem 39(43,47) sts.
Cut off yarn and leave rem sts on a holder.

Pocket linings (make 2)

Using 5mm needles cast on 39 sts.
Work in patt as given for back for 13cm/5in
ending with a WS row.
Cut off yarn and leave sts on a holder.

Left front

★ Using 3¼mm needles cast on
49(53,57) sts.
Work 5cm/2in rib as given for back, ending
with rib row 1.
Inc row K2(4,6), * M1, k5, rep from * to last
2(4,6) sts, M1, k2(4,6). 59(63,67) sts.
Change to 5mm needles.
Work in patt as given for back until front
measures 18cm/7in from cast-on edge,
ending with a WS row ★.
Place pocket
Next row Patt 6(8,10), slip the next 39 sts on
to a holder and in their place, with RS
facing, patt across 39 sts of first pocket
lining, patt to end.
★★ Cont in patt until work measures
39cm/15½in from cast-on edge, ending
with a WS row.
Mark beg of last row with a coloured thread
to indicate beg of neck shaping. (For right
front, mark end of row.)
Shape neck
Dec 1 st at neck edge on next and every foll
4th row until 39(43,47) sts rem.

Work straight until front measures same as
back to shoulders, ending with a WS row.
Cast off in patt. ★★

Right front

Work as given for left front from ★ to ★.
Place pocket
Next row Patt 14(16,18), slip the next 39 sts
on to a holder and in their place, with RS
facing, patt across 39 sts of second pocket
lining, patt to end.
Complete as given for left front from ★★ to
★★ noting exception given in brackets.

Sleeves

Using 3¼mm needles cast on
55(57,59) sts.
Work 6cm/2½in rib as given for back,
ending with rib row 1.
Inc row K5(6,7), * M1, k5, rep from * to last
5(6,7) sts, M1, k5(6,7). 65(67,69) sts.
Change to 5mm needles.
Working in patt as given for back, inc and
work into patt 1 st each end of 3rd and every
foll 4th row until there are 73(77,81) sts, then
each end of every foll 6th row until there are
101(105,109) sts.

Work straight until sleeve measures
47(48,50)cm/18½(19,19¾)in from cast-on
edge, ending with a WS row.
Cast off in patt.

Button and buttonhole border

Join shoulder seams.
With RS facing and using 3¼mm circular
needle, pick up and k86 sts up right front
edge to marker, 80(84,88) sts up right neck
edge, k35(37,39) sts from back neck holder,
pick up and k80(84,88) sts down left neck
edge to marker, then 86 sts down left front
to lower edge. 367(377,387) sts.
Working backwards and forwards in rows.
work 3 rows rib as given for back.
Buttonhole row 1 Rib to last 86 sts, [cast
off 2, rib 18 including st used in casting off]
4 times, cast off 2, rib to end.
Buttonhole row 2 Rib to end, casting on 2 sts
over those cast off in previous row.
Work 2 more rows in rib.
Cast off in rib.

Pocket tops

With RS facing and using 3¼mm needles,
slip the 39 sts on holder for pocket top on to
a needle.
Work 6 rows in rib as given for back.
Cast off in rib.

To make up

Fold sleeves in half lengthwise, then placing
folds to shoulder seams, sew into place.
Join side and sleeve seams. Slipstitch
pocket tops and linings into place. Sew on
buttons.

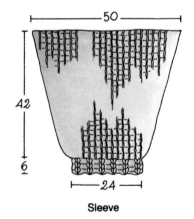

├─ 20·5 ─┼─ 17·5 ─┼─ 20·5 ─┤

66

5

├──── 58·5 ────┤

Back

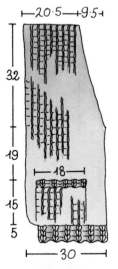

├─20·5─┼─9·5─┤

32

19

├── 18 ──┤

15

5

├── 30 ──┤

Right Front

├──── 50 ────┤

42

6

├── 24 ──┤

Sleeve

Measurements given in cm for second size

JERSEY IN CABLE AND GARTER STITCH BLOCKS

✳✳

A bold cable twist is used to contrast with the garter stitch blocks on this jersey knitted in an Aran weight yarn.

Materials
25(27)×50g balls of Jaeger Sport
A pair each of 3¾mm/No9 and
4½mm/No7 knitting needles
Cable needle

Measurements
To fit chest 96(112)cm/38(44)in
Actual measurements
Chest 112(128)cm 44(50)in
Length to shoulders 64(67)cm 25(26½)in
Sleeve seam 51.5(54.5)cm/20¼(21½)in

Tension
20 sts and 28 rows to 10cm/4in measured
over patt worked on 4½mm needles

Special abbreviation
C10 Cable 10 as follows: slip next 5 sts on
to cable needle and leave at front of work.
k5. then k5 from cable needle

Back
Using 3¾mm needles cast on
106(122) sts.
Rib row 1 K2 * p2. k2, rep from * to end.
Rib row 2 P2 * k2. p2, rep from * to end.
Rep these 2 rows for 6cm/2½in, ending
with rib row 1.
Inc row Rib 3(11). * M1, rib 20, rep from
* to last 3(11) sts. M1, rib to end.
112(128) sts.
Change to 4½mm needles.
Row 1 (RS) * K14(16), p14(16). rep from
* to end.
Row 2 * K14(16). p14(16), rep from * to
end.
Rows 3 to 5 Beg with a k row, work 3 rows
st st.
Row 6 * K14(16). p14(16), rep from * to
end.
Row 7 * K14(16). p14(16), rep from * to
end.
Row 8 P to end.
Row 9 K2(3). * C10, k18(22), rep from * to
last 26(29) sts. C10, k to end.
Row 10 P to end.
Rows 11 to 18 Rep rows 1 to 8.
Row 19 * P14(16), k14(16), rep from * to
end.
Row 20 * P14(16). k14(16), rep from * to
end.
Rows 21 to 23 Beg with a k row, work 3
rows st st.
Row 24 * P14(16). k14(16), rep from * to
end.
Row 25 * P14(16). k14(16), rep from * to
end.
Row 26 P to end.
Row 27 K16(19). * C10, k18(22), rep from
* to last 12(13) sts. C10, k to end.
Row 28 P to end.
Rows 29 to 36 As rows 19 to 26.
These 36 rows form the patt.
Cont in patt until back measures
64(67)cm/25(26)in from cast-on edge.
ending with a WS row.
Cast off.
Place a marker on 37th(43rd) st from each
end.

Front
Work as given for back until front measures
55(58)cm/21½(22¾)in from cast-on edge,
ending with a WS row.
Shape neck
Next row Patt 46(52), turn and leave rem
sts on a spare needle.
★ Cast off 3 sts at beg of next and foll 2 alt
rows. 37(43) sts.
Work straight until front measures same as
back to shoulders, ending with a WS row.
Cast off. ★
Return to sts on spare needle.

With RS facing, join yarn and cast off first
20(24) sts. then patt to end. 46(52) sts.
Patt 1 row. then complete to match first
side of neck as given from ★ to ★.

Sleeves
Using 3¾mm needles cast on 38(46) sts.
Work 6.5cm/2½in rib as given for back,
ending with a RS row.
Inc row Rib 2(6). * M1, rib 2. rep from *
to last 2(6) sts, M1, rib to end.
56(64) sts.
Change to 4½mm needles.
Row 1 (RS) [K14(16), p14(16) sts] twice.
Row 2 As row 1.
Row 3 K to end.
Row 4 P to end.
Row 5 Inc in first st, k to last st, inc in last
st. 58(66) sts.
Row 6 P1. [k14(16), p14(16)] twice, k1.
Row 7 As row 6.
Row 8 P to end.
Row 9 K3(4), C10, k18(22), C10, k17(20).
Row 10 P to end.
Row 11 Inc in first st, [k14(16), p14(16) sts]
twice, inc in last st. 60(68) sts.
Row 12 P2, [k14(16), p14(16) sts] twice,
k2.
Rows 13 to 15 Beg with a k row, work 3
rows st st.
Row 16 As row 12.
Row 17 Inc in first st, p1, [k14(16),
p14(16) sts] twice, k1, inc in last st.
62(70) sts.
Row 18 P to end.
Row 19 K3, [p14(16), k14(16) sts] twice,
p3.
Row 20 As row 19.
Rows 21 and 22 Beg with a k row, work 2
rows st st.
Row 23 Inc in first st, k to last st, inc in last
st. 64(72) sts.

Measurements given in cm for larger size

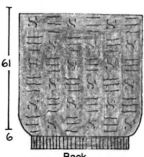

Back

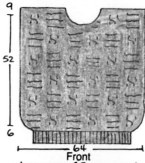

Front

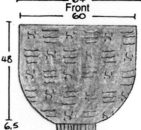

Sleeve

Row 24 K4, [p14(16), k14(16) sts] twice,
p4.
Row 25 As row 24.
Row 26 P to end.
Row 27 K20(23), C10. k18(22), C10, k6(7).
Row 28 P to end.
Row 29 Inc in first st, k3, [p14(16),
k14(16) sts] twice, p3, inc in last st.
66(74) sts.
Row 30 K5, [p14(16), k14(16) sts] twice,
p5.
Rows 31 and 32 Beg with a k row, work 2
rows st st.
Row 33 Inc in first st, k to last st, inc in last
st. 68(76) sts.
Row 34 K6, [p14(16), k14(16) sts] twice.
p6.
Row 35 Inc in first st, k5, [p14(16),
k14(16) sts] twice, p5, inc in last st.
70(78) sts.
Row 36 P to end.
Row 37 P7, [k14(16), p14(16) sts] twice.
k7.
Row 38 P7, [k14(16), p14(16) sts] twice.
k7.
Row 39 K to end.
Row 40 P to end.
Row 41 Inc in first st, k to last st, inc in last
st. 72(80) sts.
Row 42 P8, [k14(16), p14(16) sts] twice.
k8.
Row 43 As row 42.
Row 44 P to end.
Row 45 Inc in first st, k9(10), C10, k18(22),
C10, k24(26), inc in last st. 74(82) sts.
Row 46 P to end.
Row 47 P9, [k14(16), p14(16) sts] twice.
k9.
Row 48 As row 47.
Row 49 Inc in first st, k to last st, inc in last
st. 76(84) sts.
Rows 50 to 51 Beg with a p row work 2
rows st st.
Row 52 P10, [k14(16), p14(16) sts] twice.
k10.
Row 53 Inc in first st, p9, [k14(16),
p14(16) sts] twice, k9, inc in last st.
78(86) sts.
Row 54 P to end.
Row 55 K11, [p14(16), k14(16) sts] twice.
p11.
Row 56 As row 55.
Rows 57 to 59 As rows 49 to 51. 80(88) sts.
Row 60 K12, [p14(16), k14(16) sts] twice,
p12.
Continuing in patt, inc and work into patt
1 st each end of next and every foll 4th row
until there are 112(120) sts.
Work straight in patt until sleeve measures
51.5(54.5)cm/20¼(21½)in from cast-on
edge, ending with a WS row.
Cast off.

Neckband
Join right shoulder seam to marker.
With RS facing and using 3¾mm needles,
pick up and k20 sts down left side of front
neck, 16(18) sts from front neck, 20 sts up
right side of front neck, then 30(32) sts
from back neck. 86(90) sts.
Beg with rib row 2, work 3cm/1in rib as
given for back.
Cast off in rib.

To make up
Join left shoulder and neckband seam.
Fold sleeves in half lengthwise, then
placing folds to shoulder seams, sew into
place. Join side and sleeve seams.

JERSEY WITH A TRAVELLING STITCH PATTERN

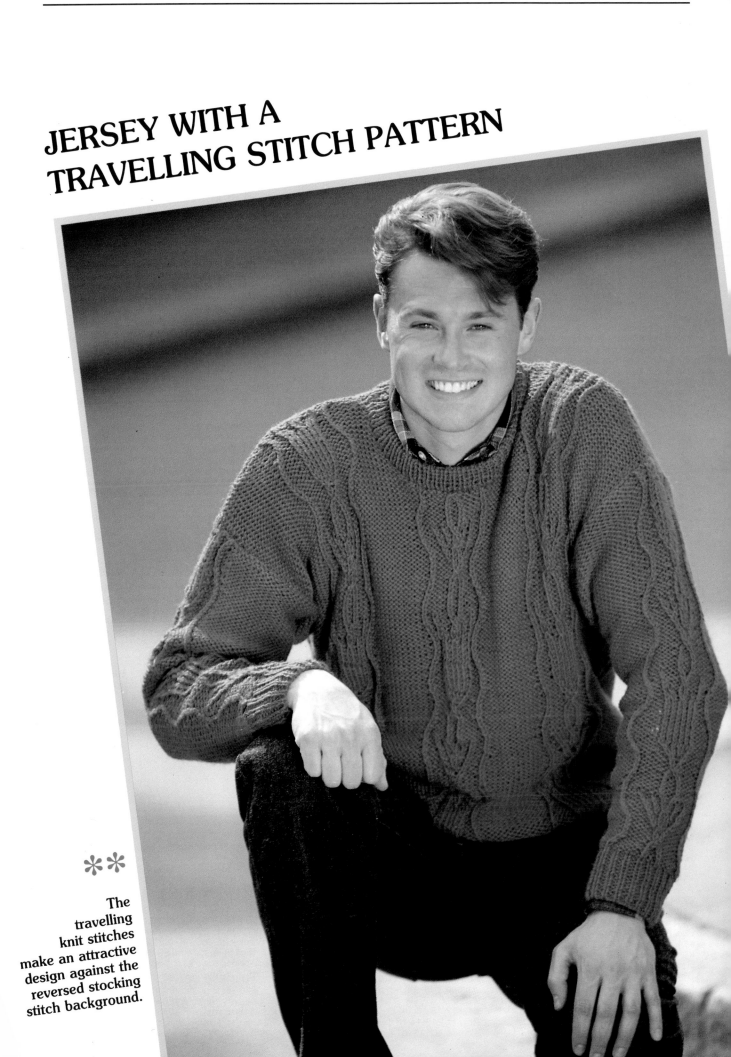

**

The travelling knit stitches make an attractive design against the reversed stocking stitch background.

Materials

8(8,9,9)×100g balls of Water Wheel Concorde Chunky
A pair each of 4½mm/No7 and 5½mm/No5 knitting needles   Cable needle

Measurements

To fit chest 97(101,106,111)cm/
38(40,42,44)in

Actual measurements
Chest 101(106,112,117)cm/40(42,44,46)in
Length to shoulders 70(72,74,76)cm/
27½(28½,29,30)in
Sleeve seam 46(47,49,49)cm/
18(18½,19,19)in

Tension

15 sts and 20 rows to 10cm/4in measured over rev st st worked on 5½mm needles

Special abbreviations

Tw2R Twist 2 right as follows: k into front of second st on left-hand needle, then k first st, slipping both sts off needle tog
Tw2L Twist 2 left as follows: k into back of second st on left-hand needle, then k first st, slipping both sts off needle tog
Cr2L Cross 2 left as follows: slip next st on to cable needle and leave at front of work, p1, then k1 from cable needle
Cr2R Cross 2 right as follows: slip next st on to cable needle and leave at back of work, k1, then p1 from cable needle
Cr4 Cross 4 sts as follows: slip next st on to cable needle and leave at front of work, slip next st on to same cable needle and leave at front, k1, then [k1, p1] from cable needle
Cr3R Cross 3 right as follows: slip next st on to cable needle and leave at back of work, k2, then p1 from cable needle
Cr3L Cross 3 left as follows: slip next 2 sts on to cable needle and leave at front of work, p1, then k2 from cable needle

Back

Using 4½mm needles cast on 76(80,84,88) sts. Work 5cm/2in k1, p1 rib, ending with a WS row.
Change to 5½mm needles.
Beg with a p row, work in rev st st until back measures 70(72,74,76)cm/
27½(28½,29,30)in from cast-on edge, ending with a WS row.

Shape shoulders
Cast off 29(30,32,33) sts at beg of next 2 rows. Cut off yarn and leave rem 18(20,20,22) sts on a holder.

Front

Using 4½mm needles cast on 82(86,90,94) sts. Work 5cm/2in k1, p1 rib, ending with a RS row.
Inc row Rib 1(3,5,7), * M1, rib 16, rep from * to last 1(3,5,7) sts, M1, rib to end. 88(92,96,100) sts.
Change to 5½mm needles.
Row 1 P10(12,14,16), * k1, p5, k1, p2, k1, p5, k1, p10, rep from * to last 26(28,30,32) sts, k1, p5, k1, p2, k1, p5, k1, p10(12,14,16).
Row 2 K10(12,14,16), * p1, k5, p1, k2, p1, k5, p1, k10, rep from * to last 26(28,30,32) sts, p1, k5, p1, k2, p1, k5, p1, k10(12,14,16).
Rows 3 and 4 As rows 1 and 2.
Row 5 P10(12,14,16), * Cr2L, p4, Cr4, p4, Cr2R, p10, rep from * to last 26(28,30,32) sts, Cr2L, p4, Cr4, p4, Cr2R, p to end.
Row 6 K11(13,15,17), * p1, k5, p2, k5, p1, k12, rep from * to last 25(27,29,31) sts, p1, k5, p2, k5, p1, k11(13,15,17).
Row 7 P11(13,15,17), * Cr2L, p4, k2, p4, Cr2R, p12, rep from * to last 25(27,29,31) sts, Cr2L, p4, k2, p4, Cr2R, p11(13,15,17).
Row 8 K12(14,16,18), * p1, k4, p2, k4, p1, k14, rep from * to last 24(26,28,30) sts, p1, k4, p2, k4, p1, k12(14,16,18).
Row 9 P12(14,16,18), * k1, p3, k4, p3, k1, p14, rep from * to last 24(26,28,30) sts, k1, p3, k4, p3, k1, p12(14,16,18).
Row 10 K12(14,16,18), * p1, k3, p4, k3, p1, k14, rep from * to last 24(26,28,30) sts, p1, k3, p4, k3, p1, k12(14,16,18).
Row 11 P11(13,15,17), * Cr2R, p2, Cr2R,

Tw2L, Cr2L, p2, Cr2L, p12, rep from * to last 25(27,29,31) sts, Cr2R, p2, Cr2R, Tw2L, Cr2L, p2, Cr2L, p11(13,15,17).
Row 12 K11(13,15,17), * p1, k3, p1, k1, k1, p1, k3, p1, k12, rep from * to last 25(27,29,31) sts, p1, k3, p1, k1, p2, k1, p1, k3, p1, k11(13,15,17).
Row 13 P10(12,14,16), * Cr2R, p2, Cr2R, k4, Cr2L, p2, Cr2L, p10, rep from * to last 26(28,30,32) sts, Cr2R, p2, Cr2R, k4, Cr2L, p2, Cr2L, p10(12,14,16).
Row 14 K10(12,14,16), * p1, k3, p1, k1, p4, k1, p1, k3, p1, k10, rep from * to last 26(28,30,32) sts, p1, k3, p1, k1, p4, k1, p1, k3, p1, k10(12,14,16).
Row 15 P10(12,14,16), * k1, p2, [Cr2R] twice, k2, [Cr2L] twice, p2, k1, p10, rep from * to last 26(28,30,32) sts, k1, p2, [Cr2R] twice, k2, [Cr2L] twice, p2, k1, p to end.
Row 16 K10(12,14,16), * p1, k2, [p1, k1] twice, p2, [k1, p1] twice, k2, p1, k10, rep from * to last 26(28,30,32) sts, p1, k2, [p1, k1] twice, p2, [k1, p1] twice, k2, p1, k10(12,14,16).
Row 17 P10(12,14,16), * k1, p5, Cr2R, Cr2L, p5, k1, p10, rep from * to last 26(28,30,32) sts, k1, p5, Cr2R, Cr2L, p5, k1, p10(12,14,16).
Row 18 As row 2.
Row 19 P10(12,14,16), * Cr2L, p4, k1, p2, k1, p4, Cr2R, p10, rep from * to last 26(28,30,34) sts, Cr2L, p4, k1, p2, k1, p4, Cr2R, p10(12,14,16).
Row 20 K11(13,15,17), * p1, k4, p1, k2, k4, p1, k12, rep from * to last 25(27,29, 31) sts, p1, k4, p1, k2, p1, k4, p1, k to end.
Row 21 P11(13,15,17), * Cr2L, p3, k1, p2, k1, p3, Cr2R, p12, rep from * to last 25(27,29,31) sts, Cr2L, p3, k1, p2, k1, p3, Cr2R, p11(13,15,17).
Row 22 K12(14,16,18), * p1, k3, p1, k2, p1, k3, p1, k14, rep from * to last 24(26,28, 30) sts, p1, k3, p1, k2, p1, k3, p1, k to end.
Row 23 P12(14,16,18), * k1, p3, Cr4, p3, k1, p14, rep from * to last 24(26,28,30) sts, k1, p3, Cr4, p3, k1, p12(14,16,18).
Row 24 K12(14,16,18), * p1, k4, p2, k4, p1, k14, rep from * to last 24(26,28,30) sts, p1, k4, p2, k4, p1, k12(14,16,18).
Row 25 P12(14,16,18), * k1, p4, k2, p4, k1, p14, rep from * to last 24(26,28,30) sts, k1, p4, k2, p4, k1, p12(14,16,18).
Row 26 As row 24.
Row 27 P11(13,15,17), * Cr2R, p3, Cr2R, Cr2L, p3, Cr2L, p12, rep from * to last 25(27,29,31) sts, Cr2R, p3, Cr2R, Cr2L, p3, Cr2L, p11(13,15,17).
Row 28 K11(13,15,17), * p1, k4, p1, k2, p1, k4, p1, k12, rep from * to last 25(27,29,31) sts, p1, k4, p1, k2, p1, k4, p1, k11(13,15,17).
Row 29 P10(12,14,16), * Cr2R, p3, Tw2R, k2, Tw2L, p3, Cr2L, p10, rep from * to last 26(28,30,32) sts, Cr2R, p3, Tw2R, k2, Tw2L, p3, Cr2L, p10(12,14,16).
Row 30 K10(12,14,16), * p1, k4, p6, k4, p1, k10, rep from * to last 26(28,30,32) sts, p1, k4, p6, k4, p1, k10(12,14,16).
Row 31 P10(12,14,16), * k1, p4, k6, p4, k1, p10, rep from * to last 26(28,30,32) sts, k1, p4, k6, p4, k1, p10(12,14,16).
Rows 32 and 33 As rows 30 and 31.
Row 34 As row 30.
Row 35 P10(12,14,16), * Cr2L, p3, k6, p3, Cr2R, p10, rep from * to last 26(28,30, 32) sts, Cr2L, p3, k6, p3, Cr2R, p to end.
Row 36 K11(13,15,17), * p1, k3, p6, k3, p1, k12, rep from * to last 25(27,29,31) sts, p1, k3, p6, k3, p1, k11(13,15,17).
Row 37 P11(13,15,17), * Cr2L, p2, k6, p2, Cr2R, p12, rep from * to last 25(27,29, 31) sts, Cr2L, p2, k6, p2, Cr2R, p to end.
Row 38 K12(14,16,18), * p1, k2, p6, k2, p1, k14, rep from * to last 24(26,28,30) sts, p1, k2, p6, k2, p1, k12(14,16,18).
Row 39 P12(14,16,18), * k1, p1, Cr3R, Tw2L, Cr3L, p1, k1, p14, rep from * to last 24(26,28,30) sts, k1, p1, Cr3R, Tw2L, Cr3L, p1, k1, p12(14,16,18).
Row 40 K12(14,16,18), * p1, k1, [p2, k1] 3 times, p1, k14, rep from * to last 24(26,28,30) sts, p1, k1, [p2, k1] 3 times, p1, k12(14,16,18).
Row 41 P12(14,16,18), * k1, [p1, k2] 3 times, p1, k1, p14, rep from * to last

24(26,28,30) sts, k1, [p1, k2] 3 times, p1, k1, p12(14,16,18).
Row 42 As row 40.
Row 43 P11(13,15,17), * Cr2R, p1, k1, p2, Tw2L, p2, k1, p1, Cr2L, p12, rep from * to last 25(27,29,31) sts, Cr2R, p1, k1, p2, Tw2L, p2, k1, p1, Cr2L, p11(13,15,17).
Row 44 K11(13,15,17), * [p1, k2] twice, p2, k2, p1, k2, p1, k12, rep from * to last 25(27,29,31) sts, [p1, k2] twice, p2, k2, p1, k11(13,15,17).
Row 45 P10(12,14,16), * Cr2R, p2, k1, p1, Cr2R, p2, Cr2L, p1, k1, p2, Cr2L, p10, rep from * to last 26(28,30,32) sts, Cr2R, p2, k1, p1, Cr2R, Cr2L, p1, k1, p2, Cr2L, p to end.
Row 46 K10(12,14,16), * p1, k3, p1, k1, p1, k2, p1, k1, p1, k3, p1, k10, rep from * to last 26(28,30,32) sts, p1, k3, p1, k1, p1, k2, p1, k1, p1, k3, p1, k10(12,14,16).
These 46 rows form the patt.
Cont in patt until work measures 56(58,60,52)cm/22(23,23½,24½)in from cast-on edge, ending with a WS row.

Shape neck
Next row Patt 39(41,42,44), turn and leave rem sts on a spare needle.
★ Keeping patt correct, dec 1 st at neck edge on next and every foll alt row until 33(35,36,38) sts rem. Work straight until front measures same as back to shoulder, ending with a WS row. Cast off. ★
Return to sts on spare needle.
With RS facing, slip first 10(10,12,12) sts on to a holder, join on yarn and patt to end. 39(41,42,44) sts.
Patt 1 row, then complete to match first side of neck from ★ to ★.

Sleeves

Using 4½mm needles cast on 40(42,44,46) sts. Work 5cm/2in rib as given for back, ending with a RS row.
Inc row Rib 2(3,4,5), * M1, rib 4, rep from * to last 2(3,4,5) sts, M1, rib to end. 50(52,54,56) sts. Change to 5½mm needles.
Row 1 P17(18,19,20), k1, p5, k1, p2, k1, p5, k1, p17(18,19,20).
Row 2 K17(18,19,20), p1, k5, p1, k2, p1, k5, p1, k17(18,19,20) sts.
Rows 3 and 4 As rows 1 and 2.
These 4 rows set the 46 row patt as given for back.
Continuing in patt, inc and work into rev st st 1 st each end of next and every foll 6th row until there are 78(80,84,86) sts.
Work straight until sleeve measures 46(47,49,49)cm/18(18½,19,19)in from cast-on edge, ending with a WS row. Cast off.

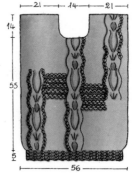

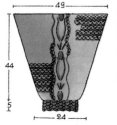

Measurements given in cm for third size

Back/ Front

Sleeve

Neckband

Join right shoulder seam.
With RS facing and using 4½mm needles, pick up and k23(25,25,27) sts down left side of front neck, k across 10(10,12,12) sts from front neck holder, pick up and k23(25,25,27) sts up right side of front neck, then k across 18(20,20,22) sts from back neck holder. 74(80,82,88) sts.
Work 14 rows in k1, p1 rib. Cast off in rib.

To make up

Join left shoulder and neckband seam. Fold sleeves in half lengthwise, then placing folds to shoulder seams, sew into place. Join side and sleeve seams. Fold neckband in half to WS and slipstitch into position.

PASTEL PATTERNED JERSEY

***

A bolder
use of colour will
give a completely
different look to
this casual jersey.

Materials

6(6,7)×50g balls of Emu Superwash DK in main shade A
3(4,4) balls of same in contrast colour B
2(2,2) balls of same in contrast colour C
1(2,2) balls of same in contrast colour D
1(1,1) balls of same in contrast colour E
3(4,4) balls of same in contrast colour F
A pair each of 3¼mm/No10 and 4½mm/No7 knitting needles

Measurements

To fit chest 97(102,107)cm/38(40,42)in
Actual measurements
Chest 99(106,114)cm/39(42,45)in
Length to shoulders 73cm/28¾in
Sleeve seam 48.5cm/19in

Tension

22 sts and 24 rows to 10cm/4in measured over patt on 4½mm needles

Back

★ Using 3¼mm needles and A, cast on 99(107,115) sts.
Rib row 1 K1, * p1, k1, rep from * to end.
Rib row 2 P1, * k1, p1, rep from * to end.
Rep these 2 rows for 9cm/3½in, ending with rib row 1.
Inc row Rib 4(4,3), * M1, rib 10(11,12), rep from * to last 5(4,4) sts, M1, rib to end. 109(117,125) sts.
Change to 4½mm needles.
Join on and cut off colours as required. Carrying yarn not in use loosely across WS, work in patt from chart 1 as follows:
Row 1 (RS) *For 3rd size only* k4C, then *for all sizes* k3(7,7)B, [7C, 7B] 7 times, 7C, 1(5,7)B, then *for 3rd size only* 2C.
Row 2 *For 3rd size only* p3C, then *for all sizes* p2(6,7)B, [7C, 7B] 7 times, 7C, 2(6,7)B then *for 3rd size only* 3C.
Row 3 *For 3rd size only* k2C, then *for all sizes* k1(5,7)B, [7C, 7B] 7 times, 7C, 3(7,7)B, then *for 3rd size only* 4C.
Row 4 *For 2nd and 3rd sizes only* p1(5)C, then *for all sizes* p4(7,7)B, [7C, 7B] 7 times, 7C, *for 2nd and 3rd sizes only* 4(7)B, then *for 3rd size only* 1C.
Beg with row 5, cont in patt from chart shaping for armholes and neck as indicated for back.

Front

Work as given for back, shaping for armholes and neck as indicated for front.

Sleeves

Using 3¼mm needles and A, cast on 49 sts.
Work 6cm/2½in rib as given for back,
ending with rib row 1.
Inc row Rib 4, * M1, rib 2, M1, rib 1, rep from * to last 3 sts, rib to end. 77 sts.
Change to 4½mm needles.
Work in patt from chart 1 for sleeve as follows:
Row 1 (RS) K1B, [7C, 7B] 5 times, 6C.
Row 2 P7C, [7B, 7C] to end.
Row 3 K6C, [7B, 7C] 5 times, 1B.
Row 4 P2B, [7C, 7B] 5 times, 5C.
Cont in patt from chart 1, shaping as indicated, until row 78 has been completed. Now cont in patt from chart 2 until row 34 has been completed.   Cast off.

Neckband

Join right shoulder seam.
With RS facing, using 3¼mm needles and A, pick up and k20 sts down left side of front neck, 37 sts across front neck, 20 sts up right side of front neck and 60 sts across back neck. 137 sts.
Work 3cm/1¼in rib as given for back.
Cast off in rib.

To make up

Join left shoulder and neckband seam. Set in sleeves, sewing row ends at top of sleeves to cast-off sts on back/front. Join side and sleeve seams.

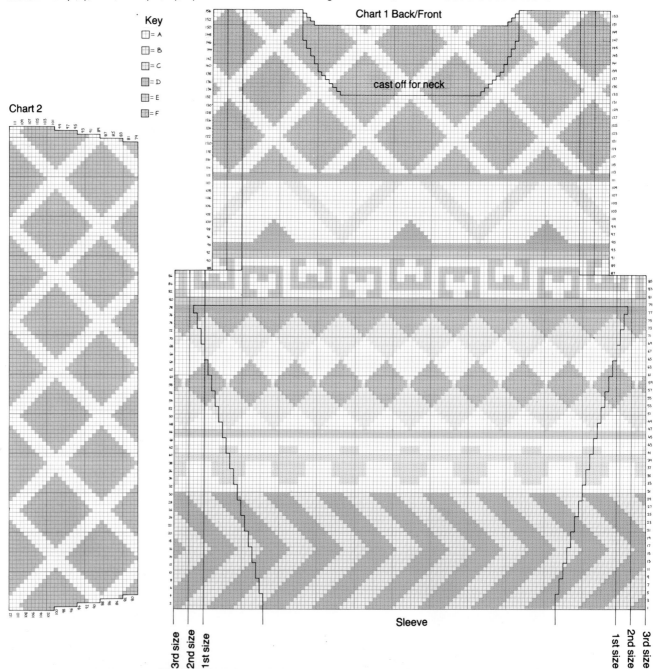

Key
□ = A
□ = B
□ = C
▨ = D
▨ = E
▨ = F

Chart 2

Chart 1 Back/Front

cast off for neck

Sleeve

3rd size 2nd size 1st size

1st size 2nd size 3rd size

FISHERMAN'S RIB CARDIGAN

✳✳

The badge
is a purchased
patch which
is sewn on to this
otherwise classic
ribbed cardigan.

Materials

6(7,8)×100g balls of Robin Good News
  DK
A pair each of 3¼mm/No10 and 4½mm/
  No7 knitting needles
5 buttons

Measurements

To fit chest 97–102(107–112,117–122)cm/
38–40(42–44,46–48)in
Actual measurements
Chest 112(121,132)cm/44(47½,52)in
Length to shoulders 71(72,73)cm/
28(28½,28¾)in
Sleeve seam 42(44,45)cm/16½(17¼,17¾)in

Tension

20 sts and 38 rows to 10cm/4in measured
over fisherman's rib worked on 4½mm
needles

Special abbreviation

k1B Knit 1 below as follows: k into st below
next st on left-hand needle in the usual way,
allowing st above to drop off needle

Back

Using 3¼mm needles cast on
113(123,133) sts
★ Rib row 1 P1, * k1, p1, rep from * to end.
Rib row 2 K1, * p1, k1, rep from * to end.
Rep these 2 rows for 11cm/4¼in, ending
with rib row 2.
Change to 4½mm needles.
Work in fisherman's rib as follows:
Row 1 (RS) K to end.
Row 2 K1, * p1, k1B, rep from * to last 2 sts,
p1, k1.
These 2 rows form the patt.
Cont in patt until work measures
42cm/16½in from cast-on edge, ending with
a WS row. ★
Shape armholes
Cast off in rib 6 sts at beg of next 2 rows.
101(111,121) sts.
Work straight until back measures
29(30,31)cm/11½(11¾,12¼)in from beg of
armhole shaping, ending with a WS row.
Cast off in rib.

Left front

Using 3¼mm needles cast on 57(61,67) sts.
Work as given for back from ★ to ★.
Shape armhole
Cast off in rib 6 sts at beg next row. 51(55,
61) sts.
Patt 7 rows.
Mark beg of last row with a coloured thread
to denote beg of neck shaping.
Shape neck
Row 1 K to last 3 sts, k2 tog, k1.
Row 2 K1, p2, [k1B, p1] to last st, k1.
Row 3 K to end
Row 4 As row 2.
Row 5 As row 1.
Row 6 K1, p1, [k1B, p1] to last st, k1.
Row 7 K to end.
Row 8 As row 6.
★★ Rep the last 8 rows until 28(31,36) sts

rem.
Work straight until front measures same as
back to shoulders, ending with a WS row.
Cast off in rib. ★★

Measurements given in cm for largest size.

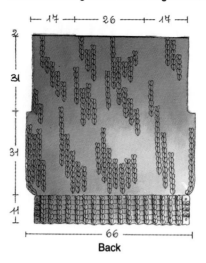

Back

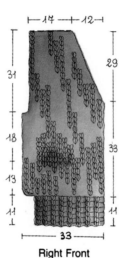

Right Front

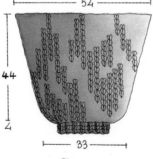

Sleeve

Right front

Using 3¼mm needles cast on 57(61,67) sts.
Work as given for back from ★ to ★.
Next row K to end.
Shape armhole
Cast off in rib 6 sts at beg of next row. 51(55,
61) sts.
Patt 6 rows.
Mark end of last row with a coloured thread
to denote beg of neck shaping.
Shape neck
Row 1 K1, skpo, k to end.
Row 2 K1, [p1, k1B] to last 3 sts, p2, k1.
Row 3 K to end.
Row 4 As row 2.
Row 5 As row 1.
Row 6 K1, p1, [k1B, p1] to last st, k1.
Row 7 K to end.
Row 8 As row 6.
Now complete as given for left front from ★★
to ★★.

Sleeves

Using 3¼mm needles cast on 65(67,69) sts.
Work 4cm/1½in rib as given for back,
ending with rib row 2.
Change to 4½mm needles.
Working in fisherman's rib as given for back,
inc and work into patt 1 st each end of 5th
and every foll 6th row until there are
115(119,121) sts.
Work straight until sleeve measures
45(47,48)cm/17¾(18½,19)in from cast-on
edge, ending with a WS row.
Cast off in rib.

Buttonhole border

Join shoulder seams.
Using 3¼mm needles cast on 13 sts.
Work 4 rows in rib as given for back.
Buttonhole row 1 Rib 6, cast off 2 sts, rib to
end.
Buttonhole row 2 Rib 5, cast on 2, rib 6.
Cont in rib until border measures 10cm/4in
from base of previous buttonhole, ending
with rib row 2.
Work 4 more buttonholes, working 10cm/4in
in between, then cont in rib until border,
slightly stretched, fits up front edge to centre
back neck.
Cast off in rib.

Button border

Work as given for buttonhole border omitting
the buttonholes.

To make up

Fold sleeves in half lengthwise, then placing
folds to shoulder seams sew into place
joining cast-off sts at armhole to row ends at
top of sleeve. Join side and sleeve seams.
Sew on front borders, joining seam at centre
back neck. Sew on buttons.

AN ARAN JERSEY IN A DOUBLE KNIT YARN

***

Traditional Aran stitch patterns have been used to knit this jersey, but using a finer yarn than is usual.

Materials

6(7)×100g balls of Spectrum Detroit DK
A pair each of 3¼mm/No10 and 4½mm/
No7 knitting needles
2 cable needles

Measurements

To fit chest 101(106)cm/40(42)in
Actual measurements
Chest 110(116)cm/43¼(45¾)in
Length to shoulders 72cm/28¼in
Sleeve seam 48cm/19in

Tension

21 sts and 27 rows to 10cm/4in measured
over rev st st worked on 4½mm needles

Special abbreviations

C4F Cable 4 front as follows: slip next 2 sts
on to cable needle and leave at front of
work, k2, then k2 from cable needle
C4B Cable 4 back as follows: slip next
2 sts on to cable needle and leave at back
of work, k2, then k2 from cable needle
C5F Cable 5 front as follows: slip next 2 sts
on to first cable needle and leave at front of
work, slip next st on to 2nd cable needle
and leave at back of work, k2, then p1 from
2nd cable needle and k2 from first cable
needle
Cr3R Cross 3 right as follows: slip next st
on to cable needle and leave at back of
work, k2, then k1 from cable needle
Cr3L Cross 3 left as follows: slip next 2 sts
on to cable needle and leave at front of
work, k1, then k2 from cable needle
Cr3Rp Cross 3 right purlwise as follows:
slip next st on to cable needle and leave at
back of work, k2, then p1 from cable
needle
Cr3Lp Cross 3 left purlwise as follows: slip
next 2 sts on to cable needle and leave at
front of work, p1, then k2 from cable needle
k1B Knit 1 below as follows: insert right-
hand needle into st below next st on left-
hand needle and knit in the usual way,
allowing st above to drop off needle

Back

Using 3¼mm needles cast on 108(114) sts.

Work 5cm/2in k1, p1 rib, ending with a RS
row.
Inc row Rib 8(12), * M1, rib 7, [M1, rib 2]
3 times, M1, rib 3, M1, rib 1, M1, rib 4, M1,
rib 7, M1, rib 6, M1, rib 13, M1, rib 11,
[M1, rib 7] twice, M1, rib 4, M1, rib 1, M1,
rib 4, [M1, rib 2] 3 times, M1, rib 5, M1,
rib 6, M1, rib 2(6). 130(138) sts.
Change to 4½mm needles.
Foundation row (RS) P3(7), k1, p3, k4, p3,
k1, p11, k2, C5F, k2, p11, k1, p3, k4, p3,
k1, p3, k8, p3, k1, p3, k4, p3, k1, p11, k2,
C5F, k2, p11, k1, p3, k4, p3, k1, p3(7).
Foundation row 2 K3(7), p1, k3, p4, k3, p1,
k11, p4, k1, p4, k11, p1, k3, p4, k3, p1, k3,
p8, k3, p1, k3, p4, k3, p1, k11, p4, k1, p4,
k11, p1, k3, p4, k3, p1, k3(7).
Work in patt as follows:
Row 1 P3(7), k1B, p3, C4F, p3, k1B, p11,
k1, Cr3R, p1, Cr3L, k1, p11, k1B, p3, C4F,
p3, k1B, p3, C4B, C4F, p3, k1B, p3, C4F,
p3, k1B, p11, k1, Cr3R, p1, Cr3L, k1, p11,
k1B, p3, C4F, p3, k1B, p3(7).
Row 2 K3(7), p1, k3, p4, k3, p1, k11, p3,
k1, p1, k1, p3, k11, p1, k3, p4, k3, p1, k3,
p8, k3, p1, k3, p4, k3, p1, k11, p3, k1, p1,
k1, p3, k11, p1, k3, p4, k3, p1, k3(7).
Row 3 P3(7), k1B, p3, k4, p3, k1B, p11,
Cr3Rp, k1, p1, k1, Cr3Lp, p11, k1B, p3, k4,
p3, k1B, p3, k8, p3, k1B, p3, k4, p3, k1B,
p11, Cr3Rp, k1, p1, k1, Cr3Lp, p11, k1B,
p3, k4, p3, k1B, p3(7).
Row 4 K3(7), p1, k3, p4, k3, p1, k11, p3,
k1, p1, k1, p3, k11, p1, k3, p4, k3, p1, k3,
p8, k3, p1, k3, p4, k3, p1, k11, p3, k1, p1,
k1, p3, k11, p1, k3, p4, k3, p1, k3(7).
Row 5 P3(7), k1B, p3, k4, p3, k1B, p10,
Cr3R, [p1, k1] twice, p1, Cr3L, p10, k1B,
p3, k4, p3, k1B, p3, k8, p3, k1B, p3, k4, p3,
k1B, p10, Cr3R, [p1, k1] twice, p1, Cr3L,
p10, k1B, p3, k4, p3, k1B, p3(7).
Row 6 K3(7), p1, k3, p4, k3, p1, k10, p2,
[k1, p1] 3 times, k1, p2, k10, p1, k3, p4, k3,
p1, k3, p8, k3, p1, k3, p4, k3, p1, k10, p2,
[k1, p1] 3 times, k1, p2, k10, p1, k3, p4, k3,
p1, k3(7).
Row 7 P3(7), k1B, p3, C4F, p3, k1B, p9,
Cr3Rp, [k1, p1] 3 times, k1, Cr3Lp, p9,
k1B, p3, C4F, p3, k1B, p3, C4B, C4F, p3,
k1B, p3, C4F, p3, k1B, p9, Cr3Rp, [k1, p1]

3 times, k1, Cr3Lp, p9, k1B, p3, C4F, p3,
k1B, p3(7).
Row 8 K3(7), p1, k3, p4, k3, p1, k9, p3,
[k1, p1] 3 times, k1, p3, k9, p1, k3, p4, k3,
p1, k3, p8, k3, p1, k3, p4, k3, p1, k9, p3,
[k1, p1] 3 times, k1, p3, k9, p1, k3, p4, k3,
p1, k3(7).
Row 9 P3(7), k1B, p3, k4, p3, k1B, p8,
Cr3R, [p1, k1] 4 times, p1, Cr3L, p8, k1B,
p3, k4, p3, k1B, p3, k8, p3, k1B, p3, k4, p3,
k1B, p8, Cr3R, [p1, k1] 4 times, p1, Cr3L,
p8, k1B, p3, k4, p3, k1B, p3(7).
Row 10 K3(7), p1, k3, p4, k3, p1, k8, p2,
[k1, p1] 5 times, k1, p2, k8, p1, k3, p4, k3,
p1, k3, p8, k3, p1, k3, p4, k3, p1, k8, p2,
[k1, p1] 5 times, k1, p2, k8, p1, k3, p4, k3,
p1, k3(7).
Row 11 P3(7), k1B, p3, k4, p3, k1B, p7,
Cr3Rp, [k1, p1] 5 times, k1, Cr3Lp, p7,
k1B, p3, k4, p3, k1B, p3, k8, p3, k1B, p3,
k4, p3, k1B, p7, Cr3Rp, [k1, p1] 5 times,
k1, Cr3Lp, p7, k1B, p3, k4 p3, k1B, p3(7).
Row 12 K3(7), p1, k3, p4, k3, p1, k7, p3,
[k1, p1] 5 times, k1, p3, k7, p1, k3, p4, k3,
p1, k3, p8, k3, p1, k3, p4, k3, p1, k7, p3,
[k1, p1] 5 times, k1, p3, k7, p1, k3, p4, k3,
p1, k3(7).
Row 13 P3(7), k1B, p3, C4F, p3, k1B, p6,
Cr3R, [p1, k1] 6 times, p1, Cr3L, p6, k1B,
p3, C4F, p3, k1B, p3, C4B, C4F, p3, k1B,
p3, C4F, p3, k1B, p6, Cr3R, [p1, k1]
6 times, p1, Cr3L, p6, k1B, p3, C4F, p3,
k1B, p3(7).
Row 14 K3(7), p1, k3, p4, k3, p1, k6, p2,
[k1, p1] 7 times, k1, p2, k6, p1, k3, p4, k3,
p1, k3, p8, k3, p1, k3, p4, k3, p1, k6, p2,
[k1, p1] 7 times, k1, p2, k6, p1, k3, p4, k3,
p1, k3(7).
Row 15 P3(7), k1B, p3, k4, p3, k1B, p5,
Cr3Rp, [k1, p1] 7 times, k1, Cr3Lp, p5,
k1B, p3, k4, p3, k1B, p3, k8, p3, k1B, p3,
k4, p3, k1B, p5, Cr3Rp, [k1, p1] 7 times,
k1, Cr3Lp, p5, k1B, p3, k4, p3, k1B, p3(7).
Row 16 K3(7), p1, k3, p4, k3, p1, k5, p3,
[k1, p1] 7 times, k1, p3, k5, p1, k3, p4, k3,
p1, k3, p8, k3, p1, k3, p4, k3, p1, k5, p3,
[k1, p1] 7 times, k1, p3, k5, p1, k3, p4, k3,
p1, k3(7).
Row 17 P3(7), k1B, p3, k4, p3, k1B, p4,

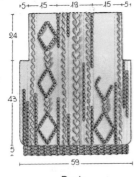

Back

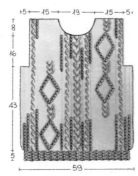

Front

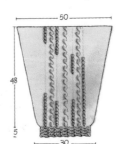

Measurements given in cm for smaller size

Sleeve

Cr3R, [p1, k1] 8 times, p1, Cr3L, p4, k1B, p3, k4, p3, k1B, p3, k8, p3, k1B, p3, k4, p3, k1B, p4, Cr3R, [p1, k1] 8 times, p1, Cr3L, p4, k1B, p3, k4, p3, k1B, p3(7).

Row 18 K3(7), p1, k3, p4, k3, p1, k4, p2, [k1, p1] 9 times, k1, p2, k4, p1, k3, p4, k3, p1, k3, p8, k3, p1, k3, p4, k3, p1, k4, p2, [k1, p1] 9 times, k1, p2, k4, p1, k3, p4, k3, p1, k3(7).

Row 19 P3(7), k1B, p3, C4F, p3, k1B, p3, Cr3Rp, [k1, p1] 9 times, k1, Cr3Lp, p3, k1B, p3, C4F, p3, k1B, p3, C4B, C4F, p3, k1B, p3, C4F, p3, k1B, p3, Cr3Rp, [k1, p1] 9 times, k1, Cr3Lp, p3, k1B, p3, C4F, p3, k1B, p3(7).

Row 20 K3(7), p1, k3, p4, k3, p1, k3, p3, [k1, p1] 9 times, k1, p3, k3, p1, k3, p4, k3, p1, k3, p8, k3, p1, k3, p4, k3, p1, k3, p3, [k1, p1] 9 times, k1, p3, k3, p1, k3, p4, k3, p1, k3(7).

Row 21 P3(7), k1B, p3, k4, p3, k1B, p3, Cr3Lp, [k1, p1] 9 times, k1, Cr3Rp, p3, k1B, p3, k4, p3, k1B, p3, k8, p3, k1B, p3, k4, p3, k1B, p3, Cr3Lp, [k1, p1] 9 times, k1, Cr3Rp, p3, k1B, p3, k4, p3, k1B, p3(7).

Row 22 As row 18.

Row 23 P3(7), k1B, p3, k4, p3, k1B, p4, Cr3Lp, [p1, k1] 8 times, p1, Cr3Rp, p4, k1B, p3, k4, p3, k1B, p3, k8, p3, k1B, p3, k4, p3, k1B, p4, Cr3Lp, [p1,k1] 8 times, p1, Cr3Rp, p4, k1B, p3, k4, p3, k1B, p3(7).

Row 24 As row 16.

Row 25 P3(7), k1B, p3, C4F, p3, k1B, p5, Cr3Lp, [k1, p1] 7 times, k1, Cr3Rp, p5, k1B, p3, C4F, p3, k1B, p3, C4B, C4F, p3, k1B, p3, C4F, p3, k1B, p5, Cr3Lp, [k1, p1] 7 times, k1, Cr3Rp, p5, k1B, p3, C4F, p3, k1B, p3(7).

Row 26 As row 14.

Row 27 P3(7), k1B, p3, k4, p3, k1B, p6, Cr3Lp, [p1, k1] 6 times, p1, Cr3Rp, p6, k1B, p3, k4, p3, k1B, p3, k8, p3, k1B, p3, k4, p3, k1B, p6, Cr3Lp, [p1, k1] 6 times, p1, Cr3Rp, p6, k1B, p3, k4, p3, k1B, p3(7).

Row 28 As row 12.

Row 29 P3(7), k1B, p3, k4, p3, k1B, p7, Cr3Lp, [k1, p1] 5 times, k1, Cr3Rp, p7, k1B, p3, k4, p3, k1B, p3, k8, p3, k1B, p3, k4, p3, k1B, p7, Cr3Lp, [k1, p1] 5 times, k1, Cr3Rp, p7, k1B, p3, k4, p3, k1B, p3(7).

Row 30 As row 10.

Row 31 P3(7), k1B, p3, C4F, p3, k1B, p8, Cr3Lp, [p1, k1] 4 times, p1, Cr3Rp, p8, k1B, p3, C4F, p3, k1B, p3, C4B, C4F, p3, k1B, p3, C4F, p3, k1B, p8, Cr3Lp, [p1, k1] 4 times, p1, Cr3Rp, p8, k1B, p3, C4F, p3, k1B, p3(7).

Row 32 As row 8.

Row 33 P3(7), k1B, p3, k4, p3, k1B, p9, Cr3Lp, [k1, p1] 3 times, k1, Cr3Rp, p9, k1B, p3, k4, p3, k1B, p3, k8, p3, k1B, p3, k4, p3, k1B, p9, Cr3Lp, [k1, p1] 3 times, k1, Cr3Rp, p9, k1B, p3, k4, p3, k1B, p3(7).

Row 34 As row 6.

Row 35 P3(7), k1B, p3, k4, p3, k1B, p10, Cr3Lp, [p1, k1] twice, p1, Cr3Rp, p10, k1B, p3, k4, p3, k1B, p3, k8, p3, k1B, p3, k4, p3, k1B, p10, Cr3Lp, [p1, k1] twice, p1, Cr3Rp, p10, k1B, p3, k4, p3, k1B, p3(7).

Row 36 As row 4.

Row 37 P3(7), k1B, p3, C4F, p3, k1B, p11, Cr3L, k1, p1, k1, Cr3R, p11, k1B, p3, C4F, p3, k1B, p3, C4B, C4F, p3, k1B, p3, C4F, p3, k1B, p11, Cr3L, k1, p1, k1, Cr3R, p11, k1B, p3, C4F, p3, k1B, p3(7).

Row 38 As row 2.

Row 39 P3(7), k1B, p3, k4, p3, k1B, p11, k1, Cr3L, p1, Cr3R, k1, p11, k1B, p3, k4, p3, k1B, p3, k8, p3, k1B, p3, k4, p3, k1B, p11, k1, Cr3L, p1, Cr3R, k1, p11, k1B, p3, k4, p3, k1B, p3(7).

Row 40 K3(7), p1, k3, p4, k3, p1, k11, p4, k1, p4, k11, p1, k3, p4, k3, p1, k3, p8, k3, p1, k3, p4, k3, p1, k11, p4, k1, p4, k11, p1, k3, p4, k3, p1, k3(7).

Row 41 P3(7), k1B, p3, k4, p3, k1B, p11, k2, C5F, k2, p11, k1B, p3, k4, p3, k1B, p3, k8, p3, k1B, p3, k4, p3, k1B, p11, k2, C5F, k2, p11, k1B, p3, k4, p3, k1B, p3(7).

Row 42 K3(7), p1, k3, p4, k3, p1, k11, p4, k1, p4, k11, p1, k3, p4, k3, p1, k3, p8, k3, p1, k3, p4, k3, p1, k11, p4, k1, p4, k11, p1, k3, p4, k3, p1, k3(7).

Row 43 P3(7), k1B, p3, C4F, p3, k1B, p11, C4B, p1, C4F, p11, k1B, p3, C4F, p3, k1B, p3, C4B, C4F, p3, k1B, p3, C4F, p3, k1B, p11, C4B, p1, C4F, p11, k1B, p3, C4F, p3, k1B, p3(7).

Row 44 K3(7), p1, k3, p4, k3, p1, k11, p4, k1, p4, k11, p1, k3, p4, k3, p1, k3, p8, k3,
p1, k3, p4, k3, p1, k11, p4, k1, p4, k11, p1, k3, p4, k3, p1, k3(7).

Row 45 P3(7), k1B, p3, k4, p3, k1B, p11, k4, p1, k4, p11, k1B, p3, k4, p3, k1B, p3, k8, p3, k1B, p3, k4, p3, k1B, p11, k4, p1, k4, p11, k1B, p3, k4, p3, k1B, p3(7).

Row 46 K3(7), p1, k3, p4, k3, p1, k11, p4, k1, p4, k11, p1, k3, p4, k3, p1, k3, p8, k3, p1, k3, p4, k3, p1, k11, p4, k1, p4, k11, p1, k3, p4, k3, p1, k3(7).

Row 47 P3(7), k1B, p3, k4, p3, k1B, p11, k4, p1, k4, p11, k1B, p3, k4, p3, k1B, p3, k8, p3, k1B, p3, k4, p3, k1B, p11, k4, p1, k4, p11, k1B, p3, k4, p3, k1B, p3(7).

Row 48 K3(7), p1, k3, p4, k3, p1, k11, p4, k1, p4, k11, p1, k3, p4, k3, p1, k3, p8, k3, p1, k3, p4, k3, p1, k11, p4, k1, p4, k11, p1, k3, p4, k3, p1, k3(7).

Rows 49 to 54 Rep rows 43 to 48.

Rows 55 to 58 Rep rows 43 to 46.

Row 59 P3(7), k1B, p3, k4, p3, k1B, p11, k2, C5F, k2, p11, k1B, p3, k4, p3, k1B, p3, k8, p3, k1B, p3, k4, p3, k1B, p11, k2, C5F, k2, p11, k1B, p3, k4, p3, k1B, p3(7).

Row 60 As row 42.

These 60 rows form the patt.

Cont in patt until work measures 48cm/19in from cast-on edge, ending with a WS row.

Shape armholes

Cast off 11 sts at beg of next 2 rows. 108(116) sts.

Cont in patt until work measures 72cm/28¼in from cast-on edge, ending with a WS row.

Shape shoulders

Cast off 32(36) sts at beg of next 2 rows. Cut off yarn and leave rem 44 sts on a holder.

Front

Work as given for back until front measures 64cm/25in from cast-on edge, ending with a WS row.

Shape neck

Next row Patt 43(47), turn and leave rem sts on a spare needle.

★ Cast off 2 sts at beg of next and foll 2 alt rows. 37(41) sts.

Keeping patt correct, dec 1 st at neck edge on next and every foll alt row until

32(36) sts rem.
Work straight until front measures same as back to shoulder, ending with a WS row.
Cast off. ★
Return to sts on spare needle.
With RS facing, slip first 22 sts on to a holder, join on yarn and patt to end.
43(47) sts.
Patt 1 row, then work as given for first side of neck from ★ to ★.

Sleeves

Using 3¼mm needles cast on 52 sts.
Work 5cm/2in rib as given for back, ending with a RS row.
Inc row Rib 1, [M1, rib 2] 4 times, M1, rib 5, M1, rib 10, M1, rib 2, M1, rib 1, M1, rib 9, M1, rib 7, [M1, rib 2] 3 times, M1, rib 3.
66 sts.
Change to 4½mm needles.
Foundation row 1 (RS) P14, k1, p3, k4, p3, k1, p3, k8, p3, k1, p3, k4, p3, k1, p14.
Foundation row 2 K14, p1, k3, p4, k3, p1, k3, p8, k3, p1, k3, p4, k3, p1, k14.
Work in patt as follows:
Row 1 P14, k1B, p3, C4F, p3, k1B, p3, C4B, C4F, p3, k1B, p3, C4F, p3, k1B, p14.
Row 2 and every foll alt row K14, p1, k3, p4, k3, p1, k3, p8, k3, p1, k3, p4, k3, p1, k14.
Row 3 P14, k1B, p3, k4, p3, k1B, p3, k8, p3, k1B, p3, k4, p3, k1B, p14.
Row 5 As row 3.
Row 6 As row 2.
These 6 rows form the patt.
Continuing in patt, inc and work into rev st st 1 st each end of next and every foll 6th row until there are 86 sts, then each end of every foll 4th row until there are 110 sts.
Work straight until sleeve measures 53cm/21in from cast-on edge, ending with a WS row.
Cast off.

Neckband

Join right shoulder seam.
With RS facing and using 3¼mm needles, pick up and k20 sts down left side of front neck, k across 22 sts from front neck holder, pick up and k20 sts up right side of front neck, then k across 44 sts from back neck holder. 106 sts.
Work 5cm/2in k1, p1 rib.
Cast off in rib.

To make up

Join left shoulder and neckband seam.
Joining row ends at top of sleeves to cast-off sts at armholes on back and front, sew in the sleeves. Join side and sleeve seams. Fold neckband in half to WS and slipstitch into position.

KNIT TIP

An alternative cable panel

If you like to memorise a knitting pattern rather than read every row, you may find the diamond and moss stitch cable panel too complicated to remember.
Try this 8 row linked cable panel over the 31 sts of the diamond and moss stitch cable panel as follows:
Cast on and work increase row as given in pattern.
Change to 4½mm needles.
Foundation row 1 (RS) P3(7), k1, p3, k4, p3, k1, instead of next 31 sts work: p2, k12, p3, k12, p2, then from patt work: k1, p3, k4, p3, k1, p3, k8, p3, k1, p3, k4, p3, k1, instead of next 31 sts work: p2, k12, p3, k12, p2, then from patt work: k1, p3, k4, p3, k1, p3(7).
Foundation row 2 K3(7), p1, k3, p4, k3, p1, instead of next 31 sts work: k2, p12, k3, p12, k2, then from patt work: p1, k3, p4, k3, p1, k3, p8, k3, p1, k3, p4, k3, p1, instead of next 31 sts work: k2, p12, k3, p12, k2, then from patt work: p1, k3, p4, k3, p1, k3(7).
Continuing in main patt as given, work over 31 sts of diamond and moss stitch cable panel as follows:
Row 1 P2, k12, p3, k12, p2.
Row 2 K2, p12, k3, p12, k2.
Rows 3 and 4 As rows 1 and 2.
Row 5 P2, C6F (slip next 3 sts on to cable needle and leave at front of work, k3, then k3 from cable needle), C6B (slip next 3 sts on to cable needle and leave at back of work, k3, then k3 from cable needle), p3, C6F, C6B, p2.
Row 6 K2, p12, k3, p12, k2.
Rows 7 and 8 As rows 1 and 2.
These 8 rows form the cable panel.

SPORTING SLIPOVER

✳✳

This slipover is knitted in a broken rib, with every other row a knit row, which you may find quicker to work than a regular rib stitch.

Materials

5(6,7)×50g balls of Wendy Family Choice
4 ply in main colour A
1(2,2) balls of same in contrast colour B
A pair each of 2¾mm/No12 and
3¼mm/No10 knitting needles
Cable needle

Measurements

To fit chest 97(102,107)cm/38(40,42)in
Actual measurements
Chest 104(109,114)cm/41(43,45)in
Length to shoulders 70(71,73)cm/
27½(28,28¾)in

Tension

28 sts and 40 rows to 10cm/4in measured
over rib patt worked on 3¼mm needles
Cable (14 sts) measures 3.5cm/1¼in

Special abbreviation

C10 Cable 10 as follows: slip next 5 sts on
to cable needle and leave at front of work,
k5, then k5 from cable needle

Front

★ Using 2¾mm needles and A, cast on
145(151,159) sts.
Rib row 1 K1, * p1, k1, rep from * to end.
Rib row 2 P1, * k1, p1, rep from * to end.
Rep these 2 rows for 5cm/2in, ending with
rib row 1.
Inc row Rib 31(33,35), [M1, rib 2] 4 times,
M1, rib 66(68,72), [M1, rib 2] 4 times, M1,
rib 32(34,36). 155(161,169) sts.
Change to 3¼mm needles.
Cut off A, join on B.
Work in patt as follows:
Row 1 (RS) K31(33,35), p2, k10, p2,
k65(67,71), p2, k10, p2, k31(33,35).
Row 2 P1, [k1, p1] 15(16,17) times, k2,
p10, k2, p1, [k1, p1] 32(33,35) times, k2,
p10, k2, p1, [k1, p1] 15(16,17) times.
Rows 3 to 6 Rep rows 1 and 2 twice.
Row 7 K31(33,35), p2, C10, p2, k65(67,71),
p2, C10, p2, k31(33,35).
Row 8 As row 2.
Rows 9 to 14 Rep rows 1 and 2 three times.
These 14 rows form the patt.
Cut off B, join on A.
Work rows 1 to 14 once more.
Cut off A, join on B.
Work rows 1 to 14 once more.
Cut off B, join on A.
Cont in patt until work measures 41cm/16in
from cast-on edge, ending with a WS row. ★
Divide for neck
Next row Patt 77(80,84), turn and leave
rem sts on a spare needle.
Patt 1 row.
Dec 1 st at neck edge on next and every foll
4th row until 72(75,79) sts rem.
Patt 1 row, so ending at side edge.
Shape armhole
Cast off 7 sts at beg of next row.
Patt 1 row.
★★ Continuing to dec 1 st at neck edge on
next and every foll 4th row, dec 1 st at
armhole edge on next and every foll alt row
until 54(57,61) sts rem.
Keeping armhole edge straight, cont to dec

1 st at neck edge on every 4th row until
48(50,52) sts rem.
Now dec 1 st at neck edge on every foll 6th
row until 41(43,45) sts rem.
Work straight in patt until front measures
70(71,73)cm/27½(28,28¾)in from cast-on
edge, ending with a WS row.
Cast off. ★★
Return to sts on spare needle.
With RS facing, slip next st on to a safety-pin,
join on A and patt to end. 77(80,84) sts.
Patt 1 row.
Dec 1 st at neck edge on next and every foll
4th row until 72(75,79) sts rem.
Patt 2 rows, so ending at side edge.
Shape armhole
Cast off 7 sts at beg of next row.
Now complete as given for first side of neck
from ★★ to ★★.

Back

Work as given for front from ★ to ★.
Cont in patt until back measures same as
front to armholes, ending with a WS row.
Shape armholes
Cast off 7 sts at beg of next 2 rows.
Dec 1 st each end of next and every foll alt
row until 127(133,141) sts rem.
Work straight until back measures same as
front to shoulders, ending with a WS row.
Shape shoulders
Cast off 41(43,45) sts, patt until there are
45(47,51) sts on the right-hand needle, cast
off rem 41(43,45) sts.
Cut off yarn and leave rem sts on a holder.

Neckband

Join right shoulder seam.
With RS facing, using 2¾mm needles and A,
pick up and k91(95,99) sts down left side of
front neck, k st from safety-pin and mark
this st with a coloured thread to denote
centre st, pick up and k91(95,99) sts up
right side of front neck, then k the back
neck sts from holder. 228(238,250) sts.
Cut off A, join on B.
Rib row 1 (WS) [P1, k1] to within 2 sts of
centre st, p2 tog, p centre st, p2 tog tbl, k1,
[p1, k1] to end.
Rib row 2 Rib to within 2 sts of centre st,
p2 tog tbl, k centre st, p2 tog, rib to end.
Rep these 2 rows once more.
Cut off B, join on A.
Rep the 2 rib rows twice.
Cut off A, join on B.
Work 3 more rows rib, decreasing 1 st each
side of centre st as before.
With B, cast off in rib, decreasing 1 st each
side of centre st as before.

Armhole borders

Join left shoulder and neckband seam.
With RS facing, using 2¾mm needles and A,
pick up and k151(159,167) sts evenly round
armhole edge.
Beg with rib row 2 as given for front, work
4 rows B, 4 rows A and 3 rows B.
With B, cast off in rib.

To make up

Join side and armhole border seams.

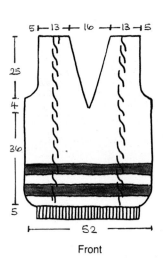

Front

Measurements given in cm for smallest size

WARM JERSEY IN A TWO COLOUR SLIP STITCH

✳

Although the stitch pattern gives a two colour effect, only one colour yarn is used on a row which makes it an easy pattern to knit.

Materials

11(12,13)×50g balls of Jaeger Sport in main colour A
8(9,10) balls of same in contrast colour C
A pair each of 4mm/No8 and 6mm/No4 knitting needles

Measurements

To fit chest 96(101,107)cm/38(40,42)in

Actual measurements

Chest 109(118,128)cm/43(46½,50½)in
Length to shoulders 74cm/29in
Sleeve seam 50cm/19¾in

Tension

13 sts and 30 rows to 10cm/4in measured over patt worked on 6mm needles

Special abbreviation

k1B Knit one below as follows: insert right-hand needle into st below next st on left-hand needle and knit it in the usual way, slipping st above off needle

Back

Using 4mm needles and A, cast on 98(102,106) sts.
Work 6cm/2½in k1, p1 rib, ending with a WS row.
Dec row K3(2,3), k2 tog, * k1, k2 tog, k2(3,4), k2 tog, rep from * to last 2 sts, k2. 71(77,83) sts.
Change to 6mm needles.
Carrying yarn not in use loosely up side, work in patt as follows:
Foundation row (WS) With A, k to end.
Row 1 With C, k1, * k1B, k1, rep from * to end.
Row 2 With C, k to end.
Row 3 With A, k2, * k1B, k1, rep from * to last 3 sts, k1B, k2.
Row 4 With A, k to end.
These 4 rows form the patt.
Cont in patt until back measures 74cm/29in from cast-on edge, ending with a RS row.

Shape shoulders

Cast off 21(23,25) sts at beg of next 2 rows.
Cut off yarns and leave rem 29(31,33) sts on a holder.

Front

Work as given for back until front measures 59cm/23¼in from cast-on edge, ending with a WS row.

Shape neck

Next row Patt 28(30,32) sts, turn and leave rem sts on a spare needle.
Keeping patt correct, dec 1 st at neck edge on next and every foll alt row until 21(23,25) sts rem.
Work straight until front measures same as back to shoulder, ending with a WS row. Cast off.
Return to sts on spare needle.
With RS facing, slip first 15(17,19) sts on to a holder, join on yarns, then patt to end.
Keeping patt correct, dec 1 st at neck edge on next and every foll alt row until 21(23,25) sts rem.
Work straight until front measures same as back to shoulder, ending with a WS row. Cast off.

Sleeves

Using 4mm needles and A, cast on 45(49,53) sts.
Rib row 1 P1, * k1, p1, rep from * to end.
Rib row 2 K1, * p1, k1, rep from * to end.
Rep these 2 rows for 5cm/2in, ending with rib row 2.
Change to 6mm needles.
Carrying yarn not in use loosely up side, work in patt as follows:

Row 1 With C, k1, * k1B, k1, rep from * to end.
Row 2 With C, k to end.
Row 3 With A, k2, * k1B, k1, rep from * to last 3 sts, k1B, k2.
Row 4 With A, k to end.
These 4 rows form the patt.
Continuing in patt, inc and work into patt 1 st each end of next and every foll 10th row until there are 69(73,77) sts.
Work straight until sleeve measures 50cm/19¾in from cast-on edge, ending with a RS row.
Cast off.

Neckband

Join right shoulder seam.
With RS facing and using 4mm needles, pick up and k36 sts down left side of front neck, k15(17,19) sts from front neck holder, pick up and k36 sts up right side of front neck, then k29(31,33) sts from back neck holder. 116(120,124) sts.
Work 7cm/3in k1, p1 rib.
Cast off in rib.

To make up

Join left shoulder and neckband seam. Fold neckband in half to WS and slipstitch into position. Fold sleeves in half lengthwise, then placing folds to shoulder seams, sew into place. Join side and sleeve seams.

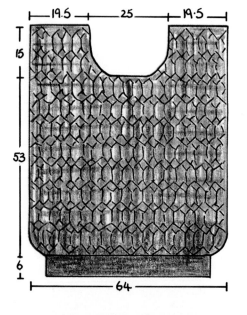

Front

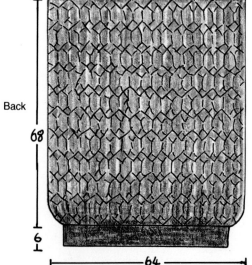

Back

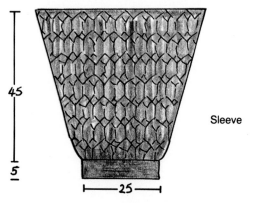

Sleeve

Measurements given in cm for third size

CABLE AND RIB SLASH NECK JERSEY

✳✳✳

A slash neck jersey has no neck or shoulder shaping so it is one of the simplest to knit – leaving you to concentrate on the stitch pattern.

Materials

5(6,6)×100g balls of Water Wheel
   Concorde DK
A pair each of 3¼mm/No10 and 4½mm/
   No7 knitting needles
Cable needle

Measurements

To fit chest 96(102,106)cm/38(40,42)in
Actual measurements
Chest 115(120.5,126)cm/45¼(47½,49¾)in
Length to shoulders 62(66,70)cm/
24½(26,27½)in
Sleeve seam 49cm/19¼in

Tension

22 sts and 28 rows to 10cm/4in measured
over st st worked on 4½mm needles
24 sts and 28 rows to 10cm/4in measured
over k1, p2 rib worked on 4½mm needles

Special abbreviations

C11F Cable 11 front as follows: slip next
6 sts on to cable needle and leave at front of
work, k5, slip the last st from cable needle
back on to left-hand needle and p this st,
then k5 from cable needle
C5F Cable 5 front as follows: slip next 3 sts
on to cable needle and leave at front of
work, k2, then k3 from cable needle
C5B Cable 5 back as follows: slip next 2 sts
on to cable needle and leave at back of
work, k3, then k2 from cable needle

Back and front (alike)

Using 3¼mm needles cast on
126(132,138) sts.
Work 5cm/2½in k1, p1 rib, ending with a RS
row.
Inc row Rib 3(6,1), * M1, rib 7(7,8), rep from
* to last 4(7,1) sts, M1, rib to end.
144(150,156) sts.
Change to 4½mm needles.
Work in patt as follows:
Row 1 (RS) K1, p2, k5, p1, k5, p2, [k1, p2]
7 times, yon, skpo, k2 tog, yf, [k1, p1] twice,
k1, yfon, skpo, k2 tog, yrn, p2, k3, yfon,
skpo, k2 tog, yf, k3, p2, [k1, p2]
5(7,9) times, k1, p2, k3, yfon, skpo, k2 tog,
yf, k3, p2, yon, skpo, k2 tog, yf, [k1, p1]
twice, k1, yfon, skpo, k2 tog, yrn, [p2, k1]
7 times, p2, k5, p1, k5, p2, k1.
Row 2 and every foll alt row P1, k2, p5, k1,
p5, k2, [p1, k2] 7 times, p5, k1, p1, k1, p5,
k2, p10, k2, [p1, k2] 5(7,9) times, p1, k2,
p10, k2, p5, k1, p1, k1, p5, [k2, p1] 7 times,
k2, p5, k1, p5, k2, p1.
Rows 3 to 6 Rep rows 1 and 2 twice.
Row 7 K1, p2, k5, p1, k5, p2, [k1, p2]
7 times, yon, skpo, k2 tog, yf, [k1, p1] twice,
k1, yfon, skpo, k2 tog, yrn, p2, C5F, C5B,
p2, [k1, p2] 5(7,9) times, k1, p2, C5F, C5B,
p2, yon, skpo, k2 tog, yf, [k1, p1] twice, k1,
yfon, skpo, k2 tog, yrn, [p2, k1] 7 times, p2,
k5, p1, k5, p2, k1.
Row 9 K1, p2, k5, p1, k5, p2, [k1, p2]
7 times, yon, skpo, k2 tog, yf, [k1, p1] twice,
k1, yfon, skpo, k2 tog, yrn, p2, k10, p2,
[k1, p2] 5(7,9) times, k1, p2, k10, p2, yon,
skpo, k2 tog, yf, [k1, p1] twice, k1, yfon,
skpo, k2 tog, yrn, [p2, k1] 7 times, p2, k5,
p1, k5, p2, k1.
Row 11 K1, p2, C11F, p2, [k1, p2] 7 times,
yon, skpo, k2 tog, yf, [k1, p1] twice, k1, yfon,
skpo, k2 tog, yrn, p2, C5F, C5B, p2, [k1, p2]
5(7,9) times, k1, p2, C5F, C5B, p2, yon,
skpo, k2 tog, yf, [k1, p1] twice, k1, yfon,
skpo, k2 tog, yrn, [p2, k1] 7 times, p2, C11F,
p2, k1.
Rows 13 to 20 Rep rows 1 and 2 four times.
Row 21 As row 7.
Row 23 K1, p2, C11F, p2, [k1, p2] 7 times,
yon, skpo, k2 tog, yf, [k1, p1] twice, k1, yfon,
skpo, k2 tog, yrn, p2, k10, p2, [k1, p2]

5(7,9) times, k1, p2, k10, p2, yon, skpo,
k2 tog, yf, [k1, p1] twice, k1, yfon, skpo,
k2 tog, yrn, [p2, k1] 7 times, p2, C11F, p2,
k1.
Row 25 As row 7.
Rows 27 to 34 Rep rows 1 and 2 four times.
Row 35 K1, p2, C11F, p2, [k1, p2] 7 times,
yon, skpo, k2 tog, yf, [k1, p1] twice, k1, yfon,
skpo, k2 tog, yrn, p2, C5F, C5B, p2, [k1, p2]
5(7,9) times, k1, p2, C5F, C5B, p2, yon,
skpo, k2 tog, yf, [k1, p1] twice, k1, yfon,
skpo, k2 tog, yrn, [p2, k1] 7 times, p2, C11F,
p2, k1.
Row 37 As row 9.
Row 39 As row 7.
Rows 41 to 46 Rep rows 1 and 2 three times.
Row 47 K1, p2, C11F, p2, [k1, p2] 7 times,
yon, skpo, k2 tog, yf, [k1, p1] twice, k1, yfon,
skpo, k2 tog, yrn, p2, k3, yfon, skpo, k2 tog,
yf, k3, p2, [k1, p2] 5(7,9) times, k1, p2, k3,
yfon, skpo, k2 tog, yf, k3, p2, yon, skpo,
k2 tog, yf, [k1, p1] twice, k1, yfon, skpo,
k2 tog, yrn, [p2, k1] 7 times, p2, C11F, p2,
k1.
Rows 49 to 52 As rows 7 to 10.
Row 53 As row 7.
Rows 55 to 58 Rep rows 1 and 2 twice.
Row 59 As row 47.
Row 61 As row 1.
Rows 63 to 66 As rows 7 to 10.
Row 67 As row 7.
Row 69 As row 1.
Row 71 As row 47.
Rows 73 to 76 Rep rows 1 and 2 twice.
Rows 77 to 80 As rows 7 to 10.
Row 81 As row 7.
Row 83 As row 47.
Row 84 As row 2.
These 84 rows form the patt.
Cont in patt until work measures
58(62,66)cm/23(24½,26)in from cast-on
edge, ending with a WS row.
Change to 3¼mm needles.
Cont in g st until work measures
62(66,70)cm/24½(26,27½)in, ending with a
WS row.
Cast off.

Sleeves

Using 3¼mm needles cast on 40 sts.
Work 4cm/1¾in k1, p1 rib, ending with a RS
row.
Inc row Rib 3, * M1, rib 1, M1, rib 2, rep from
* to last st, rib 1. 64 sts.
Change to 4½mm needles.
Work in patt as follows:
Row 1 (RS) K14, p2, [k1, p1] twice, k1, yfon,
skpo, k2 tog, yrn, p2, k3, yfon, skpo, k2 tog,
yf, k3, p2, yon, skpo, k2 tog, yf, [k1, p1]
twice, k1, p2, k14.
Row 2 P14, k2, [p1, k1] twice, p5, k2, p10,
k2, p5, [k1, p1] twice, k2, p14.
Rows 3 to 6 Rep rows 1 and 2 twice.
Row 7 Inc in first st, k13, p2, [k1, p1] twice,
k1, yfon, skpo, k2 tog, yrn, p2, C5F, C5B,
p2, yon, skpo, k2 tog, yf, [k1, p1] twice, k1,
p2, k13, inc in last st. 66 sts.
Row 8 P15, k2, [p1, k1] twice, p5, k2, p10,
k2, p5, [k1, p1] twice, k2, p15.
Row 9 K15, p2, [k1, p1] twice, k1, yfon,
skpo, k2 tog, yrn, p2, k10, p2, yon, skpo,
k2 tog, yf, [k1, p1] twice, k1, p2, k15.
Row 10 As row 8.
Row 11 Inc in first st, k14, p2, [k1, p1] twice,
k1, yfon, skpo, k2 tog, yrn, p2, C5F, C5B,
p2, yon, skpo, k2 tog, [k1, p1] twice, k1, p2,
k14, inc in last st. 68 sts.
Row 12 P16, k2, [p1, k1] twice, p5, k2, p10,
k2, p5, [k1, p1] twice, k2, p16.
Row 13 K16, p2, [k1, p1] twice, k1, yfon,
skpo, k2 tog, yrn, p2, k3, yfon, skpo, k2 tog,
yon, k3, p2, yon, skpo, k2 tog, yf, [k1, p1]
twice, k1, p2, k16.
Row 14 As row 12.

These 14 rows form the patt.
Continuing in patt, inc and work into st st 1 st
each end of next and every foll 4th row until
there are 114 sts.
Work straight until sleeve measures 49cm/
19¼in from cast-on edge, ending with a WS
row.
Cast off.

To make up

Join back and front at shoulder seams for
11cm/4½in. Fold sleeves in half lengthwise,
then placing folds to shoulder seams, sew
into place. Join side and sleeve seams.

Measurements given in cm for smallest size

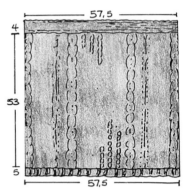

Back/Front

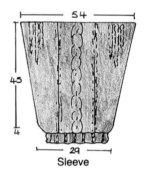

Sleeve

CHILDREN'S PATTERNS

SAND STITCH JERSEY WITH A CENTRAL CABLE

✳✳
There's no problem getting this jersey over a child's head – the slit neck and ribbed edging give a wide yet close-fitting opening.

Materials

6(7,8)×50g balls of Sirdar 80/20 DK
A pair each of 4½mm/No7 and 5mm/No6 knitting needles
Cable needle

Measurements

To fit chest 61 (66,71)cm/24 (26,28)in
Actual measurements
Chest 72 (76,80)cm/29 (30½, 32)in
Length to shoulders 41 (41,42)cm/16½ (16½,17)in
Sleeve seam 40 (41,41)cm/16 (16½,16½)in

Tension

22 sts and 28 rows to 10cm/4in measured over sand stitch on 5mm needles

Special abbreviations

C8B Cable 8 back as follows: slip next 4 sts on to cable needle and leave at back of work, k4, then k4 from cable needle
C5F Cable 5 front as follows: slip next 4 sts on to cable needle and leave at front of work, p1, then k4 from cable needle
C5B Cable 5 back as follows: slip next st on to cable needle and leave at back of work, k4, then p1 from cable needle

Front

Using 4½mm needles cast on 73 (77,81) sts.
Rib row 1 (RS) K1, * p1, k1, rep from * to end.
Rib row 2 P1, * k1, p1, rep from * to end.
Rep these 2 rows for 5 (5,6)cm/2 (2,2½)in, ending with rib row 1.
Inc row Rib 27 (29,31), inc in next st, rib 1, [inc in next st, rib 2] twice, inc into each of next 3 sts, [rib 2, inc in next st] twice, rib 1, inc in next st, rib to end. 82 (86,90) sts.
Change to 5mm needles.
Work in patt as follows:
Row 1 (RS) [K1, p1] 13 (14,15) times, k1, p2, k4, p4, k8, p4, k4, p2, [k1, p1] 13 (14,15) times, k1.
Row 2 K29 (31,33), p4, k4, p8, k4, p4, k29 (31,33).
Row 3 [K1, p1] 13 (14,15) times, k1, p2, k4, p4, C8B, p4, k4, p2, [k1, p1] 13 (14,15) times, k1.
Row 4 As row 2.
Row 5 [K1, p1] 13 (14,15) times, k1, p2, [C5F, p2, C5B] twice, p2, [k1, p1] 13 (14,15) times, k1.
Row 6 K30 (32,34) sts, [p4, k2] 3 times, p4, k30 (32,34).
Row 7 [K1, p1] 13 (14,15) times, k1, p3, C5F, C5B, p2, C5F, C5B, p3, [k1, p1] 13 (14,15) times, k1.
Row 8 K31 (33,35), p8, k4, p8, k31 (33,35).
Row 9 [K1, p1] 13 (14,15) times, k1, p4, [C8B, p4] twice, [k1, p1] 13 (14,15) times, k1.
Row 10 As row 8.
Row 11 [K1, p1] 13 (14,15) times, k1, p4, [k8, p4] twice, [k1, p1] 13 (14,15) times, k1.
Rows 12 and 13 As rows 8 and 9.
Row 14 As row 8.
Row 15 [K1, p1] 13 (14,15) times, k1, p3, C5B, C5F, p2, C5B, C5F, p3, [k1, p1] 13 (14,15) times, k1.
Row 16 As row 6.
Row 17 [K1, p1] 13 (14,15) times, k1, p2, [C5B, p2, C5F] twice, p2, [k1, p1] 13 (14,15) times, k1.

Rows 18 and 19 As rows 2 and 3.
Row 20 As row 2.
Row 21 As row 1.
Row 22 K29 (31,33), p4, k4, p8, k4, p4, k29 (31,33).
These 22 rows form the patt.
Cont in patt until front measures approx 38 (38,39)cm/15 (15,15½)in from cast-on edge, ending with row 3.
Dec row Patt 27 (29,31), k2 tog, p1, p2 tog, patt 2, k2 tog, patt 2, [p2 tog] 3 times, patt 2, k2 tog, patt 2, p2 tog, p1, k2 tog, patt to end. 73 (77,81) sts.
Beg with row 1, work 3cm/1¼in rib.
Cast off in rib.

Back

Using 4½mm needles cast on 73 (77,81) sts.
Work the 2 rib rows as given for front for 5 (5,6)cm/2 (2,2½)in, ending with rib row 1.
Inc row Rib 9 (11,13), * M1, rib 1, M1, rib 17, rep from * to last 10 (12,14) sts, M1, rib 1, M1, rib to end. 81 (85,89) sts.
Change to 5mm needles.
Work in patt as follows:
Row 1 (RS) K1, * p1, k1, rep from * to end.
Row 2 K to end.
These 2 rows form the patt.
Cont in patt until back measures same length as front up to beg of top rib, ending

with a WS row.
Beg with rib row 1, work 3cm/1¼in rib.
Cast off in rib.

Sleeves

Using 4½mm needles cast on 39 (43,43) sts.
Work the 2 rib rows as given for back for 4cm/1½in, ending with rib row 1.
Inc row Rib 7 (9,9), * M1, rib 1, M1, rib 7, rep from * to last 8 (10,10) sts, M1, rib 1, M1, rib to end. 47 (51,51) sts.
Change to 5mm needles.
Work in patt as given for back increasing and working into patt 1 st each end of 7th (7th,5th) and every foll 8th row until there are 69 (71,73) sts.
Work straight until sleeve measures 40 (41,41)cm/15¾ (16,16)in from cast-on edge, ending with a WS row.
Cast off in patt.

To make up

Join shoulder seams leaving approx 17.5 (18,18.5)cm/7 (7¼,7½)in open at centre for neck. Place markers 15.5 (16,16.5)cm/6 (6¼,6½)in below shoulders on back and front to denote beg of armholes. Set in sleeves between markers, then join side and sleeve seams.

KNIT TIP

Substituting another cable pattern

To ring the changes try using another cable pattern up the front of this attractive jersey. To fit without altering the pattern the cable should be worked over the same number or slightly fewer stitches. This cable pattern is worked over 28 sts. If you are using a pattern with fewer stitches, add sufficient reversed st st at each end to make up the total.

Plaited cable

This cable is much simpler than the one featured in the pattern as there are fewer rows to remember. Knit up a stitch sample of the cable using the centre 28 sts to see what it looks like.

Special abbreviations

C6B Cable 6 back as follows: sl next 3 sts on to cable needle and leave at back of work, k3, k3 from cable needle

C6F Cable 6 front as follows: sl next 3 sts on to cable needle and leave at front, k3, k3 from cable needle

The pattern

Row 1 (RS) [K1, p1] 13 (14,15) times, k1, p5, k18, p5, [k1, p1] 13 (14,15) times, k1.
Row 2 K27 (29,31), then k5, p18, k5, k27 (29,31).
Row 3 [K1, p1] 13 (14,15) times, k1, p5, [C6B] 3 times, p5, [k1, p1] 13 (14,15) times, k1.
Row 4 As row 2.
Row 5 [K1, p1] 13 (14,15) times, k1, p5, k18, p5, [k1, p1] 13 (14,15) times, k1.
Row 6 As row 2.
Row 7 [K1, p1] 13 (14,15) times, k1, p5, k3, [C6F] twice, k3, p5, [k1, p1] 13 (14,15) times, k1.
Row 8 K27 (29,31), then k5, p18, k5, k27 (29,31).
These 8 rows form the patt.

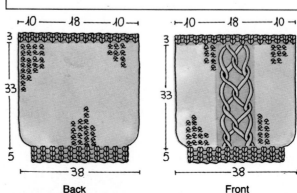

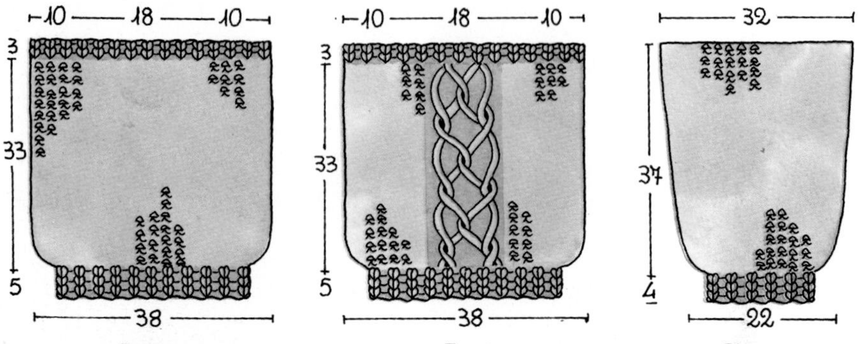

Back   Front   Sleeve
Measurements given for middle size in cm

JERSEY WITH A SOFT BRICK STITCH PATTERN

*

Two different types of yarn are used to give the three dimensional effect in this child's jersey.

Meassurements given in cm

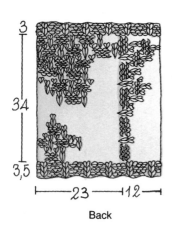

Back

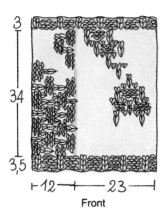

Front

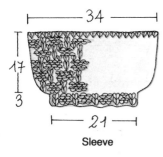

Sleeve

Materials

2×50g balls of Emu Superwash DK (SDK)
6×50g balls of Emu Cotton DK (CDK)
A pair each of 4mm/No8 and 5mm/No6
   knitting needles

Measurements

To fit chest 61cm/24in
Actual measurements
Chest 70cm/27½in
Length to shoulders 40.5cm/16in
Sleeve seam 19.5cm/7¾in

Tension

19 sts and 30 rows to 10cm/4in measured
over patt worked on 5mm needles

Back

★ Using 4mm needles and SDK, cast on
67 sts.
Rib row 1 P3, * k1, p3, rep from * to end.
Rib row 2 K3, * p1, k3, rep from * to end.
Rep these 2 rows for 3.5cm/1½in, ending
with rib row 2. ★
Change to 5mm needles.
With SDK, k 1 row and p 1 row.
With SDK cast off 23 sts, then work in patt as
follows:
Row 1 With CDK, * k5, sl 1 pw, rep from * to
last 2 sts, k2. 44 sts.
Row 2 With CDK, k2, * ytf, sl 1 pw, ytb, k5,
rep from * to end.
Row 3 With CDK, * p5, ytb, sl 1 pw, ytf, rep
from * to last 2 sts, p2.
Row 4 As row 2.
Row 5 With SDK, k to end.
Row 6 With SDK, p to end.
Row 7 With CDK, k2, * sl 1 pw, k5, rep from *
to end.
Row 8 With CDK, * k5, ytf, sl 1 pw, ytb, rep
from * to last 2 sts, k2.
Row 9 With CDK, p2, * ytb, sl 1 pw, ytf, p5,
rep from * to end.
Row 10 As row 8.
Row 11 With SDK, k to end.
Row 12 With SDK, p to end.
These 12 rows form the patt.
Cont in patt until work measures approx
37.5cm/14¾in from cast-on edge, ending
with row 4 of patt.
Cut off yarn and leave these sts on a holder.
Side panel
With RS of back facing, join on SDK at first
row of patt at right-hand edge, then using
5mm needles pick up and k68 sts up row
ends to top of back.
P 1 row.

Rep rows 1 to 12 until work measures
approx 12cm/4¾in from beg of picked up
sts, ending with row 12 of patt.
Using SDK, cast off.

Neckband

With RS facing, using 4mm needles and SDK,
pick up and k23 sts along row ends of side
panel, then k44 sts from holder. 67 sts.
Beg with rib row 2, work 3cm/1¼in rib as
given on welt, ending with rib row 2.
Cast off loosely in rib.

Front

Work as given for back from ★ to ★
Change to 5mm needles.
With SDK, k 1 row.
Next row Cast off 23 sts, p to end.
Now work in patt as given for back until work
measures approx 37.5cm/14¾in from cast-
on edge, ending with row 5 of patt.
Do not cut off yarn, but leave rem sts on a
holder.

Side panel

With RS of front facing, using 5mm needles
and SDK from end of last row worked at top of
front, pick up and k68 sts down row ends of
left-hand edge of front to top of welt.
Rep rows 1 to 12 until work measures
approx 12.5cm/5in from beg of picked up
sts, ending with row 12 of patt.
Using SDK, cast off.

Neckband

With RS facing, using 4mm needles and SDK,
k44 sts from holder, then pick up and
k23 sts along row ends of side panel. 67 sts.
Beg with rib row 2, work 3cm/1¼in rib as
given on back welt, ending with rib row 2.
Cast off loosely in rib.

Sleeves

Using 4mm needles and SDK, cast on 39 sts.
Work 3cm/1¼in rib as given for back,
ending with rib row 1.
Inc row Rib 1, M1, rib 1, * [M1, rib 1] twice,
M1, rib 2, rep from * to last st, M1, rib 1. 68 sts.
Change to 5mm needles.
With SDK, k 1 row and p 1 row.
Now rep patt rows 1 to 12, as given for back,
until sleeve measures approx 19.5cm/7¾in
from cast-on edge, ending with row 12 of patt.
Using SDK, cast off in patt.

To make up

Join shoulder seams for about 6cm/2¼in,
leaving rem 23cm/9in for neck opening.
Fold sleeves in half lengthwise, then placing
folds to shoulder seams, sew into place.
Join side and sleeve seams.

BUTTON NECK FAIR ISLE JUMPER

**
This soft, brushed yarn is used double and knits up very quickly to make an attractive child's jumper.

Materials

4×50g balls of Neveda Arosa Superwash in main colour A
4 balls of same in contrast colour B
1 ball each of same in contrast colours C, D and E
A pair each of 5mm/No6 and 6½mm/No3 knitting needles   2 buttons

Measurements

To fit chest 56–58(61–63)cm/22–23 (24–25)in

Actual measurements

Chest 67(73)cm/26½(28¾)in
Length to shoulders 31.5(34)cm/ 12½(13½)in
Sleeve seam 23.5(26)cm/9½(10¼)in

Tension

14 sts and 14 rows to 10cm/4in measured over patt worked on 6½mm needles

Note

The yarns are used double throughout.

Back

Using 5mm needles and A double, cast on 47(51) sts.
Rib row 1 (RS) K1, * p1, k1, rep from * to end.
Rib row 2 P1, * k1, p1, rep from * to end.
Rep these 2 rows for 3.5(4.5)cm/1½(1¾)in, ending with a WS row.
Change to 6½mm needles.
Joining on and cutting off colours as required and carrying yarns not in use loosely across WS of work, work in patt as follows:
Row 1 With B, k to end.
Row 2 With B, p to end.
Row 3 K1(3)B, [5A, 3B] 5 times, 5A, 1(3)B.
Row 4 P2(4)B, [3A, 5B] 5 times, 3A, 2(4)B.
Row 5 K3(5)B, [1A, 7B] 5 times, 1A, 3(5)B.
Row 6 P7(9)B, [1C, 7B] 4 times, 1C, 7(9)B.
Row 7 K6(8)B, [3C, 5B] 4 times, 3C, 6(8)B.
Row 8 P2(4)B, [3D, 5B] 5 times, 3D, 2(4)B.
Row 9 K3,(5)B, [1D, 7B] 5 times, 1D, 3(5)B.
Row 10 P7(9)B, [1A, 7B] 4 times, 1A, 7(9)B.
Row 11 K6(8)B, [3A, 5B] 4 times, 3A, 6(8)B.
Row 12 P5(7)B, [5A, 3B] 4 times, 5A, 5(7)B.
Row 13 With B, k to end.
Row 14 With B, p to end.
Row 15 With C, k to end.
Row 16 With B, p to end.
Row 17 With A, k to end.
Row 18 With A, p to end.
Row 19 K1(3)A, [5B, 3A] 5 times, 5B, 1(3)A.
Row 20 P2(4)A, [3B, 5A] 5 times, 3B, 2(4)A.
Shape armholes
Row 21 With A, cast off 3 sts, then k a further 7(9)A, [1B, 7A] 4 times, 1B, 3(5)A.
Row 22 With A, cast off 3 sts, then p a further 3(5)A, [1D, 7A] 4 times, 1D, 4(6)A.
Row 23 K3(5)A, [3D, 5A] 4 times, 3D, 3(5)A. 41(45) sts.
Row 24 P7(9)A, [3E, 5A] 3 times, 3E, 7(9)A.
Row 25 K8(10)A, [1E, 7A] 3 times, 1E, 8(10)A.
Row 26 P4(6)A, [1B, 7A] 4 times, 1B, 4(6)A.
Row 27 K3 (5)A, [3B, 5A] 4 times, 3B, 3(5)A.
Row 28 P2(4)A, [5B, 3A] 4 times, 5B, 2(4)A.
Row 29 With A, k to end.
Row 30 With A, p to end.
Row 31 With B, k to end.
Row 32 With C, p to end.
Row 33 With B, k to end.
Row 34 With B, p to end.
Row 35 K2(4)B, [5A, 3B] 4 times, 5A, 2(4)B.
Row 36 P3(5)B, [3A, 5B] 4 times, 3A, 3(5)B.
Row 37 K4(6)B, [1A, 7B] 4 times, 1A, 4(6)B.
Row 38 With B, p to end.
Second size only
With B, k 1 row and p 1 row.
Shape neck (both sizes)
With B, k12(14), turn and leave rem sts on a spare needle.

With B, p 1 row, then cast off.
Return to sts on spare needle. With RS facing, slip first 17 sts on to a holder, join B to next st and k to end. 12(14) sts.
With B, p 1 row; then cast off.

Front

Work as given for back until row 20 has been completed.
Row 21 With A, cast off 3 sts, then k a further 7(9)A, 1B, 7A, 1B, 2A, turn and leave rem sts on a spare needle.
Row 22 P6A, 1D, 7A, 1D, 4(6)A.
Row 23 K3(5)A, 3D, 5A, 3D, 5A.
Row 24 P1A, 3E, 5A, 3E, 7(9)A.
Row 25 K8(10)A, 1E, 7A, 1E, 2A.
Row 26 P6A, 1B, 7A, 1B, 4(6)A.
Row 27 K3(5)A, [3B, 5A] twice.
Row 28 P4A, 5B, 3A, 5B, 2(4)A.
Row 29 With A, k to end.
Row 30 With A, p to end.
Row 31 With B, k to end.
Row 32 With C, p to end.
Row 33 With B, k to end.
Shape neck
Row 34 With B, cast off 4 sts, p to end.
Row 35 K2(4)B, 5A, 3B, 5A.
Row 36 With A, cast off 2 sts, then p a further 1A, 5B, 3A, 3(5)B.
Row 37 K4(6)B, 1A, 7B, 1A.
Row 38 With B, p2 tog, then p to end.
Using B only, work 2(4) rows st st. Cast off.
Return to sts on spare needle. With RS facing, join on A and cast off 3 sts, then k a further 1A, [1B, 7A] twice, 11B, 3(5)A.
Row 22 With A, cast off 3 sts, then p a further 3(5)A, 1D, 7A, 1D, 6A.
Row 23 [K5A, 3D] twice, 3(5)A.
Row 24 P7(9)A, 3E, 5A, 3E, 1A.
Row 25 K2A, 1E, 7A, 1E, 8(10)A.
Row 26 P4(6)A, 1B, 7A, 1B, 6A.
Row 27 [K5A, 3B] twice, 3(5)A.
Row 28 P2(4)A, 5B, 3A, 5B, 4A.
Row 29 With A, k to end.
Row 30 With A, p to end.
Row 31 With B, k to end.
Row 32 With C, p to end.
Row 33 With B, k to end.
Row 34 With B, p to end.
Shape neck
Row 35 With B, cast off 4 sts, then k a further 4A, 3B, 5A, 2(4)B.
Row 36 P3(5)B, 3A, 5B, 3A, 1B.
Row 37 With B, cast off 2 sts, then k a further 7B, 1A, 4(6)B.
Row 38 With B, p to end.
Row 39 With B, k2 tog, k to end.
Using B only, work 1(3) rows st st. Cast off.

Sleeves

Using 5mm needles and A, cast on 25 sts.
Work 3.5(4.5)cm/1½(1¾)in rib as given for back, ending with a WS row. Change to 6½mm needles. Cut off A and join in B.
Inc row K5, [M1, k5] 4 times. 29 sts.
P 1 row. Now work in patt as follows:
Row 1 K5A, [3B, 5A] 3 times.
Row 2 P1B, [3A, 5B] 3 times, 3A, 11B.
Row 3 With B inc in first st, k1B, [1A, 7B] 3 times, 1A, 2B, with B inc in last st. 31 sts.
Row 4 P7B, [1C, 7B] 3 times.
Row 5 K6B, [3C, 5B] twice, 3C, 6B.
Row 6 P2B, [3D, 5B] 3 times, 3D, 2B.
Row 7 With B inc in first st, k2B, [1D, 7B] 3 times, 1D, 2B, with B inc in last st. 33 sts.
Row 8 P8B, [1A, 7B] twice, 1A, 8B.
Row 9 K7B, [3A, 5B] twice, 3A, 7B.
Row 10 P6B, [5A, 3B] twice, 5A, 6B.
Row 11 With B, inc in first st, k31, inc in last st. 35 sts.
Row 12 With B, p to end.
Row 13 With C, k to end.
Row 14 With B, p to end.
Row 15 With A, inc in first st, k33, inc in last st. 37 sts.

Row 16 With A, p to end.
Row 17 K4A, [5B, 3A] 3 times, 5B, 4A.
Row 18 P5A, [3B, 5A] 4 times.
Row 19 With A, inc in first st, k5A, [1B, 7A] 3 times, 1B, 5A, with A inc in last st. 39 sts.
Row 20 P11A, [1D, 7A] twice, 1D, 11A.
Row 21 K10A, [3D, 5A] twice, 3D, 10A.
Row 22 P6A, [3E, 5A] 3 times, 3E, 6A.
Row 23 With A inc in first st, k6A, [1E, 7A] 3 times, 1E, 6A, with A inc in last st. 41 sts.
First size only
Next row With A, p to end.
Next row With A, k to end.
Next row With B, p to end, then cast off.
Second size only
Row 24 P4A, [1B, 7A] 4 times, 1B, 4A.
Row 25 K3A, [3B, 5A] 4 times, 3B, 3A.
Row 26 K2A, [5B, 3A] 4 times, 5B, 2A.
Row 27 With A, inc in first st, k39, inc in last st. 43 sts.
Row 28 With B, p to end, then cast off.

Buttonhole border

With RS facing and using 5mm needles and A, pick up and k15 sts evenly along right front neck opening.
Beg with rib row 2, work 2 rows in rib as given for back.
Buttonhole row [Rib 4, yf, k2 tog] twice, rib 3.
Rib 1 row. Cut off A and join in B.
P 2 rows. Cast off.

Button border

Work as given for buttonhole border, omitting buttonholes.

Collar

Join shoulder seams.
With RS facing and using 5mm needles and A, pick up and k49 sts evenly round neck edge.
Work 12 rows rib as given for back.
Cut off A and join on B. K 2 rows. Cast off.
Collar edging
With RS facing and using 5mm needles and B, pick up and k12 sts along row ends of one collar edge. K 1 row, then cast off.
Rep along 2nd edge.

To make up

Lapping right over left, sew down row ends of button and buttonhole borders to cast off sts of front opening. Fold sleeves in half lengthwise, then placing folds to shoulder seams, sew into place.
Join side and sleeve seams.

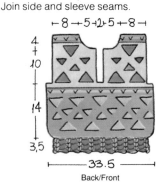

Back/Front

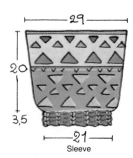

Sleeve

Measurements given in cm for smaller size

SUMMER COTTON TOP WITH FISHES

✳

his summer beach top, with fishes on both front and back, is quick and easy to knit.

Materials

4(4,5)×50g balls of Scheepjeswol
Mayflower Helarsgarn in main colour A
1(2,2)×50g balls of same in contrast
colours B and C
A pair each of 3¼mm/No10 and 4mm/No8
knitting needles

Measurements

To fit chest 56(61,66)cm/22(24,26)in
Actual measurements
Chest 64(69,75)cm/25¼(27¼,29½)in
Length to shoulders 36cm/14in
Sleeve seam 11.5cm/4½in

Tension

21 sts and 29 rows to 10cm/4in measured
over st st using 4mm needles

Note

The chart is given for the smallest size only.
For the middle and larger sizes add extra
sts as indicated to each side.

Back and front (alike)

Using 3¼mm needles and B, cast on
67(73,79) sts.
Work 7 rows g st.
Change to 4mm needles.
Cut off B. Join on A.
Beg with a k row, work 3 rows st st.
Use separate small balls of yarn for each
area of colour and twist yarns together on
WS of work when changing colour to avoid
making a hole.
Beg at row 4, work in st st from chart as
follows:
Next row P8(11,14)A, 4B, [6A, 4B] twice,
35(38,41)A.
Cont in this way, working 3(6) sts more each
side for 2nd and 3rd sizes until row 94 has
been completed.
Working in B only, work in rib as follows:
Rib row 1 K1, * p1, k1, rep from * to end.
Rib row 2 P1, * k1, p1, rep from * to end.
Rep these 2 rows twice more.
Cast off in rib.

Sleeves

Using 3¼mm needles and B, cast on
54(59,64) sts.
Work 7 rows g st.
Change to 4mm needles.
Cut off B, join on A.
Beg with a k row, work 4 rows st st.
Join on C and work 2 rows st st.
Cont in st st, work 4 rows A, 2 rows C, 4 rows
A, 2 rows C and 4 rows A.
Cut off A and C, join on B.
Work 6 rows g st.
Cast off.

To make up

Join shoulder seams leaving approx 17cm/
8in open at centre for neck.
Fold sleeves in half lengthwise, then placing
folds to shoulder seams, sew into place.
Join side and sleeve seams.

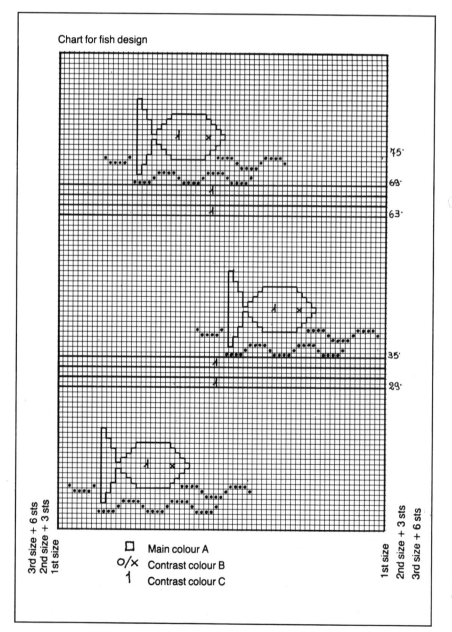

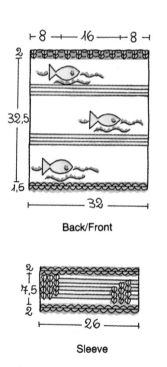

Back/Front

Sleeve

Measurements given in
cm for smallest size

JERSEY WITH RANDOM CABLES, TWISTS AND RIBS

***

This classic Aran
style
jersey
is a
little different
as the cables are
set at random over
the front, back
and sleeves.

Materials

9×50g balls of Emu Superwash Chunky
A pair each of 3¼mm/No10 and 5½mm/No5 knitting needles
Cable needle

Measurements

One size only to fit chest 71cm/28in

Actual measurements

Chest 82cm/32¼in
Length to shoulders 51cm/20in
Sleeve seam 34cm/13½in

Tension

20 sts and 21 rows to 10cm/4in measured over patt using 5½mm needles

Special abbreviations

C6 Cable 6 as follows: slip next 3 sts on to cable needle and leave at front of work, k3, then k3 from cable needle
Cr2 Cross 2 as follows: ytb, sl 1 kw, k1, yarn forward and over needle to make a st, psso

Back

Using 3¼mm needles cast on 76 sts.
Work 4cm/1½in k1, p1 rib, ending with a WS row.
Change to 5½mm needles.
Work in patt as follows:
Row 1 [K1, p2] 11 times, k6, [p2, k1] 5 times, p3, k6, [p2, k1] 4 times, p1.
Row 2 and every alt row K all the knit sts and p all the purl sts.
Rows 3, 5, 7 and 9 As row 1.
Row 11 Inc in first st, p2, k1, p1, k6, p1, [k1, p2] 7 times, C6, [p2, k1] 5 times, p3, C6, [p2, k1] 4 times, inc in last st. 78 sts.
Row 13 P1, k1, p2, k1, p1, k6, p1, [k1, p2] 7 times, k6, [p2, k1] 5 times, p3, k6, [p2, k1] 4 times, p2.
Row 15 P1, k1, p2, k1, p1, k6, p2, k6, [p2, k1] 4 times, p2, k6, [p2, k1] 5 times, p3, k6, [p2, k1] 4 times, p2.
Row 17 As row 15.
Row 19 P1, k1, p2, k1, p1, [k6, p2] twice, k6, p3, k1, p2, k6, [p2, k1] 5 times, p3, k6, [p2, k1] 4 times, p2.
Row 21 Inc in first st, k1, p2, k1, p1, C6, [p2, k6] twice, p3, k1, p2, C6, [p2, k1] 5 times, p3, C6, [p2, k1] 4 times, p1, inc in last st. 80 sts.
Row 23 [P2, k1] twice, p1, [k6, p2] 3 times, [Cr2, p2] 3 times, k6, p3, k1, p2, k1, p3, [Cr2, p2] twice, k6, p2, Cr2, p2, k1.
Row 25 [P2, k1] twice, p1, k6, p2, C6, p2, k6, p2, [Cr2, p2] 3 times, k6, p3, k1, p2, k1, p3, [Cr2, p2] twice, k6, p2, Cr2, p2, k1.
Row 27 [P2, k1] twice, p1, [k6, p2] 3 times, [Cr2, p2] 3 times, [k6, p2] twice, [Cr2, p2] twice, k6, p2, Cr2, p2, k1.
Row 29 [P2, k1] twice, p1, [k6, p2] twice, C6, p2, [Cr2, p2] 3 times, [k6, p2] twice, [Cr2, p2] twice, k6, p2, Cr2, p2, k1.
Row 31 Inc in first st, p1, k1, p2, k1, p1, C6, p2, [k6, p2] twice, [Cr2, p2] 3 times, [k6, p2] twice, [Cr2, p2] twice, k6, p2, Cr2, p2, inc in last st. 82 sts.
Row 33 [K1, p2] twice, k1, p1, [k6, p2] 3 times, [Cr2, p2] 3 times, C6, p2, k6, p2, [Cr2, p2] twice, C6, p2, Cr2, p2, k1, p1.
Row 35 [K1, p2] twice, k1, p1, k6, p2, C6, p2, [Cr2, p2] 3 times, [k6, p2] twice, [Cr2, p2] twice, k6, p2, Cr2, p2, k1, p1.
Row 37 [K1, p2] twice, k1, p1, [k6, p2] 3 times, [Cr2, p2] 3 times, k6, p2, C6, p2, [Cr2, p2] twice, k6, p2, Cr2, p2, k1, p1.
Row 39 [K1, p2] twice, k1, p1, [k6, p2] twice, C6, p2, [Cr2, p2] 3 times, [k6, p2] twice, [Cr2, p2] twice, k6, p2, Cr2, p2, k1, p1.
Row 41 [K1, p2] twice, k1, p1, C6, p2, k6, p2, [Cr2, p2] 5 times, [k6, p2] twice, [Cr2, p2] twice, k6, p2, Cr2, p2, k1, p1.

Row 43 [K1, p2] twice, k1, p1, [k6, p2] twice, [Cr2, p2] 5 times, C6, p2, k6, p2, [Cr2, p2] twice, C6, p2, Cr2, p2, k1, p1.
Row 45 [K1, p2] twice, k1, p1, k6, p2, C6, p2, [Cr2, p2] 5 times, [k6, p2] twice, [Cr2, p2] twice, k6, p2, Cr2, p2, k1, p1.
Row 47 [K1, p2] twice, k1, p1, k6, p2, [Cr2, p2] twice, k6, p2, C6, p2, [Cr2, p2] twice, k6, p2, Cr2, p2, k1, p1.
Row 49 [K1, p2] twice, k1, p1, k6, p2, [Cr2, p2] 7 times, k6, p2, [Cr2, p2] 4 times, k6, p2, Cr2, p2, k1, p1.
Row 51 [K1, p2] twice, k1, p1, C6, p2, [Cr2, p2] 7 times, k6, p2, [Cr2, p2] 4 times, k6, p2, Cr2, p2, k1, p1.
Row 53 [K1, p2] twice, k1, p1, [Cr2, p2] 9 times, C6, p2, [Cr2, p2] 4 times, C6, p2, Cr2, p2, k1, p1.

Shape raglans

Row 55 Cast off 5 sts, then k1, p1, [Cr2, p2] 9 times, k6, p2, [Cr2, p2] 7 times, k1, p1. 77 sts.
Row 56 Cast off 5 sts, patt to end. 72 sts.
Row 57 P1, Cr2 for border, skpo, p2, [Cr2, p2] 8 times, k6, p2, [Cr2, p2] 5 times, k2 tog, then Cr2, p1 for border.
Row 58 and every foll alt row K the knit sts and p the purl sts as before.
Keeping patt correct and working cables on the 5th and every foll 10th row, cont to dec 1 st within the border at each end of next

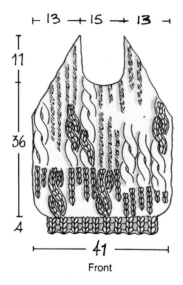

├ 13 ─┤├ 15 ─┤├ 13 ─┤

11

36

4

├── 41 ──┤
Front

and every foll alt row until 30 sts rem, ending with a WS row.
Cut off yarn and leave rem sts on a holder.

Front

Work as given for back until 52 sts rem, ending with a WS row.

Shape neck

Next row P1, Cr2, skpo, k2, p2, [Cr2, p2] 3 times, turn and leave rem sts on a spare needle.
Keeping patt and raglan shaping correct, dec 1 st at beg of next and every foll alt row until 5 sts rem.
Keeping neck edge straight, cont raglan shaping until 2 sts rem, ending with a WS row.
K2 tog and fasten off.
Return to sts on spare needle.
With RS facing, slip first 10 sts on to holder, join on yarn and work as follows:
K4, [p2, Cr2] twice, p2, k2, k2 tog, sl 1, k1, yf, psso, k1.
Now complete to match first side of neck.

Sleeves

Using 3¼mm needles cast on 40 sts.
Work 5cm/2in k1, p1 rib ending with a WS row.
Change to 5½mm needles.
Work in patt as follows:
Row 1 [P2, k1] 5 times, p2, [k6, p2] twice, [k1, p2] twice, k1.
Row 2 and every alt row K the knit sts and p the purl sts.
These 2 rows establish the position of the patt.
Keeping patt correct and working C6 on row 11, inc and work into patt 1 st each end of 3rd and every foll 5th row until there are 52 sts, ending with a WS row.
Row 31 K1, * p2, Cr2, rep from * to last 3 sts, p2, k1.
Row 32 P1, * k2, p2, rep from * to last 3 sts, k2, p1.

Measurements given in cm

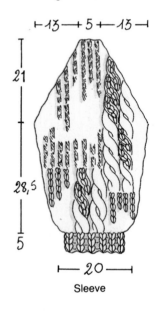

├─13─┤─5─├─13─┤

21

28,5

5

├── 20 ──┤
Sleeve

These 2 rows set the cable and cross st rib patt.
Continuing in cross st rib patt, inc and work into patt 1 st each end of 3rd and every foll 5th row until there are 62 sts.
Work 4 rows straight, so ending with a WS row.

Shape raglan

Keeping patt correct, cast off 5 sts at beg of next 2 rows.
Next row P1, Cr2 for border, skpo, [p2, Cr2] 10 times, p2, k2 tog, then Cr2, p1 for border.
Next and every foll alt row K the knit sts and p the purl sts as before.
Keeping patt correct, dec 1 st within the border at each end of next and every foll alt row until 10 sts rem.
Cut off yarn and leave rem sts on holder.

Neckband

Join raglan seams, leaving left back raglan seam open.
With RS facing, and using 3¼mm needles, k across 10 sts from holder at top of left sleeve, pick up and k17 sts down left front neck, k10 sts from front neck holder, pick up and k17 sts up right front neck, then k10 sts from holder at top of right sleeve and 30 sts from back neck holder. 94 sts.
Work in k1, p1, rib for 3cm/1¼in.
Cast off in rib.

To make up

Join left back raglan and neckband seam.
Join side and sleeve seams.

RABBITS GALORE!

**

The rabbits are only worked on the front of this polo neck jersey but you could continue them across the back as well.

Materials
2(2,3)×100g balls of Sunbeam Scoop DK in main colour A
1 ball of same in contrast colour B
1 ball of same in contrast colour C
A pair each of 3¼mm/No10, 4mm/No8 and 4½mm/No7 knitting needles

Measurements
To fit chest 61(63,66)cm/24(25.26)in
Actual measurements
Chest 74(78,82)cm/29(30¾,32¼)in
Length to shoulders 37(41,44)cm/14½(16¼,17¼)in
Sleeve seam 29(30,33)cm/11½(12,13)in

Tension
22 sts and 30 rows to 10cm/4in measured over st st worked on 4mm needles

Back
★ Using 3¼mm needles and B, cast on 71(75,79) sts.
Rib row 1 K1, * p1, k1, rep from * to end.
Rib row 2 P1, * k1, p1, rep from * to end.
Rep these 2 rows for 4cm/1¾in, ending with rib row 1.
Inc row Rib 6(2,5), * M1, rib 6(7,7), rep from * to last 5(3,4) sts, M1, rib to end. 82(86,90) sts. ★
Change to 4mm needles.
Beg with a k row, work 27(31,35) rows st st, so ending with a k row.
Cut off B. Join on C.
Beg with a p row, work 27(31,35) rows st st, so ending with a p row.
Cut off C. Join on A.
Shape raglans
Cast off 4 sts at beg of next 2 rows.
Next row K1, k2 tog, k to last 3 sts, skpo, k1.
Next row P to end.
Rep the last 2 rows until 30(32,34) sts rem, ending with a p row.
Cut off yarn and leave sts on a holder.

Front
Work as given for back from ★ to ★.
Change to 4mm needles.
Beg with a k row, work 2(4,6) rows st st, so ending with a p row.
Change to 4½mm needles.
Join on and cut off colours as required.
Use separate small balls of yarn for each area of colour and twist yarns together at back of work when changing colour to avoid making a hole.
Working odd numbered (k) rows from right to left and even numbered (p) rows from left to right, work first set of 3 rabbits from chart as follows:
Row 1 K3(5,7)B, working across row 1 of chart * k4B, 1A, 4C, 1A, 3C, 2A, 10C *, rep from * to * twice more, k4(6,8)B.
Row 2 P4(6,8)B, working across row 2 of chart * p9C, 2A, 4C, 1A, 1C, 1A, 7B *, rep from * to * twice more. p3(5,7)B.

Row 3 K3(5,7)B, working across row 3 of chart * k9B, 1C, 1A, 5C, 1A, 7C 1B *, rep from * to * twice more, k4(6,8)B.
Row 4 P4(6,8), working across row 4 of chart * p1B, 7C, 1A, 4C, 1A, 1C, 1A, 3C, 6B *, rep from * to * twice more, p3(5,7)B.
Cont in this way, working from chart, until row 23 has been completed.
Change to 4mm needles.
With B and beg with a p row, work 2(4.6) rows st st, so ending with a k row.
With C and beg with a p row, work 2(4,6) rows st st, so ending with a k row.
Change to 4½mm needles.
Working odd numbered (p) rows from right to left and even numbered (k) rows from left to right, work second set of 3 rabbits from chart as follows:
Row 1 P3(5,7)C, working across row 1 of chart * p4C, 1B, 4A, 1B, 3A, 2B, 10A *, rep from * to * twice more, p4(6,8)C.
Row 2 K4(6,8)C, working across row 2 of chart * k9A, 2B, 4A, 1B, 1A, 1B, 7C *, rep from * to * twice more, k3(5,7)C.
Cont in this way, working from chart, until row 23 has been completed.
Change to 4mm needles.
With C and beg with a k row, work 2(4,6) rows st st, so ending with a p row.
Shape raglans
With A. cast off 4 sts at beg of next 2 rows.
Next row With A, k1, k2 tog, k to last 3 sts, skpo, k1.
Next row With A, p to end.
Rep the last 2 rows once more.
Change to 4½mm needles.
Working odd numbered (k) rows from right to left and even numbered (p) rows from left to right, position last rabbit as follows:
Row 1 With A, k1, k2 tog, k19(21,23), working across row 1 of chart k4A, 1C, 4B, 1C, 3B, 2C, 10B, with A, k20(22,24), skpo, k1.
Row 2 With A, p22(24,26), working across. row 2 of chart p9B, 2C, 4B, 1C, 1B, 1C, 7A, with A, p21(23,25).
Cont in this way, working rabbit from chart as set, dec 1 st within raglan border as before, each end of next and every foll alt row until 42(44,46) sts rem, ending with a p row.
Change to 4mm needles.
Shape neck
Next row K1, k2 tog, k7, turn and leave rem sts on a spare needle.
Next row P2 tog, p to end.
Next row K1, k2 tog, k to last 2 sts, k2 tog.
Next row P to end.
Next row K1, [k2 tog] twice.
Next row P to end.
Next row K2 tog, k1. 2 sts.
P2 tog and fasten off.
Return to sts on spare needle.
With RS facing, slip first 22(24,26) sts on to a holder, join on yarn and k to last 3 sts, skpo, k1.

Next row P to last 2 sts, p2 tog.
Next row K2 tog, k to last 3sts, skpo, k1.
Next row P to last 2 sts, p2 tog.
Next row K2 tog, skpo, k1.
Next row P to end.
Next row K1, skpo. 2 sts.
P2 tog and fasten off.

Right sleeve
★★ Using 3¼mm needles and A, cast on 33(35.37) sts.
Rib row 1 K1. * p1, k1. rep from * to end.
Rib row 2 P1, * k1, p1. rep from * to end.
Rep these 2 rows for 4(5,5)cm/1¾(2,2)in, ending with rib row 1.
Inc row Rib 1(2,3). * M1, rib 6, rep from * to last 2(3,4) sts. M1, rib to end. 39(41,43) sts.
Change to 4mm needles.
Working in st st, inc 1 st each end of 3rd(7th,3rd) row and every foll 6th(6th,8th) row until there are 59(61,63) sts.
Work straight until sleeve measures 30(33,37)cm/12(13.14½)in from cast-on edge, ending with a p row.
Shape raglan
Cast off 4 sts at beg of next 2 rows.
Next row K1, k2 tog, k to last 3 sts, skpo, k1.
Next row P to end. ★★
Rep the last 2 rows until 13 sts rem, ending with a p row.
Next row Cast off 5 sts, k to last 3 sts, skpo, k1.
Next row P to end.
Next row Cast off 4 sts, k to last 3 sts, skpo, k1. 2 sts.
P2 tog and fasten off.

Left sleeve
Work as given for right sleeve from ★★ to ★★.
Rep the last 2 rows until 13 sts rem, ending with a k row.
Next row Cast off 5 sts, p to end.
Next row K1, k2 tog, k to end.
Next row Cast off 4 sts, p to end.
Next row K2 tog, k1. 2 sts.
P2 tog and fasten off.

Collar
Join raglan seams, leaving left back raglan open.
With RS facing. using 3¼mm needles and A, pick up and k8 sts across left sleeve top, 9 sts down left front neck, k across 22(24,26) sts from front holder, pick up and k9 sts up right front neck, 8 sts across right sleeve top and k across 30(32,34) sts from back holder. 86(90,94) sts. Work 9cm/3½in k1, p1 rib.
Cast off in rib.

To make up
Join left back raglan and collar seam, reversing seam on last 4cm/1¾in of collar. Join side and sleeve seams. Embroider French knots for eyes using B on first 2 rows of rabbits and C on single rabbit.

Chart for rabbit motif

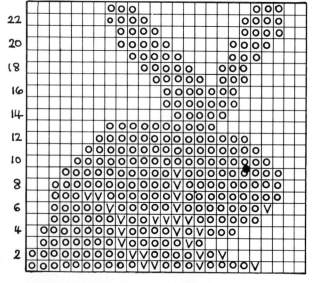

Key

1st row rabbits
V =
O =
□ =

2nd row rabbits
o =
V =
□ =

3rd row rabbit
O =
V =
□ =

● French knot

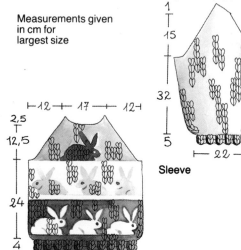

Measurements given in cm for largest size

Sleeve

Back/Front

ROSES FOR
A LITTLE GIRL

✳✳✳

This charming
crossover cardigan
has a simple
repeating rose
motif.

Materials

4(5,5)×50g balls of Patons Diploma DK in main colour A
1 ball of same in contrast colour B
2 balls of same in contrast colour C
A pair each of 3¼mm/No10 and 4mm/No8 knitting needles
4 buttons

Measurements

To fit chest 61(66,71)cm/24(26,28)in
Actual measurements
Chest 68.5(72,75.5)cm/27(28½,30)in
Length to shoulders 38(40,41)cm/ 15(15¾, 16¼)in
Sleeve seam 30(32,34.5)cm/ 11¾(12¾,13½)in

Tension

23 sts and 26 rows to 10cm/4in measured over st st worked on 4mm needles

Left front

Using 3¼mm needles and A, cast on 43(47,51) sts.
Rib row 1 (RS) K1, * p1, k1, rep from * to end.
Rib row 2 P1, * k1, p1, rep from * to end.
Rep these 2 rows 3(4,5) times more, then work rib row 1 again.
Inc row Rib 4(3,5), * M1, rib 7(8,8), rep from * to last 4(4,6) sts, M1, rib to end. 49(53,57) sts.
Change to 4mm needles.
K 1 row and p 1 row.
Use separate small balls of yarn for each area of colour and twist yarns together on WS of work when changing colour to avoid making a hole.
Reading odd numbered (k) rows from right to left and even numbered (p) rows from left to right, work motifs from chart as follows:
Row 1 K3(5,7)A, working across row 1 of chart, [k1A, 5B] twice, 19A, 5B, 1A, 5B, 3A, then k1(3,5)A.
Row 2 P1(3,5)A, working across row 2 of chart, k2A, 5B, 3A, 5B, 17A, 5B, 3A, 5B, then k3(5,7)A.
Cont in this way, working motifs from chart until row 14 has been completed.

Shape front edge

Next row Patt to last 4 sts, with A, k2 tog, k2.
Next row Patt to end.
Continuing to work motifs from chart, rep the last 2 rows until 31(31,33) sts rem. Now dec 1 st at front edge, as before, on every foll 4th row until 24(26,28) sts rem.
Work straight in patt until front measures approx 39(40,41)cm/15¼(15¾, 16¼)in from cast-on edge, ending with row 13.
With A, p 1 row.
Cast off.

Right front

Using 3¼mm needles and A, cast on 43(47,51) sts.
Rib row 1 (RS) K1, * p1, k1, rep from * to end.
Rib row 2 P1, * k1, p1, rep from * to end.
Rep these 2 rows once more.
Buttonhole row Rib 4, yf, k2 tog, rib 8(10,12), yf, k2 tog, rib to end.
Work 4(6,8) rows rib, so ending with rib row 1.
Inc row Rib 4(3,5), * M1, rib 7(8,8), rep from * to last 4(4,6) sts, M1, rib to end. 49(53,57) sts.
Change to 4mm needles.
K 1 row and p 1 row.
Reading odd numbered (k) rows from left to right and even numbered (p) rows from right to left, work motifs from chart as follows:
Row 1 K1(3,5)A, working across row 1 of chart, k3A, 5B, 1A, 5B, 19A, [5B, 1A] twice, then k3(5,7)A.
Row 2 P3(5,7)A, working across row 2 of chart, p5B, 3A, 5B, 17A, 5B, 3A, 5B, 2A, then p1(3,5)A.
Cont in this way, working motifs from chart until row 12 has been completed.
Buttonhole row Patt 4, yf, k2 tog, patt 10(12,14), yf, k2 tog, patt to end.
Patt 1 row.

Shape front

Next row K2, skpo, patt to end.
Next row Patt to end.
Now complete to match left front.

Back

Using 3¼mm needles and A, cast on 73(77,81) sts.
Rib row 1 (RS) K1, * p1, k1, rep from * to end.
Rib row 2 P1, * k1, p1, rep from * to end.
Rep these 2 rows 3(4,5) times more, then work rib row 1 again.
Inc row Rib 6(6,5), * M1, rib 12(13,14), rep from * to last 7(6,6) sts, M1, rib to end. 79(83,87) sts.
Change to 4mm needles.
K 1 row, p 1 row and k 1 row.
Reading odd numbered (k) rows from right to left and even numbered (p) rows from left to right and beginning at row 14, work motifs from chart as follows:
Next row P1(3,5)A, working across row 14 of chart p15A, [p3A, 5B, 1A, 5B, 16A] twice, then p3(5,7)A.
Next row K3(5,7)A, working across row 15 of chart [k15A, 5B, 3A, 5B, 2A] twice, k15A, then k1(3,5)A.
Keeping the 26 row patt correct, cont in patt from chart until back measures the same length as fronts, ending with row 26.
Cast off.

Sleeves

using 3¼mm needles and A, cast on 39(43,47) sts.
Work 3cm/1¼in rib as given for back, ending with rib row 1.
Inc row Rib 1(3,5), * M1, rib 4, rep from * to last 2(4,6) sts, M1, rib to end. 49(53,57) sts.
Change to 4mm needles.
K 1 row, p 1 row and k 1 row.
Reading odd numbered (k) rows from right to left and even numbered (p) rows from left to right and beginning with row 14, work motifs from chart as follows:
Next row P1(3,5)A, working across row 14 of chart p18A, 5B, 1A, 5B, 16A, then p3(5,7)A.
Next row K3(5,7)A, working across row 15 of chart k15A, 5B, 3A, 5B, 17A, then k1(3,5)A.
Keeping the 26 row patt correct, cont in patt from chart increasing and working into patt 1 st each end of 3rd and every foll 6th row until there are 69(73,77) sts.
Work straight until sleeve measures 30(32,34.5)cm/11¾(12¾,13½)in from cast-on edge, ending with a WS row.
Cast off.

Right front border

Join shoulder seams.
With RS facing, using 3¼mm needles and A, pick up and k21(23,25) sts up right front to beg of front shaping, 79 sts up right front shaping to shoulder and 15(17,17) sts to centre back neck. 115(119,121) sts.
Rib row 1 P1, * k1, p1, rep from * to end.
Rib row 2 K1, * p1, k1, rep from * to end.
Rep these 2 rows once more then work rib row 1 again.
Cast off in rib.

Left front border

With RS facing, using 3¼mm needles and A, pick up and k15(17,17) sts from centre back neck to shoulder, 79 sts down left side of front shaping and 21(23,25) sts down left front to cast-on edge. 115(119,121) sts.
Now complete to match right front border.

To make up

Fold sleeves in half lengthwise, then placing folds to shoulder seams sew sleeves in place. Join side and sleeve seams. Sew border seam at centre back neck. Sew on the buttons. Neaten buttonholes.

Chart for motifs

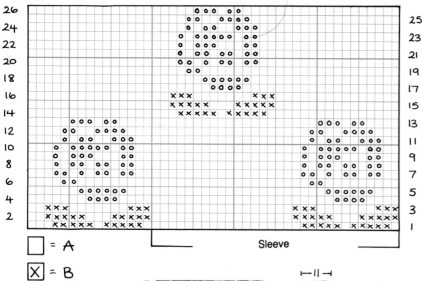

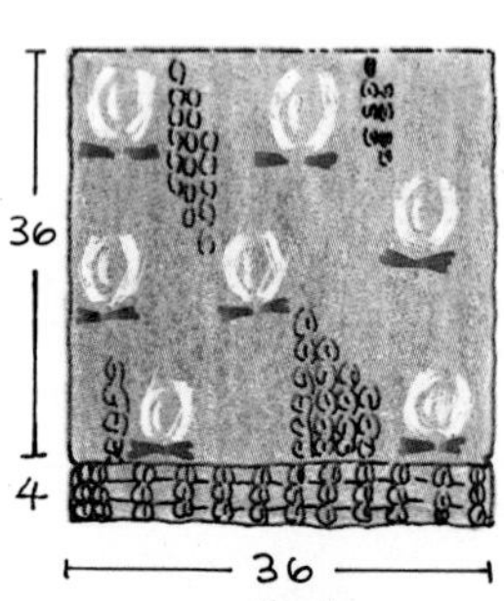

□ = A
X = B
O = C

Measurements given in cm for second size

36
4
Back

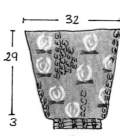

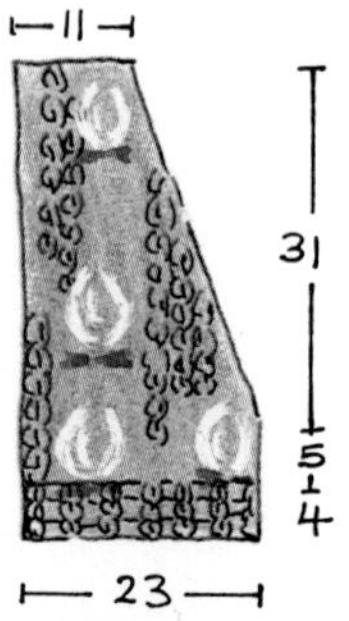

31
5
4
23
Right front

32
29
3
22
Sleeve

ARAN STYLE JERSEY

* The central cable is bordered by an easy-to-knit textured slip stitch pattern.

Materials

10(11, 12)×50g balls of Emu Superwash Aran
A pair each of 4½mm/No7 and 6mm/No4
knitting needles
Cable needle

Measurements

To fit chest 66(71,76)cm/26(28,30)in
Actual measurements
Chest 74(84,93)cm/29(33,36½)in
Length to shoulders 50(53,57)cm/
19¾(21,22½)in
Sleeve seam 35(39,41)cm/13¾(15½,16)in

Tension

17 sts and 28 rows to 10cm/4in measured
over main patt worked on 6mm needles
Centre cable panel (24 sts) measures
10cm/4in worked on 6mm needles

Special abbreviations

C6F Cable 6 front as follows: slip next 3 sts
on to cable needle and leave at front of
work, k3, then k3 from cable needle
C6B Cable 6 back as follows: slip next 3 sts
on to cable needle and leave at back of
work, k3, then k3 from cable needle

Back

Using 4½mm needles, cast on
59(65,73) sts.
Rib row 1 K1, * p1, k1, rep from * to end.
Rib row 2 P1, * k1, p1, rep from * to end.
Rep these 2 rows for 4(4,5)cm/1½(1½,2)in,
ending with rib row 1.
Inc row Rib 4(2,6), [inc in next st, rib 4]
10(12,12) times, inc in next st, rib 4(2,6).
70(78,86) sts.
Work in patt as follows:
Row 1 (RS) K3, [ytf, sl 2 pw, ytb, k2]
5(6,7) times, sl 3 pw, k18, sl 3 pw, [k2, ytf,
sl 2 pw, ytb] 5(6,7) times, k3.
Row 2 and every foll alt row P to end.
Row 3 K1, ytf, sl 2 pw, [ytb, k2, ytf, sl 2 pw]
5(6,7) times, ytb, sl 3 pw, [C6F] 3 times,
sl 3 pw, [ytf, sl 2 pw, ytb, k2] 5(6,7) times,
ytf, sl 2 pw, ytb, k1.
Row 5 As row 1.
Row 7 K1, ytf, sl 2 pw, [ytb, k2, ytf, sl 2 pw]
5(6,7) times, ytb, sl 3 pw, k18, sl 3 pw, [ytf,
sl 2 pw, ytb, k2] 5(6,7) times, ytf, sl 2 pw,
ytb, k1.
Row 9 K3, [ytf, sl 2 pw, ytb, k2] 5(6,7) times,
sl 3 pw, k3, [C6B] twice, k3, sl 3 pw, [k2, ytf,
sl 2 pw, ytb] 5(6,7) times, k3.
Row 11 As row 7.
Row 12 P to end.
These 12 rows form the patt.
Cont in patt until work measures
50(53,57)cm/19¾(21,22½)in from cast-on
edge, ending with a p row.
Cast off 16(20,24) sts at beg of next 2 rows.
Cast off.

Front

Work as given for back until front measures
44(47,51)cm/17¼(18½,20)in from cast-on
edge, ending with a p row.

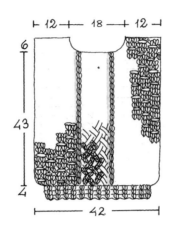

|←12→|←18→|←12→|

Back/Front

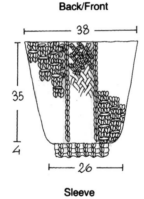

|←38→|

|←26→|

Sleeve

Measurements given in cm for second size

Shape neck

Next row Patt 24(28,32), turn and leave rem
sts on a spare needle.
★ Cast off 2 sts at beg of next and foll 2 alt
rows.
Dec 1 st at neck edge on every foll alt row
until 16(20,24) sts rem.
Work straight until front measures same as
back to shoulder, ending with a p row.
Cast off. ★
Return to sts on spare needle.
With RS facing, slip the first 22 sts on to a
holder, join on yarn and patt to end.
24(28,32) sts.
P 1 row.
Now complete as given for left side of neck
from ★ to ★.

Sleeves

Using 4½mm needles cast on
31(33,35) sts.
Work 4(4,5)cm/1½(1½,2)in rib as given for
back, ending with rib row 1
Inc row Rib 4(6,8), k twice into each of next
23(21,19) sts, rib 4(6,8). 54 sts.
Change to 6mm needles.
Work in patt as follows:
Row 1 K3, [ytf, sl 2 pw, ytb, k2] 3 times,
sl 3 pw, k18, sl 3 pw, [k2, ytf, sl 2 pw, ytb]
3 times, k3.
Row 2 and every foll alt row P to end.
Row 3 K1, M1, ytf, sl 2 pw, [ytb, k2, ytf,
sl 2 pw] 3 times, ytb, sl 3 pw, [C6F] 3 times,
sl 3 pw, [ytf, sl 2 pw, ytb, k2] 3 times, ytf,
sl 2 pw, ytb, M1, k1. 56 sts.
Row 5 K4, [ytf, sl 2 pw, ytb, k2] 3 times,
sl 3 pw, k18, sl 3 pw, [k2, ytf, sl 2 pw, ytb]
3 times, k4.
Row 7 [K2, ytf, sl 2 pw, ytb] 4 times, sl 3 pw,
k18, sl 3 pw, [ytf, sl 2 pw, ytb, k2] 4 times.
Row 9 K4, [ytf, sl 2 pw, ytb, k2] 3 times,
sl 3 pw, k3, [C6B] twice, k3, sl 3 pw, [k2, ytf,
sl 2 pw, ytb] 3 times, k4.
Row 11 As row 7.
Row 12 P to end.
Continuing in patt, inc and work into the slip
stitch patt 1 st each end of next and every
foll 10th(8th,8th) row until there are
68(72,76) sts.
Work straight until sleeve measures
35(39,41)cm/13¾(15½,16)in from cast-on
edge, ending with a p row.
Cast off.

Neckband

Join right shoulder seam.
With RS facing and using 4½mm needles,
pick up and k16 sts down left side of front
neck, k22 sts from holder, then pick up and
k16 sts up right side of front neck and 35 sts
across back neck. 89 sts.
Work 3cm/1in rib as given for back.
Cast off in rib.

To make up

Join left shoulder and neckband seam.
Fold sleeves in half lengthwise, then placing
folds to shoulder seams, sew into place.
Join side and sleeve seams.

STRAWBERRY MOTIF TWIN SET

✳✳✳✳

The strawberry motifs are worked across the top of the jersey and all over the cardigan. Several other motif designs are given – or you could try designing your own.

Materials
Cardigan
3(4, 4, 5)×50g balls of Emu Superwash DK in main colour A (black)

2 balls of same in contrast colour C (green)

1 ball of same in each of contrast colours B (yellow), D (peach), E (red), F (pink), G (sky blue) and H (turquoise)

7 buttons

Jersey
4(5,5,6)×50g balls of Emu Superwash DK in main colour A (black)

Small amounts each of contrast colours C (green), D (peach), E (red), F (pink) and G (sky blue)

Note If you are knitting both the cardigan and the jersey you will need the same amount of A and C as quoted for each garment but only 1 ball each of all the other contrasts

A pair each of 3¼mm/No10 and 4½mm/ No7 knitting needles

Measurements
To fit chest 56(61,66,71)cm/22(24,26,28)in

Actual measurements for cardigan

Chest 71(76,81,86)cm/28(30,32,34)in

Length to shoulders 43(44.5, 46.5, 48)cm/ 17(17½m 18¼,19)in

Sleeve seam 26(28,29.5,32)cm/ 10¼(11,11½,12½)in

Actual measurements for jersey

Chest 64(69,74,79)cm/25¼, 29,31)in

Length to shoulders 39(41,43,45)cm/ 15¼(16¼,17,17¾)in

Sleeve seam 26(27.5,29,31.5)cm/ 10¼(10¾,11½,12½)in

Tension
Cardigan
22 sts and 24 rows to 10cm/4in measured over strawberry motifs worked on 4½mm needles

Jersey
22 sts and 30 rows to 10cm/4in measured over st st worked on 4mm needles

Cardigan back and fronts (worked in one piece)
Using 3¼mm needles and A, cast on 155(167,177,189) sts.

Rib row 1 K1, * p1, k1, rep from * to end.

Rib row 2 P1, * k1, p1, rep from * to end.

Rep these 2 rows three times more, increasing 1 st at centre of last row *for 1st and 3rd sizes only*. 156(167,178,189) sts.

Change to 4½mm needles.

2nd, 3rd and 4th sizes only
Work 2(4,6) rows st st, so ending with a p row.

All sizes
Join on and cut off colours as required and carry yarns not in use loosely across the WS of work, weaving yarns in when passing across more than 5 sts.

Reading odd numbered (k) rows from right to left and even numbered (p) rows from left to right, work from chart as follows:

Row 1 (RS) With A, k to end.

Row 2 With A, p to end.

Row 3 Work across the first edge sts as follows: k6A, 1B, 5A, work across patt rep as follows: * k5A, 1B, 5A, rep from * to last 12 sts, work across the rem edge sts as follows: k5A, 1B, 6A.

Row 4 Work across the first edge sts as

follows: p5A, 3B, 4A, work across patt rep as follows: * p4A, 3B, 4A, rep from * to last 12 sts, work across the rem edge sts as follows: p4A, 3B, 5A.

Cont in this way, working from chart until row 32 has been completed.

Using E instead of B and F instead of D, rep the first 20(22,24,28) rows again.

Divide for right front
Next row Patt 40(42,45,47), turn and leave rem sts on a spare needle.

Cont in patt until row 32 of chart has been completed.

Using G instead of B and H instead of D, rep the first 12(16,20,24) rows of chart.

★ Shape neck
Cast off in patt 7(7,8,8) sts at beg of next row.

Keeping patt correct, cast off 3 sts at beg of foll 2 alt rows. 27(29,31,33) sts.

Dec 1 st at neck edge on next 5 rows, 22(24,26,28) sts, ending with row 22(26,30,2) of chart. (For left front end with row 21(25,29,1) here.)

1st, 2nd and 3rd sizes only
Cont in patt until row 32 of chart has been completed.

2nd and 3rd sizes only
Using A only, work 2(4) rows st st, so ending with a p row.

4th size only
Using A only, work 4 rows st st, so ending with a p row. (For left front work 1 more row here, so ending with a p row.)

All sizes
Cast off. ★

Return to sts on spare needle.

With RS facing, join on yarn and patt 76(83,88,95), turn and leave rem sts on a spare needle.

Measurements given in cm for third size

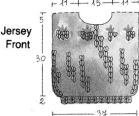

Jersey Front

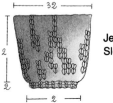

Jersey Sleeve

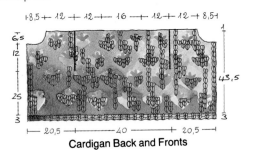

Cardigan Back and Fronts

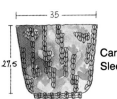

Cardigan Sleeve

Strawberry motif chart

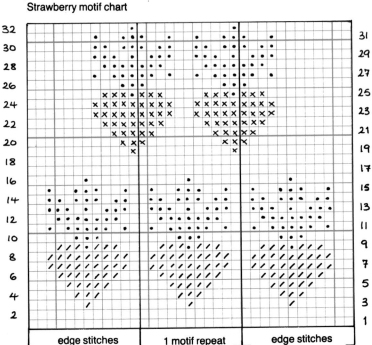

edge stitches   1 motif repeat   edge stitches

/ = B

• = C

X = D

V = E

I = F

Λ = G

— = H

⊙ = I

Cont in patt until row 32 of chart has been completed.

Using G instead of B and H instead of D, rep rows 1 to 32.

2nd, 3rd and 4th sizes only
Using A only, work 2(4,6) rows st st, so ending with a p row.

All sizes
Cast off.

Return to sts on spare needle.

With RS facing, join on yarn and patt to end. 40(42,45,47) sts.

Cont in patt until row 32 of chart has been completed.

Using G instead of B and H instead of D, rep the first 11(15,19,23) rows of chart.

Now work as given for right front from ★ to ★ and *for the 4th size only* noting the exception in brackets.

Cardigan sleeves

Using 3¼mm needles and A, cast on 41(41,51,51) sts.

Rep the 2 rib rows twice, then work rib row 1 again.

Inc row Rib 4(4,5,5), * M1, rib 8, rep from * to last 5(5,6,6) sts, M1, rib to end. 46(46,57,57) sts.

Change to 4½mm needles.

Working in patt from chart as given for back and fronts, inc and work into patt 1 st each end of 3rd and every foll 4th(4th,6th,6th) row until there are 72(74,77,79) sts.

Work straight until sleeve measures 26(28,29.5,32)cm/10¼(11,11½,12½)in from cast-on edge, ending with a p row. Using A, cast off.

Cardigan neckband

Join shoulder seams.

With RS facing, using 3¼mm needles and A, pick up and k29(29,30,30) sts up right side of front neck, 31(33,35,37) sts across back neck and 29(29,30,30) sts down left side of front neck. 89(91,95,97) sts.

Beg with rib row 2, rib 7 rows.

Cast off in rib.

Cardigan button border

With RS facing, using 3¼mm needles and A, pick up and k91(97,97,103) sts down left front edge.

Beg with rib row 2, work 7 rows rib.

Cast off in rib.

Cardigan buttonhole border

With RS facing, using 3¼mm needles and A, pick up and k91(97,97,103) sts up right front edge.

Beg with rib row 2, work 3 rows rib.

Buttonhole row (RS) Rib 3, * yf, k2 tog, rib 12(13,13, 14), rep from * to last 4 sts, yf, k2 tog, rib 2.

Rib 3 rows.

Cast off in rib.

To make up cardigan

Fold sleeves in half lengthwise, then placing folds to shoulder seams, sew into place. Join sleeve seams. Sew on the buttons.

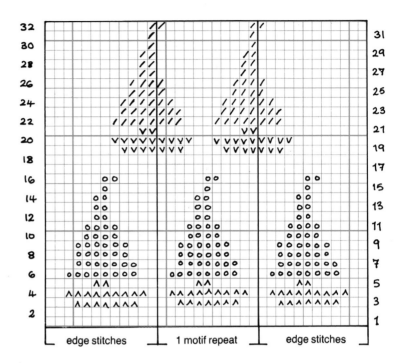

edge stitches | 1 motif repeat | edge stitches

Alternative motifs

The strawberry motif can be replaced with other small repeating motifs. If you would like to work out your own, make sure they fit over exactly the same number of squares as the strawberry.

Or you can use one of the three charts given on this page and overleaf. Suggested colours are given for the boats, robots and snowmen but you could, of course, use any colours to match your chosen background.

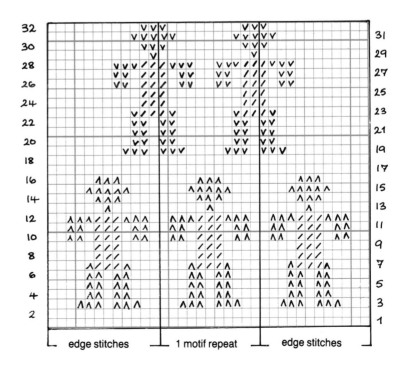

edge stitches | 1 motif repeat | edge stitches

Jersey front

★ Using 3¼mm needles and A, cast on 68(72,78,84) sts.
Work 5 rows k1, p1 rib.
Inc row Rib 12(12,13,14), * M1, rib 22(24,26,28), rep from * to last 12(12,13,14) sts, M1, rib to end. 71(75,81,87) sts. ★
Change to 4mm needles.
Work in st st until front measures 27(29,31,33)cm/10½(11½,12¼,13)in from cast-on edge, ending with a p row.
Join on and cut off colours as required. Use separate small balls for each area of colour and twist yarns together at wrong side of work when changing colour to avoid making a hole.
Reading odd numbered (k) rows from right to left and even numbered (p) rows from left to right, work from chart as follows:
Row 1 (RS) K12(14,17,20)A, using D instead of B work across the 11 st motif from row 3 of chart as follows: * k5A, 1D, 5A * k1A, using E instead of D rep from * to * once, k1A, using F instead of D rep from * to * once, k1A, using G instead of D rep from * to * once, then k12(14,17,20)A.
Row 2 P12(14,17,20)A, using G instead of B work across the 11 st motif from row 4 of chart as follows: * p4A, 3G, 4A *, p1A, using F instead of G rep from * to * once, p1A, using E instead of G rep from * to * once, p1A, using D instead of G rep from * to * once, then p12(14,17,20)A.

These 2 rows set the position of the motifs.
Cont in this way, working from chart until row 16 has been completed.
Using A only, work 4 rows st st, so ending with a p row.

Shape neck

Next row K28(30,32,35), turn and leave rem sts on a spare needle.
Dec 1 st at neck edge on every row until 20(22,24,27) sts rem.
Work straight until first side of neck measures 5cm/2in from beg of shaping, ending with a p row.
Cast off.
Return to sts on spare needle.
With RS facing, slip first 15(15,17,17) sts on to a holder, join on A and k to end. 28(30,32,35) sts.
Now complete to match first side of neck.

Jersey back

Work as given for front from ★ to ★.
Change to 4mm needles.
Work in st st until back measures same as front to shoulders, ending with a p row.

Shape shoulders

Cast off 20(22,24,27) sts at beg of next 2 rows.
Cut off yarn and leave rem 31(31,33,33) sts on a holder.

Jersey sleeves

Using 3¼mm needles and A, cast on 42(44,46,48) sts.

Work 5 rows k1, p1 rib.
Inc row Rib 6(5,8,6), * M1, rib 10(11,10,12), rep from * to last 6(6,8,6) sts, M1, rib to end. 46(48,50,52) sts.
Change to 4mm needles.
Working in st st, inc 1 st each end of 3rd(7th,3rd,3rd) and every foll 6th(6th,8th,8th) row until there are 66(68,70,72) sts.
Work straight until sleeve measures 26(27.5,29,31.5)cm/10¼(10¾,11½,12½)in from cast-on edge, ending with a p row.
Cast off.

Jersey neckband

Join right shoulder seam.
With RS facing, using 3¼mm needles and A, pick up and k16(16,17,17) sts down left side of front neck, k the front neck sts from holder, pick up and k16(16,17,17) sts up right side of front neck, then k the back neck sts from holder. 78(78,84,84) sts.
Work 7 rows k1, p1 rib.
Cast off in rib.

To make up jersey

Join left shoulder and neckband seam. Fold sleeves in half lengthwise, then placing folds to shoulder seams, sew into place. Join side and sleeve seams.

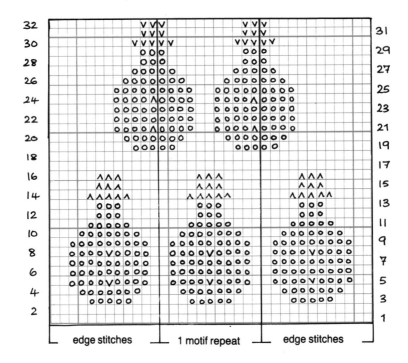

edge stitches · 1 motif repeat · edge stitches

CARDIGAN IN RIB AND CABLE PATTERN

✳✳✳

This
practical
cardigan
for summer,
or winter,
is knitted
in an interesting
stitch pattern.

Materials
10(12,14)×20g balls of Sunbeam Scoop DK
A pair each of 3¼mm/No10 and 4mm/No8 knitting needles
Cable needle
5 buttons

Measurements
To fit chest 61(66,71)cm/24(26,28)in
Actual measurements
Chest 68(72,76)cm/26¾(28½,30)in
Length to centre back neck 36(37.5,39)cm/14(14¾,15½)in
Sleeve seam 23(27,31)cm/9(10½,12)in

Tension
30 sts and 29 rows to 10cm/4in measured over patt worked on 4mm needles

Special abbreviation
C15B Cable 15 back as follows: slip next 9 sts on to cable needle and leave at back of work, [p2, k1] twice, then work [p2, k1] 3 times across sts from cable needle

Back
With 3¼mm needles, cast on 91(97,101) sts.
Rib row 1 K1, * p1, k1, rep from * to end.
Rib row 2 P1, * k1, p1, rep from * to end.
Rep these 2 rows for 5(6,7)cm/2(2¼,2¾)in, ending with rib row 1.
Inc row Rib 4(8,6), * M1, rib 9(9,8), rep from * to last 6(8,7) sts, M1, rib to end.
101(107,113) sts.
Change to 4mm needles.
Work in patt as follows:
Row 1 P2, * k1, p2, rep from * to end.
Row 2 K2, * p1, k2, rep from * to end.
Rows 3 to 16 Rep rows 1 and 2 seven times.
Row 17 [P2, k1] 2(3,4) times, * C15B, [p2, k1] 3 times, rep from * twice more, C15B, [p2, k1] 2(3,4) times, p2.
Row 18 As row 2.
Rows 19 to 34 Rep rows 1 and 2 eight times.
Row 35 [P2, k1] 2(3,4) times, * p17, k1, [p2, k1] twice, rep from * twice more, p17, [k1, p2] 2(3,4) times.
Row 36 [K2, p1] 2(3,4) times, * k17, p1, [k2, p1] twice, rep from * twice more, k17, [p1, k2] 2(3,4) times.
Rows 37 to 46 Rep rows 35 and 36 five times.
Rows 47 to 50 Rep rows 1 and 2 twice.
Shape raglans
Keeping p2, k1 rib patt correct, cast off 3 sts at beg of next 2 rows.
Next row K2, skpo, patt to last 4 sts, k2 tog, k2.
Next row P2, p2 tog, patt to last 4 sts, p2 tog tbl, p2.
Rep the last 2 rows until 79(85,91) sts rem, so ending with a WS row.
Next row K2, skpo, [p2, k1] 5(6,7) times, C15B, [p2, k1] 3 times, C15B, [p2, k1] 5(6,7) times, p2, k2 tog, k2.
Keeping rib patt correct, dec 1 st within the st st border on every row, as before, until 19(21,23) sts rem, so ending with a WS row.
Cut off yarn and leave rem sts on a holder.

Right front
★ Using 3¼mm needles, cast on 45(49,51) sts.
Work 5(6,7)cm/2(2¼,2¾)in rib as given for back, ending with rib row 1.
Inc row Rib 6, * M1, rib 8(12,10), rep from * to last 7(7,5) sts, M1, rib to end.
50(53,56) sts.
Change to 4mm needles.
Work in patt as follows:
Row 1 P2, * k1, p2, rep from * to end.
Row 2 K2, * p1, k2, rep from * to end.
Rows 3 to 16 Rep rows 1 and 2 seven times. ★
Row 17 P2, k1, C15B, [p2, k1] 3 times, C15B, [p2, k1] 2(3,4) times, p2.
Row 18 As row 2.
Rows 19 to 34 Rep rows 1 and 2 eight times.
Row 35 P2, k1, p17, [k1, p2] twice, k1, p17, [k1, p2] 2(3,4) times.
Row 36 [K2, p1] 2(3,4) times, k17, p1, [k2, p1] twice, k17, p1, k2.

Rows 37 to 46 Rep rows 35 and 36 five times.
Rows 47 to 50 Rep rows 1 and 2 twice.
Row 51 As row 1.
Shape raglan
Keeping rib patt correct, cast off 3 sts at beg of next row.
Next row Patt to last 4 sts, k2 tog, k2.
Next row P2, p2 tog, patt to end.
Rep the last 2 rows until 39(42,45) sts rem, so ending with a WS row.
Next row P2, k1, C15B, [p2, k1] 5(6,7) times, p2, k2 tog, k2.
Keeping rib patt correct, dec 1 st within the st st border on every row, as before, until 25(28,31) sts rem, so ending with a WS row.
Shape neck
Next row Cast off 4 sts, patt to last 4 sts, k2 tog, k2.
Decreasing at raglan edge as before, dec 1 st at neck edge on every row until 12(13,14) sts rem.
Keeping neck edge straight, cont to dec at raglan edge only until 2 sts rem.
Cast off.

Left front
Work as given for right front from ★ to ★.
Cont in patt as follows:
Row 17 [P2, k1] 2(3,4) times, C15B, [p2, k1] 3 times, C15B, [p2, k1], p2.
Row 18 As row 2.
Rows 19 to 34 Rep rows 1 and 2 eight times.
Row 35 [P2, k1] 2(3,4) times, p17, k1, [p2, k1] twice, p17, k1, p2.
Row 36 K2, p1, k17, p1, [k2, p1] twice, k17, [p1, k2] 2(3,4) times.
Rows 37 to 46 Rep rows 35 and 36 five times.
Rows 47 to 50 Rep rows 1 and 2 twice.
Shape raglan
Keeping rib patt correct, cast off 3 sts at beg of next row.
Next row Patt to end.
Next row K2, skpo, patt to end.
Next row Patt to last 4 sts, p2 tog tbl, p2.
Rep the last 2 rows until 39(42,45) sts rem, so ending with a WS row.
Next row K2, skpo, [p2, k1] 5(6,7) times, C15B, p2, k1, p2.
Keeping rib patt correct, dec 1 st within the st st border on every row, as before, until 24(27,30) sts rem, so ending with a RS row.
Shape neck
Next row Cast off 4 sts, patt to last 4 sts, p2 tog tbl, p2.
Decreasing at raglan edge as before, dec 1 st at neck edge on every row until 11(12,13) sts rem.
Keeping neck edge straight, cont to dec at raglan edge only until 2 sts rem.
Cast off.

Sleeves
Using 3¼mm needles, cast on 41(45,49) sts.
Work 5(6,7)cm/2(2¼,2¾)in rib as given for back, ending with rib row 1.
Inc row Rib 4, * M1, rib 1, M1, rib 2, rep from * to last 1(2,3) sts, rib to end. 65(71,77) sts.
Change to 4mm needles.
Work in patt as follows:
Row 1 P2, * k1, p2, rep from * to end.
Row 2 K2, * p1, k2, rep from * to end.
These 2 rows form the rib patt.
Continuing in rib patt, inc and work into patt 1 st each end of 5th(15th, 23rd) and foll 4th row.
Patt 3 rows.
Next row Inc in first st, rib 13(16,19), p17, rib 7, p17, rib to last st, inc in last st.
Next row Rib 15(18,21), k17, rib 7, k17, rib to end.
The last 2 rows set the rib patt with rev st st squares.
Keeping rib and rev st st patt correct, inc and work into rib patt 1 st each end of 3rd and foll 4th row.
Patt 3 rows.
Continuing in rib patt only, inc 1 st each end of next and every foll 4th row until there are 85(91,97) sts.
Patt 3 rows.

Next row For first and 2nd sizes only inc in first st, for all sizes rib 21(24,28), C15B, rib 9, C15B, rib 23(26,30), then for first and 2nd sizes only inc in last st.
Patt 3 rows.
First size only
Inc each end of next row.
All sizes
89(93,97) sts.
Patt 5(6,6) rows.
Shape raglan
Keeping patt correct, cast off 3 sts at beg of next 2 rows.
Next row K2, skpo, patt to last 4 sts, k2 tog, k2.
Next row P2, p2 tog, patt to last 4 sts, p2 tog tbl, p2.
Keeping patt correct, dec 1 st within the st st border on every row, as before, until 71 sts rem.
Next row K2, skpo, p1, [k1, p2] 3 times, k1, p17, k1, [p2, k1] twice, p17, k1, [p2, k1] 3 times, p1, k2 tog, k2.
Next row P2, p2 tog, [p1, k2] 3 times, p1, k17, p1, [k2, p1] twice, k17, [p1, k2] 3 times, p1, p2 tog tbl, p2.
These 2 rows set the 2 rev st st blocks.
Keeping patt correct, dec 1 st within the st st border on every row until 47 sts rem.
Now continuing in rib patt only, dec 1 st within the st st border on every row, as before, until 7(9,11) sts rem, ending with a WS row.
Cut off yarn and leave rem sts on a holder.

Neckband
Join raglan seams.
With RS facing and using 3¼mm needles, pick up and k20(22,24) sts up right side of front neck, k7(9,11) sts from right sleeve holder, 19(21,23) sts from back neck holder and 7(9,11) sts from left sleeve holder, then pick up and k20(22,24) sts down left side of front neck. 73(83,93) sts.
Work 4cm/1½in rib as given for back.
Cast off in rib.
Fold neckband in half to WS and slipstitch into position.

Buttonhole border
With RS facing and using 3¼mm needles,

Measurements given in cm for smallest size

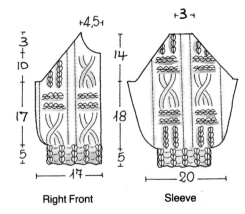

Right Front   Sleeve

pick up and k91 sts up right front edge and neckband
Beg with rib row 2, work 3 rows rib as given for back.
Buttonhole row Rib 5, * yf, k2 tog, rib 18, rep from * to last 6 sts, yf, k2 tog, rib 4.
Work 4 more rows rib.
Cast off in rib.

Button border
Work as given for buttonhole border, omitting buttonholes.

To make up
Join side and sleeve seams. Sew on buttons.

COTTON JERSEY IN A BOLD GEOMETRIC DESIGN

**

The striking design on this cotton jersey will appeal to boys and girls alike.

Materials

3(3,5)×50g balls of Pingouin Corrida 4 (Aran weight cotton) in main colour A

2(3,3) balls of same in each of contrast colours B and C

A pair each of 3¼mm/No10 and 4mm/No8 knitting needles

Measurements

To fit chest 61(66,71)cm/24(26,28)in

Actual measurements

Chest 66(71,76)cm/26(28,30)in

Length to shoulders 39(42,47)cm/ 15½(16½,19)in

Sleeve seam 26(28,30)cm/10¼(11,11¾)in

Tension

23 sts and 30 rows to 10cm/4in measured over st st worked on 4mm needles

Back and front (alike)

Using 3¼mm needles and A, cast on 69(75,81) sts.

Rib row 1 K1, * p1, k1, rep from * to end.

Rib row 2 P1, * k1, p1, rep from * to end.

Rep these 2 rows for 4cm/1½in, ending with rib row 1.

Inc row Rib 7, * M1, rib 9(10,11) rep from * to last 8 sts, M1, rib 8. 76(82,88) sts.

Change to 4mm needles.

Joining on and cutting off colours as required and using separate balls of yarn for each area of colour, work in square patt as follows:

Row 1 K12(13,14)A, * 13(14,15)B, 13(14,15)A, rep from * once more, 12(13,14)B.

Row 2 P12(13,14)B, * 13(14,15)A, 13(14,15)B, rep from * once more, 12(13,14)A.

Rep the last 2 rows 6(7,9) times more.

Next row K12(13,14)B, * 13(14,15)A, 13(14,15)B, rep from * once more, 12(13,14)A.

Next row P12(13,14)A, * 13(14,15)B, 13(14,15)A, rep from * once more, 12(13,14)B.

Rep the last 2 rows 6(7,9) times more.

Work triangle patt as follows:

Row 1 K15(17,18)C, * 1B, 29(31,33)C, rep from * once more, 1(1,2)B.

Row 2 P1(1,2)B, * 29(31,33)C, 1B, rep from * once more, 15(17,18)C.

Row 3 K14(16,17)C, * 3B, 27(29,31)C, rep from * once more, 2(2,3)B.

Row 4 P2(2,3)B, * 27(29,31)C, 3B, rep from * once more, 14(16,17)C.

Row 5 K13(15,16)C, * 5B, 25(27,29)C, rep from * once more, 3(3,4)B.

Row 6 P3(3,4)B, * 25(27,29)C, 5B, rep from * once more, 13(15,16,)C.

Row 7 K12(14,15)C, * 7B, 23(25,27)C, rep from * once more, 4(4,5)B.

Row 8 P4(4,5)B, * 23(25,27)C, 7B, rep from * once more, 12(14,15)C.

Row 9 K11(13,14)C, * 9B, 21(23,25)C, rep from * once more, 5(5,6)B.

Row 10 P5(5,6)B, * 21(23,25)C, 9B, rep from * once more, 11(13,14)C.

Row 11 K10(12,13)C, * 11B, 19(21,23)C, rep from * once more, 6(6,7)B.

Row 12 P6(6,7)B, * 19(21,23)C, 11B, rep

from * once more, 10(12,13)C.

Cont in this way, working 1 more st in B and 1 st less in C each side of every triangle on every RS row until the row: p15(16,18)B, * 1C, 29(31,33)B, rep from * once more, 1(2,2)C, has been worked.

With B, k 1 row and p1 row.

Next row K16(17,19)A, 15(16,17)C, 15(16,17)A, 15(16,17)C, 15(17,18)A.

Next row P15(17,18)A, 15(16,17)C, 15(16,17)A, 15(16,17)C,16(17,19)A.

Rep the last 2 rows 6(7,9) times more.

Next row K16(17,19)C, 15(16,17)B, 15(16,17)C, 15(16,17)B, 15(17,18)C.

Next row P15(17,18)C, 15(16,17)B, 15(16,17)C, 15(16,17)B, 16(17,19)C.

Rep the last 2 rows 6(7,9) times more.

With A, k1 row and p1 row, decreasing 1 st at centre of 2nd row. 75(81,87) sts.

With A, work 5cm/2in rib as given for back and front, ending with rib row 2.

Cast off in rib.

Sleeves

Using 3¼mm needles and A, cast on 41(43,45) sts.

Work 4cm/1½in rib as given for back and front, ending with rib row 1.

Inc row Rib 4(5,6), * M1, rib 4, rep from * to last 5(6,7) sts, M1, rib 5(6,7). 50(52,54) sts.

Change to 4mm needles.

Work in square patt as follows:

Row 1 K12A, 13(14,15)B, 13(14,15)A, 12B.

Row 2 P12B, 13(14,15)A, 13(14,15)B, 12A.

Rows 3 to 6 Rep rows 1 and 2 twice.

Row 7 With A inc in first st, k11A, 13(14,15)B, 13(14,15)A, 11B, with B inc in last st. 52(54,56) sts.

Row 8 P13B, 13(14,15)A, 13(14,15)B, 13A.

Measurements given in cm for smallest size

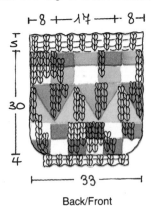

Back/Front

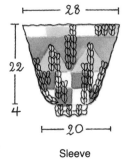

Sleeve

Row 9 K13A, 13(14,15)B, 13(14,15)A, 13B.

Row 10 P13B, 13(14,15)A, 13(14,15)B, 13A.

Rep the last 2 rows twice more.

Next row With B inc in first st, k12B, 13(14,15)A, 13(14,15)B, 12A, with A inc in last st. 54(56,58) sts.

Next row P14A, 13(14,15)B, 13(14,15)A, 14B.

Next row K14B, 13(14,15)A, 13(14,15)B, 14A.

Next row P14A, 13(14,15)B, 13(14,15)A, 14B.

Rep the last 2 rows twice more.

Next row With B inc in first st, k13B, 13(14,15)A, 13(14,15)B, 13A, with A inc in last st. 56(58,60) sts.

Next row P15A, 13(14,15)B, 13(14,15)A, 15B.

Next row K15B, 13(14,15)A, 13(14,15)B, 15A.

Next row P15A, 13(14,15)B, 13(14,15)A, 15B.

Rep the last 2 rows once more.

Work in triangle patt as follows:

Row 1 K1(2,1)B, 26(26,28)C, 2B, 26(26,28)C, 1(2,1)B.

Row 2 P1(2,1)B, 26(26,28)C, 2B, 26(26,28)C, 1(2,1)B.

Row 3 With B inc in first st, k1(2,1)B, 24(24,26)C, 4B, 24(24,26)C, 1(2,1)B, with B inc in last st. 58(60,62) sts.

Row 4 P3(4,3)B, 24(24,26)C, 4B, 24(24,26)C, 3(4,3)B.

Row 5 K4(5,4)B, 22(22,24)C, 6B, 22(22,24)C, 4(5,4)B.

Row 6 P4(5,4)B, 22(22,24)C, 6B, 22(22,24)C, 4(5,4)B.

Row 7 K5(6,5)B, 20(20,22)C, 8B, 20(20,22)C, 5(6,5)B.

Row 8 P5(6,5)B, 20(20,22)C, 8B, 20(20,22)C, 5(6,5)B.

Row 9 K6(7,6)B, 18(18,20)C, 10B, 18(18,20)C, 6(7,6)B.

Row 10 P6(7,6)B, 18(18,20)C, 10B, 18(18,20)C, 6(7,6)B.

Continuing in this way, working 1 more st in B and 1 st less in C each side of every triangle, inc and work into patt 1 st each end of next and every foll 8th row until there are 62(64,68) sts.

Patt 7(7,1) rows, so working the row: p16(17,18)B, 2C, 26(26,28)B, 2C, 16(17,18)B.

Continuing to inc 1 st each end of every 8th row as before, work 2(6,8) rows st st with B, so ending with a p row. 64(66,70) sts.

Now work in colour blocks as follows:

Next row K16(16,17)A, 16(17,18)C, 16(17,18)A, 16(16,17)C.

Next row P16(16,17)C, 16(17,18)A, 16(17,18)C, 16(16,17)A.

These 2 rows set the colour blocks. Continuing to inc at each end of every foll 8th row as before, patt 10(12,14) rows, so ending with a WS row. 66(70,74) sts. Cast off.

To make up

Join shoulder seams leaving 17cm/6¾in open at centre for neck. Fold sleeves in half lengthwise, then placing folds to shoulder seams, sew into place. Join side and sleeve seams.

TARTAN SQUARES JERSEY

***

Pick a
selection
of bright colours
to work the
squares formed
where the lines
cross each other.

Materials
5(6,6)×50g balls of Patons Beehive Soft
Blend DK in main colour A
2×50g balls of same in contrast colour B
1×50g ball each of same in each of contrast
colours C, D, E and F
A pair each of 4½mm/No7 and 6mm/No5
knitting needles

Measurements
To fit chest 66(71,76)cm/26(28,30)in
Actual measurements
Chest 78(82,87)cm/30¾(32¼,34¼)in
Length to shoulders 44(48,52)cm/
17¼(19,20½)in
Sleeve seam 26(29,31)cm/
10¼(11½,12¼)in

Tension
17 sts and 20 rows to 10cm/4in measured
over patt worked on 6mm needles using
yarn double

Note
All yarns are used double throughout.

Back
★ Using 4½mm needles and A double, cast
on 56(60,64) sts.
Work 5cm/2in k1, p1 rib, ending with a
RS row.
Inc row Rib 1(3,5), * M1, rib 6, rep from * to
last 1(3,5) sts, M1, rib 1(3,5). 66(70,74) sts.
Change to 6mm needles.
Join on and cut off colours as required.
Using separate small balls of double yarn
for each area of colour and twisting yarns
tog on WS of work when changing colour to
avoid making a hole, work in patt as follows:
Row 1 (RS) K13(14,15)B, 4F, 12(13,14)B,
4D, 12(13,14)B, 4E, 12(13,14)B, 5C.
Row 2 P5C, 12(13,14)B, 4E, 12(13,14)B, 4D,
12(13,14)B, 4F, 13(14,15)B.
Rows 3 and 4 As rows 1 and 2.
Row 5 K13(14,15)A, [4B, 12(13,14)A]
3 times, 5B.
Row 6 P5B, [12(13,14)A, 4B] 3 times,
13(14,15)A.
Rep the last 2 rows 6(7,8) times more.
Next row K13(14,15)B, 4E, 12(13,14)B, 4C,
12(13,14)B, 4F, 12(13,14)B, 5D.

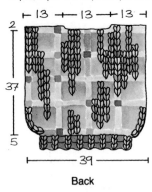

Back

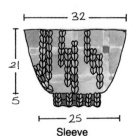

Sleeve

Next row P5D, 12(13,14)B, 4F, 12(13,14)B,
4C, 12(13,14)B, 4E, 13(14,15)B.
Rep the last 2 rows once more, then rep
rows 5 and 6 seven(eight,nine) times.
Next row K13(14,15)B, 4D, 12(13,14)B, 4F,
12(13,14)B, 4C 12(13,14)B, 5E.
Next row P5E, 12(13,14)B, 4C, 12(13,14)B,
4F, 12(13,14)B, 4D, 13(14,15)B.
Rep the last 2 rows once more, then rep
rows 5 and 6 seven(eight,nine) times.
Next row K13(14,15)B, 4C, 12(13,14)B, 4E,
12(13,14)B, 4D, 12(13,14)B, 5F.
Next row P5F, 12(13,14)B, 4D, 12(13,14)B,
4E, 12(13,14)B, 4C, 13(14,15)B.
Rep the last 2 rows once more. ★
Rep rows 5 and 6 seven(eight,nine) times.
Next row K13(14,15)B, 4F, 12(13,14)B, 4D,
12(13,14)B, 4E, 12(13,14)B, 5C.
Next row P5C, 12(13,14)B, 4E, 12(13,14)B,
4D, 12(13,14)B, 4F, 13(14,15)B.
Shape neck
Next row K13(14,15)B, 4F, 5(5,6)B, turn and
leave rem sts on a spare needle.
Work 3 rows in colours as set by previous
row.
Cast off.
Return to sts on spare needle.
With RS facing, slip first 22(24,24) sts on to a
holder, then patt as follows: k1(1,2)B, 4E,
12(13,14)B, 5C.
Work 3 rows in colours as set by previous
row.
Cast off.

Front
Work as given for back from ★ to ★.
Rep rows 5 and 6 three times.
Shape neck
Next row K13(14,15)A, 4B, 12(12,13)A, turn
and leave rem sts on a spare needle.
★★ Continuing in colours as set, cast off
2 sts at beg of next and foll 2 alt rows.
Patt 1 row, then dec 1 st at beg of foll row.
22(23,25) sts. ★★
Work 6(8,10) rows straight, completing patt
to match back.
Cast off.
Return to sts on spare needle.
With RS facing, slip the first 8(10,10) sts on
to a holder, patt to end. 29(30,32) sts.
Work one row.
Now complete to match first side of neck as
given from ★★ to ★★.
Work 5(7,9) rows straight.
Cast off.

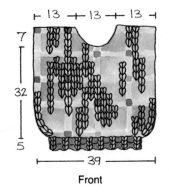

Front

Measurements given in cm for smallest size

Sleeves
Using 4½mm needles and A double, cast
on 34,(38,42) sts.
Work 5cm/2in k1, p1 rib ending with a
RS row.
Inc row Rib 3(5,7), * M1, rib 4, rep from * to
last 3(5,7) sts, M1, rib 3(5,7). 42(46,50) sts.
Change to 6mm needles.
Row 1 (RS) K3(4,5)A, [4B, 12(13,14)A]
twice, 4B, 3(4,5)A.
Row 2 P3(4,5)A, 4B, [12(13,14)A, 4B] twice,
3(4,5)A.
Rep the last 2 rows 4 times more, increasing
in A each end of the 5th row. 44(48,52) sts.
Next row With B inc in first st, k3(4,5)B, 4E,
12(13,14)B, 4C, 12(13,14)B, 4F, 3(4,5)B,
with B inc in last st. 46(50,54) sts.
Next row P5(6,7)B, 4F, 12(13,14)B, 4C,
12(13,14)B, 4E, 5(6,7)B.
Next row K5(6,7)B, 4E, 12(13,14)B, 4C,
12(13,14)B, 4F, 5(6,7)B.
Next row P5(6,7)B, 4F, 12(13,14)B, 4C,
12(13,14)B, 4E, 5(6,7)B.
Next row K5(6,7)A, [4B, 12(13,14)A] twice,
4B, 5(6,7)A.
Next row P5(6,7)A, [4B, 12(13,14)A] twice,
4B, 5(6,7)A.
Working in colour blocks as set and
increasing 1 st in A at each end of
next(next,3rd) and foll 6th(8th, 8th) row,
work 12(14,16) rows. 50(54,58) sts.
Next row K7(8,9)B, 4D, 12(13,14)B, 4F,
12(13,14)B, 4C, 7(8,9)B.
Next row P7(8,9)B, 4C, 12(13,14)B, 4F,
12(13,14)B, 4D, 7(8,9)B.
Next row With B inc in first st, k6(7,8)B, 4D,
12(13,14)B, 4F, 12(13,14)B, 4C, 6(7,8)B,
with B inc in last st. 52(56,60) sts.
Next row P8(9,10)B, 4C, 12(13,14)B, 4F,
12(13,14)B, 4D, 8(9,10)B.
Next row K8(9,10)A, 4B, [12(13,14)A, 4B]
twice, 8(9,10)A.
Next row P8(9,10)A, 4B, [12(13,14)A, 4B]
twice, 8(9,10)A.
Working in colour blocks as set and
increasing 1 st in A at each end of 5th row,
work 8(12,14) rows. 54(58,62) sts.
Cast off.

Neckband
Join right shoulder seam.
With RS facing, using 4½mm needles and A
double, pick up and k16(17,19) sts down
left side of front neck, k the front neck sts
from holder, pick up and k16(17,19) sts up
right side of front neck, 2 sts down right side
of back neck, k the back neck sts from
holder, then pick up and k2 sts up left side
of back neck. 66(72,76) sts.
Work 8 rows k1, p1 rib.
Cast off in rib.

To make up
Join left shoulder and neckband seam. Fold
sleeves in half lengthwise, then placing
folds to shoulder seams, sew into place.
Join side and sleeve seams. Fold neckband
in half to WS and slipstitch into position.

STRIPED COTTON TOP

✳

This bright
summer top
s quick to make
as the sleeves
are knitted
as part of the
back and front.

Materials

1(2,2)×100g balls of Twilleys Pegasus (chunky cotton) in main colour A
1 ball of same in each of contrast colours B and C
A pair each of 3¼mm/No10 and 4mm/No8 knitting needles

Measurements

To fit chest 61(66,71)cm/24(26,28)in
Actual measurements
Chest 68(74,80)cm/27(29,31½)in
Length to shoulders 35(38,40)cm/14(15,16)in

Tension

17 sts and 22 rows to 10cm/4in measured over patt worked on 4mm needles

Back

★★ Using 3¼mm needles and A, cast on 57(61,67) sts.
Rib row 1 P1, * k1, p1, rep from * to end.
Rib row 2 K1, * p1, k1, rep from * to end.
Rep these 2 rows 3 times more.
Join on and cut off colours as required.
With B, rep rib rows 1 and 2 twice.
With C, rep rib rows 1 and 2 again increasing 1 st at centre of last row. 58(62,68) sts.
Change to 4mm needles.
Work in patt as follows:
With A, work 10(10,12) rows st st, so ending with a p row.
★ Cut off A, join on B.
Next row K to end.
Next row * P1, k1, rep from * to end.
Work in moss st as follows:
Row 1 * K1, p1, rep from * to end.
Row 2 * P1, k1, rep from * to end.
First size only
Rep row 1 again.
Cut off B, join on C and rep row 2.
2nd and 3rd sizes only
Rep rows 1 and 2 once more.
Cut off B, join on C.
All sizes
Rep rows 1 and 2 two(three,three) times more. ★
With A, work 10(10,12) rows st st, so ending with a p row.
Rep from ★ to ★ again.
Place markers each end of last row.
With A, work 6 rows st st.
Using separate balls of yarn for each area of B and C, work in check patt as follows:
Row 1 K1(3,6)A, * 4C, 8A, rep from * to last 9(11,14) sts, k4C, 5(7,10)A.
Row 2 P5(7,10)A,* 4C, 8A, rep from * to last

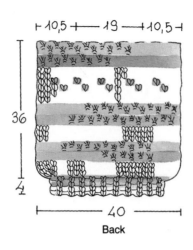

Back

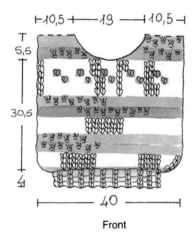

Front

Measurements given in cm for third size

5(7,10) sts, p4C, 1(3,6)A.
Rows 3 and 4 As rows 1 and 2.
Row 5 K5(7,10)A, * k4B, 8A, rep from * to last 5(7,10) sts, k4B, 1(3,6)A.
Row 6 P1(3,6)A,* p4B, 8A, rep from * to last 9(11,14) sts, p4B, 5(7,10)A.
Rows 7 and 8 As rows 5 and 6.
With A, work 6 rows st st, so ending with a p row. ★★
Now rep from ★ to ★ again.
Shape shoulders
With B, cast off in patt 14(16,18) sts at beg of next 2 rows.
Cut off yarn and leave rem 30(30,32) sts on a holder.

Front

Work as given for back from ★★ to ★★, so ending with a WS row.
Shape neck
Next row Patt 23(25,28), turn and leave rem sts on a spare needle.
★★★ Keeping patt correct, dec 1 st at neck edge on every row until 14(16,18) sts rem.
Work straight until front measures same as back to shoulder, ending at sleeve edge.
Cast off in patt. ★★★
Return to sts on spare needle.
With RS facing, slip first 12 sts on to a holder, join on B and then patt to end. 23(25,28) sts.
Now work as given for first side of neck from ★★★ to ★★★.

Neckband

Join right shoulder seam.
With RS facing, using 3¼mm needles and A, pick up and k15(16,16) sts down left side of front neck, k the sts from front neck holder, pick up and k15(16,16) sts up right side of front neck, then increasing 1 st at centre k the sts from back neck holder. 73(75,77) sts.
Beg with rib row 2 and working in rib as given for back, work 4 rows A, 2 rows B and 1 row C.
With C, cast off in rib.

Armhole borders

Join left shoulder and neckband seam.
With RS facing, using 3¼mm needles and A, pick up and k47(51,51) sts between markers at sleeve edge.
Beg with rib row 2 and working in rib as given for back, work 4 rows A, 2 rows B and 1 row C.
With C, cast off in rib.

To make up

Join side and armhole border seams.

JERSEY WITH MOUNTAIN PEAKS DESIGN

**

Bold, bright colours make an impact on this colourful jumper.

Materials
3(4,5,6)×50g balls of Wendy Family Choice
  Aran in main colour A
1(1,1,2) balls of same in each of contrast
  colours B, C and D
A pair each of 3¼mm/No 10 and 4mm/No8
  knitting needles

Measurements
To fit chest 61(66,71,76)cm/24(26,28,30)in
Actual measurements
Chest 68(74,78, 84)cm/27(29,31,33)in
Length to shoulders 38(42,46,51)cm/
  15(16½,18,20)in
Sleeve seam 29(32,35,38)cm/
  11½(12½,13½,15)in

Tension
18 sts and 24 rows to 10cm/4in measured
over st st worked on 4mm needles

Back
Using 3¼mm needles and A, cast on
53(57,61,65) sts.
Rib row 1 K1, * p1, k1, rep from * to end.
Rib row 2 P1, * k1, p1, rep from * to end.
Rep these 2 rows for 5cm/2in, ending with
rib row 1.
Inc row Rib 7(9,7,2), * M1, rib 5(5,6,6), rep
from * to last 6(8,6,3) sts, M1, rib to end.
62(66,70,76) sts.
Change to 4mm needles.
Using separate small balls of yarn for each
area of colour and twisting yarns together
on WS of work when changing colour to
avoid making a hole, work in patt as follows:
For 2nd, 3rd and 4th sizes only
Row 1 K20(22,24,27)B, 17C, 25(27,29,32)A.
Row 2 and every foll alt row P to end,
working in colours as set.
Row 3 As row 1.
Row 5 K21(23,25,28)B, 17C, 24(26,28,31)A.
Row 7 K22(24,26,29)B, 16C, 24(26,28,31)A.
Row 8 P to end, working in colours as set.
For all sizes
Row 9 K23(25,27,30)B, 16C, 1B,
22(24,26,29)A.
Row 10 and every foll alt row P to end,
working in colours as set.
Row 11 K24(26,28,31)B, 2D, 13C, 2B,
21(23,25,28)A.
Row 13 K2(4,6,9)A, 21B, 4D, 11C, 4B,
20(22,24,27)A.
Row 15 K3(5,7,10)A, 19B, 6D, 9C, 6B,
19(21,23,26)A.
Row 17 K4(6,8,11)A, 17B, 8D, 7C, 8B,
18(20,22,25)A.
Row 19 K5(7,9,12)A, 16B, 9D, 5C, 1D, 9B,
15A, 2(4,6,9)B.
Row 21 K6(8,10,13)A, 13B, 3A, 8D, 4C, 2D,
10B, 14A, 2(4,6,9)B.
Row 23 K7(9,11,14)A, 11B, 5A, 8D, 2C, 4D,
10B, 12A, 3(5,7,10)B.
Row 25 K2(4,6,9)D, 6A, 9B, 7A, 14D, 10B,
10A, 4(6,8,11)B.
Row 27 K3(5,7,10)D, 6A, 7B, 8A, 2B, 13D,
10B, 9A, 4(6,8,11)B.
Row 29 K4(6,8,11)D, 6A, 5B, 8A, 4B, 13D,
10B, 7A, 5(7,9,12)B.
Row 31 K5(7,9,12)D, 6A, 3B, 8A, 6B, 12D,
1C, 10B, 5A, 6(8,10,13)B.
Row 33 K7(9,11,14)D, 5A, 1B, 7A, 1D, 8B,
10D, 3C, 10B, 3A, 5B, 2(4,6,9)C.
Row 35 K7(9,11,14)D, 12A, 4D, 6B, 9D, 5C,
10B, 1A, 5B, 3(5,7,10)C.
Row 37 K2(4,6,9)A, 7D, 9A, 5D, 7B, 6D, 2B,
6C, 14B, 4(6,8,11)C.
Row 39 K3(5,7,10)A, 7D, 7A, 7D, 7B, 5D,
3B, 5C, 14B, 4(6,8,11)C.
Row 41 K4(6,8,11)A, 7D, 5A, 8D, 1A, 6B,
4D, 5B, 5C, 12B, 5(7,9,12)C.
Row 43 K5(7,9,12)A, 7D, 3A, 9D, 2A, 6B,
3D, 5B, 5C, 10B, 7(9,11,14)C.
Row 45 K6(8,10,13)A, 7D, 1A, 9D, 4A, 6B,
1D, 7B, 5C, 8B, 8(10,12,15)C.
Row 47 K8(10,12,15)A, 14D, 6A, 14B, 4C,
8B, 8(10,12,15)C.
Row 49 K10(12,14,17)A, 11D, 7A, 14B, 1A,
4C, 6B, 9(11,13,16)C.
Row 51 K12(14,16,19)A, 7D, 10A, 12B, 3A,
4C, 5B, 9(11,13,16)C.
Row 53 K13(15,17,20)A, 5D, 12A, 10B, 4A,
5C, 3B, 10(12,14,17)C.
Row 55 K14(16,18,21)A, 3D, 14A, 9B, 5A,
5C, 1B, 11(13,15,18)C.

Row 57 K15(17,19,22)A, 1D, 16A, 7B, 6A,
17(19,21,24)C.
Row 59 K33(35,37,40)A, 5B, 8A,
16(18,20,23)C.
Row 61 K34(36,38,41)A, 3B, 10A,
15(17,19,22)C.
Row 63 K35(37,39,42)A, 1B, 12A, 12C,
2(4,6,9)A.
Row 65 K49(51,53,56)A, 10C, 3(5,7,10)A.
Row 67 K50(52,54,57)A, 8C, 4(6,8,11)A.
Row 69 K51(53,55,58)A, 6C, 5(7,9,12)A.
Row 71 K52(54,56,59)A, 4C, 6(8,10,13)A.
Row 73 K53(55,57,60)A, 2C, 7(9,11,14)A.
Row 74 P to end, working in colours as set.
Using A only and beg with a k row, cont in
st st until back measures 36(40,44,49)cm/
14¼(15¾,17¼,19¼)in from cast-on edge,
ending with a WS row.
Shape neck
Next row K21(22,23,25), turn and leave rem
sts on a spare needle.
Dec 1 st at neck edge on next 3 rows.
Cast off.
Return to sts on spare needle.
With RS facing, slip first 20(22,24,26) sts on
to a holder, join on yarn and k to end.
Now complete to match first side of neck.

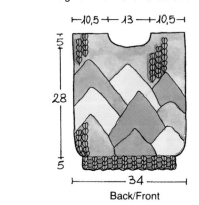

Measurements given in cm for smallest size

├─10,5─┼─ 13 ─┼─10,5─┤

28

├──── 34 ────┤

Back/Front

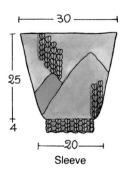

├── 30 ──┤

25

├──20──┤

Sleeve

Front
Work as given for back until row 74 has
been completed.
Using A only and beg with a k row, cont in
st st until work measures 33(37,41,46)cm/
13(14½,16,18)in from cast-on edge, ending
with a WS row.
Shape neck
Next row K22(23,24,26), turn and leave rem
sts on spare needle.
Dec 1 st at neck edge on foll 4 alt rows.
Work 3 rows st st.
Cast off.
Return to sts on spare needle. With RS
facing, slip first 18(20,22,24) sts on to a

holder, join on yarn and k to end.
Now complete to match first side of neck.

Left sleeve
Using 3¼mm needles and A, cast on
31(35,39,43) sts.
Rib row 1 K1, * p1, k1, rep from * to end.
Rib row 2 P1, * k1, p1, rep from * to end.
Rep these 2 rows for 4cm/1½in, ending with
rib row 1.
Inc row Rib 6(8,8,8), * M1, rib 5(5,6,7), rep
from * to last 5(7,7,7) sts, M1, rib to end.
36(40,44,48) sts.
Change to 4mm needles.
Work in patt as follows:
Row 1 K34(38,42,46)C, 2D.
Row 2 and every foll alt row P to end working
colours as set.
Row 3 K33(37,41,45)C, 3D.
Row 5 K32(36,40,44)C, 4D.
Row 7 With C inc in first st, k30(34,38,42)C,
4D, with D inc in last st.
Row 9 K31(35,39,43)C, 7D.
Row 11 K30(34,38,42)C, 8D.
Row 13 With C inc in first st, k28(32,36,40)C,
8D, with D inc in last st.
Row 15 K29(33,37,41)C, 10D, 1A.
Row 17 K28(32,36,40)C, 10D, 2A.
Row 19 With C inc in first st, k26(30,34,38)C,
10D, 2A, with A inc in last st.
Row 21 K27(31,35,39)C, 10D, 5A.
Row 23 K26(30,34,38)C, 10D, 6A.
Row 25 With C inc in first st, k24(28,32,36)C,
10D, 6A, with A inc in last st.
Row 27 K25(29,33,37)C, 10D, 9A.
Row 29 K1A, 23(27,31,35)C, 2A, 8D, 10A.
Row 31 With A inc in first st, k1A,
21(25,29,33)C, 4A, 6D, 10A, with A inc in
last st.
Row 33 K5A, 18(22,26,30)C, 6A, 4D, 13A.
Row 35 K7A, 15(19,23,27)C, 8A, 2D, 14A.
Row 37 With A inc in first st, k8A,
12(16,20,24)C, 24A, with A inc in last st.
Row 39 K12A, 9(13,17,21)C, 27A.
Row 41 K14A, 6(10,14,18)C, 28A.
Row 43 With A inc in first st, k15A,
3(7,11,15)C, 28A, with A inc in last st.
50(54,58,62) sts.
Row 45 K18A, 1(5,9,13)C, 31A.
2nd, 3rd and 4th sizes only
Row 47 K19A, 3(7,11)C, 32A.
Row 49 With A inc in first st, k19A, 1(5,9)C,
32A, with A inc in last st. 56(60,64) sts.
For 3rd and 4th sizes only
Row 51 K22A, 3(7)C, 35A.
Row 53 K23A, 1(5)C, 36A.
For 4th size only
Row 55 With A inc in first st, k23A, 3C, 36A,
with A inc in last st.
Row 57 K26A, 1C, 39A. 66 sts.
All sizes
Using A only and beg with a p row, work
3(5,1,1) rows st st.
Continuing in A only and working in st st, inc
1 st each end of next row. 52(58,62,68) sts.
Work straight until sleeve measures
29(32,35,38)cm/11½(12½,13½,15)in from
cast-on edge, ending with a WS row.
Cast off.

Right sleeve
Using B instead of D work as given for left
sleeve but purling every knit row and
knitting every purl row.

Neckband
Join right shoulder seam. With RS facing,
using 3¼mm needles and A, pick up and
k14 sts down left side of front neck,
k18(20,22,24) sts from front neck holder,
pick up and k14 sts up right side of front
neck and 7 sts down right side of back
neck, k20(22,24,26) sts from back neck
holder, then pick up and k7 sts up left side
of back neck. 80(84,88,92) sts.
Work 6cm/2½in k1, p1, rib.
Cast off in rib.

To make up
Join left shoulder and neckband seam. Fold
neckband in half to WS and slipstitch into
place. Fold sleeves in half lengthwise, then
placing folds to shoulder seams, sew into
place. Join side seams.

TWEEDY ARAN JERSEY

**

A warm jumper to
wear outdoors on a
cold winter's day.

Materials
6(7,8)×50g balls of Sunbeam Aran Tweed
A pair each of 4mm/No8 and 5mm/No6
  knitting needles

Measurements
To fit chest 56(61,66)cm/22(24,26)in
Actual measurements
Chest 65(70,75)cm/25½(27½,29½)in
Length to shoulders 33(38,42)cm/
13(15,16½)in
Sleeve seam 22(26,30)cm/8¾(10¼,11¾)in

Tension
16 sts and 22 rows to 10cm/4in measured
over st st worked on 5mm needles

Special abbreviations
Mb Make bobble as follows: into next st
work [k1, yf and k1], turn and p3, turn and
k3, then pass 2nd and 3rd sts over first and
off needle
C6F Cable 6 front as follows: slip next 3 sts
on to cable needle and leave at front of
work, k3, then k3 from cable needle

Back
Using 4mm needles, cast on 55(59,63) sts.
Rib row 1 K1, * p1, k1, rep from * to end.
Rib row 2 P1, * k1, p1, rep from * to end.
Rep these 2 rows for 3cm/1¼in, ending with
rib row 1.
Inc row Rib 2(4,4), * M1, rib 10(10,11), rep
from * to last 3(5,4) sts, M1, rib to end.
61(65,69) sts.
Change to 5mm needles.
Work in patt as follows:
Row 1 K2, [p1, k1] 3(4,5) times p1,
[k2 tog, yf] twice, k1, p2, k6, p2, k3,
[k2 tog, yf] twice, k1, yfon, skpo, k3, p2,
k6, p2, k1, [yfon, skpo] twice, p1, [k1, p1]
3(4,5) times, k2.
Row 2 P3, k1, [p1, k1] 2(3,4) times, [p6, k2]
twice, p13, [k2, p6] twice, [k1, p1] 2(3,4)
times, k1, p3.
Row 3 K2, [p1, k1] 3(4,5) times, [k2 tog, yf]
twice, k2, p2, k6, p2, k2, [k2 tog, yf] twice,
k1, [yfon, skpo] twice, k2, p2, k6, p2, k2,
[yfon, skpo] twice, [k1, p1] 3(4,5) times, k2.
Row 4 As row 2.
Row 5 K2, [p1, k1] 2(3,4) times, p1,
[k2 tog, yf] twice, k3, p2, C6F, p2, k1,
[k2 tog, yf] twice, k3, [yfon, skpo] twice,
k1, p2, C6F, p2, k3, [yfon, skpo] twice, p1,
[k1, p1] 2(3,4) times, k2.
Row 6 P3, k1, [p1, k1] 1(2,3) times, p8, k2,
p6, k2, p13, k2, p6, k2, p8, [k1, p1]
1(2,3) times, k1, p3.
Row 7 K2, [p1, k1] 2(3,4) times, [k2 tog, yf]
twice, k4, p2, k6, p2, [k2 tog, yf] twice, k5,
[yfon, skpo] twice, p2, k6, p2, k4, [yfon,
skpo] twice, [k1, p1] 2(3,4) times, k2.
Row 8 As row 2.
Row 9 K2, [p1, k1] 1(2,3) times, p1,
[k2 tog, yf] twice, k5, p2, k6, p2, k1, k2 tog,
yf, k3, Mb, k3, yfon, skpo, k1, p2, k6, p2,
k5, [yfon, skpo] twice, p1, [k1, p1] 1(2,3)
times, k2.
Row 10 P3, k1, *for 2nd and 3rd sizes only*
[p1, k1] 1(2) times, *for all sizes* p10, k2, p6,
k2, p13, k2, p6, k2, p10, *for 2nd and 3rd
sizes only* [k1, p1] 1(2) times, then *for all
sizes* k1, p3.

Row 11 K2, [p1, k1] 1(2,3) times,
[k2 tog, yf] twice, [k6, p2] twice, k2 tog, yf,
k9, yfon, skpo, [p2, k6] twice, [yfon, skpo]
twice, [k1, p1] 1(2,3) times, k2.
Row 12 As row 10.
Row 13 K2, *for 2nd and 3rd sizes only*
[p1, k1] 1(2) times, *for all sizes* p1,
[k2 tog, yf] twice, k7, p2, C6F, p2, k13, p2,
C6F, p2, k7, [yfon, skpo] twice, p1, *for 2nd
and 3rd sizes only* [k1, p1] 1(2) times, then
for all sizes k2.
Row 14 *For 2nd and 3rd sizes only* p3, k1,
for 3rd size only p1, k1, *for all sizes*
p14(12,12), k2, p6, k2, p13, k2, p6, k2,
p14(12,12), *for 3rd sizes only* k1, p1, then
for 2nd and 3rd sizes only k1, p3.
Row 15 K2, *for 2nd and 3rd sizes only*
[p1, k1] 1(2) times, *for all sizes* [k2 tog, yf]
twice, k8, p2, k6, p2, k13, p2, k6, p2, k8,
[yfon, skpo] twice, *for 2nd and 3rd sizes
only* [k1, p1] 1(2) times, then *for all sizes* k2.
Row 16 As row 14.
Row 17 K2, *for 2nd and 3rd sizes only*
[p1, k1] 1(2) times, *for all sizes* [yfon, skpo]
twice, k8, p2, k6, p2, k3, [k2 tog, yf] twice,
k1, yfon, skpo, k3, p2, k6, p2, k8, [k2 tog, yf]
twice, *for 2nd and 3rd sizes only* [k1, p1]
1(2) times, then *for all sizes* k2.
Row 18 As row 14.
Row 19 K2, *for 2nd and 3rd sizes only*
[p1, k1] 1(2) times, *for all sizes* p1, yon,
skpo, yfon, skpo, k7, p2, k6, p2, k2,
[k2 tog, yf] twice, k1 [yfon, skpo] twice,
k2, p2, k6, p2, k7, k2 tog, yf, k2 tog, yrn, p1,
for 2nd and 3rd sizes only [k1, p1]
1(2) times, then *for all sizes* k2.
Row 20 As row 10.
Row 21 K2, [p1, k1] 1(2,3) times, [yfon,
skpo] twice, k6, p2, C6F, p2, k1, [k2 tog, yf]
twice, k3, [yfon, skpo] twice, k1, p2, C6F,
p2, k6, [k2 tog, yf] twice, [k1, p1] 1(2,3)
times, k2.
Row 22 As row 10.
Row 23 K2, [p1, k1] 1(2,3) times, p1, yon,
skpo, yfon, skpo, k5, p2, k6, p2, [k2 tog, yf]
twice, k5, [yfon, skpo] twice, p2, k6, p2, k5,
k2 tog, yf, k2 tog, yrn, p1, [k1, p1] 1(2,3)
times, k2.
Row 24 As row 6.
Row 25 K2, [p1, k1] 2(3,4) times,
[yfon, skpo] twice, k4, p2, k6, p2, k1, k2 tog,
yf, k3, Mb, k3, yfon, skpo, k1, p2, k6, p2, k4,
[k2 tog, yf] twice, [k1, p1] 2(3,4) times, k2.
Row 26 As row 6.
Row 27 K2, [p1, k1] 2(3,4) times, p1, yon,
skpo, yfon, skpo, k3, p2, k6, p2, k2 tog, yf,
k9, yfon, skpo, p2, k6, p2, k3, k2 tog, yf,
k2 tog, yrn, p1, [k1, p1] 2(3,4) times, k2.
Row 28 As row 2.
Row 29 K2, [p1, k1] 3(4,5) times,
[yfon, skpo] twice, k2, p2, C6F, p2, k13,
p2, C6F, p2, k2, [k2 tog, yf] twice, [k1, p1]
3(4,5) times, k2.
Row 30 As row 2.
Row 31 K2, [p1, k1] 3(4,5) times, p1, yon,
skpo, yfon, skpo, k1, p2, k6, p2, k13, p2, k6,
p2, k1, k2 tog, yf, k2 tog, yrn, p1, [k1, p1]
3(4,5) times, k2.
Row 32 P3, k1, [p1, k1] 3(4,5) times, p4, k2,
p6, k2, p13, k2, p6, k2, p4 [k1, p1] 3(4,5)
times, k1, p3.
These 32 rows form the patt.
Cont in patt until back measures

33(38,42)cm/13(15,16½)in from cast-on
edge, ending with a WS row.
Shape shoulders
Keeping patt correct, cast off 16(17,18) sts
at beg of next 2 rows.
Cut off yarn and leave rem 29(31,33) sts on
a holder.

Front
Work as given for back until front measures
27(32,36)cm/10¾(12¾,14¼)in from
cast-on edge, ending with a WS row.
Shape neck
Next row Patt 24(25,26) sts, turn and leave
rem sts on a spare needle.
Keeping patt correct, dec 1 st at neck edge
on next 8 rows. 16(17,18) sts.
Work straight until front measures same as
back to shoulder, ending with a WS row.
Cast off.
Return to sts on spare needle.
With RS facing, slip first 13(15,17) sts on to
a holder, join on yarn and patt to end.
Keeping patt correct, dec 1 st at neck edge
on next 8 rows. 16(17,18) sts.
Work straight until front measures same as
back to shoulder, ending with a WS row.
Cast off.

Sleeves
Using 4mm needles cast on 25(27,29) sts.
Work 4cm/1½in rib as given for back,
ending with rib row 1.
Inc row Rib 4(3,4), * M1, rib 2. rep from * to
last 5(4,5) sts, M1, rib to end. 34(38,40) sts.
Change to 5mm needles.
Beg with a k row and working in st st, inc 1 st
each end of 7th(5th,3rd) and every foll
4th(6th,8th) row until there are 48(52,54) sts.
Work straight until sleeve measures
22(26,30)cm/8¾(10¼,11¾)in from cast-on
edge, ending with a WS row.
Cast off.

Neckband
Join right shoulder seam.
With RS facing and using 4mm needles,
pick up and k17(19,21) sts down left side of
front neck, k across 13(15,17) sts from front
neck holder, pick up and k17(19,21) sts up
right side of front neck, then decreasing 1 st
each end and 1 st at centre k across
29(31,33) sts from back neck holder.
75(83,91) sts.
Beg with rib row 2, work 5cm/2in rib as
given for back.
Cast off in rib.

To make up
Join left shoulder and neckband seam. Fold
sleeves in half lengthwise, then placing
folds to shoulder seams, sew into place.
Join side and sleeve seams. Fold neckband
in half to WS and slipstitch into place.

Measurements given in cm for second size

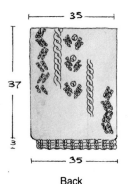

Back

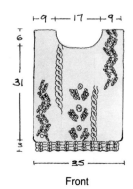

Front

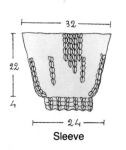

Sleeve

SPOTTED JERSEY WITH HEART MOTIF BORDER

***

This little girl's jumper in a simple repeating spot pattern is not as difficult to knit as it looks and would look just as pretty worked in bright contrasting colours.

Materials
4(4,5)×50g balls of Patons Diploma Gold DK in main colour A
1 ball of same in each of contrast colours B and C
A pair each of 3¼mm/No10 and 4mm/No8 knitting needles

Measurements
To fit chest 56(61,66)cm/22(24,26)in
Actual measurements
Chest 61(68,75)cm/24(26¾,29½)in
Length to shoulders 34(38.5,43)cm/13½(15¼,17)in
Sleeve seam 24.5(28.5,33)cm/9¾(11¼,13)in

Tension
22 sts and 30 rows to 10cm/4in measured over patt worked on 4mm needles

Back
★ Using 3¼mm needles and A, cast on 62(70,76) sts.
Work 3(3,4)cm/1¼(1¼,1¾)in k1, p1 rib.
Inc row Rib 7(7,8), * M1, rib 12(14,10), rep from * to last 7(7,8) sts, M1, rib to end. 67(75,83) sts.
Change to 4mm needles.
Join on and cut off colours as required. Carrying yarn not in use loosely across WS, work in dot patt as follows:
Row 1 (RS) K3A, * 1B, 3A, rep from * to end.
Row 2 With A, p to end.
Row 3 With A, k to end.
Rows 4 and 5 As rows 2 and 3.
Row 6 P1A, * 1B, 3A, rep from * to last 2 sts, 1B, 1A.
Row 7 With A, k to end.
Row 8 With A, p to end.
Rows 9 and 10 As rows 7 and 8.
These 10 rows form the patt.
Cont in patt until back measures approx 16(19.5,22)cm/6¼(7¾,8¾)in from cast-on edge, ending with row 10(10,4).
Use separate small balls of yarn for each area of colour and twist yarns together at back of work when changing colour to avoid making a hole.
Reading odd numbered (k) rows from right to left and even numbered (p) rows from left to right, work from chart as follows:
Row 1 For 1st size only k1B, 3A, for 2nd size only k4A, 1B, 3A, for 3rd size only k2A, 1B, 5A, 1B, 3A, then for all sizes * k2A, 5A, 1B, 3A, rep from * to last 3(7,11) sts, for 1st size only k2A, 1B, for 2nd size only k2A, 1B, 4A, for 3rd size only k2A, 1B, 5A, 1B, 2A.
Row 2 For 1st size only P1C, 1B, 1A, for 2nd size only p3A, 1B, 1C, 1B, 1A, for 3rd size only p1A, 1B, 1C, 1B, 3A, 1B, 1C, 1B, 1A,

then for all sizes * p2A 1B, 1C, 1B, 3A, 1B, 1C, 1B, 1A, rep from * to last 4(8,12) sts, for 1st size only p2A, 1B, 1A, for 2nd size only p2A, 1B, 1A, 1B, 3A, for 3rd size only p2A, 1B. 1C. 1B. 3A. 1B. 1C. 1B. 1A.
Cont in patt from chart until row 18 has been completed.
Shape armholes
With A, cast off 5 sts at beg of next 2 rows.
With A, k 1 row and p 1 row. ★
Rep rows 1 to 6(8,10) of dot patt.
3rd size only
Work rows 1 to 4 again.
All sizes
Divide for opening
Next row Patt 26(30,34), turn and leave rem sts on a spare needle.
Work straight until armhole measures 10(11,13)cm/4(4½,5¼)in from beg of shaping, ending at inner edge.
Shape neck
Cast off in patt 4(5,6) sts at beg of next row and 3 sts at beg of foll alt row.
Dec 1 st at neck edge on next 2 rows. 17(20,23) sts.
Cast off.
Return to sts on spare needle.
With RS facing and using A, cast off first 5 sts, then patt to end. 26(30,34) sts.
Now complete to match first side of opening.

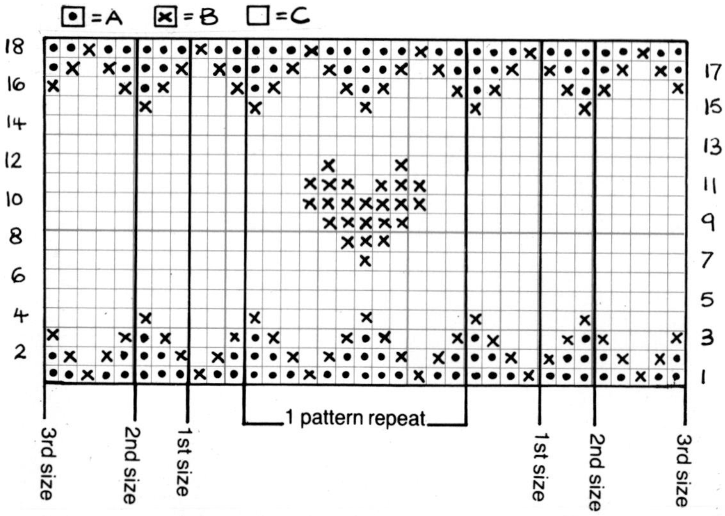

Front
Work as given for back from ★ to ★.
Beg with row 1, cont in dot patt until armhole measures 6(6.5,7.5)cm/2¼(2½,3)in from beg of shaping, ending with a p row.
Shape neck
Next row Patt 22(25,29), turn and leave rem sts on a spare needle.
Keeping patt correct, dec 1 st at neck edge on next 2 rows. 20(23,27) sts.
Dec 1 st at neck edge on every foll alt row until 17(20,23) sts rem.
Work straight until front measures same as back to shoulder, ending with a p row.
Cast off.
Return to sts on spare needle.
With RS facing, slip first 13(15,15) sts on to a holder, then patt to end. 22(25,29) sts.
Now complete to match first side of neck.

Sleeves
Using 3¼mm needles and A, cast on 36(38,40) sts.
Work 4(4,5)cm/1¾(1¾,2)in k1, p1 rib.
Inc row Rib 4(3,4), * M1, rib 7(4,4), rep from * to last 4(3,4) sts, M1, rib to end. 41(47,49) sts.
Change to 4mm needles.
Working in dot patt as given for back, inc

and work into patt 1 st each end of 7th(9th,5th) and every foll 10th(10th,8th) row until there are 51(59,67) sts.
Work straight until sleeve measures 26.5(30.5,35)cm/10½(12,13¾)in from cast-on edge, ending with a p row. Cast off.

Neckband
Join shoulder seams.
With RS facing, using 3¼mm needles and A, pick up and k13(14,15) sts up left side of back neck from beg of neck shaping, 15(16,18) sts down left side of front neck, k the front neck sts from holder, pick up and k15(16,18) sts up right side of front neck and 13(14,15) sts down left side of back neck to beg of neck shaping. 69(75,81) sts.
Rib row 1 P1, * k1, p1, rep from * to end.
Rib row 2 K1, * p1, k1, rep from * to end.
Rep these 2 rows once more, then work rib row 1 again. Cast off in rib.

Button border
Using 3¼mm needles and A, cast on 7 sts.
Rib row 1 (RS) K1, * p1, k1, rep from * to end.
Rib row 2 P1, * k1, p1, rep from * to end.
Rep these 2 rows until border, slightly stretched, fits up back neck opening to top of neckband.
Cast off in rib. Sew on the border.
Mark 3 button positions on this border. The first one 1.5cm/¾in from base of opening, the top one 1cm/½in from cast-off edge and the 3rd evenly spaced between.

Buttonhole border
Work as given for button border, making buttonholes to correspond with markers as follows:
Buttonhole row (RS) Rib 3, yf, k2 tog, rib 2.

To make up
Fold sleeves in half lengthwise, then placing folds to shoulder seams and row ends at top of sleeves to cast-off edges for armholes, sew into place. Join side and sleeve seams. Sew on the buttonhole border, then sew on the buttons.

Measurements given in cm for second size

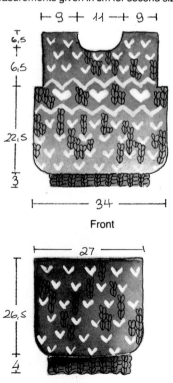

Front

Sleeve

Chart

•=A   ☒=B   ☐=C

1 pattern repeat

3rd size 2nd size 1st size 1st size 2nd size 3rd size

FAIR ISLE POLO NECK JUMPER

**

Suitable for either a boy or a girl, this Fair Isle jumper is simple enough for a beginner to try.

Materials

6(7,8,9)×50g balls of Emu Superwash Chunky in main colour A
2(2,2,3) balls of same in each of contrast colours B, C and D
A pair each of 4½mm/No7 and 6½mm/No3 knitting needles

Measurements

To fit chest 61(66,71,76)cm/24(26,28,30)in
Actual measurements
Chest 64(71,78,86)cm/25¼(28,31,34)in
Length to shoulders 39(42,44,46)cm/
15½(16½,17½,18¼)in
Sleeve seam 27(30,36,40)cm/
10½(12,14,16)in

Tension

16 sts and 18 rows to 10cm/4in measured over Fair Isle worked on 6½mm needles

Back

Using 4½mm needles and A, cast on 47(53,59,65) sts.
Rib row 1 K1, * p1, k1, rep from * to end.
Rib row 2 P1, * k1, p1, rep from * to end.
Continuing in rib, work 4(4,6,6) more rows A, then work 2 rows B and 5(5,7,7) rows A.
Inc row With A, rib 8(12,12,14), * M1, rib 10(10,12,13), rep from * to last 9(11,11,12) sts, M1, rib to end.
51(57,63,69) sts.
Change to 6½mm needles.
K 1 row and p 1 row.
Join on and cut off colours as required.
Carrying yarns not in use loosely across WS of work, weaving them in when passing across 5 sts or more, work in patt as follows:
Row 1 (RS) K1C, * 1A, 1C, rep from * to end.
Row 2 P1A, * 1C, 1A, rep from * to end.
Rows 3 and 4 As rows 1 and 2.
Row 5 With A, k to end.
Row 6 With A, p to end.
Row 7 K2A, * 1B, 3A, rep from * to last 1(3,1,3) sts, k1B, then for 2nd and 4th sizes only k2A.
Row 8 For 1st and 3rd sizes only p2A, then for all sizes p1B, * 3A, 1B, rep from * to end.
Row 9 * K1B, 3A, rep from * to last 3(1,3,1) sts, k1B, then for 1st and 3rd sizes only k2A.
Row 10 For 2nd and 4th sizes only p2A, then for all sizes * p1B, 3A, rep from * to last 3 sts, p1B, 2A.
Rows 11 and 12 As rows 5 and 6.
Row 13 K3A, * 3D, 3A, rep from * to end.
Row 14 * P1D, 1A, 1D, 3A, rep from * to last 3 sts, 1D, 1A, 1D.
Row 15 * K1D, 1A, 1D, 3A, rep from * to last 3 sts, 1D, 1A, 1D.
Row 16 P3A, * 3D, 3A, rep from * to end.
Rows 17 and 18 As rows 5 and 6.
Row 19 K1C, * 1A, 5C, rep from * to last 2 sts, 1A, 1C.
Row 20 P3A, * 1C, 1A, 1C, 3A, rep from * to end.
Row 21 K3A, * 1C, 1A, 1C, 3A, rep from * to end.
Row 22 P1C, * 1A, 5C, rep from * to last 2 sts, 1A, 1C.
Rows 23 and 24 As rows 5 and 6.
Row 25 K2A, * 2B, 4A, rep from * to last st, 1B.
Row 26 P4A, * 1B, 5A, rep from * to last 5 sts, 1B, 4A.

Row 27 * K5A, 1B, rep from * to last 3 sts, 3A.
Row 28 P1A, 2B, * 4A, 2B, rep from * to end.
Rows 29 and 30 As rows 5 and 6.
Row 31 K4A, * 1D, 5A, rep from * to last 5 sts, 1D, 4A.
Row 32 P3A, * 3D, 3A, rep from * to end.
Row 33 K3D, * 3A, 3D, rep from * to end.
Row 34 P1A, * 1D, 5A, rep from * to last 2 sts, 1D, 1A.
Rows 35 and 36 As rows 5 and 6.
Row 37 K3A, * 1C, 1A, 1C, 3A, rep from * to end.
Row 38 * P1C, 1A, 1C, 3A, rep from * to last 3 sts, 1C, 1A, 1C.
Rows 39 and 40 As rows 37 and 38.
Rows 41 and 42 As rows 5 and 6.
Row 43 K3A, * 3B, 3A, rep from * to end.
Row 44 P4A, * 1B, 5A, rep from * to last 5 sts, 1B, 4A.
Row 45 K1A, * 1B, 5A, rep from * to last 2 sts, 1B, 1A.
Row 46 P3B, * 3A, 3B, rep from * to end.
Rows 47 and 48 As rows 5 and 6.
Row 49 K1D, * 2A, 2D, rep from * to last 2(4,2,4) sts, k2A, then for 2nd and 4th sizes only k2D.
Row 50 For 2nd and 4th sizes only p2A, then for all sizes * p2D, 2A, rep from * to last 3 sts, p2D, 1A.
Rows 51 and 52 As rows 49 and 50.
Rows 53 and 54 As rows 5 and 6.
First size only
With A, k 1 row and p 1 row.
2nd, 3rd and 4th sizes only
Row 55 K1A, * 1C, 5A, rep from * to last 2 sts, 1C, 1A.
Row 56 * P1C, 1A, 1C, 3A, rep from * to last 3 sts, 1C, 1A, 1C.
Row 57 K3A, * 1C, 1A, 1C, 3A, rep from * to end.
Row 58 P4A, * 1C, 5A, rep from * to last 5 sts, 1C, 4A.
Rows 59 and 60 As rows 5 and 6.
2nd size only
With A, k 1 row and p 1 row.
3rd and 4th sizes only
Row 61 K3B, * 3A, 3B, rep from * to end.
Row 62 P3A, * 3B, 3A, rep from * to end.
Rows 63 and 64 As rows 61 and 62.
4th size only
Using A only and beginning with a k row, work 4 rows st st.
Shape shoulders
All sizes
Using A, cast off 15(18,20,22) sts at beg of next 2 rows.
Cut off yarn and leave rem 21(21,23,25) sts on a holder.

Front

Work as given for back until row 50(52,54,58) has been completed
Shape neck
Next row Patt 17(20,22,25), turn and leave rem sts on a spare needle.
Keeping patt correct, dec 1 st at neck edge on every row until 15(18,20,22) sts rem.
Work straight until front measures same as back to shoulder, ending with a WS row.
Cast off.
Return to sts on spare needle.
With RS facing, slip first 17(17,19,19) sts on to a holder, join on yarn and patt to end.
Now complete to match first side of neck.

Sleeves

Using 4½mm needles and A, cast on 21(27,33,39) sts.
Work 13(13,17,17) rows rib as given for back.
Inc row Rib 4, * M1, rib 3(4,5,6), rep from * to last 2(3,4,5) sts, M1, rib to end.
27(33,39,45) sts.
Change to 6½mm needles.
K 1 row and p 1 row.
Working in patt as given for back, inc and work into patt 1 st each end of 3rd(3rd,3rd,7th) and every foll 2nd row to 47(45,45,49) sts, then on every foll 4th row until there are 51(57,63,69) sts.
Work 3(1,3,7) rows straight, so ending with row 34(40,48,58).
Using A, cast off.

Collar

Join right shoulder seam.
With RS facing, using 4½mm needles and A, pick up and k8(14,18,22) sts down left side of front neck, k17(17,19,19) sts from front neck holder, pick up and k8(14,18,22) sts up left side of front neck, then k21(21,23,25) sts from back neck holder. 54(66,78,88) sts.
Beg with rib row 2, work 7(9,9,11) rows rib as given for back, then continuing in rib work 2 rows B and 8(10,10,12) rows A.
Using A, cast off in rib.

To make up

Join left shoulder and collar seam. Fold sleeves in half lengthwise, then placing folds to shoulder seams, sew into place.
Join side and sleeve seams.

Measurements given in cm for third size

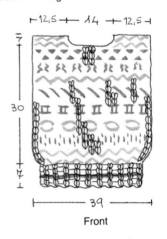

Front

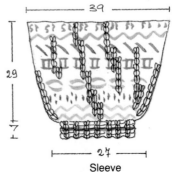

Sleeve

SIMPLE SLIPOVER IN TWO COLOURS

⁂

This smart little slipover looks particularly good knitted in bright contrasting colours.

Materials

2(3,3)×50g balls of Patons Beehive Soft Blend DK in main colour A
1 ball of same in contrast colour B
A pair each of 3¼mm/No10 and 4mm/No8 knitting needles

Measurements

To fit chest 61(66,71)cm/24(26,28)in
Actual measurements
Chest 66(72,80)cm/26(28¼,31½)in
Length to shoulders 37(40,45)cm/
14½(15¾,17¾)in

Tension

25 sts and 27 rows to 10cm/4in measured over patt worked on 4mm needles

Back

Using 3¼mm needles and A, cast on 77(85,93) sts.
Rib row 1 K1, * p1, k1, rep from * to end.
Rib row 2 P1, * k1, p1, rep from * to end.
Rep these 2 rows for 4(5,6)cm/
1½(2, 2½)ins, ending with rib row 1.
Inc row Rib 8(7,9), * M1, rib 12(14,15), rep from * to last 9(8,9) sts, M1, rib 9(8,9). 83(91,99) sts.
Change to 4mm needles.
Beg with a k row, work 2(2,4) rows st st.
Carrying yarn not in use loosely across WS of work, proceed in patt as follows:
Row 1 With A, k to end.
Row 2 With A, p to end.
Row 3 K1A, * 1B, 1A, rep from * to end.
Row 4 With A, p to end.
Row 5 With A, k to end.
Row 6 For 2nd size only p1B, for all sizes p1(2,2)A, * p1B, 2A, rep from * to last 3(4,2) sts, p1B, 2(2,1)A, then for 2nd size only p1B.
Row 7 For 1st size only k1B, 2A, for 2nd size only k3A, then for all sizes * k1B, 1A, 1B, 3A, rep from * to last 1(5,3) sts, k1B, then for 2nd size only k1A, 1B, 2A and for 3rd size only k1B, 1A, 1B.
Row 8 For 2nd size only p1A, 1B, for all sizes p1(3,3)A, * p1B, 1A, 1B, 3A, rep from * to last 4(2,6) sts, for 1st and 3rd sizes only p1B, 1A, 1B, 1(3)A and for 2nd size only p1B, 1A.

Row 9 For 2nd size only k1B, for all sizes k2(5,4)A, * k1B, 5A, rep from * to last 3(7,5) sts, k1B, 2(5,4)A, then for 2nd size only k1B.
Row 10 With A, p to end.
Row 11 With A, k to end.
Row 12 P1A, * 1B, 1A, rep from * to end.
Row 13 With A, k to end.
Row 14 With A, p to end.
Row 15 K1A, * 1B, 3A, rep from * to last 2 sts, 1B, 1A.
Row 16 P3A, * 1B, 3A, rep from * to end.
Rows 17 and 18 As rows 15 and 16.
Rows 19 and 20 As rows 1 and 2.
Row 21 K3A, * 1B, 3A, rep from * to end.
Row 22 P1B, * 1A, 1B, rep from * to end.
Row 23 K1A, 1B, * 3A, 1B, rep from * to last st, 1A.
Row 24 With A, p to end.
Row 25 With A, k to end.
Row 26 P1A, * 1B, 3A, rep from * to last 2 sts, 1B, 1A.
Row 27 K3A, * 1B, 3A, rep from * to end.
Row 28 P1A, * 1B, 3A, rep from * to last 2 sts, 1B, 1A.
These 28 rows form the patt.
Cont in patt until back measures approx 20(22,23)cm/8(8¾,9)in from cast-on edge, ending with a WS row.
Shape armholes
Keeping patt correct, cast off 3 sts at beg of next 2 rows.
Dec 1 st each end of next 2 rows. 73(81,89) sts.
Work straight until back measures 37(40,45)cm/14½(15¾,17¾)in from cast-on edge, ending with row 2(10,20). Cut off B.
Shape shoulders
Using A only, cast off 20(24,27) sts at beg of next 2 rows.
Cut off yarn and leave rem 32(32,34) sts on a holder.

Front

Work as given for back until front measures same as back to armholes, ending with a WS row.
Shape armholes and neck
Next row (RS) Cast off 3 sts, patt 38(42,46) sts (including st used in casting

off), turn and leave rem sts on a spare needle.
Next row P2 tog, patt to end.
Next row K2 tog, patt to end.
Dec 1 st each end of next row.
★ Keeping armhole edge straight, dec 1 st at neck edge on every foll alt row until 20(24,27) sts rem.
Work straight until front measures same as back to shoulder, ending at side edge.
Cast off. ★
Return to sts on spare needle.
With RS facing, slip first st on to a safety-pin, join on yarns and patt to end. 41(45,49) sts.
Next row Cast off 3 sts, patt to last 2 sts, p2 tog.
Next row Patt to last 2 sts, k2 tog.
Dec 1 st at end of next row, then at each end of foll row.
Now work as given for first side of neck from ★ to ★.

Neckband

Join right shoulder seam.
With RS facing, using 3¼mm needles and A, pick up and k46(50,54) sts evenly down left side of front neck, k into back and front of st from safety-pin and mark these sts with a coloured thread, pick up and k46(50,54) sts up right side of front neck, then k the sts from back neck holder. 127(135,143) sts.
Rib row 1 [K1, p1] to within 2 sts of marked sts, skpo, p2, k2 tog, [p1, k1] to end.
Rib row 2 Rib to within 2 sts of marked sts, skpo, k2, k2 tog, rib to end.
Rep these 2 rows for 2cm/¾in.
Cast off in rib, decreasing as before.

Armhole borders

Join left shoulder and neckband seam.
With RS facing, using 3¼mm needles and A, pick up and k93(101,109) sts evenly along armhole edge.
Work 2cm/¾in rib as given for back.
Cast off in rib.

To make up

Join side and armhole border seams.

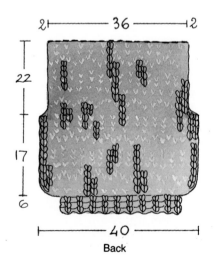

Back

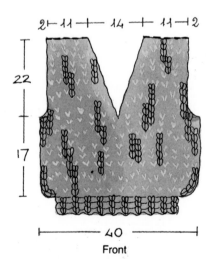

Front

Measurements given in cm for largest size

SIMPLE MOTIF JUMPER

**

The yarn is stranded across the back when knitting these simple single colour motifs.

Materials

4(5,6)×50g balls of Jaeger Matchmaker DK in main colour A

1 ball each of same in contrast colours B, C and D

A pair each of 3¼mm/No10 and 4mm/No8 knitting needles

Measurements

To fit chest 56(61,66)cm/22(24,26)in

Actual measurements

Chest 64(69,76)cm/25(27,30)in

Length to shoulders 34(38,43)cm/ 13¼(15,17)in

Sleeve seam 26.5(30,32)cm/ 10½(11¾,12½)in

Tension

22 sts and 30 rows to 10cm/4in measured over patt worked on 4mm needles

Back

Using 3¼mm needles and A, cast on 69(75,83) sts.

Rib row 1 K1, * p1, k1, rep from * to end.

Rib row 2 P1, * k1, p1, rep from * to end.

Rep these 2 rows for 5cm/2in, ending with rib row 2 and increasing 1 st at centre of last row. 70(76,84) sts.

Change to 4mm needles.

Join on and cut off colours as required and carry yarns not in use loosely across WS of work, weaving them in when passing across more than 5 sts.

Work in patt as follows:

Row 1 With A, k to end.

Row 2 With A, p to end.

Rows 3 to 8 Rep rows 1 and 2 three times.

Row 9 K6(4,4)A, * 7B, 10(8,10)A, rep from * to last 13(12,12) sts, 7B, 6(5,5)A.

Row 10 P6(5,5)A, * 7B, 10(8,10)A, rep from * to last 13(11,11) sts, 7B, 6(4,4)A.

Row 11 K7(5,5)A, * 5B, 12(10,12)A, rep from * to last 12(11,11) sts, 5B, 7(6,6)A.

Row 12 P7(6,6)A, * 5B, 12(10,12)A, rep from * to last 12(10,10) sts, 5B, 7(5,5)A.

Row 13 K8(6,6)A, * 3B, 14(12,14)A, rep from * to last 11(10,10) sts, 3B, 8(7,7)A.

Row 14 P8(7,7)A, * 3B, 14(12,14)A, rep from * to last 11(9,9) sts, 3B, 8(6,6)A.

Row 15 K9(7,7)A, * 1B, 16(14,16)A, rep from * to last 10(9,9) sts, 1B, 9(8,8)A.

Row 16 P9(8,8)A, * 1B, 16(14,16)A, rep from * to last 10(8,8) sts, 1B, 9(7,7)A.

Rows 17 to 22 Rep rows 1 and 2 three times.

Row 23 As row 1.

Row 24 P8(5,8)A, * 2C, 5A, 2C, 14(10,11)A, rep from * to last 16(14,16) sts, 2C, 5A, 2C, 7(5,7)A.

Row 25 K5(3,5)A, * 13C, 10(6,7)A, rep from * to last 19(16,19) sts, 13C, 6(3,6)A.

Row 26 P6(3,6)A, * 13C, 10(6,7)A, rep from * to last 18(16,18) sts, 13C, 5(3,5)A.

Row 27 K7(5,7)A, * 2C, 2A, 1C, 2A, 2C, 14(10,11)A, rep from * to last 17(14,17) sts, 2C, 2A, 1C, 2A, 2C, 8(5,8)A.

Row 28 P8(5,8)A, * 2C, [2A, 1C] twice, 15(11,12)A, rep from * to last 16(14,16) sts, 2C, [2A, 1C] twice, 8(6,8)A.

Row 29 K8(6,8)A, * 8C, 15(11,12)A, rep

from * to last 16(13,16) sts, 8C, 8(5,8)A.

Row 30 P8(5,8)A, * 7C, 16(12,13)A, rep from * to last 16(14,16) sts, 7C, 9(7,9)A.

Rows 31 to 36 Rep rows 1 and 2 three times.

Row 37 As row 1.

Row 38 P4A, * 8D, 10(7,9)A, rep from * to last 12 sts, 8D, 4A.

Row 39 K4A, * 8D, 10(7,9)A, rep from * to last 12 sts, 8D, 4A.

Row 40 P4A, * 8D, 10(7,9)A, rep from * to last 12 sts, 8D, 4A.

These 40 rows form the patt.

Cont in patt until back measures approx 34(38,43)cm/13¼(15,17)in from cast-on edge, ending with a WS row in A.

Shape shoulders

Using A only, cast off 21(23,26) sts at beg of next 2 rows.

Cut off yarn and leave rem 28(30,32) sts on a holder.

Front

Work as given for back until front measures approx 29(32,37)cm/11½(12½,14½)in from cast-on edge ending with a WS row in A.

Shape neck

Next row Patt 31(34,38), turn and leave rem sts on a spare needle.

★ Keeping patt correct dec 1 st at neck edge on every row until 21(23,26) sts rem. Work straight until front measures same as back to shoulder, ending at side edge. Cast off. ★

Return to sts on spare needle.

With RS facing, slip first 8 sts on to a holder, join on yarn and patt to end. 31(34,38) sts.

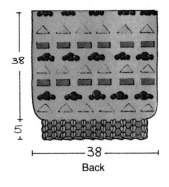

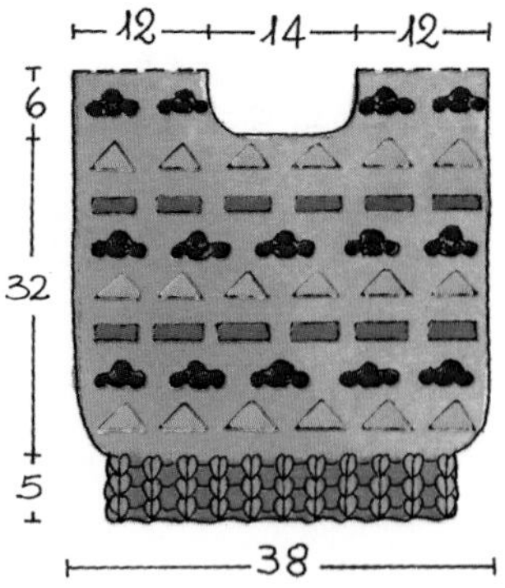

38

38

Back

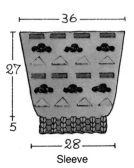

36

27

5

28

Sleeve

12   14   12

6

32

5

38

Front

Measurements given in cm for largest size

Now work as given for first side of neck from ★ to ★.

Sleeves

Using 3¼mm needles and A, cast on 49(51,57) sts.

Work 5cm/2in rib as given for back, ending with rib row 1.

Inc row Rib 12(4,4), [M1, rib 24(6,7) sts] 1(7,7) times, M1, rib 13(5,4). 51(59,65) sts.

Change to 4mm needles.

Beginning with a k row and increasing 1 st each end of 5th row, work 8 rows st st.

Beginning with row 9 and working in patt as given for back, inc and work into patt 1 st each end of 3rd(5th,7th) and every foll 6th(8th,10th) row until there are 69(73,79) sts.

Work straight until sleeve measures approx 26.5(30,32)cm/10½(11¾,12½)in from cast-on edge, ending with a WS row in A.

Cast off.

Neckband

Join right shoulder seam.

With RS facing, using 3¼mm needles and A, pick up and k15(17,19) sts down left side of front neck, k8 sts from front neck holder, pick up and k15(17,19) sts up right side of front neck, then increasing 1 st at centre k the sts from back neck holder. 61(73,79) sts.

Work 6cm/2½in k1, p1 rib.

Cast off in rib.

To make up

Join left shoulder and neckband seam. Fold sleeves in half lengthwise, then placing folds to shoulder seams, sew into place. Join side and sleeve seams. Fold neckband in half to WS and slipstitch into position.

MOSS STITCH JERSEY WITH AN ARAN PANEL

✳✳✳

The back and
sleeves
are
knitted
in moss stitch
with the pattern
panel worked
down the centre
of the front.

Materials

4(5, 5, 6)×50g balls of Robin Good News DK
A pair each of 3¾mm/No9 and 4½mm/No7
knitting needles   Cable needle

Measurements

To fit chest 61(66,71,76)cm/24(26,28,30)in
Actual measurements
Chest 74(78,82,86)cm/29(30¾,32¼,34)in
Length to shoulders 37(39,41,44)cm/
14½(15¼,16¼,17¼)in
Sleeve seam 29(31,33,35)cm/
11½(12¼,13,13¾)in

Tension

19 sts and 34 rows to 10cm/4in measured
over moss st worked on 4½mm needles

Special abbreviations

C4B Cable 4 back as follows: slip next 2 sts
on to cable needle and leave at back of
work, k2, then k2 from cable needle
C4F Cable 4 front as follows: slip next 2 sts
on to cable needle and leave at front of
work, k2, then k2 from cable needle
Cr3L Cross 3 left as follows: slip next 2 sts
on to cable needle and leave at front of
work, p1, then k2 from cable needle
Cr3R Cross 3 right as follows: slip next st on
to cable needle and leave at back of work,
k2, then p1 from cable needle
Tw2R Twist 2 right as follows: k into front of
2nd st on left-hand needle, then k the first st,
letting both sts drop off needle together
pick up 1 as follows: pick up the loop
between st just worked and next st on
left-hand needle and k this loop
Tw3R Twist 3 right as follows: k into front of
3rd st on left-hand needle, then k the first
2 sts tog, letting all 3 sts drop off left-hand
needle together

Front

Using 3¾mm needles cast on
74(78,82,86) sts.
Rib row 1 K2, * p2, k2, rep from * to end.
Rib row 2 P2, * k2, p2, rep from * to end.
Rep these 2 rows for 4cm/1½in, ending with
rib row 1.
Inc row [Rib 10(11,12,13), M1] twice, rib 9,
M1, rib 16, M1, rib 9,
[M1, rib 10(11,12,13) sts] twice.
80(84,88,92) sts.
Change to 4½mm needles.
Work in patt as follows:
Row 1 [K1, p1] 7(8,9,10) times, k8, p2,
[Cr3L, p10, Cr3R] twice, p2, k8, [p1, k1]
7(8,9,10) times.
Row 2 [K1, p1] 6(7,8,9) times, k2, p8, k3,
p2, k10, p2, k2, p2, k10, p2, k3, p8, k2,
[p1, k1] 6(7,8,9) times.
Row 3 [K1, p1] 7(8,9,10) times, C4B, C4F,
p3, Cr3L, p8, Cr3R, p2, Cr3L, p8, Cr3R, p3,
C4B, C4F, [p1, k1] 7(8,9,10) times.
Row 4 [K1, p1] 6(7,8,9) times, k2, p8, k4,
[p2, k8, p2, k4] twice, p8, k2, [p1, k1]
6(7,8,9) times.
Row 5 [K1, p1] 7(8,9,10) times, k8,
[p4, Cr3L, p6, Cr3R] twice, p4, k8, [p1, k1]
7(8,9,10) times.
Row 6 [K1, p1] 6(7,8,9) times, k2, p8, k5,
[p2, k6] 3 times, p2, k5, p8, k2, [p1, k1]
6(7,8,9) times.
Row 7 [K1, p1] 7(8,9,10) times, C4F, C4B,
p5, Cr3L, p4, Cr3R, p2, Tw2R, p2, Cr3L, p4,
Cr3R, p5, C4F, C4B, [p1, k1] 7(8,9,10)
times.
Row 8 [K1, p1] 6(7,8,9) times, k2, p8, k6,
p2, k4, p2, [k3, p2] twice, k4, p2, k6, p8, k2,
[p1, k1] 6(7,8,9) times.
Row 9 [K1, p1] 7(8,9,10) times, k8, p6,
Cr3L, p2, Cr3R, p3, k1, pick up 1, k1, p3,
Cr3L, p2, Cr3R, p6, k8, [p1, k1] 7(8,9,10)
times.

Row 10 [K1, p1] 6(7,8,9) times, k2, p8, k7,
p2, k2, p2, k4, p3, k4, p2, k2, p2, k7, p8, k2,
[p1, k1] 6(7,8,9) times.
Row 11 [K1, p1] 7(8,9,10) times, C4F, C4B,
p7, Cr3L, Cr3R, p4, Tw3R, p4, Cr3L, Cr3R,
p7, C4F, C4B, [p1, k1] 7(8,9,10) times.
Row 12 [K1, p1] 6(7,8,9) times, k2, p8, k8,
p4, k5, p2, k5, p4, k8, p8, k2, [p1, k1]
6(7,8,9) times.
Row 13 [K1, p1] 7(8,9,10) times, k8, p8,
C4B, p5, k1, pick up 1, k1, p5, C4B, p8, k8,
[p1, k1] 7(8,9,10) times.
Row 14 [K1, p1] 6(7,8,9) times, k2, p8, k8,
p4, k5, p3, k5, p4, k8, p8, k2, [p1, k1]
6(7,8,9) times.
Row 15 [K1, p1] 7(8,9,10) times, C4B, C4F,
p7, Cr3R, Cr3L, p4, Tw3R, p4, Cr3R, Cr3L,
p7, C4B, C4F, [p1, k1] 7(8,9,10) times.
Row 16 [K1, p1] 7(8,9,10) times, k2, p8, k7,
p2, k2, [p2, k4] twice, p2, k2, p2, k7, p8, k2,
[p1, k1] 6(7,8,9) times.
Rows 1 to 16 form the moss st and cable
side panels.

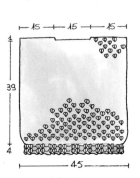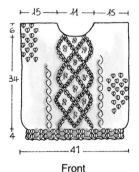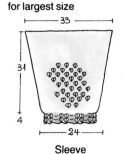

Measurements given in cm
for largest size

15	15	15
39		
45		

Back

15	11	15
6		
34		
41		

Front

33		
34		
24		

Sleeve

Keeping patt correct over side panels, cont
with centre panel as follows:
Row 17 Patt 22(24,26,28), p6, Cr3R, p2,
Cr3L, p8, Cr3R, p2, Cr3L, p6, patt to end.
Row 18 Patt 22(24,26,28), k6, p2, k4, p2, k8,
p2, k4, p2, k6, patt to end.
Row 19 Patt 22(24,26,28), p5, Cr3R, p4,
Cr3L, p6, Cr3R, p4, Cr3L, p5, patt to end.
Row 20 Patt 22(24,26,28), k5, [p2, k6]
3 times, p2, k5, patt to end.
Row 21 Patt 22(24,26,28), [p4, Cr3R, p2,
Tw2R, p2, Cr3L] twice, p4, patt to end.
Row 22 Patt 22(24,26,28), [k4, p2, k3, p2,
k3, p2] twice, k4, patt to end.
Row 23 Patt 22(24,26,28), p3, Cr3R, p3, k1,
pick up 1, k1, p3, Cr3L, p2, Cr3R, p3, k1,
pick up 1, k1, p3, Cr3L, p3, patt to end.
Row 24 Patt 22(24,26,28), k3, p2, k4, p3, k4,
p2, k2, p2, k4, p3, k4, p2, k3, patt to end.
Row 25 Patt 22(24,26,28), p2,
[Cr3R, p4, Tw3R, p4, Cr3L] twice, p2, patt to
end.
Row 26 Patt 22(24,26,28), k2, [p2, k5] twice,
p4, [k5, p2] twice, k2, patt to end.
Row 27 Patt 22(24,26,28), p2, k2, p5, k1,
pick up 1, k1, p5, C4F, p5, k1, pick up 1, k1,
p5, k2, p2, patt to end.
Row 28 Patt 22(24,26,28), k2, p2, k5, p3, k5,
p4, k5, p3, k5, p2, k2, patt to end.
Row 29 Patt 22(24,26,28), p2,
[Cr3L, p4, Tw3R, p4, Cr3R] twice, p2, patt to
end.
Row 30 Patt 22(24,26,28), k3, p2, [k4, p2]
twice, k2, [p2, k4] twice, p2, k3, patt to end.
Rows 3 to 30 form the centre panel patt.
Keeping patt panels correct, cont in patt
until front measures 32(34,36,38)cm/
12½(13¼,14¼,15)in, from cast-on edge,
ending with a WS row.
Shape neck
Next row Patt 36(38,40,42), turn and leave
rem sts on a spare needle.
Keeping patt correct, dec 1 st at neck edge
on every row until 26(27,28,30) sts rem.

Work 9(9,7,7) rows straight.   Cast off.
Return to sts on spare needle.
With RS facing, slip first 8 sts on to a holder,
join on yarn and patt to end.
36(38,40,42) sts.
Now complete to match first side of neck.

Back

Using 3¾mm needles cast on
74(78,82,86) sts.
Work 4cm/1½in rib as given for front,
ending with rib row 2 and decreasing 1 st at
centre of last row. 73(77,81,85) sts.
Change to 4½mm needles.
Work in patt as follows:
Row 1 K1, * p1, k1, rep from * to end.
This row forms the patt.
Cont in patt until back measures
36(38,40,43)cm/14¼(15,15¾,17)in from
cast-on edge, ending with a WS row.
Shape neck
Next row Patt 25(26,27,29), turn and leave
rem sts on a spare needle.

Keeping patt correct, dec 1 st at neck edge
on next row. 24(25,26,28) sts.
Work 2 rows straight.   Cast off.
Return to sts on spare needle.
With RS facing, slip first 23(25,27,27) sts on
to a holder, join on yarn and patt to end.
25(26,27,29) sts.
Now complete to match first side of neck.

Sleeves

Using 3¾mm needles cast on
38(42,42,46) sts. Work 4cm/1½in rib as
given for front, ending with rib row 2 and
decreasing 1 st at centre of last row.
37(41,41,45) sts.
Change to 4½mm needles.
Working in patt as given for back, inc and
work into patt 1 st each end of 3rd and every
foll 8th(10th,8th,10th) row until there are
55(57,61,63) sts.
Cont in patt until sleeve measures
29(31,33,35)cm/11½(12¼,13,13¾)in from
cast-on edge, ending with a WS row.
Cast off in patt.

Neckband

Join right shoulder seam.
With RS facing and using 3¾mm needles,
pick up and k21(22,23,25) sts evenly down
left side of front neck, k the front neck sts
from holder, pick up and k21(22,23,25) sts
up right side of front neck and 2 sts down
right side of back neck, then increasing 1 st
at centre k the back neck sts from holder,
78(82,86,90) sts.
Work 5cm/2in rib as given for front.
Cast off in rib.

To make up

Join left shoulder and neckband seam. Fold
sleeves in half lengthwise, then placing
folds to shoulder seams, sew into place.
Join side and sleeve seams. Fold neckband
in half to WS and slipstitch into position.

BASKET STITCH JUMPER

*

Basket stitch is a simple but effective pattern to use on a classic round necked jersey.

Materials

2(2,3)×100g balls of Water Wheel Concorde DK
A pair each of 3¼mm/No10 and 4mm/No8 knitting needles

Measurements

To fit chest 61(66,71)cm/24(26,28)in
Actual measurements
Chest 70(75,81)cm/27½(29½,32)in
Length to shoulders 38(43,46)cm/15(17,18)in
Sleeve seam 29(32,36)cm/11½(12½,14)in

Tension

22 sts and 30 rows to 10cm/4in measured over patt worked on 4mm needles

Front

★ Using 3¼mm needles cast on 70(74,78) sts.
Rib row 1 K2, * p2, k2, rep from * to end.
Rib row 2 P2, * k2, p2, rep from * to end.
Rep these 2 rows for 3cm/1¼in, ending with rib row 2.
Inc row K5(5,4), * M1, k10(8,7), rep from * to last 5(5,4) sts, M1, k to end. 77(83,89) sts.
Next row P to end. ★
Change to 4mm needles.
Work in basket st patt as follows:
Row 1 (RS) K4, * p3, k3, rep from * to last st, k1.
Row 2 P4, * k3, p3, rep from * to last st, p1.
Rows 3 to 6 Rep rows 1 and 2 twice.
Row 7 As row 1.
Row 8 P to end.
Row 9 P4, * k3, p3, rep from * to last st, p1.
Row 10 K4, * p3, k3, rep from * to last st, k1.
Rows 11 to 14 Rep rows 9 and 10 twice.
Row 15 As row 9.
Row 16 P to end.
These 16 rows form the patt.
Cont in patt until work measures approx 22(24,26)cm/8¾(9½,10¼)in from cast-on edge, ending with a WS row.
Shape armholes
Cast off 3 sts at beg of next 2 rows. 71(77,83) sts.
Cont in patt until work measures 10(12,13)cm/4(4¾,5)in from beg of armhole shaping, ending with a WS row.
Shape neck
Next row Patt 32(35,37) sts, turn and leave rem sts on a spare needle.
Cast off 4 sts at beg of next row, 3 sts at beg of foll alt row and 2 sts at beg of foll alt row. 23(26,28) sts.
Dec 1 st at neck edge on next and every foll alt row until 19(21,23) sts rem.
Work straight until front measures approx 16(19,20)cm/6¼(7½,8)in from beg of armhole shaping, ending with row 8(8,16).
Cast off in patt.
Return to sts on spare needle.
With RS facing, slip first 7(7,9) sts on to a holder, join on yarn and patt to end.
Next row Patt to end.
Now complete as given for first side of neck.

Back

Work as given for front from ★ to ★.
Change to 4mm needles.
Beg with row 9, work in patt as given for front until back measures approx 15(18,19)cm/5¾(7,7½)in from beg of armhole shaping, omitting front neck shaping and ending with row 12(12,14).
Shape neck
Next row Patt 23(25,27) sts, turn and leave rem sts on a spare needle.
Cast off 3 sts at beg of next row, then dec 1 st at end of foll row.
Patt 1 row. 19(21,23) sts.
Cast off in patt.
Return to sts on spare needle.
With RS facing, slip first 25(27,29) sts on to a holder, join on yarn and cast off 3 sts, then patt to end.
Next row Patt to end.
Next row Work 2 tog, patt to end. 19(21,23) sts.
Patt 1 row.
Cast off in patt.

Sleeves

Using 3¼mm needles, cast on 42(46,46) sts.
Work 2cm/¾in rib as given for front, ending with rib row 2.
Inc row K5, * M1, k8(6,6), rep from * to last 5 sts, M1, k5. 47(53,53) sts.
Next row P to end.
Change to 4mm needles.
Working in patt as given for front, inc and work into patt 1 st each end of 3rd and every foll 6th row until there are 71(83,87) sts.
Work straight until sleeve measures approx 29(32,36)cm/11½(12½,14)in from cast-on edge, ending with row 16(8,8).
Cast off in patt.

Neckband

Join right shoulder seam.
With RS facing and using 3¼mm needles, pick up and k16(20,22) sts down left side of front neck, k7(7,9) sts from front neck holder, pick up and k16(20,22) sts up right side of front neck and 4 sts down right side of back neck, k25(27,29) from back neck holder, then pick up and k4 sts up left side of back neck. 72(82,90) sts.
Work 2.5cm/1in rib as given for front.
Cast off in rib.

To make up

Join left shoulder and neckband seam. Fold sleeves in half lengthwise, then placing folds to shoulder seams, sew into place, joining row ends at top of sleeves to cast-off sts at underarm on back and front. Join side and sleeve seams.

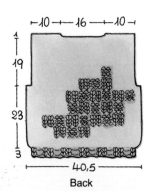

Back

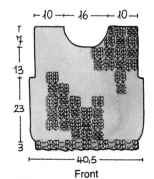

Front

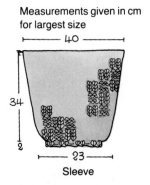

Measurements given in cm for largest size

Sleeve

SLIPOVER WITH A SIMPLE FAIR ISLE PATTERN

✳✳

These simple bands of Fair Isle are easy to knit. If you wish, a single contrast colour could be used.

Materials

3(4,5)×50g balls of Sunbeam 1st Edition (DK) in main colour A
1 ball of same in each of contrast colours B, C, and D
A pair each of 3¼mm/No10 and 4mm/No8 knitting needles

Measurements

To fit chest 61(66,71)cm/24(26,28)in

Actual measurements
Chest 73(76,80)cm/28¾(30,31¼)in
Length to shoulders 38(40,44)cm/15(15¾,17¼)in

Tension

22 sts and 28 rows to 10cm/4in measured over st st worked on 4mm needles

Back

★ Using 3¼mm needles and A, cast on 66(70,74) sts.
Work 4cm/1¼in k1, p1 rib, ending with a RS row.
Inc row Rib 7(3,5), * M1, rib 4(5,5) rep from * to last 7(2,4) sts, M1, rib to end. 80(84,88) sts.
Change to 4mm needles.
Using A and beginning with a k row, work 8(10,12) rows st st.
Join on and cut off colours as required. Carrying yarn not in use loosely across WS, work in patt as follows:
Row 1 K3(5,7)A, * 2B, 6A, rep from * to last 5(7,9) sts, 2B, 3(5,7)A.
Row 2 P3(5,7)A, * 2B, 6A, rep from * to last 5(7,9) sts, 2B, 3(5,7)A.
Row 3 K1(3,1)A, * 2B, 2A, rep from * to last 3(5,3) sts, 2B, 1(3,1)A.
Row 4 P1(3,1)A, * 2B, 2A, rep from * to last 3(5,3) sts, 2B, 1(3,1)A.
Row 5 K7(1,3)A, * 2B, 6A, rep from * to last 9(3,5) sts, 2B, 7(1,3)A.
Row 6 P7(1,3)A, * 2B, 6A, rep from * to last 9(3,5) sts, 2B, 7(1,3)A.
Using A only and beginning with a k row, work 6(8,10) rows st st.
Rep rows 1 to 6 once more.
Using A only and beginning with a k row, work 8(10,12) rows st st.
Now work in patt as follows:
Row 1 K4(2,4)A, * 1C, 3A, rep from * to last 4(2,4) sts, 1C, 3(1,3)A.
Row 2 With A, p to end.
Row 3 With A, k to end.
Row 4 P1(3,1))A, * 1C, 3A, rep from * to last 2(4,2) sts, 1C, 2(4,2)A.
Row 5 With A, k to end.
Row 6 With A, p to end.
These 6 rows form the patt.
Cont in patt until back measures approx 21(22,26)cm/8¼(8¾,10¼)in from cast-on edge, ending with row 4.

Shape armholes

Continuing in patt, cast off 2 sts at beg of next 2 rows, then dec 1 st each end of foll 1(2,3) alt rows. 74(76,78) sts. ★
Work straight in patt until back measures 26(28,32)cm/10¼(11,12½)in from cast-on edge, ending with a WS row.
Using A only and beginning with a k row, work 8(10,12) rows st st.
Now work in patt as follows:
Row 1 K3(2,1)A, * 1D, 1A, rep from * to last 5(2,3) sts, 1D, 4(1,2)A.
Row 2 P5(2,3)A, * 1D, 3A, rep from * to last 5(2,3) sts, 1D, 4(1,2)A.
Row 3 As row 1.
Rows 4 to 7 Using A only and beginning with a p row, work 4 rows st st.
Row 8 As row 2.
Rows 9 and 10 As rows 1 and 2.
Rows 11 to 14 Using A only and beginning with a k row work 4 rows st st.
Rows 15 to 17 As rows 1 to 3.
Using A only and begining with a p row, work in st st until back measures 38(40,44)cm/15(15¾,17¼)in from cast-on edge, ending with a WS row.

Shape shoulders

Cast off 23(24,25) sts at beg of next 2 rows.
Cut off yarn and leave rem 28 sts on a holder.

Front

Work as given for back from ★ to ★.

Shape neck

Next row Patt 36(37,38), turn and leave rem sts on a spare needle.
Next row Patt to end.
Next row Patt to last 3 sts, k2 tog, k1. 35(36,37) sts.
Patt 3 rows.
Next row Patt to last 3 sts, k2 tog, k1. 34(35,36) sts.
Patt 1 row.
★★ Continuing in patt as given for back, rep the last 6 rows until 23(24,25) sts rem.
Work straight until front measures same as back to shoulders, ending with a WS row.
Cast off. ★★
Return to sts on spare needle.
With RS facing, slip first 2 sts on to a safety-pin, join on yarn and patt to end. 36(37,38) sts.
Patt 1 row.
Next row K1, skpo, patt to end. 35(36,37) sts.
Patt 3 rows.
Next row K1, skpo, patt to end. 34(35,36) sts.
Patt 1 row.
Now complete as given for first side of neck from ★★ to ★★.

Neckband

Join right shoulder seam.
With RS facing, using 3¼mm needles and A, pick up and k40 sts down left side of front neck, k the 2 sts from safety-pin and

mark with a coloured thread, pick up and k40 sts up right side of front neck, then k back neck sts from holder. 110 sts.
Row 1 (WS) [K1, p1] to within 2 sts of marked sts, skpo, p2, k2 tog, [p1, k1] to end.
Row 2 Rib to within 2 sts of marked sts, skpo, k2, k2 tog, rib to end.
Rep these 2 rows twice more, then row 1 again.
Decreasing each side of marked sts as before, cast off in rib.

Armhole borders

Join left shoulder and neckband seam.
With RS facing, using 3¼mm needles and A, pick up and k84(88,92) sts evenly round armhole edge.
Work 5 rows k1, p1 rib.
Cast off in rib.

To make up

Join side and armhole border seams.

Measurements given in cm for second size

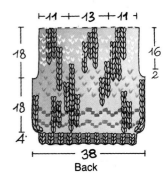

Back

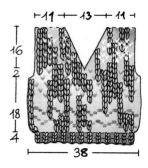

Front

BABIES' PATTERNS

A FIRST OUTFIT

✳

A jacket, trousers and bootees make up this charming outfit. The jacket has a single cable trim and the trousers and bootees are in garter stitch.

Materials

5×50g balls of Wendy Family Choice DK
A pair of 3¾mm/No9 knitting needles
Cable needle

Measurements

To fit chest 46(51)cm/18(20)in
Actual measurements
Jacket:
Chest 50(59)cm/19½(23)in
Length to shoulders 26cm/10in
Sleeve seam (with cuff turned
back) 15cm/6in
Trousers:
Waist to crutch 20cm/8in
Inner leg seam 20cm/8in

Tension

21 sts and 40 rows to 10cm/4in measured
over g st worked on 3¾mm needles
Cable panel (6 sts) measures 2cm/¾in

Special abbreviations

C6F Cable 6 front as follows: slip next 3 sts
on to cable needle and leave at front of
work, k3, then k3 from cable needle

Right front

Using 3¾mm needles cast on 30(34) sts.
Work in patt as follows:
Row 1 K to end.
Row 2 K6(8), p6, k8(10), p6, k4.
Rows 3 and 4 As rows 1 and 2.
Row 5 K4, C6F, k8(10), C6F, k6(8).
Row 6 As row 2.
These 6 rows form the patt.
Cont in patt until work measures 16.5cm/
6½in, ending with a RS row.
Shape for sleeve
Next row Cast on 36 sts, over these 36 sts
work k28, p6, k2, then patt to end. 66(70) sts.
Next row Patt to end.
Cont in patt as set until work measures
21.5cm/8½in, ending with a WS row.
Shape neck
Next row Cast off 10 sts, patt to end of row.
56(60) sts.
Cont in patt as now set until work measures
27cm/11in from cast-on edge, ending with a
WS row.
Cut off yarn and leave sts on a spare
needle.

Left front

Using 3¾mm needles cast on 30(34) sts.
Work in patt as follows:
Row 1 K to end.
Row 2 K4, p6, k8(10), p6, k6(8).
Rows 3 and 4 As rows 1 and 2.
Row 5 K6(8), C6F, k8(10), C6F, k4.
Row 6 As row 2.
These 6 rows form the patt.
Cont in patt until work measures 16.5cm/
6½in, ending with a WS row.
Shape for sleeve
Next row Cast on 36 sts, k these 36 sts, then
patt to end. 66(70) sts.
Next row Patt 30(34) sts, k2, p6, k to end.
Cont in patt as set until work measures
21.5cm/8½in, ending with a RS row.
Shape neck
Next row Cast off 10 sts, patt to end of row.
56(60) sts.
Cont in patt as now set until work measures
27cm/11in from cast-on edge, ending with a
WS row.

Join left and right front

Patt across 56(60) sts of left front, turn and
cast on 20(22) sts for back neck, then turn
work again and patt across 56(60) sts of
right front. 132(142) sts.
Next row K28, [p6, k8(10) sts] 5 times, p6,
k28.
Cont in patt as now set until sleeve edges
measure 19cm/7½in, ending with a WS row.
Shape sleeves
Cast off 36 sts at beg of next 2 rows. 60(70)
sts.
Cont in patt until back measures 16.5cm/
6½in from cast-off sts for sleeve, ending
with a WS row.
Cast off.

Trousers

Using 3¾mm needles cast on 53 sts.
Work 20cm/8in g st.
Shape crutch
Cast off 2 sts at beg of next 2 rows.
Dec 1 st each end of next and foll alt row.
45 sts.
Cont in g st until work measures 37cm/
14½in from cast-on edge, ending with a WS
row.
Eyelet hole row K4, * yf, k2 tog, k4, rep from
* to last 5 sts, yf, k2 tog, k3.
Cont in g st until work measures 40cm/16in
from cast-on edge, ending with a WS row.
Cast off.
Work second leg in the same way.

Bootees

Using 3¾mm needles cast on 29 sts.
Work 7cm/2¾in g st, ending with a WS row.
Shape foot
Next row K19, turn and leave rem sts on
spare needle.
Next row K9, turn and leave rem sts on
spare needle.
Work a further 6cm/2¼in g st on rem 9 sts,
ending with a WS row and dec 1 st each end
of last row. 7 sts.
Cut off yarn and leave sts on the needle.
With RS facing, join on yarn at inner end of
right-hand spare needle, then using the
right-hand needle holding 10 sts, pick up
and k12 sts up side edge of centre panel, k7

from needle at top of centre panel, pick up
and k12 sts down second side edge of
centre panel, then k10 sts from second
spare needle. 51 sts.
Work in g st for 2.5cm/1in, ending with a WS
row.
Shape sole
Next row K28, k2 tog, turn and leave rem 21
sts on left-hand needle.
Next row K6, k2 tog, turn and leave rem 20
sts on needle.
Next row K6, k2 tog tbl, turn and leave rem
20 sts on needle.
Next row K6, k2 tog, turn and leave rem 19
sts on needle.
Cont in this way, rep the last 2 rows until the
row 'k6, k2 tog, turn and leave rem 5 sts on
needle' has been worked.
Next row K6, k2 tog tbl, k rem 5 sts.
Cast off all 17 sts.

To make up

Join side and sleeve seams of jacket.
Joint front and back seam of trousers, then
join inner leg seam.
Make a twisted cord approx 85cm/34in
long, and thread through holes at waist.
Join seams at back of bootees.

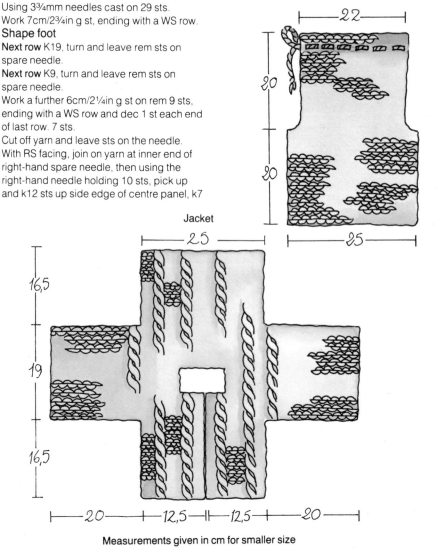

Trousers

Jacket

Measurements given in cm for smaller size

BOBBLE STITCH CARDIGAN AND MATCHING TROUSERS

**

An attractive textured stitch has been used as an all-over pattern on this matching outfit.

Materials

4(4,5) x 50g balls of Patons Fairytale 4 ply
A pair each of 2¾mm/No12 and 3¼mm/No10 knitting needles
5 buttons
Waist length of 2cm/¾in wide elastic

Measurements

To fit chest 48(51,54)cm/19(20,21)in
Actual measurements
Chest 59(62,65)cm/23(24½,25½)in
Length to shoulders 30(32,34)cm/12(12½,13½)in
Sleeve seam 15(17,20)cm/6(6¾,8)in
Outside leg length 34(36,38)cm/13½(14,15)in

Tension

25 sts and 32 rows to 10cm/4in measured over patt worked on 3¼mm needles

Special abbreviation

M3 Make 3 as follows: all into next st work [k1, yf and k1]

Cardigan back

Using 2¾mm needles cast on 75(79,83) sts.
Rib row 1 K1, * p1, k1, rep from * to end.
Rib row 2 P1, * k1, p1, rep from * to end.
Rep these 2 rows for 4(4,5)cm/1½(1½,2)in, ending with rib row 2.
Change to 3¼mm needles.
Work in patt as follows:
Row 1 P3, * M3, p3, rep from * to end.
Row 2 K3, * p3, k3, rep from * to end.
Row 3 P3, * k3, p3, rep from * to end.
Row 4 K3, * p3 tog, k3, rep from * to end.
Row 5 P to end.
Row 6 K to end.
Row 7 P1, * M3, p3, rep from * to last 2 sts, M3, p1.
Row 8 K1, * p3, k3, rep from * to last 4 sts, p3, k1.
Row 9 P1, * k3, p3, rep from * to last 4 sts, k3, p1.
Row 10 K1, * p3 tog, k3, rep from * to last 4 sts, p3 tog, k1.
Row 11 P to end.
Row 12 K to end.
These 12 rows form the patt.
Cont in patt until back measures approx 16.5(18,19)cm/6½(7,7½)in from cast-on edge, ending with row 4(10,10).
Shape armholes
Cast off 4 sts at beg of next 2 rows.
67(71,75) sts.
Keeping patt correct, work straight until back measures approx 30(32,34)cm/12(12½,13½)in from cast-on edge, ending with row 10(4,10).
Shape shoulders
Cast off 21(22,23) sts at beg of next 2 rows.
Cut off yarn and leave rem 25(27,29) sts on a holder.

Cardigan left front

★ Using 2¾mm needles cast on 35(37,39) sts.
Work 4(4,5)cm/1½(1½,2)in rib as given for back, ending with rib row 2.★
Change to 3¼mm needles.
Work in patt as follows:
Row 1 P3, * M3, p3, rep from * to last 4(6,4) sts, M3, p3, then for 2nd size only p2.
Row 2 K3(5,3), * p3, k3, rep from * to end.
Row 3 P3, * k3, p3, rep from * to last 6(8,6) sts, k3, p3, then for 2nd size only p2.
Row 4 K3(5,3), * p3 tog, k3, rep from * to end.
Row 5 P to end.
Row 6 K to end.
Row 7 P1, * M3, p3, rep from * to last 2(4,2) sts, M3, p1(3,1).
Row 8 K1(3,1), * p3, k3, rep from * to last 4 sts, p3, k1.
Row 9 P1, * k3, p3, rep from * to last 4 (6, 4) sts, k3, p1(3, 1).

Row 10 K1(3,1), * p3 tog, k3, rep from * to last 4 sts, p3 tog, k1.
Row 11 P to end.
Row 12 K to end.
These 12 rows form the patt.
Cont in patt until front measures same as back to armhole shaping, ending with row 4(10,10).
Shape armhole
Cast off 4 sts at beg of next row.
31(33,35) sts.
Work straight until front measures approx 24(26,29)cm/9½(10¼,11½)in from cast-on edge, ending with row 5(11,5).
Shape neck
Cast off 3(4,5) sts at beg of next row.
Dec 1 st at neck on next 4 rows, then dec 1 st at neck edge on every foll alt row until 21(22,23) sts rem.
Keeping patt correct, work straight until front measures same as back to shoulder, ending with row 10(4,10).
Cast off.

Cardigan right front

Work as given for left front from ★ to ★.
Change to 3¼mm needles.
Work in patt as follows:
Row 1 P3(5,3), * M3, p3, rep from * to end.
Row 2 K3, * p3, k3, rep from * to last 6(8,6) sts, p3, k3, then for 2nd size only k2.
Row 3 P3(5,3), * k3, p3, rep from * to end.
Row 4 K3, * p3 tog, k3, rep from * to last 6(8,6) sts, p3 tog, k3, then for 2nd size only k2.
Row 5 P to end.
Row 6 K to end.
Row 7 P1(3,1), * M3, p3, rep from * to last 2 sts, M3, p1.
Row 8 K1, * p3, k3, rep from * to last 4(6,4) sts, p3, k1(3,1).
Row 9 P1(3,1), * k3, p3, rep from * to last 4 sts, k3, p1.
Row 10 K1, * p3 tog, k3, rep from * to last 4(6,4) sts, p3 tog, k1(3,1).
Row 11 P to end.
Row 12 K to end.
These 12 rows form the patt.
Cont in patt until front measures same as back to armhole shaping, ending with row 5(11,11).
Shape armhole
Cast off 4 sts at beg of next row.
31(33,35) sts.
Keeping patt correct, work straight until front measures approx 24(26,29)cm/9½(10¼,11½)in from cast-on edge, ending with row 4(10,4).
Shape neck
Cast off 3(4,5) sts at beg of next row.
Dec 1 st at neck edge on next 4 rows, then dec 1 st at neck edge on every foll alt row until 21(22,23) sts rem.
Work straight until front measures same as back to shoulder, ending with row 10(4,10).
Cast off.

Cardigan sleeves

Using 2¾mm needles cast on 39(43,47) sts.
Work 4(4,5)cm/1½(1½,2)in rib as given for back, ending with rib row 2.
Change to 3¼mm needles.
Working in patt as given for back, inc and work into patt 1 st each end of 3rd and every foll alt row until there are 71(75,79) sts.
Work straight until sleeve measures approx 15(17,20)cm/6(6¾,8)in from cast-on edge, ending with row 12(6,12).
Cast off.

Neckband

Join shoulder seams.
With RS facing and using 2¾mm needles, pick up and k18(19,20) sts up right side of front neck, k25(27,29) sts from back neck holder, then pick up and k18(19,20) sts down left side of front neck. 61(65,69) sts.
Beg with rib row 2, work 8 rows rib as given

for back. Cast off in rib.

Buttonhole border

With RS facing and using 2¾mm needles, pick up and k77(83,89) sts up edge of right front to top of neckband.
Beg with rib row 2, work 3 rows rib as given for back.
Buttonhole row 1 Rib 4(5,4), * cast off 2, then rib 15(16,18), rep from * 3 times more, cast off 2, rib to end.
Buttonhole row 2 Rib to end, casting on 2 sts over those cast off in previous row.
Work 3 more rows rib.
Cast off in rib.

Button border

Work as given for buttonhole border, omitting buttonholes.

To make up

Fold sleeves in half lengthwise, then placing folds to shoulder seams, sew into place. Join side and sleeve seams. Sew on buttons.

Trousers first leg (back and front alike)

Using 2¾mm needles cast on 35(37,39) sts.
Work 4(4,5)cm/1½(1½,2)in rib as given for cardigan back, ending with rib row 2.
Change to 3¼mm needles.
Working in patt as given for cardigan right front, inc and work into patt 1 st at beg of 3rd and every foll 6th(8th,8th) row until there are 43(45,47) sts.
Work straight until leg measures 15(16,17)cm/6(6¼,6¾)in from cast-on edge, ending with row 10(4,4).
Shape crutch
Cast off 3 sts at beg of next row, then dec 1 st at same edge on next and foll alt row.
38(40,42) sts.
Patt 2 rows, so ending with row 4(10,10).
Cut off yarn and leave these sts on a holder.

Trousers second leg (back and front alike)

Using 2¾mm needles cast on 35(37,39) sts.
Work 4(4,5)cm/1½(1½,2)in rib as given for cardigan back, ending with rib row 2.
Change to 3¼mm needles.
Working in patt as given for cardigan left front, inc and work into patt 1 st at end of 3rd and every foll 6th(8th,8th) row until there are 43(45,47) sts.
Work straight until leg measures approx 15(16,17)cm/6(6¼,6¾)in from cast-on edge, ending with row 11(5,5).
Shape crutch
Cast off 3 sts at beg of next row, then dec 1 st at same edge on next and foll alt row.
38(40,42) sts.
Patt 1 row, so ending with row 4(10,10).
Join legs
Next row Patt across 37(39,41) sts of second leg, with RS of first leg facing p tog last st of 2nd leg with first st of first leg from holder, then patt across rem 37(39,41) sts of first leg. 75(79,83) sts.
Keeping patt correct, work straight until outer edge measures approx 34(36,38)cm/13½(14,15)in from cast-on edge, ending with row 12(6,12).
Change to 2¾mm needles.
Work 5cm/2in rib as given for cardigan back.
Cast off in rib.

To make up

Join first and second legs together at crutch shaping. Join inner and outer leg seams.
Fold waist ribbing in half to WS and slipstitch into place, leaving an opening for elastic.
Insert elastic and close opening.

SHORT SLEEVED TOP WITH COLLAR

**

A simple
loop
stitch is carried
over the contrast
colour band to add
interest to a
plain cotton top.

Materials

3(3,4)×50g balls of Twilleys Stalite
    Perlespun (4 ply cotton) in main colour A
1 ball of same in contrast colour B
A pair each of 2¼mm/No13 and 3¼mm/
    No10 knitting needles
A 3.00mm/No10 crochet hook
2 buttons

Measurements

To fit chest 53(58,63)cm/21(23,25)in
Actual measurements
Chest 58(63,68)cm/22¾(24¾,26¾)in
Length to shoulders 26.5(29,31.5)cm/
10½(11½,12½)in
Sleeve seam 7.5cm/3in

Tension

28 sts and 32 rows to 10cm/4in measured
over patt worked on 3¼mm needles

Special abbreviation

Cr4F Cross 4 front as follows: drop the
elongated loop off left-hand needle and
leave at front of work, k3, then being careful
not to twist the loop slip it back on to
left-hand needle and knit it in the usual way

Front

★ Using 2¼mm needles and A, cast on
82(90,94)sts.
Work 3cm/1½in k1, p1 rib.
Change to 3¼mm needles.
Join on and cut off colours as required.
Work in patt as follows:
Row 1 (RS) With A, k to end.
Row 2 With A, p to end.
Rows 3 to 8 Rep rows 1 and 2 three times.
Row 9 With A, k1, * k next st winding yarn
3 times round needle, k3, rep from * to last 5
sts, k next st winding yarn 3 times round
needle, k4.
Row 10 With A, p4, * dropping extra loops
off needle sl 1 pw, p3, rep from * to last
2 sts, sl 1 pw, p1.
Row 11 With B, k1, * sl 1 pw, k3, rep from
* to last 5 sts, sl 1 pw, k4.
Row 12 With B, p4, * sl 1 pw, p3, rep from
* to last 2 sts, sl 1 pw, p1.
Row 13 With A, k1, * Cr4F, rep from * to
last st, k1.
Row 14 With A, p to end.
These 14 rows form the patt. ★
Cont in patt until front measures approx
12(15,17)cm/4¾(6,6¾)in from cast-on
edge, ending with row 2(10,4).
Divide for opening
Next row Patt 38(42,44), turn and leave
rem sts on a spare needle.
Patt 13(9,7) rows. so ending with a WS row.
Shape armhole
Cast off in patt 3(4,5) sts at beg of next row.
Patt 1 row.
Keeping patt correct, dec 1 st at armhole
edge on next and every foll alt row until
30(33,34) sts rem, ending with a RS row.
2nd and 3rd sizes only
Patt 4(6) rows, ending with a RS row.
All sizes
Cont in patt as follows:
Shape neck
Cast off in patt 6(7,8) sts at beg of next row.
Dec 1 st at neck edge on next and every foll
alt row until 18(20,20)sts rem.

Patt 9 rows.
Cast off.
Return to sts on spare nedle.
With RS facing, join on A(B,A) and cast off
first 6 sts, then patt to end of row.
38(42,44) sts.
Patt 14(10,8) rows, so ending with a RS row.
Shape armhole
Cast off in patt 3(4,5) sts at beg of next row.
Dec 1 st at armhole edge on next and every
foll alt row until 30(33,34) sts rem, ending
with a RS row.
Patt 1(5,7) rows, so ending at inner edge.
Shape neck
Cast off in patt 6(7,8) sts at beg of next row.
Dec 1 st at neck edge on every row until
18(20,20) sts rem.
Patt 9 rows.
Cast off.

Back

Work as given for front from ★ to★.
Cont in patt until back measures same as
front up to beg of armhole shaping, ending
with a WS row.
Shape armholes
Cast off in patt 3(4,5) sts at beg of next
2 rows.
Dec 1 st each end of next and every foll alt
row until 66(72,74) sts rem.
Work straight until back measures same as
front to cast-off edge, ending with a WS row.
Shape shoulders
Cast off in patt 18(20,20) sts at beg of next
2 rows.
Cut off yarn and leave rem 30(32,34) sts on
a holder.

Sleeves

Using 2¼mm needles and A, cast on
58(62,66) sts.
Work 2.5cm/1in k1, p1 rib.
Change to 3¼mm needles.
Work in patt as given for front until sleeve
measures approx 7.5cm/3in from cast-on
edge, ending with a WS row.
Shape top
Cast off 3(4,5) sts at beg of next 2 rows.
Dec 1 st each end of next and every foll alt
row until 42(44,46) sts rem, ending with a
WS row.
Cast off 6 sts at beg of next 4 rows.
Cast off.

Collar

Join shoulder seams.
With RS facing, using 2¼mm needles
and A, pick up and k29(30,31) sts up right
side of front neck, increasing 1 st each end
k the back neck sts from holder, then pick
up and k29(30,31) sts down left side of front
neck. 90(94,98) sts.
K 20 rows.
Cast off loosely.

Button border

Using 2¼mm needles and B, cast on 6 sts.
K 1 row and mark the ridge with a coloured
thread to denote right side.
Cont in g st until border, slightly stretched,
fits up opening to beg of neck shaping,
ending with a RS row.
Cast off.
Sew on the border.
Mark 2 button positions on the border. The
first one 3cm/1¼in from base of opening
and the second one 2cm/¾in below cast-off
edge.

Buttonhole border

Work as given for button border making
buttonholes to correspond with markers as
follows:
Buttonhole row (RS) K2, k2 tog, yf, k2.

Collar edging

With right side facing, using 3.00mm
crochet hook and B, work 12 dc up first side
of collar, 1 dc into corner, 55 dc along edge
of collar, 1 dc into corner, then 12 dc down
second side, turn.

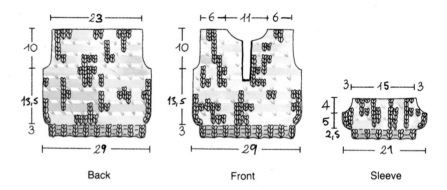

| Back | Front | Sleeve |

Next row Work 1 dc into first dc, * 4 ch, miss
3 dc, 1 dc into next dc, rep from * to end.
Fasten off.

To make up

Set in the sleeves, then join side and sleeve
seams. Sew on the buttonhole border. Sew
on buttons.

PRACTICAL DUNGAREES

*

These
enchanting
dungarees have
a simple eyelet
hole pattern.
The design
allows plenty of
room for a nappy
and the straps
are adjustable.

Materials

5×50g balls of Emu Cotton DK
A pair each of 3mm/No11 and 3¾mm/No9 knitting needles
2 buttons

Measurements

To fit chest 51cm/20in
Actual measurements
Chest 64cm/25in
Length 49cm/19¼in
Leg length to crutch 23cm/9in

Tension

21 sts and 27 rows to 10cm/4in measured over patt worked on 3¾mm needles

Back of right leg

★ Using 3mm needles cast on 30 sts.
Work 3cm/1¼in k1, p1 rib, ending with a RS row.
Inc row P5, * M1, p3, rep from * to last 4 sts, M1, p4. 38 sts.
Change to 3¾mm needles.
Work in patt as follows:
Row 1 K.
Row 2 P.
Rows 3 and 4 As rows 1 and 2.
Row 5 K8, * yf, k2 tog, k8, rep from * to end.
Row 6 P.
Rows 7 to 12 Rep rows 1 and 2 three times.
Row 13 K2, * skpo, yf, k8, rep from * to last 6 sts, skpo, yf, k4.
Row 14 As row 6.
Rows 15 and 16 As rows 1 and 2.
These 16 rows form the patt. ★
Rep rows 1 to 16 twice, then rows 1 to 5 again.
Shape crutch
Next row Cast off 2 sts, p to end.
K 1 row.
Dec 1 st at beg of next and foll alt row. 34 sts.
K 1 row.
Cut off yarn and leave sts on a holder.

Back of left leg

Work as given for back of right leg from ★ to ★.
Rep rows 1 to 16 twice, then rows 1 to 6 again.
Shape crutch
Next row Cast off 2 sts, k to end.
P 1 row.
Dec 1 st at beg of next and foll alt rows. 34 sts.
Join legs
Next row P across sts of left leg, then p across sts of right leg from holder. 68 sts.
Next row K2, [skpo, yf, k8] twice, skpo, yf, k18, skpo, [yf, k8, skpo] twice, yf, k4.
Cont in patt until work measures 46cm/18in from cast-on edge, ending with a WS row.
Dec row K3, * k2 tog, rep from * to last 3 sts, k3. 37 sts.
Change to 3mm needles.
Top border
Rib row 1 K1, * p1, k1, rep from * to end.
Rib row 2 K2, * p1, k1, rep from * to last st, k1.

Rep these 2 rows 4 times more.
Cast off loosely in rib.

Front

Work as given for back, placing 2 buttonholes on 5th row of top border as follows:
Rib row 5 Rib 6, yf, k2 tog, rib to last 8 sts, skpo, yf, rib to end.
Work 5 more rows in rib.
Cast off loosely in rib.

Shoulder straps (both alike)

Using 3mm needles cast on 19 sts.
Rib row 1 K2, * p1, k1, rep from * to last st, k1.
Rib row 2 K1, * p1, k1, rep from * to end.
Rep these 2 rows until strap measures 16cm/6¼in.
Cast off in rib.

To make up

Join seams at crutch shaping.
Join side leg seams, leaving the top 10cm/4in open for armholes. Join inner leg seam. Sew one shoulder strap at each end of the top border on the back, then sew on a button to the other end of each strap, adjusting position to fit baby.

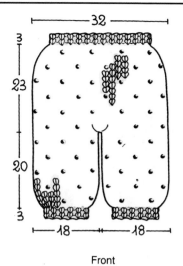

Front

Measurements given in cm

Back

KNIT TIP

Neat buttonholes

To strengthen the edges of the buttonholes, embroider them with buttonhole stitch. Use the yarn the garment is knitted in, if it is not too thick, or a cotton thread of the same colour. Fan out the stitches at each end of the slit as shown above.

CARDIGAN WITH BONNET AND BOOTEES TO MATCH

**

The back and fronts are knitted as one piece, dividing at the armholes. A bonnet and bootees make up the set.

Materials
Cardigan
3(4)×50g balls of Emu Baby (DK)
5 buttons
Oddments of embroidery wool
Bonnet
1×50g ball of Emu Baby
50cm/19¾in of 2.5cm/1in wide ribbon
Bootees
1×50g ball of Emu Baby
50cm/19¾in of narrow ribbon
A pair each of 3¼mm/No10 and 4mm/No8 knitting needles

Measurements
To fit chest 51(53.5)cm/20(21)in
Actual measurements
Chest 54.5(57)cm/21½(22½)in
Length to shoulders 24(26.5)cm/9½(10½)in
Sleeve seam 18(19.5)cm/7(7¾)in

Tension
22 sts and 30 rows to l0cm/4in measured over st st worked on 4mm needles

Special abbreviation
loop 3 as follows: insert right-hand needle under the 3 horizontal loops at front of work, pick them up then knit these 3 loops tog with next st on left-hand needle

Back and fronts
Using 3¼mm needles cast on 113(121) sts.
Rib row 1 K1, * p1, k1, rep from * to end.
Rib row 2 [K1, p1] twice, k2, * k1, k1, rep from * to last 7 sts, p1, k2, [p1, k1] twice.
Buttonhole row (RS) K1, p1, yrn, p2 tog, k1, * p1, k1, rep from * to end.
Beg with rib row 2, cont in rib with moss st borders until work measures 4cm/1½in from cast-on edge, ending with rib row 2.
Next row Rib to last 5 sts, turn and leave rem 5 sts on a safety-pin for button border. 108(116) sts.
Inc row Rib 1(3), [M1, rib 2(3) sts] 3(2) times, * M1, rib 9, M1, rib 4, M1, rib 5, [M1, rib 4(5) sts] twice *, M1, rib 9, M1, rib 5, M1, rib 4, [M1, rib 5] twice, rep from * to * once, M1, rib 9, [M1, rib 2(3) sts] 3(2) times, M1, rib 1(3), turn and leave rem 5 sts on a safety-pin for buttonhole border. 126(132) sts.
Change to 4mm needles.
Row 1 (RS) K12(13), * p1, k5, p1, k24(26), p1, k5, p1 *, k26, rep from * to * once, k12(13).
Row 2 and every foll alt row P12(13), * k1, p5, k1, p24(26), k1, p5, k1 *, p26, rep from * to * once, p12(13).
Row 3 K12(13), * p1, k1, ytf, sl 3 pw, ytb, k1, p1, k24(26), p1, k1, ytf, sl 3 pw, ytb, k1, p1 *, k26, rep from * to * once, k12(13).
Row 5 As row 3.
Row 7 As row 3.
Row 9 K12(13), * p1, k2, loop 3, k2, p1, k24(26), p1, k2, loop 3, k2, p1 *, k26, rep from * to * once, k12(13).
Row 10 As row 2.
These 10 rows form the slip stitch panels with st st.
Cont in patt until body measures approx 14.5(16.5)cm/5¾(6½)in from cast-on edge, ending with row 2(8).
Divide for right front
Next row K2 tog, patt 25(27), turn and leave rem sts on a spare needle.
Keeping patt correct and decreasing 1 st at inner edge on every row, dec 1 st at front edge on every foll alt row until 19(21) sts rem.
Keeping armhole edge straight, cont to dec at front edge only until 15(16) sts rem.
Patt 3 rows.
Dec 1 st at front edge on next and foll 4th row. 13(14) sts.
Patt 7 rows, so ending with a WS row.
Cast off in patt.
Return to sts on spare needle.
With RS facing, join on yarn and cast off first 8 sts, then patt until there are 56(58) sts on right-hand needle, turn and leave rem sts on a spare needle.
Keeping patt correct, dec 1 st each end of

next 5 rows. 46(48) sts.
Work straight until back measures same as right front to shoulder, ending with a WS row.
Cast off in patt.
Return to sts on spare needle.
With RS facing, join on yarn and cast off first 8 sts, then patt to last 2 sts, k2 tog. 26(28) sts.
Now complete to match right front.

Sleeves
Using 3¼mm needles cast on 33 sts.
Rib row 1 P1, * k1, p1, rep from * to end.
Rib row 2 K1, * p1, k1, rep from * to end.
Rep these 2 rows for 4cm/1½in, ending with rib row 1.
Inc row Rib 4, M1, rib 1, M1, rib 3, [M1, rib 1] 1(2) times, M1, rib 3(2), [M1, rib 1, M1, rib 3] twice, M1, rib 1, M1, rib 3(2), [M1, rib 1] 1(2) times, M1, rib 3, M1, rib 1, M1, rib 4. 47(49) sts.
Change to 4mm needles.
Work in patt as follows:
Row 1 (RS) K2, p1, k5, p1, * k11(12), p1, k5, p1 *, rep from * to * once more, k2.
Row 2 P2, k1, p5, k1, * p11(12), k1, p5, k1 *, rep from * to * once more, p2.
Row 3 Inc in first st, k1, p1, k1, ytf, sl 3 pw, ytb, k1, p1, * k11(12), p1, k1, ytf, sl 3 pw, ytb, k1, p1 *, rep from * to * once more, k1, inc in last st. 49(51) sts.
These 3 rows set the position of the slip stitch patt panel.
Continuing in patt, inc and work into st st side panels 1 st each end of every foll 8th(10th) row until there are 53(55) sts.
Work straight until sleeve measures approx 18(19.5)cm/7(7¾)in from cast-on edge, ending with row 2(6) of slip stitch panel.
Shape top
Cast off in patt 4 sts at beg of next 2 rows.
Keeping patt correct, dec 1 st each end of every row to 19(17) sts, then each end of every foll alt row until 9 sts rem.
Cast off in patt.

Button border
Join shoulder seams.
With RS facing and using 3¼mm needles, work across sts from safety-pin as follows: [k1, p1] twice, k1. 5 sts.
Cont in moss st until border, slightly stretched, fits up front and round to centre back neck.
Cast off in patt.
Sew on the border.
Mark 5 button positions on this border. The first one to correspond with buttonhole, the top one just below beg of front edge shaping and the others evenly spaced between.

Buttonhole border
With WS facing and using 3¼mm needles, work across sts from safety-pin as follows: [k1, p1] twice, k1. 5 sts.
Continuing in moss st, complete to match button border working buttonholes to correspond with markers as follows:
Buttonhole row (RS) K1, p1, yrn, p2 tog, k1.

To make up
Sew in sleeves, then join sleeve seams.
Sew on the buttonhole border, joining seam at centre back neck. Sew on the buttons.
Using the embroidery wools, work an initial or motif on right front.

Bonnet
Using 3¼mm needles cast on 69 sts.
Row 1 K1, * p1, k1, rep from * to end.
This row forms the moss st.
Cont in moss st until work measures 2cm/¾in from cast-on edge, increasing 1 st at centre of last row. 70 sts.
Change to 4mm needles.
Work in patt as follows:
Row 1 (RS) K3, * p1, k5, p1, k12, rep from * to last 10 sts, p1, k5, p1, k3.
Row 2 and every foll alt row P3, * k1, p5, k1, p12, rep from * to last 10 sts, k1, p5, k1, p3.
Row 3 K3, * p1, k1, ytf, sl 3 pw, ytb, k1, p1,

k12, rep from * to last 10 sts, p1, k1, ytf, sl 3 pw, ytb, k1, p1, k3.
Row 5 As row 3.
Row 7 As row 3.
Row 9 K3, * p1, k2, loop 3, k2, p1, k12, rep from * to last 10 sts, p1, k2, loop 3, k2, p1, k3.
Row 10 As row 2.
These 10 rows form the patt.
Cont in patt until bonnet measures approx 12cm/4¾in from cast-on edge, ending with row 10.
Shape for centre back panel
Cast off 22 sts at beg of next 2 rows. 26 sts.
Work in patt as follows:
Row 1 * K1, p1, rep from * to end.
This row forms the patt.
Keeping patt correct, dec 1 st each end of next and every foll 4th row until 12 sts rem.
Work straight until centre back panel measures 9cm/3½in from beg of shaping, ending with a WS row.
Cast off in patt.

To make up
Join cast-off edges of side panels to row ends of centre back panel. Cut ribbon in half and sew to row ends of moss st border.

Bootees
Using 3¼mm needles cast on 31 sts.
Row 1 Inc in first st, k14, yf, k1, yf, k14, inc in last st. 35 sts.
Row 2 and every foll alt row K to end.
Row 3 Inc in first st, k15, yf, k3, yf, k15, inc in last st. 39 sts.
Row 5 Inc in first st, k16, yf, k5, yf, k16, inc in last st. 43 sts.
Row 7 Inc in first st, k17, yf, k7, yf, k17, inc in first st. 47 sts.
Row 9 Inc in first st, k18, yf, k9, yf, k18, inc in last st. 51 sts.
Row 10 K to end.
Next row K1, * p1, k1, rep from * to end.
Rep the last row 7 times more.
Next row K21 and leave these 21 sts on a spare needle with the point at inner edge, k9, then turn and leave rem 21 sts on a spare needle with the point at inner edge.
Next row P8, p tog last st on left-hand needle with first st from spare needle and turn.
Next row K to last st, k tog last st on left-hand needle with first st from spare needle and turn.
Cont in this way, working 1 st from spare needle with the last st on left-hand needle on every row until 11 sts rem on each spare needle, ending with a RS row.
Next row With RS still facing and using the 4mm needles, k11 from second spare needle. 20 sts.
Next row P20, then p11 from first spare needle. 31 sts.
Next row K to end.
Next row P to end.
Eyelet hole row K2, * yf, k2 tog, rep from * to last st, k1.
Next row P to end.
Change to 4mm needles.
Rib row 1 K1, * p1, k1, rep from * to end.
Rib row 2 P1, * k1, p1, rep from * to end.
Rep these 2 rows 10 times more.
Next row Pl, * kl, pl, rep from * to end.
Rep the last row 3 times more.
Cast off in patt.

To make up
Join seam for sole, back of heel and ankle.
Cut ribbon in half and thread half through eyelets of each bootee, leaving ends free to tie at front.

JERSEY AND SHORTS SET

**

The
lace
triangles
e worked up the
sides of the legs
as well as the
body and sleeves
of this outfit.

Materials
4(5)×50g balls of Water Wheel Comfy Baby DK in main colour A
1 ball of same in contrast colour B
A pair each of 3¼mm/No10 and 4mm/No8 knitting needles
5 buttons
Shirring elastic

Measurements
To fit chest 48(53)cm/19(21)in
Actual measurements
Chest 53.5(59)cm/21(23¼)in
Length to shoulders 25.5(26.5)cm/10(10½)in
Sleeve seam 10(11)cm/4(4½)in
Length of shorts 33(35)cm/13¼(14)in

Tension
22 sts and 33 rows to 10cm/4in measured over patt worked on 4mm needles

Jersey
Back and front
(Knitted in 1 piece to armholes)
Using 4mm needles and A, cast on 118(130) sts.
K 4 rows.
Buttonhole row K to last 4 sts, k2 tog, yf, k2.
K 3(5) more rows.
P 1 row.
Work in patt as follows:
Row 1 (RS) K9(15), * yfon, skpo, k9, rep from * to last 10(16) sts, yfon, skpo, k8(14).
Row 2 and every foll alt row K4, p to last 4 sts, k4.
Row 3 K8(14), * [yfon, skpo] twice, k7, rep from * to last 11(17) sts, [yfon, skpo] twice, k7(13).
Row 5 K7(13), * [yfon, skpo] 3 times, k5, rep from * to last 12(18) sts, [yfon, skpo] 3 times, k6(12).
Row 7 K6(12), * [yfon, skpo] 4 times, k3, rep from * to last 13(19) sts, [yfon, skpo] 4 times, k5(11).
Row 9 K to end.
Row 11 K15(10), * yfon, skpo, k9, rep from * to last 15(10) sts, yfon, skpo, k13(8).
Row 13 K14(9), * [yfon, skpo] twice, k7, rep from * to last 16(11) sts, [yfon, skpo] twice, k12(7).
Row 15 K2, yf, k2 tog, k9(4), * [yfon, skpo] 3 times, k5, rep from * to last 17(12) sts, [yfon, skpo] 3 times, k11(6).
Row 17 K12(7), * [yfon, skpo] 4 times, k3, rep from * to last 18(13) sts, [yfon, skpo] 4 times, k10(5).
Row 19 K to end.
Row 20 As row 2.
These 20 rows form the patt.
Work rows 1 to 18 once more.
Shape armholes
Next row K28(31) sts, turn and leave rem sts on a spare needle.
Keeping patt correct, dec 1 st at beg of next and every foll alt row until 23(26) sts rem.
Work 2 rows straight, so ending with row 10.
Cut off yarn and leave these sts on a holder.
Return to spare needle.
With RS facing, join on yarn and cast off first st, k to last 29(32) sts, turn and leave rem sts on a spare needle. 60(66) sts.
Keeping patt correct, dec 1 st each end of next and every foll alt row until 50(56) sts rem.
Work 2 rows straight, so ending with row 10.
Cut off yarn and leave these sts on a holder.
Return to sts on spare needle.
With RS facing, join on yarn and cast off first st, k to end. 28(31) sts.
Keeping patt correct, dec 1 st at end of next and every foll alt row until 23(26) sts rem.
Work 2 rows straight, so ending with row 10.
Cut off yarn and leave these sts on a holder.

Sleeves
Using 4mm needles and A, cast on 30 sts.
K 6(8) rows.
Inc row K2, * M1, k2, rep from * to end. 44 sts.
K 1 row and p 1 row.
Work in patt as follows:
Row 1 K5, * yfon, skpo, k9, rep from * to last 6 sts, yfon, skpo, k4.
Row 2 and every foll alt row P to end.

Row 3 K4, * [yfon, skpo] twice, k7, rep from * to last 7 sts, [yfon, skpo] twice, k3.
Row 5 K3, * [yfon, skpo] 3 times, k5, rep from * to last 8 sts, [yfon, skpo] 3 times, k2.
Row 7 K2, * [yfon, skpo] 4 times, k3, rep from * to last 9 sts, [yfon, skpo] 4 times, k1.
Row 9 K to end.
Row 11 K11, * yfon, skpo, k9, rep from * to end.
Row 13 K10, * [yfon, skpo] twice, k7, rep from * to last 12 sts, [yfon, skpo] twice, k8.
Row 15 K9, * [yfon, skpo] 3 times, k5, rep from * to last 13 sts, [yfon, skpo] 3 times, k7.
Row 17 K8, * [yfon, skpo] 4 times, k3, rep from * to last 14 sts, [yfon, skpo] 4 times, k6.
Row 19 K to end.
Row 20 As row 2.
These 20 rows form the patt.
Rep rows 1 to 8 once more.
Shape top
Continuing in patt, dec 1 st each end of next and every foll alt row until 34 sts rem.
Work 2 rows straight, so ending with row 20.
Cut off yarn and leave rem sts on a holder.

Yoke
With RS facing, using 3¼mm needles and A, work across sts from left back holder as follows: k2, yf, k2 tog, k19(22), k the 34 sts from left sleeve holder, increasing 3(1) sts evenly k across sts from front holder, then k34 sts from right sleeve holder and 23(26) from right back holder. 167(177) sts.
Next row K5, * p1, k1, rep from * to last 4 sts, k4.
2nd size only
Dec row K4, [p1, k1] twice, p3 tog, [k1, p1] 18 times, k1, rep from * to last 9 sts, p3 tog, k1, p1, k4. 167 sts.
Next row K4, rib to last 4 sts, k4.
Both sizes
Joining on and cutting off colours as required, cont in striped rib as follows:
Next row With B, k4, rib to last 4 sts, k4.
Rep last row once more.
Dec row With A, k4, [p1, k1] 3 times, * p3 tog, [k1, p1] 7 times, k1, rep from * to last 13 sts, p3 tog, [k1, p1] 3 times, k4. 149 sts.
Next row With A, k4, rib to last 4 sts, k4.
Using B instead of A, rep last row twice more.
Dec row With A, k4, p1, k1, p1, * k3 tog, [p1, k1] 4 times, p1, rep from * to last 10 sts, k3 tog, p1, k1, p1, k4. 125 sts.
Next row With A, k4, rib to last 4 sts, k4.
Using B instead of A, rep last row twice more.
Dec row With A, k4, p1, k1, * p3 tog, [k1, p1] 3 times, k1, rep from * to last 9 sts, p3 tog, k1, p1, k4. 101 sts.
Next row With A, k4, rib to last 4 sts, k4.
Using B instead of A, rep last row twice more.
Buttonhole and dec row With A, k2, yf, * k2 tog, rep from * to last st, k1. 53 sts.
Using A, k 4 rows.
Cast off.

To make up
Join raglan seams. Join sleeve seams. Sew on buttons.

Shorts back
Left back leg
★ Using 3¼mm needles and A, cast on 29(33) sts.
Rib row 1 With A, k1, * p1, k1, rep from * to end.
Rib row 2 With B, p1, * k1, p1, rep from * to end.
Rib row 3 With B, k1, * p1, k1, rep from * to end.
Rib row 4 With A, p1, * k1, p1, rep from * to end.
Rep last 4 rows once more. ★
Change to 4mm needles.
Using A only, work 10 rows st st.
Cut off yarn and leave these sts on a spare needle.
Right back leg
Work as given for left back leg, but do not cut off the yarn.
Join legs and shape gusset
With RS facing k across sts of right leg, turn

and cast on 13 sts, then turn and k across sts of left leg. 71(79) sts.
Next row P to end.
Next row K28(32), skpo, k11, k2 tog, k to end.
Next row P to end.
Next row K28(32), skpo, k9, k2 tog, k to end.
★★ Cont decreasing 1 st each side of gusset on every alt row until 59(67) sts rem, ending with a WS row.
Next row K28(32), sl 1, k2 tog, psso, k to end. 57(65) sts.
Work straight until back measures 27(29)cm/10½(11½)in from cast-on edge, ending with a RS row.
Change to 3¼mm needles.
Rep the 4 rib rows as given for left back leg 3 times.
Cast off in rib. ★★

Shorts front
Right front leg
Work as given for left back leg from ★ to ★.
Change to 4mm needles.
Using A only, work 10 rows patt as follows:
Row 1 K to end.
Row 2 and every foll alt row P to end.
Row 3 K22(26), yfon, skpo, k to end.
Row 5 K21(25), [yfon, skpo] twice, k to end.
Row 7 K20(24), [yfon, skpo] 3 times, k to end.
Row 9 K19(23), [yfon, skpo] 4 times, k to end.
Row 10 As row 2.
Cut off yarn and leave these sts on a spare needle.
Left front leg
Work as given for left back leg from ★ to ★.
Change to 4mm needles.
Using A only, work 10 rows patt as follows:
Row 1 K to end.
Row 2 and every foll alt row P to end.
Row 3 K5, yfon, skpo, k to end.
Row 5 K4, [yfon, skpo] twice, k to end.
Row 7 K3, [yfon, skpo] 3 times, k to end.
Row 9 K2, [yfon, skpo] 4 times, k to end.
Row 10 As row 2.
Join legs and shape gusset
Next row K across sts of left leg, turn and cast on 13 sts, then turn and k across sts of right leg. 71(79) sts.
Next row P to end.
Next row K5, yfon, skpo, k21(25), skpo, k11, k2 tog, k to last 7 sts, yfon, skpo, k5.
Next row P to end.
Next row K4, [yfon, skpo] twice, k20(24), skpo, k9, k2 tog, k to last 8 sts, [yfon, skpo] twice, k4.
Keeping patt correct, complete to match back from ★★ to ★★.

To make up
Join side seams. Join inner leg and gusset seams. Thread 2 rows of shirring elastic through knit sts of ribbed waistband.

LACY EDGED DRESS WITH A FLOWER BORDER

**

The sleeves and lower edge of this dress are knitted in a diagonal lace pattern and the yoke is in a seeded stitch. The flower motifs can be omitted if you prefer.

Materials

2(2)×50g balls of Patons Fairytale 4 ply in main colour A

Oddments of 4 ply yarn in contrast colours B, C and D for embroidery

A pair each of 2¾mm/No12 and 3¼mm/No10 knitting needles

3 buttons

Measurements

To fit chest 48(53.5)cm/19(21)in

Actual measurements

Skirt width 76(84)cm/30(33)in

Length to shoulders 33(34)cm/13(13½)in

Sleeve seam 6cm/2½in

Tension

28 sts and 36 rows to 10cm/4in measured over st st worked on 3¼mm needles

Special abbreviation

K1B Knit one below as follows: insert right-hand needle into st below next st on left-hand needle and knit in the usual way slipping st above off needle

Front

Using 2¾mm needles cast on 107(117) sts.

K 7 rows.

Change to 3¼mm needles.

Work in diagonal lace patt as follows:

Row 1 (RS) P1, * yon, skpo, p3, rep from * to last 6 sts, yon, skpo, p4.

Row 2 K4, * p2, k3, rep from * to last 3 sts, p2, k1.

Row 3 P2, * yon, skpo, p3, rep from * to end.

Row 4 * K3, p2, rep from * to last 2 sts, k2.

Row 5 * P3, yon, skpo, rep from * to last 2 sts, p2.

Row 6 K2, * p2, k3, rep from * to end.

Row 7 P4, * yon, skpo, p3, rep from * to last 3 sts, yon, skpo, p1.

Row 8 K1, * p2, k3, rep from * to last 6 sts, p2, k4.

Row 9 P5, * yon, skpo, p3, rep from * to last 7 sts, yon, skpo, p5.

Row 10 K5, * p2, k3, rep from * to last 7 sts, p2, k5.

These 10 rows form the patt.

Cont in patt until front measures 6.5cm/2¾in from cast-on edge, ending with a WS row.

Beg with a k row, work in st st until front measures 23.5(24)cm/9¼(9½)in from cast-on edge, ending with a p row.

Shape armholes

Cast off 5(6) sts at beg of next 2 rows, then 2 sts at beg of foll 4 rows. 89(97) sts.

Work 4 rows st st, so ending with a p row.

Dec row K1, * k2 tog, rep from * to end. 45(49) sts.

Next row K to end.

Work in yoke patt as follows:

Row 1 K1, * k1B, k1, rep from * to end.

Row 2 K to end.

Row 3 K2, * k1B, k1, rep from * to last 3 sts, k1B, k2.

Row 4 K to end.

These 4 rows form the patt.

Cont in patt until armholes measure 7(7.5)cm/2¾(3)in from beg of shaping, ending with a WS row.

Shape neck

Next row Patt 16(17), turn and leave rem sts on a spare needle

Keeping patt correct, cast off 2 sts at beg of next and foll alt row.

Dec 1 st at neck edge on foll 2 alt rows. 10(11) sts.

Work straight until armhole measures 11(11.5)cm/4¼(4½)in from beg of shaping, ending with a WS row.

Cast off in patt.

Return to sts on spare needle.

With RS facing, slip first 13(15) sts on to a holder, then patt to end. 16(17) sts.

Patt 1 row.

Now complete to match first side of neck.

Back

Work as given for front until back measures 19.5(20)cm/7¾(8)in from cast-on edge, ending with a p row.

Divide for opening

Next row K51(56), turn and leave rem sts on a spare needle.

Work straight until back measures same as front to beg of armhole shaping, ending at side edge.

Shape armhole

Cast off 5(6) sts at beg of next row and 2 sts at beg of foll 2 alt rows. 42(46) sts.

Work 5 rows st st, so ending with a p row.

Dec row * K2 tog, rep from * to end. 21(23) sts.

Work in yoke patt as given for front until armhole measures 8(8.5)cm/3(3¼)in from beg of shaping, ending at inner edge.

Shape neck

Cast off 7(8) sts at beg of next row and 2 sts at beg of foll 2 alt rows. 10(11) sts.

Work straight until back measures same as front to shoulder, ending with a WS row.

Cast off in patt.

Measurements given in cm for second size

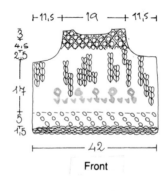

Front

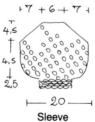

Sleeve

Chart for Swiss darning

Return to sts on spare needle.

With RS facing, join on yarn and cast off 5 sts, patt to end. 51(56) sts.

Work as given for first side of opening to beg of armhole shaping, ending at side edge.

Shape armhole

Cast off 5(6) sts at beg of next row and 2 sts at beg of foll 2 alt rows. 42(46) sts.

Work 4 rows st st, so ending with a p row.

Dec row * K2 tog, rep from * to end. 21(23) sts.

Working in yoke patt as given for front, complete to match first side of neck.

Sleeves

Using 2¾mm needles cast on 28(30) sts.

K 10 rows.

Inc row K2, * M1, k1, rep from * to last 3(2) sts, M1, k to end. 52(57) sts.

Change to 3¼mm needles.

Work in diagonal lace patt as given for front until sleeve measures 6cm/2½in from cast-on edge, ending with a WS row.

Shape top

Keeping patt correct, cast off 5(6) sts at beg of next 2 rows and 2 sts at beg of every row until 14(17) sts rem.

Cast off in patt.

Neckband

Join shoulder seams.

With RS facing and using 2¾mm needles, pick up and k15(16) sts up left side of back neck, 19 sts down left side of front neck, k the front neck sts from holder, pick up and k 19 sts up right side of front neck and 15(16) sts down right side of back neck. 81(85) sts.

K 6 rows. Cast off.

Button border

With RS facing and using 2¾mm needles, pick up and k45(47) sts from base of opening to top of neckband.

K 6 rows. Cast off.

Buttonhole border

With RS facing and using 2¾mm needles, pick up and k45(47) sts from top of neckband to base of opening.

K 3 rows.

Buttonhole row (RS) K3, [yf, k2 tog, k13(14) sts] twice, yf, k2 tog, k to end.

K 2 rows. Cast off.

To make up

Sew in sleeves, gathering tops to fit armholes. Join side and sleeve seams. Lapping buttonhole border over button border, sew row ends of borders in position at base of opening. Sew on buttons. Using oddments of yarn and centring the chart with 27(32) sts in A each side, Swiss darn the motifs on to front of dress, working the first row of chart on the 9th row of st st.

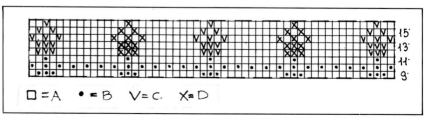

□ = A • = B V = C X = D

MATCHING JUMPER AND SHORTS

**

This
matching
set is knitted
in two colours
with the lacy
front panel edged
with chain stitch.

Materials
3(4,4)×50g balls of Robin Bambino 50 DK in main colour A
1×50g ball of same in contrast colour B
A pair each of 3mm/No11 and 3¾mm/No9 knitting needles
2 buttons   A waist length of elastic

Measurements
To fit chest 51(56,61)cm/20(22,24)in
Actual measurements
Chest 56(61,66)cm/22(24,26)in
Length to shoulders 25(27,29)cm/10(10½,11½)in
Sleeve seam 12(15,18)cm/4¾(6,7)in
Outside leg seam 21(22,23)cm/8¼(8¾,9)in

Tension
23 sts and 31 rows to 10cm/4in measured over st st worked on 3¾mm needles

Jersey back
★ Using 3mm needles and A, cast on 57(63,69) sts.
Rib row 1 With B, k1, * p1, k1, rep from * to end.
Rib row 2 With B, p1, * k1, p1, rep from * to end.
Continuing in rib work 2 rows A, then with B work rib row 1 again.
Inc row With B, rib 8(11,10) * M1, rib 6(6,7), rep from * to last 1(4,3) sts, rib 1(4,3). 65(71,77) sts.
Cut off B. Change to 3¾mm needles. ★
Using A only and beg with a k row, work 42(44,46) rows st st.
Shape armholes
Cast off 7 sts at beg of next 2 rows. 51(57,63) sts.
Divide for back neck opening
Next row K23(26,29), turn and leave rem sts on a spare needle.
Next row Cast on 5 sts, k these 5 sts, then p to end. 28(31,34) sts.
Next row K to end. **Next row** K5, p to end.
Rep these 2 rows until armhole measures 8(9,10)cm/3¼,3½,4)in from beg of shaping, ending with a RS row.
Shape neck
Next row Cast off 11(12,13) sts, p to end.
Next row K to end. **Next row** P to end.
Shape shoulder
Cast off 6(6,7) sts at beg of next and foll alt row. P 1 row. Cast off.
Return to sts on spare needle.
With RS facing, join on yarn and k to end.
Next row P23(26,29), k5.
Next row K to end.
Rep these 2 rows 6 times more.
Buttonhole row P23(26,29), k1, k2 tog, yf, k2.
Next row K to end. **Next row** P23(26,29), k5.
Rep the last 2 rows until armhole measures 8(9,10)cm/3¼(3½,4)in from beg of shaping, ending with a WS row.
Shape neck
Next row Cast off 11(12,13) sts, k to end.
Next row P to end. **Next row** K to end.
Shape shoulder
Cast off 6(6,7) sts at beg of next and foll alt row. K 1 row. Cast off.

Jersey front
Work as given for back from ★ to ★.
Using A only, work 2(4,6) rows st st.
Row 1 K30(33,36), k2 tog, yf, k1, yf, skpo, k30(33,36).
Row 2 and every foll alt row P to end.
Row 3 K to end.
Row 5 K29(32,35), k2 tog, yf, k3, yf, skpo, k29(32,35). **Row 7** K to end.
Row 9 K28(31,34), k2 tog, yf, k5, yf, skpo, k28(31,34). **Row 11** K to end.
Row 13 K27(30,33), k2 tog, yf, k3, yf, skpo, k2, yf, skpo, k27(30,33).
Row 15 K31(34,37), [yf, skpo] twice, k to end.
Row 17 K26(29,32), k2 tog, yf, k2, [yf, skpo] 3 times, k1, yf, skpo, k26(29,32).
Row 19 As row 15.
Row 21 K25(28,31), k2 tog, yf, k5, yf, skpo, k4, yf, skpo, k25(28,31).
Row 23 K to end.

Row 25 K24(27,30), k2 tog, yf, k6, yf, skpo, k5, yf, skpo, k24(27,30).
Row 27 As row 15.
Row 29 K23(26,29), k2 tog, yf, k5, [yf, skpo] 3 times, k4, yf, skpo, k23(26,29).
Row 31 As row 15.
Row 33 K22(25,28), k2 tog, yf, k8, yf, skpo, k7, yf, skpo, k22(25,28).
Row 35 K to end.
Row 37 K21(24,27), k2 tog, yf, k3, [yf, skpo, k4] twice, yf, skpo, k2, yf, skpo, k21(24,27).
Row 39 K25(28,31), * [yf, skpo] twice, k2, rep from * once more, [yf, skpo] twice, k to end. **Row 40** P to end.
Shape armholes
Row 41 Cast off 7 sts, then k12(15,18), k2 tog, yf, k2, [yf, skpo] 9 times, k1, yf, skpo, k20(23,26).
Row 42 Cast off 7 sts, p to end. 51(57,63) sts.
Row 43 K18(21,24), * [yf, skpo] twice, k2, rep from * once more, [yf, skpo] twice, k to end.
Row 44 and every foll alt row P to end.
Row 45 K12(15,18), k2 tog, yf, k5, [yf, skpo, k4] 3 times, yf, skpo, k12(15,18).
Row 47 K to end.
Row 49 K11(14,17), k2 tog, yf, k6, [yf, skpo, k4] twice, yf, skpo, k5, yf, skpo, k11(14,17).
Row 51 K18(21,24), * [yf, skpo] twice, k2, rep from * once more, [yf, skpo] twice, k to end.
Row 53 K10(13,16), k2 tog, yf, k5, [yf, skpo] 9 times, k4, yf, skpo, k10(13,16).
Row 55 As row 51.
Row 57 K9(12,15), k2 tog, yf, k8, [yf, skpo, k4] twice, yf, skpo, k7, yf, skpo, k9(12,15).
Row 59 K to end. **Row 60** P to end.
Shape neck
Row 61 K8(11,14), k2 tog, yf, k2, yf, skpo, k3, turn and leave rem sts on a spare needle.
Row 62 and every foll alt row P to end.
Row 63 K11(14,17), [yf, skpo] twice, k2.
Row 65 K7(10,13), k2 tog, yf, k1, [yf, skpo] 3 times, k1.
Row 67 K11(14,17), [yf, skpo] twice, k2.
Row 69 For 1st size only cast off 6 sts, then for all sizes k5(15,18), yf, skpo, k3.
Row 70 P to end.
First size only Cast off 6 sts at beg of next row. K 1 row. Cast off.
2nd size only Cast off 6 sts at beg of next and foll alt row. Work 1 row. Cast off.
3rd size only Beg with a k row work 4 rows st st. Cast off 7 sts at beg of next and foll alt row. Work 1 row. Cast off.
Return to sts on spare needle.
With RS facing, slip first 17 sts on to a holder, join on yarn and cont as follows:
Row 61 K3, yf, skpo, k2, yf, skpo, k8(11,14).
Row 62 and every foll alt row P to end.
Row 63 K2, [yf, skpo] twice, k to end.
Row 65 K1, [yf, skpo] 3 times, k1, yf, skpo, k7(10,13). **Row 67** As row 63.
Row 69 K3, yf, skpo, k to end.
2nd and 3rd sizes only Work 2(6) rows st st.
All sizes Cast off 6(6,7) sts at beg of next and foll alt rows. Work 1 row. Cast off.

Jersey sleeves
Using 3mm needles and A, cast on 29(31,33) sts. Work 5 rows in rib as given for back.
Inc row With B, rib 9(10,11) * M1, rib 6, rep from * to last 2(3,4) sts, rib 2(3,4). 32(34,36) sts. Change to 3¾mm needles.
Working in st st stripes of 2 rows A, 2 rows B, inc 1 st each end of 5th and every foll 4th(6th,6th) row until there are 42(46,50) sts. Work straight until sleeve measures 12(15,18)cm/4¾(6,7)in from cast-on edge, ending with a WS row.
Shape top
Cast off 5(6,7) sts at beg of next 2 rows.
Dec 1 st each end of next and every foll alt row until 12 sts rem, ending with a WS row. Cast off.

Neckband
Join shoulder seams. With RS facing, using 3mm needles and B, pick up and k17(18,19) sts across left back neck, 10 sts down left side of front neck; k17 sts from front neck holder, then pick up and k10 sts up right side of front neck and 17(18,19) sts across right back neck. 71(73,75) sts.
Rib row 1 With B, k1, * p1, k1, rep from * to end.
Rib row 2 With B, p1, k1, p1, yrn, p2 tog, * k1, p1, rep from * to end. Continuing in rib, work 2 rows A.
Using A, cast off in rib.

To make up
Slipstitch cast-on edge of button border into place on WS of work. Set in sleeves, then join side and sleeve seams. Sew on buttons. Using B, work chain st along eyelet holes each side of lacy pattern on front to form a V shape.

Shorts back and front (alike)
First leg Using 3mm needles and A, cast on 31(33,35) sts. Working in rib as given for back of jersey, work 2 rows B and 2 rows A, then increasing 1 st at centre of 2nd row, work 2 rows B. 32(34,36) sts. Change to 3¾mm needles. Using A only, work in patt as follows:
Row 1 K15(16,17), yf, skpo, k15(16,17).
Row 2 and every foll alt row P to end.
Row 3 K14(15,16), [yf, skpo] twice, k14(15,16).
Row 5 K13(14,15), [yf, skpo] 3 times, k13(14,15). **Row 7** As row 3.
Row 9 As row 1. **Row 10** P to end.
Cut off yarn and leave sts on a holder.
Second leg Work as given for first leg, but do not cut off yarn.
Join legs
Row 11 K across 32(34,36) sts of second leg, turn and cast on 13 sts, turn work again, then with RS facing k32(34,36) sts of first leg from holder. 77(81,85) sts.
Row 12 and every foll alt row P to end.
Row 13 K15(16,17), yf, skpo, k14(15,16), k2 tog, k11, skpo, k14(15,16), yf, skpo, k15(16,17).
Row 15 K14(15,16), [yf, skpo] twice, k13(14,15), k2 tog, k9, skpo, k13(14,15), [yf, skpo] twice, k14(15,16).
Row 17 K13(14,15), [yf, skpo] 3 times, k12(13,14), k2 tog, k7, skpo, k12(13,14), [yf, skpo] 3 times, k13(14,15).
Row 19 K14(15,16), [yf, skpo] twice, k13(14,15), k2 tog, k5, skpo, k13(14,15), [yf, skpo] twice, k14(15,16).
Row 21 K15(16,17), yf, skpo, k14(15,16), k2 tog, k3, skpo, k14(15,16), yf, skpo, k15(16,17).
Row 23 K31(33,35), k2 tog, k1, skpo, k31(33,35).
Row 25 K15(16,17), yf, skpo, k14(15,16), sl 1, k2 tog, psso, k14(15,16), yf, skpo, k15(16,17). 63(67,71) sts.
Row 27 K14(15,16), [yf, skpo] twice, k29(31,33), [yf, skpo] twice, k14(15,16).
Row 29 K13(14,15), [yf, skpo] 3 times, k27(29,31), [yf, skpo] 3 times, k13(14,15).
Row 31 As row 27.
Row 33 K15(16,17), yf, skpo, k31(33,35), yf, skpo, k15(16,17).
Row 35 K to end. Continuing in patt as set, work straight until shorts measure 24(25,26)cm/9½(9¾,10¼)in from cast-on edge, ending with a RS row.
Dec row P2 tog, p to last 2 sts, p2 tog. 61(65,69) sts. Change to 3mm needles.
Rib row 1 K1, * p1, k1, rep from * to end.
Rib row 2 P1, * k1, p1, rep from * to end.
Rep these 2 rows for 6cm/2¼in, ending with rib row 2. Cast off in rib.

To make up
Join outside leg seams, then join inside leg and crutch seam. Fold waist rib in half to WS, then slipstitch into position, leaving an opening for elastic to be inserted. Insert elastic and close opening.

WINTER JUMPER WITH HOOD

**

This warm jersey has a knitted-on hood for extra warmth on cold winter days.

Materials

2×50g balls of Emu Superwash Chunky in main colour A
2 balls of same in contrast colour B
1 ball of same in each of contrast colours C and D
A pair each of 4½mm/No7 and 5½mm/No5 knitting needles

Measurements

One size only to fit chest 51–56cm/20–22in
Actual measurements
Chest 65cm/25½in
Length to shoulders 42cm/16½in
Sleeve seam 20cm/8in

Tension

15 sts and 19 rows to 10cm/4in measured over patt worked on 5½mm needles

Back

★ Using 4½mm needles and A, cast on 49 sts.
Rib row 1 K1, * p1, k1, rep from * to end.
Rib row 2 P1, * k1, p1, rep from * to end.
Rep these 2 rows for 3cm/1¼in, ending with rib row 2.
Change to 5½mm needles.
Beg with a k row, work in st st and colour patt as follows:
Row 1 (RS) With A, k to end.
Row 2 With A, p to end.
Rows 3 and 4 As rows 1 and 2.
Row 5 K1C, * 15A, 1C, rep from * to end.
Row 6 P2C, * 13A, 3C, rep from * to last 15 sts, 13A, 2C.
Row 7 K3C, * 11A, 5C, rep from * to last 14 sts, 11A, 3C.
Row 8 P4C, * 9A, 7C, rep from * to last 13 sts, 9A, 4C.
Row 9 K5C, * 7A, 9C, rep from * to last 12 sts, 7A, 5C.
Row 10 P6C, * 5A, 11C, rep from * to last 11sts, 5A, 6C.
Row 11 K7C,* 3A, 13C, rep from * to last 10 sts, 3A, 7C.
Row 12 P8C, * 1A, 15C, rep from * to last 9 sts, 1A, 8C.
Rows 13 to 16 With C, work 4 rows st st.
Row 17 K1D, * 15C, 1D, rep from * to end.
Row 18 P2D, * 13C, 3D, rep from * to last 15 sts, 13C, 2D.
Row 19 K3D, * 11C, 5D, rep from * to last 14 sts, 11C, 3D.
Row 20 P4D, * 9C, 7D, rep from * to last 13 sts, 9C , 4D.
Row 21 K5D, * 7C, 9D, rep from * to last 12 sts, 7C, 5D.
Row 22 P6D, * 5C, 11D, rep from * to last 11 sts, 5C, 6D.
Row 23 K7D, * 3C, 13D, rep from * to last 10 sts, 3C, 7D.
Row 24 P8D, * 1C, 15D, rep from * to last 9 sts, 1C, 8D.
Rows 25 to 28 With D, work 4 rows st st.
Row 29 K1B, * 15D, 1B, rep from * to end.
Row 30 P2B, * 13D, 3B, rep from * to last 15 sts, 13D, 2B.
Row 31 K3B, * 11D, 5B, rep from * to last 14 sts, 11D, 3B.
Row 32 P4B, * 9D, 7B, rep from * to last 13 sts, 9D, 4B.
Row 33 K5B, * 7D, 9B, rep from * to last 12 sts, 7D, 5B.
Row 34 P6B, * 5D, 11B, rep from * to last 11 sts, 5D, 6B.
Row 35 K7B, * 3D, 13B, rep from * to last 10 sts, 3D, 7B.
Row 36 P8B, * 1D, 15B, rep from * to last 9 sts, 1D, 8B.
Rows 37 to 40 With B, work 4 rows st st.
Row 41 K1A, * 15B, 1A, rep from * to end.
Row 42 P2A, * 13B, 3A, rep from * to last 15 sts, 13B, 2A.
Row 43 K3A, * 11B, 5A, rep from * to last 14 sts, 11B, 3A.
Row 44 P4A, * 9B, 7A, rep from * to last 13 sts, 9B, 4A.
Row 45 K5A, * 7B, 9A, rep from * to last 12 sts, 7B, 5A.
Row 46 P6A, * 5B, 11A, rep from * to last 11 sts, 5B, 6A.

Row 47 K7A, * 3B, 13A, rep from * to last 10 sts, 3B, 7A.
Row 48 P8A, * 1B, 15A, rep from * to last 9 sts, 1B, 8A.
Shape armholes
Using A only, cast off 5 sts at beg of next 2 rows. 39 sts. ★
Cont in st st until work measures 14cm/5½in from beg of armhole, ending with a p row.
Shape shoulders
Cast off 10 sts at beg of next 2 rows. Cut off yarn and leave rem 19 sts on a holder.

Front

Work as given for back from ★ to ★.
Work 4 rows st st, ending with a p row.
Neck inset
Next row K10A, 19B, turn and leave rem sts on a spare needle.

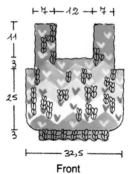

Back

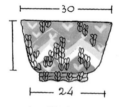

Front

Sleeve

Measurements given in cm

Next row K19B, p10A.
Next row K10A, 19B.
Next row K19B, p10A.
Buttonhole row 1 (RS) With A k10, with B k2, cast off the next 2 sts, k to last 4 sts, cast off 2, k to end.
Buttonhole row 2 With B, k19 casting on 2 sts over those cast off in previous row, with A, p10.
Next row K10A, 19B.
Next row K19B, p10A.
Rep last 2 rows until front measures 4 rows less than back to shoulder, ending with a WS row. Rep the 2 buttonhole rows once more.

Next row K to end.
Shape neck
Next row Cast off 7 sts, k to end. 22 sts.
Shape shoulder
Next row Cast off 10 sts, leave the rem 12 sts on a holder.
Return to sts on spare needle. Using 5½mm needles and B, cast on 19 sts, then with RS facing, using A and on to same needle, k across 10 sts from spare needle. 29 sts.
Next row P10A, k19B.
Next row K19B, p10A.
Rep the last 2 rows until work measures 2 rows less than back to shoulder, ending with a WS row.
Shape neck
Next row Cast off 7 sts, k to end. 22 sts.
Shape shoulder
Next row Cast off 10 sts, k to end. 12 sts.
Hood
Using B only, cont in g st as follows:
Next row Cast off 2 sts, k to end, then with RS facing, work across sts from back neck holder as follows: k1, [M1, k1] 18 times, now with RS facing, k12 across sts from left front holder, 59 sts.
Next row Cast off 2 sts, k13, M1, [k6, M1] 5 times, k to end. 62 sts.
Cast off 2 sts at beg of next 2 rows, then dec 1 st each end of next and foll 2 alt rows. 52 sts. K 29 rows.
Shape top
Next row K24, k2 tog, skpo, k24. 50 sts.
Next row K to end.
Next row K23, k2 tog, skpo, k23. 48 sts.
Next row K to end. Cast off.

Sleeves

Using 4½mm needles and A, cast on 29 sts.
Work 3cm/1¼in rib as given for back, ending with rib row 2.
Inc row K2, [M1, k5] 5 times, M1, k2. 35 sts.
Change to 5½mm needles. P1 row.
Beg with a k row, work in patt as follows:
Row 1 K17A, 1C, 17A.
Row 2 P16A, 3C, 16A.
Row 3 K15A, 5C, 15A.
Row 4 P1C, 13A, 7C, 13A, 1C.
Row 5 K2C, 11A, 9C, 11A, 2C.
Row 6 P3C, 9A, 11C, 9A, 3C.
Row 7 Using C, inc in first st, k3C, 7A, 6C, 1D, 6C, 7A, 3C, using C, inc in last st. 37 sts.
Row 8 P6C, 5A, 6C, 3D, 6C, 5A, 6C.
Row 9 K1D, 6C, 3A, 6C, 5D, 6C, 3A, 6C, 1D.
Row 10 P2D, 6C, 1A, 6C, 7D, 6C, 1A, 6C, 2D.
Row 11 K3D, 11C, 9D, 11C, 3D.
Row 12 P4D, 9C, 11D, 9C, 4D.
Row 13 Using D, inc in first st, k4D, 7C, 6D, 1B, 6D, 7C, 4D, using D inc in last st. 39 sts.
Row 14 P1B, 6D, 5C, 6D, 3B, 6D, 5C, 6D, 1B.
Row 15 K2B, 6D, 3C, 6D, 5B, 6D, 3C, 6D, 2B.
Row 16 P3B, 6D, 1C, 6D, 7B, 6D, 1C, 6D, 3B.
Row 17 K4B, 9D, 11B, 9D, 4B.
Row 18 P5B, 9D, 11B, 9D, 5B.
Row 19 Using B inc in first st, k5B, 7D, 6B, 1A, 6B, 7D, 5B, using B inc in last st. 41 sts.
Row 20 P2A, 6B, 5D, 6B, 3A, 6B, 5D, 6B, 2A.
Row 21 K3A, 6B, 3D, 6B, 5A, 6B, 3D, 6B, 3A.
Row 22 P4A, 6B, 1D, 6B, 7A, 6B, 1D, 6B, 4A.
Row 23 K5A, 11B, 9A, 11B, 5A.
Row 24 P6A, 9B, 11A, 9B, 6A.
Row 25 Using A, inc in first st, k6A, 7B, 13A, 7B, 6A, using A inc in last st. 43 sts.
Row 26 P9A, 5B, 15A, 5B, 9A.
Row 27 K10A, 3B, 17A, 3B, 10A.
Row 28 P11A, 1B, 19A, 1B, 11A.
Using A and beg with a k row, work 6 rows st st. Cast off.

To make up

Swiss darn the single sts 3 sts apart as shown in the picture. Join shoulder seams. Sew in sleeves, joining last few rows at top of sleeve to cast-off sts at underarm on front and back. Join side and sleeve seams. Catch down right neck inset behind left inset at base. Join seam at top of hood. Sew buttons to right neck inset.

ARAN JERSEY, HAT AND BOOTEES

**

Several sizes have been given for this delightful matching Aran outfit.

Materials

4(5,5,6)×50g balls of Wendy Peter Pan Darling DK for jersey

2 balls of same for hat, 1 ball of same for bootees

A pair each of 4mm/No8 and 5mm/No6 knitting needles for jersey and hat

A pair of 3¾mm/No 9 knitting needles for bootees

Cable needle

2 buttons for jersey

Measurements

To fit chest 41(46,51,56)cm/16(18,20,22)in

Actual measurements

Chest 48.5(52.5,57,61)cm/19(20¾,22½,24)in

Length to shoulders 23(25,27,28)cm/9¼(9¾,10½,11)in

Sleeve seam 16(18,20,22)cm/6¼(7,8,8½)in

Tension

Central pattern panel for jersey (36 sts) measures 19.5cm/7¾in worked on 5mm needles using yarn double

30 rows to 10cm/4in measured over patt worked on 5mm needles using yarn double

Special abbreviations

C4F Cable 4 front as follows: slip next 2 sts on to cable needle and leave at front of work, k2, then k2 from cable needle

C4B Cable 4 back as follows: slip next 2 sts on to cable needle and leave at back of work, k2, then k2 from cable needle

C8 Cable 8 as follows: slip next 4 sts on to cable needle and leave at front of work, k4, then k4 from cable needle

Note

The yarn is used double throughout for the jersey and hat and single for the bootees.

Jersey front

Using 4mm needles and 2 strands of yarn together throughout, cast on 43(47,51,55) sts.

Rib row 1 (RS) K1, * p1, k1, rep from * to end.

Rib row 2 P1, * k1, p1, rep from * to end.

Rep these 2 rows for 3cm/1¼in, ending with rib row 1.

Inc row Rib 11(13,15,17) sts, [inc in next st, rib 9] twice, inc in next st, rib 11(13,15,17). 46(50,54,58) sts.

Change to 5mm needles.

Foundation row 1 [K1, p1] 7(8,9,10) times, k1, yf, k2 tog, p1, k10, p1, k1, yf, k2 tog, [p1, k1] 7(8,9,10) times.

Foundation row 2 [K1, p1] 2(3,4,5) times, k2, p1, k1, p1, k2, [p1, k1] 4 times, p8, [k1, p1] 4 times, k2, p1, k1, p1, k2, [p1, k1] 2(3,4,5) times.

Rep the last 2 rows once more.

Work in patt as follows:

Row 1 [K1, p1] 7(8,9,10) times, k1, yf, k2 tog, p1, k1, C4F, C4B, k1, p1, k1, yf, k2 tog, [p1, k1] 7(8,9,10) times.

Row 2 [K1, p1] 2(3,4,5) times, k2, p1, k1, p1, k2, [p1, k1] 4 times, p8, [k1, p1] 4 times, k2, p1, k1, p1, k2, [p1, k1] 2(3,4,5) times.

Row 3 [K1, p1] 7(8,9,10) times, k1, yf,

k2 tog, p1, k10, p1, k1, yf, k2 tog, [p1, k1] 7(8,9,10) times.

Rows 4 and 5 As rows 2 and 3.

Row 6 [K1, p1] 2(3,4,5) times, k2, p1, k1, p1, k2, [p1, k1] 4 times, p8, [k1, p1] 4 times, k2, p1, k1, p1, k2, [p1, k1] 2(3,4,5) times.

These 6 rows form the patt.

Cont in patt until front measures 13(14,15,15.5)cm/5(5½,6,6¼)in from cast-on edge, ending with a WS row.

Place a marker at each end of last row to denote beg of raglan shaping.

Shape raglans

Keeping patt correct, dec 1 st each end of next and every foll alt row until 28(32,34,36) sts rem, ending with a WS row.

Shape neck

Next row Work 2 tog, patt 9(11,12,12), turn and leave rem sts on a spare needle.

Patt 1 row.

Continuing to dec at raglan edge on next and every foll alt row as before, dec 1 st at neck edge on next and every foll alt row until 4(4,3,3) sts rem.

Keeping neck edge straight, dec 1 st at raglan edge on foll alt row 2(2,1,1) times, so ending with a RS row. 2 sts.

Work 2 tog and fasten off.

Return to sts on spare needle.

With RS facing, slip first 6 sts on to a holder, join on yarn and patt to last 2 sts, work 2 tog. 10(12,13,13) sts.

Now complete to match first side of neck.

Jersey back

Work as given for front until 30(32,34,36) sts rem, ending with a WS row.

Divide for opening

Next row Work 2 tog, patt 11(12,13,14), k4 for buttonhole border, turn and leave rem sts on a spare needle.

Next row K4, patt to end.

Next row Work 2 tog, patt to last 4 sts, k4.

Next row K4, patt to end.

Buttonhole row Work 2 tog, patt to last 4 sts, k1, yf, k2 tog, k1.

Next row K4, patt to end.

Next row Work 2 tog, patt to last 4 sts, k4.

Cont in this way, repeating the last 2 rows until 9(10,11,12) sts rem, ending with a RS row.

Next row K4 and leave these sts on a safety-pin, then cast off rem sts for back neck.

Return to sts on spare needle.

With RS facing, join on yarn and cast on 4 sts, k across these 4 sts, then patt to last 2 sts, work 2 tog. 16(17,18,19) sts.

Next row Patt to last 4 sts, k4.

Next row K4, patt to last 2 sts, work 2 tog.

Cont in this way, repeating the last 2 rows until 9(10,11,12) sts rem, ending with a RS row.

Next row Cast off in patt first 5(6,7,8) sts, then k to end.

Leave these 4 sts on a safety-pin and do not cut off yarn.

Sleeves

Using 4mm needles and 2 strands of yarn together throughout, cast on 23(23,27,27) sts.

Work 3cm/1¼in rib as given for front, ending with rib row 1.

Inc row Rib 2(2,4,4) sts, [M1, rib 2] 3 times, M1, rib 3, inc in next st, rib 3, [M1, rib 2] 3 times, M1, rib 2(2,4,4). 32(32,36,36) sts.

Change to 5mm needles.

Foundation row 1 [P1, k1] 5(5,6,6) times, p1, k10, p1 [k1, p1] 5(5,6,6) times.

Foundation row 2 [P1, k1] 1(1,2,2) times, [k1,p1] twice, k2, [p1, k1] twice, p8, [k1, p1] twice, k2, [p1, k1] twice, [k1, p1] 1(1,2,2) times.

Rep the last 2 rows once more.

Work in patt as follows:

Row 1 Inc in first st, [k1, p1] 5(5,6,6) times, k1, C4B, C4F, k1, [p1, k1] 5(5,6,6) times, inc in last st. 34(34,38,38) sts.

Row 2 [K1, p1] 1(1,2,2) times, k2, p1, k1, p1, k2, [p1, k1] twice, p8, [k1, p1] twice, k2, p1, k1, p1, k2, [p1, k1] 1(1,2,2) times.

Row 3 [K1, p1] 6(6,7,7) times, k10, [p1, k1] 6(6,7,7) times.

Rows 4 and 5 As rows 2 and 3.

Row 6 [K1, p1] 1(1,2,2) times, k2, p1, k1, p1, k2, [p1, k1] twice, p8, [k1, p1] twice, k2, p1, k1, p1, k2, [p1, k1] 1(1,2,2) times.

These 6 rows set the position of the cable and rib panel with moss st side panels.

Keeping patt correct, inc and work into moss st side panels 1 st each end of 5th(3rd,9th,7th) row and then the foll 10th(8th,12th,12th) row 1(2,1,2) times, 38(40,42,44) sts.

Cont in patt until sleeve measures 16(18,20,22)cm/6¼(7,8,8½)in from cast-on edge, ending with a WS row.

Place a marker at each end of last row to denote beg of raglan shaping.

Shape raglan

Dec 1 st each end of next and every foll alt row until 8 sts rem, ending with a WS row.

Cast off in patt.

Neckband

Join raglan seams.

With RS facing, slip the 4 sts of button border on to a 4mm needle with point of needle at centre back edge, k4, then on to same needle pick up and k5(6,7,8) sts across back neck, 7 sts across top of left sleeve, 9(10,10,10) sts down left side of front neck, decreasing 1 st at centre, k the front neck sts from holder, pick up and k9(10,10,10) sts up right side of front neck, 7 sts across top of right sleeve, 5(6,7,8) sts across back neck and then k the 4 sts from safety-pin for buttonhole border. 55(59,61,65) sts.

Next row K4, p1, * k1, p1, rep from * to last 4 sts, k4.

Buttonhole row (RS) K5, p1, * k1, p1, rep from * to last 5 sts, k2, yf, k2 tog, k1.

Rib row 1 K4, p1, * k1, p1, rep from * to last 4 sts, k4.

Rib row 2 K5, p1, * k1, p1, rep from * to last 5 sts, k5.

Cast off knitwise for border and in rib for neckband.

To make up

Join side and sleeve seams. Catch cast-on edge of button border to base of buttonhole border, then sew on the buttons.

Hat

Using 4mm needles and 2 strands of yarn together throughout, cast on 83 sts.
Rib row P1, * k1, p1, rep from * to end.
Inc row [K1, p1] twice, inc in next st, p1, k1, p1, * inc in next st, [p1, k1] 3 times, p1, [inc in next st, p1, k1, p1] twice, rep from * three times more, inc in next st, [p1, k1] 5 times. 97 sts.
Change to 5mm needles.
Work in border patt as follows:
Row 1 P3, [k1, p1] 3 times, k1, * p2, k8, p2, [k1, p1] 3 times, k1 , rep from * to last 11 sts p2, k8, p1.
Row 2 K1, p8, k2, * [p1, k1] 3 times, p1, k2, p8, k2, rep from * to last 10 sts, [p1, k1] 3 times, p1, k3.

Rows 3 to 6 Rep rows 1 and 2 twice.
Row 7 P3, [k1, p1] 3 times, k1, * p2, C8, p2, [k1, p1] 3 times, k1, rep from * to last 11 sts, p2, C8, p1.
Row 8 K1, p8, k2, * [p1, k1] 3 times, p1, k2, p8, k2, rep from * to last 10 sts, [p1, k1] 3 times, p1, k3.
Now work the cables with moss stitch panels, shaping for crown as follows:
Next row P4, * [k1, p1] twice, k1, p3, k8, p3, rep from * to last 17 sts, [k1, p1] twice, k1, p3, k8, p1.
Next row K1, * p8, k2, [p1, k1] 3 times, p1, k2, rep from * to last 20 sts, p8, k2, [p1, k1] 3 times, p1, k3.
Rep the last 2 rows twice more.
Dec row P1, * p2 tog, p1, [k1, p1] 3 times, p2 tog, C8, rep from * to last st, p1. 87 sts.
Next row K1, * p8, k3, p1, k1, p1, k3, rep

from * to last 18 sts, p8, k3, p1, k1, p1, k4.
Next row P3, * [k1, p1] twice, k1, p2, k8, p2, rep from * to last 16 sts, [k1, p1] twice, k1, p2, k8, p1.
Rep the last 2 rows twice more.
Next row K1, * p8, k3, p1, k1, p1, k3, rep from * to last 18 sts, p8, k3, p1, k1, p1, k4.
Dec row P1, * p2 tog, p2, k1, p2, p2 tog, C8, rep from * to last st, p1. 77 sts.
Next row K1, * p8, k2, p1, k1, p1, k2, rep from * to last 16 sts, p8, k2, p1, k1, p1, k3.
Next row P4, k1, p3, * k8, p3, k1, p3, rep

The five cables decrease to meet at a point on the crown of the hat. Use mattress stitch to sew the seam invisibly.
The bootees have a single cable on the outside of each leg.

from * to last 9 sts, k8, p1.
Rep the last 2 rows once more.
Dec row K1. * [p2 tog] 4 times, k2, p1, k1,
p1, k3, rep from * to end. 57 sts.
Dec row P1, p2 tog, p3, p2 tog, * C4F,
p2 tog, p3, p2 tog, rep from * to last 5 sts,
C4F, p1. 47 sts.
Next row K1, * p4, k2, p1, k2, rep from * to
last 10 sts, p4, k2, p1, k3.
Next row P6, * k4, p5, rep from * to last
5 sts, k4, p1.
Next row K1, * p4, k2, p1, k2, rep from * to
last 10 sts, p4, k2, p1, k3.
Dec row P2, p3 tog, p1, * C4F, p1, p3 tog,
p1, rep from * to last 5 sts, C4F, p1. 37 sts.
Next row K1, * p4, k3, rep from * to last
8 sts, p4, k4.
Next row P4, * k4, p3, rep from * to last
5 sts, k4, p1.
Next row K1, * p4, k3, rep from * to last
8 sts, p4, k4.
Dec row P1, p3 tog, * [k2 tog] twice, p3 tog,
rep from * to last 5 sts, [k2 tog] twice, p1.
Cut off yarn leaving a length of about
20cm/8in to thread through sts left on
needle. Draw up sts together and stitch to
secure, then sew side seam from crown to
cast-on edge.

Left bootee
★ Using 3¾mm needles cast on 44 sts.
Foundation row 1 Inc in first st, k19, inc in
next st, k2, inc in next st, k19, inc in last st.
48 sts.
Foundation row 2 P to end.
Foundation row 3 Inc in first st, k22, M1, k2,
M1, k22, inc in last st. 52 sts.
Foundation row 4 P to end.
Foundation row 5 Inc in first st, k24, M1, k2,
M1, k24, inc in last st. 56 sts.
Foundation row 6 P to end.
K 4 rows.
Beg with a k row, work 4 rows st st.
Shape for leg
Next row K22, k2 tog, k8, skpo, sl 1, turn.
Next row P2 tog tbl, p8, p2 tog, sl 1 pw, turn.
Next row K2 tog, k8, skpo, sl 1, turn.
Rep the last 2 rows three times more.
Next row P2 tog tbl, p8, p2 tog, p to end.
36 sts. ★
Work cable panel as follows:
Row 1 (RS) K7, p1, C4F, p1, k23.
Row 2 P23, k1, p4, k1, p7.
Row 3 K7, p1, k4, p1, k23.
Row 4 P23, k1, p4, k1, p7.
These 4 rows form the cable panel patt.
Cont in patt until cable panel measures
7cm/2¾in from base, ending with a WS row.
K 3 rows.
Cast off.

Right bootee
Work as given for left bootee from ★ to ★.
Work cable panel as follows:
Row 1 (RS) K23, p1, C4B, p1, k7.
Row 2 P7, k1, p4, k1, p23.
Row 3 K23, p1, k4, p1, k7.
Row 4 P7, k1, p4, k1, p23.
These 4 rows form the cable panel patt.
Now complete to match left bootee.

To make up
Join back leg and sole seam.

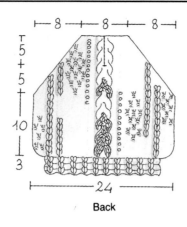

Back

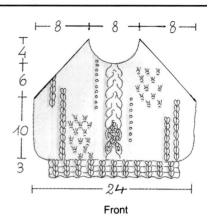

Front

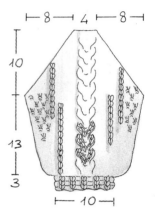

Sleeve

Measurements given in cm
for smallest size

JERSEY WITH A DUCK MOTIF

✳

This bright
summer top has a
button-neck
opening which
slips easily over a
baby's head.

Materials

2×50g balls of Twilley's Galaxia 3 in main colour A
1 ball of same in contrast colour B
A pair each of 2¼mm/No13 and 3¼mm/No10 knitting needles
3 buttons

Measurements

To fit chest 51cm/20in
Actual measurements
Chest 62cm/24½in
Length to centre back neck 27cm/10½in
Sleeve seam 6cm/2¼in

Tension

24 sts and 30 rows to 10cm/4in measured over st st worked on 3¼mm needles

Note

If preferred, this jersey may be knitted plain with the motifs Swiss darned afterwards.

Front

★ Using 2¼mm needles and A, cast on 75 sts.
Rib row 1 (RS) K1, * p1, k1, rep from * to end.
Rib row 2 P1, * k1, p1, rep from * to end.
Rep these 2 rows for 3cm/1¼in, ending with rib row 2. ★
Change to 3¼mm needles.
Work in st st until front measures 7.5cm/3in from cast-on edge, ending with a p row.
Join on and cut off colours as required.
Use separate balls of yarn for each area of colour and twist yarns together on WS of work when changing colour to avoid making a hole.
Reading odd numbered (k) rows from right to left and even numbered (p) rows from left to right, work from chart as follows:

Row 1 (RS) K14A, working across row 1 of chart k47B, then k14A.
Row 2 P14A, working across row 2 of chart p47A, then p14A.
Row 3 K14A, working across row 3 of chart k47A, then k14A.
Row 4 P14A, working across row 4 of chart p47A, then p14A.
Row 5 K14A, working across row 5 of chart k2A, 43B, 2A, then k14A.
Rows 6 and 7 As given for rows 2 and 3, working across rows 6 and 7 of chart.
Row 8 P14A, working across row 8 of chart p3A, 8B, 23A, 8B, 5A, then p14A.
Cont in this way, working from chart until row 24 has been completed.
Cut off B.
Cont in st st until front measures 16cm/6¼in from cast-on edge, ending with a p row.
Divide for opening
Next row K34, turn and leave rem sts on a spare needle.
Work 3 rows st st, so ending at side edge.
Shape armhole
Cast off 3 sts at beg of next row.
Work 1 row.
Dec 1 st at armhole edge on next and every foll alt row until 26 sts rem.
Work straight until armhole measures 7cm/2¾in from beg of shaping, ending at neck opening edge.
Shape neck
Cast off 3 sts at beg of next row and 2 sts at beg of foll alt row. 21 sts.
Dec 1 st at neck edge on next 2 rows. 19 sts.
Work straight until armhole measures 10cm/4in from beg of shaping, ending with a p row.
Cast off.
Return to sts on spare needle.
With RS facing, join A to next st and cast off

first 7 sts, then k to end of row. 34 sts.
Work 2 rows, so ending at side edge.
Now complete to match first side of neck opening from beg of armhole shaping.

Back

Work as given for front from ★ to ★.
Using A only, work in st st until back measures same length as front up to beg of armhole shaping, ending with a p row.
Shape armholes
Cast off 3 sts at beg of next 2 rows. 69 sts.
Dec 1 st at each end of next and every foll alt row until 59 sts rem.
Work straight until armholes measure same length as front to shoulders, ending with a p row.
Shape shoulders
Cast off 19 sts at beg of next 2 rows.
Cut off yarn and leave remaining 21 sts on a holder.

Sleeves

Using 2¼mm needles and A, cast on 51 sts.
Rep the 2 rib rows for 2cm/¾in, ending with rib row 2.
Change to 3¼mm needles.
Work in st st until sleeve measures 6cm/2½in from cast-on edge, ending with a p row.
Shape top
Cast off 3 sts at beg of next 2 rows.
Dec 1 st each end of next and every foll alt row until 27 sts rem, ending with a p row.
Cast off.

Button border

With RS facing, using 2¼mm needles and B, pick up and k33 sts up right side of front opening to beg of neck shaping.
Beg with rib row 2, work 9 rows rib as given for front.
Cast off in rib.

Buttonhole border

With RS facing, using 2¼mm needles and B, pick up and k33 sts down left side of front opening.
Beg with rib row 2, rib 3 rows, so ending with rib row 2.
Buttonhole row (RS) Rib 3, [yf, k2 tog, rib 10] twice, yf, k2 tog, rib 4.
Rib 4 rows.
Cast off in rib.

Collar

Join shoulder seams.
With RS facing, using 3¼mm needles and B, and beg at first row of buttonhole border, pick up and k20 sts up right side of front neck, k the back neck sts from holder, then pick up and k20 sts down left side of front neck. 61 sts.
Rib row 1 K2, * p1, k1, rep from * to last 3 sts, p1, k2.
Rib row 2 K1, * p1, k1, rep from * to end.
Rep these 2 rows for 6cm/2½in, ending with rib row 2.
Cut off B. Join on A.
K 1 row.
Beg with rib row 2, rib 3 rows.
Cast off in rib.

To make up

Gathering sleeve tops to fit armholes, sew in the sleeves, then join side and sleeve seams. Join row ends of borders to cast-off edge of opening. Sew on buttons.

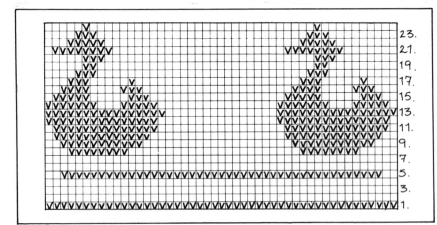

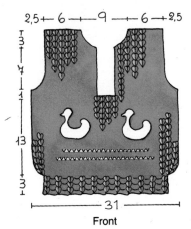

2,5 — 6 — 9 — 6 — 2,5

3
7
4
13
3

31

Front

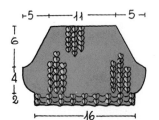

Measurements given in cm

5 — 11 — 5

6
4
2

16

Sleeve

NUMBER JUMPER

✳✳✳

pattern on the
front is knitted
from a
chart with
the single
cross stitches
broidered on the
front and sleeves
after the jumper
is complete.

Materials

2(2,3)×50g balls of Wendy Family Choice 4 ply in main colour A
1 ball of same in each of contrast colours B, C, D and E
A pair each of 2¾mm/No12 and 3¼mm/No10 knitting needles

Measurements

To fit chest 51(56,61)cm/20(22,24)in
Actual measurements
Chest 55(61,66)cm/21¾(24,26)in
Length to shoulders 29(33,35)cm/ 11½(13,13¾)in
Sleeve seam 19(25,27)cm/7½(10,10½)in

Tension

28 sts and 36 rows to 10cm/4in measured over st st worked on 3¼mm needles

Front

★ Using 2¾mm needles and A, cast on 71(79,87) sts.
Rib row 1 K1, * p1, k1, rep from * to end.
Rib row 2 P1, * k1, p1, rep from * to end.
Rep these 2 rows for 4(6,6)cm/ 1½(2½,2½)in, ending with rib row 1.
Inc row Rib 6(5,6), * M1, rib 12(14,15), rep from * to last 5(4,6) sts, M1, rib to end. 77(85,93) sts. ★
Change to 3¼mm needles.
2nd and 3rd sizes only
Beg with a k row, work 4(8) rows st st.
All sizes
Use separate small balls of yarn for each area of colour and twist yarns together on WS of work when changing colour to avoid making a hole.
Reading odd numbered (k) rows from right to left and even numbered (p) rows from left to right and beginning with a k row, work in patt from chart as follows:
Row 1 With A, k to end.

Row 2 With A, p to end.
Rows 3 to 10 Rep rows 1 and 2 four times.
Row 11 As row 1.
Row 12 P29(33,37)A, 1D, 3A, 1D, 12A, 1D, 3A, 1D, 26(30,34)A.
Beg with row 13, cont in patt from chart shaping for armholes as indicated, until row 68 has been completed. 67(71,77) sts.
Using A only, work 2(6,8) rows st st.
Shape neck
Next row K26(28,31), turn and leave rem sts on a spare needle.
★★ Cast off 3 sts at beg of next and foll alt row.
Dec 1 st at neck edge on next and every foll alt row until 14(16,19) sts rem.
Work straight until armhole measures 11(12,13)cm/4½(4¾,5)in from beg of armhole shaping, ending with a p row.
Cast off. ★★
Return to sts on spare needle.
With RS facing, slip first 15 sts on to a holder, join on A and k to end.
P 1 row.
Now complete as given for first side of neck from ★★ to ★★.

Back

Work as given for front from ★ to ★.
Change to 3¼mm needles.
Beg with a k row work in st st until back measures same as front to beg of armhole shaping, ending with a p row.
Shape armholes
Cast off 2 sts at beg of next 2 rows, then dec 1 st each end of foll 3(5,6) rows. 67(71,77) sts.
Work straight until back measures same as front to shoulders, ending with a p row.
Shape shoulders
Cast off 14(16,19) sts at beg of next 2 rows.
Cast off.

Sleeves

Using 2¾mm needles and A, cast on 41(45,49) sts.
Work 3cm/1¼in rib as given for front, ending with rib row 2.
Inc row Rib 3(2,2), * M1, rib 7(6,5), rep from * to last 3(1,2) sts, M1, rib 3(1,2). 47(53,59) sts.
Change to 3¼mm needles.
Next row P23(26,29), p1 and mark this st with a coloured thread, then p to end.
Continuing in st st, inc 1 st each end of next and every foll 6th(10th,10th) row until there are 63(67,73) sts.
Work straight until sleeve measures 19(25,27cm/7½(10,10½)in from cast-on edge, ending with a p row.
Shape top
Cast off 2 sts at beg of next 2 rows, then dec 1 st each end of foll 3(5,6) rows. 53(53,57) sts.
Cast off.

Neckband

Join right shoulder seam.
With RS facing, using 2¾mm needles and A, pick up and k20(21,22) sts down left side of front neck, k15 sts from front neck holder, then pick up and k20(21,22) sts up right side of front neck and 40 sts across back neck. 95(97,99) sts.
Work 6cm/2½in rib as given for front.
Cast off in rib.

To make up

Following chart for sleeve, and beginning at centre marked st above cuff, embroider cross sts on to sleeves. Following chart for front, embroider cross sts on to front.
Join left shoulder and neckband seam. Set in sleeves. Join side and sleeve seams.

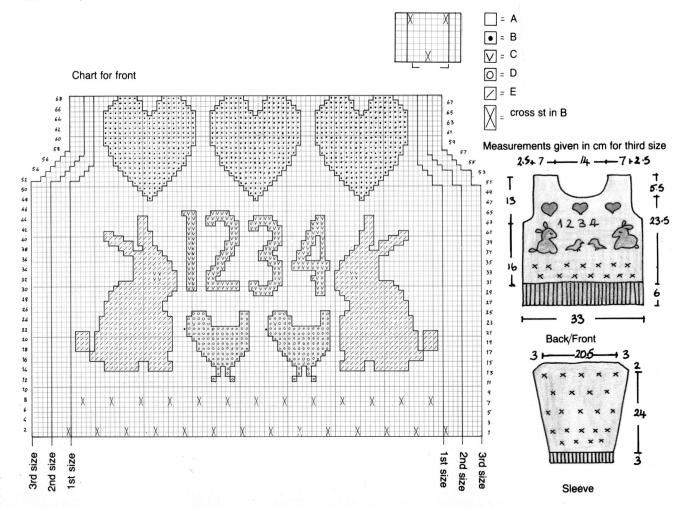

Chart for front

Sleeve

Key

☐ = A
⊡ = B
☑ = C
Ⓞ = D
⊘ = E
☒ = cross st in B

Measurements given in cm for third size

Back/Front

Sleeve

DUNGAREES AND JERSEY SET

**

A simple
basket
stitch
pattern is used
or the dungarees
while the jersey
is knitted in
stocking stitch.

Materials

Dungarees
2(3, 3) x 50g balls of Patons Fairytale 4 ply
2 buttons
Jersey
2(3,3) x 50g balls of Patons Fairytale 4 ply
3 buttons
A pair each of 2¾mm/No12 and 3¼mm/No 10
knitting needles

Measurements

To fit chest 46(48.5,51)cm/18(19,20)in
Actual measurements
Chest 50(53,56)cm/19¾(21,22)in
Length to shoulders 24(26,28)cm/
9¹/₂(10¹/₄, 11)in
Sleeve seam 15(17,19)cm/6(6¾, 7½)in
Outside leg 34(36,38)cm/13½(14,15)in

Tension

28 sts and 38 rows to 10cm/4in measured
over basket st patt worked on 3¼mm needles
28 sts and 36 rows to 10cm/4in measured
over st st worked on 3¼mm needles

Dungarees back first leg

★ Using 2¾mm needles cast on
30(32, 34) sts.
Work 2.5cm/1in g st, ending with a RS row.
Inc row K2(6,4), [M1, k5(4,5) sts] 5 times,
M1, k to end. 36(38,40) sts. ★
Change to 3¼mm needles.
Work in basket st patt as follows:
Row 1 (RS) K to end.
Row 2 * K4, p4, rep from * to last 4(6,8) sts,
k4, then *for 2nd and 3rd sizes only* p2(4).
Rows 3 to 6 Rep rows 1 and 2 twice.
Row 7 Inc in first st, k to end.
Row 8 P4, k4, rep from * to last 5(7,9) sts,
p4, k1(3,4), then *for 3rd size only* p1.
Row 9 K to end.
Row 10 As row 8.
Row 11 Inc in first st, k to end.
Row 12 * P4, k4, rep from * to last
6(8, 10) sts, p4, k2(4,4), then *for 3rd size
only* p2.
These 12 rows set the patt.
Continuing in patt, inc and work into patt 1 st
at shaped edge on 3rd and every foll
4th(5th,4th) row until there are 45(49,53) sts.
Work straight until leg measures
18(19,20)cm/7(7½,8)in from cast-on edge,
ending with a WS row.
Shape crutch
Cast off 3 sts at beg of next row, then dec 1
st at same edge on next and foll 3 alt rows.
38(42,46) sts.
Cut off yarn and leave sts on a holder.

Dungarees back second leg

Work as given for first leg from ★ to ★.
Change to 3¼mm needles.
Work in basket st patt as follows:
Row 1 (RS) K to end.
Row 2 *For 2nd and 3rd sizes only* p2(4),
then *for all sizes* k4, * p4, k4, rep from * to
end.
Rows 3 to 6 Rep rows 1 and 2 twice.
Row 7 K to last st, inc in last st.
Row 8 *For 3rd size only* p1, then *for all sizes*
k1(3,4), p4, * k4, p4, rep from * to end.
Row 9 K to end.
Row 10 As row 8.
Row 11 K to last st, inc in last st.
Row 12 *For 3rd size only* p2, then *for all
sizes* k2(4,4), p4, * k4, p4, rep from * to end.
These 12 rows set the patt.
Continuing in patt, inc and work into patt 1 st
at shaped edge and every foll
4th(5th,4th) row until there are 45(49,53) sts.
Work straight until second leg measures 1
row less than first leg, so ending with a RS
row.
Shape crutch
Cast off 3 sts at beg of next row, then dec 1
st at same edge on next and foll 3 alt rows.
38(42,46) sts.
Patt 1 row.
Join legs
Next row Patt 38(42,46) sts of second leg,
then with RS facing, patt across
38(42,46) sts from first leg holder.
76(84,92) sts.

Cont in patt until work measures 34(36, 38)cm/
13¹/₂(14¹/₄, 15)in from cast-on edge,
ending with a WS row.
Waistband
Dec row K5(1,1), * k2 tog, k2, rep from * to
last 7(3,3) sts, k to end. 60(64,70) sts.
Work 1.5cm/¾in g st, ending with a WS row.
Shape for straps
Next row Cast off 14(16,19) sts, k until there
are 6 sts on right-hand needle and slip these
sts on to a safety-pin, cast off next 20 sts, k
until there are 6 sts on right-hand needle and
slip these sts on to a safety-pin, then cast off
rem 14(16,19) sts.

Straps

With RS facing and using 2¾mm needles, k
across 6 sts of first strap from safety-pin.
Work in g st for 34(36,38)cm/13½(14¼,15)in.
Cast off.
Work second strap in the same way.

Dungarees front

Work as given for back until front measures
34(36,38)cm/13½(14¼,15)in from cast-on
edge, ending with a WS row. 76(84,92) sts.
Waistband
Dec row K6(4,2), [k2 tog, k1] 4(6,8) times,
k6, patt 28, k6, [k1, k2 tog] 4(6,8) times,
k6(4,2). 68(72,76) sts.
Next row K20(22,24), patt 28, k20(22,24).
Rep the last row for 2cm/¾in, ending with a
WS row.
Shape bib
Next row Cast off 14(16,18) sts, then k5,
patt 28, k6, cast off rem 14(16,18) sts.
With WS facing, join on yarn to rem 40 sts
and cont as follows:
Next row K6, patt 28, k6.
Rep the last row for 10cm/4in, ending with a
WS row.
K 6 rows.
Buttonhole row 1 K3, cast off 2 sts, k to last
5 sts, cast off 2 sts, k to end.
Buttonhole row 2 K to end, casting on 2 sts
over those cast off in previous row.
K 2 rows.
Cast off.

To make up

Join first and second leg seams at crutch
shaping. Join inner and outer leg seams.
Sew buttons to end of straps to fit.

Jersey back

★★ Using 2¾mm needles cast on
65(69,73) sts.
Rib row 1 K1, * p1, k1, rep from * to end.
Rib row 2 P1, * k1, p1, rep from * to end.
Rep these 2 rows for 4cm/1½in, ending with
rib row 1.
Inc row Rib 6, * M1, rib 13(14,15), rep from *
to last 7 sts, M1, rib 7. 70(74,78) sts. ★★
Change to 3¼mm needles.
Beg with a k row, work in st st until back

measures 24(26,28)cm/9½(10¼,11)in from
cast-on edge, ending with a p row.
Shape shoulders
Cast off 21(22,23) sts at beg of next 2 rows.
Cut off yarn and leave rem 28(30,32) sts on a
holder.

Jersey front

Work as given for back from ★★ to ★★.
Change to 3¼mm needles.
Beg with a k row, work in st st until front
measures 19(21,23)cm/7½(8¼,9)in from cast-
on edge, ending with a p row.
Shape neck
Next row K28(29,30), turn and leave rem sts
on a spare needle.
Dec 1 st at neck edge of next 4 rows, then
on every foll alt row until 21(22,23) sts rem.
Work straight until front measures same as
back to shoulder, ending with a p row.
Cast off.
Return to sts on spare needle.
With RS facing and using 3¼mm needles, slip
first 14(16,18) sts on to a holder, join on yarn
and k to end.
Now complete to match first side of neck.

Jersey sleeves

Using 2¾mm needles cast on 35(39,43) sts.
Work 4cm/1½in rib as given for back, ending
with rib row 1.
Inc row Rib 3(3,5), * M1, rib 7(8,8), rep from *
to last 4(4,6) sts, M1, rib 4(4,6).
40(44,48) sts.
Change to 3¼mm needles.
Beginning with a k row and working in st st,
inc 1 st each end of 3rd and every foll
2nd(3rd,3rd) row until there are 68(72,76)
sts.
Work straight until sleeve measures
15(17,19)cm/6(6¾, 7½)in from cast-on edge,
ending with a p row.
Cast off.

Neckband

Join right shoulder seam.
With RS facing and using 2¾mm needles,
pick up and k16 sts down left side of front
neck, k14(16,18) sts from front neck holder,
pick up and k16 sts up left side of front neck,
then increasing 1 st at centre k across back
neck sts from holder. 75(79,83) sts.
Work 2cm/¾in rib as given for back.
Cast off in rib.

To make up

Join left shoulder for 5cm/2in at shoulder
edge. Fold sleeves in half lengthwise, then
placing folds to shoulder seams, sew into
place. Join side and sleeve seams. Make 3
button loops on left front shoulder edge, then
sew on buttons to left back shoulder to
correspond.

Measurements given in cm for second size

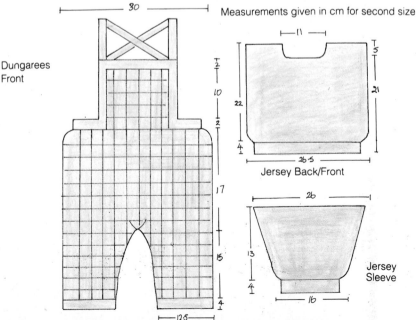

Dungarees
Front

Jersey Back/Front

Jersey
Sleeve